Readings in Career Education

A collection of articles previously published in the *Journal of Career Education*

With supplements courtesy of Sidney P. Marland, Jr. and Kenneth B. Hoyt

Compiled and edited by
H. C. KAZANAS

Chairperson of the Department of Vocational and Technical
Education, College of Education
University of Illinois at Urbana-Champaign

Ⓑ

Bennett Publishing Company

Peoria, Illinois 61615

81 82 83 84 85 KP 5 4 3 2 1

ISBN 87002-308-X

Library of Congress Catalog No.

Printed in the United States of America

Editors: Kay Huffman, Marlene Weigel
Production Manager: Gordon Guderjan
Production Assistant: Pat Schultz
Cover Design: Steve Justice

PREFACE

One day historians will undoubtedly consider career education the most powerful educational movement of this century in terms of curriculum reform. Career education came at a time when reform of the school system in the United States was very much in need. Career education is not really a new idea in American education; it was simply restated. As a result, public response was predictable and the idea was enthusiastically supported. Whether career education is ultimately going to have the impact its many proponents believe it will depends to a great extent on the federal government's commitment and on the leadership and resources provided by local school systems.

Evidence indicates that career education is indeed having an impact on education but not as drastic as its proponents had envisioned. However, its contributions to the educational system are multiplying. The public is becoming increasingly aware of and educators more concerned about career education. To keep up the momentum, there must be enlightened educational leaders who understand the conceptual structure of career education and who are familiar with what happened in its initial stages. It is in this light that this book has been put together—to provide an account of some of the views and practices of those who were active in career education during its difficult growth.

It is my belief that these writings may have historical value as well as future use, serving as a resource to many current practitioners as well as future educators.

The reader should keep in mind that most of the articles presented here were written between 1974 and 1978, as this was the most turbulent time for career education. Most were chosen on the basis of the author's qualifications. All but four of the articles appeared in the first four volumes of the University of Missouri's *Journal of Career Education (JCE)* of which I was privileged to be both founder and first editor.

I would like to express my sincere appreciation to the book's many contributors for permission to use their material, especially Drs. Sidney P. Marland, Jr., and Kenneth B. Hoyt who sent supplements not published in *The Journal*; to the Curators of the University of Missouri for making it possible to reprint *Journal* articles; again to Dr. Marland for his invaluable review and suggestions; and finally to Mike Kenny, Kay Huffman, and Marlene Weigel of Bennett Publishing Company for their help in seeing this book to its completion.

H.C. Kazanas

TABLE OF CONTENTS

The Socio-philosophic Foundations of Career Education

Career education came into being in the early 1970s. Since then, American educators have been debating its merits. Since most educational movements have their antecedents in the social and philosophic context of the society from which they spring, one effort has been to analyze the social and philosophic bases of career education in order to provide it with a solid intellectual foundation.

The three articles that comprise this chapter were written in 1975. Van Cleve Morris examines the broad meaning of work in contemporary society and its relationship to career education. He agrees that through career choice, the individual attempts to exert his/her influence upon society, and, therefore, career education is a social phenomenon, assisting individuals in making more realistic career choices. Philip Lloyd Smith examines the educational and noneducational benefits that may be derived through career education, an improvement over traditional schooling which is often associated only with educational benefits. Carl J. Dolce's analysis of career education is centered on the conceptual problems associated with it as an educational movement. He believes that society in general and educators in particular have not examined the conceptual bases of career education enough to warrant the investment of resources awarded to career education in such a short time.

CAREER EDUCATION AND THE WAY WE WORK—A NEW COINAGE IN THE REALM

Van Cleve Morris

Dr. Morris is professor of education at the University of Illinois at Chicago Circle, where he has also served as dean of the College of Education. His specialty is the philosophy of education. This article was written in 1975.

The word *career* has a faint, upper middle-class ring to it. Customarily, we do not speak of pursuing a career in bricklaying, selling shoes, or tightening bolts on a production line. These, by convention, are trades, jobs, or occupations. Of course, at the other end of the social spectrum there is something spoken of as a calling, a title for activities allegedly sponsored by a celestial voice; we are called to service as a missionary, a social worker, a nun, an evangelist, or a true-believing revolutionary. It is from this notion that we have come to use the word *vocation* (from the Latin *vocare*, to call), which sounds considerably less pretentious and is often applied to work of more prosaic origins.

Somewhere else on the socio-economic ladder of productive functioning are what we call the *professions* (medicine, law, teaching, the ministry, and a few more modern others like accounting or research science). Here is another term which, like vocation, conveys the implication of some level of personal commitment and identification not usually associated with other more modest terms. Now comes something called *career education*, two common enough words but conjoined in an unfamiliar linkage, suggesting a new context for discussing educational goals and procedures.

The very fact that we have so many words for the gainful, i.e., income-producing, side of our lives—job, trade, occupation, vocation, career, profession, calling—forces on our attention the possibility that work really cannot be understood in a generic sense but must be analyzed more cautiously in its variety of idiosyncratic forms. For example, we are mindful of the pragmatic obligation to work in order to live. But we have always attached more significance to work than the mere payoff in groceries. There is something about work, which, if not exactly ennobling in the Puritan sense, is nonetheless somehow central to our makeup. Our work yields "psychological groceries," food for the spirit and ego as much as for the digestive tract.

It is this psychological yield from our work which is really behind our continuing interest in job training, vocational preparation, and, in the present case, career education. We know that skills, abilities, and competencies are required in anything we do, and the educator is understandably attentive to those requirements. But the educator's responsibility to her or his students embraces a wider concern: to comprehend the larger dimensions of a *life work*, to understand what a life (or part-life) might be like if one spent it as an electrician, a nurse, a life insurance salesperson, a hairdresser, an accountant, a stenographer, or a TV repairer. Since educators are one of society's primary communication links to the young, they need to know what such a life would offer, what the rewards and agonies of it may be, and how best to convey these understandings—usually not found in the training manual—to their students. The phenomenon of growing up embraces a number of things, but certainly a primary element is to find a sphere of activity compatible not only with one's skills and abilities but with the subtler features of one's personality and makeup—one's views of oneself and what one wants from life. This search for compatibility is partly the teacher's responsibility.

It is in this context that the term career education, for all its upper middle-class baggage, may come closer than any of the other labels to embrace the larger perspective the educator is looking for. A career is neither a calling nor an occupation. It is both and then some. A career, at whatever level of the economic ladder, is at bottom a decision—a personal decision on what work one feels fitted for, what one will settle for in terms of economic rewards, and finally, all things considered, what one wants to do with one's life.

The word career conveys continuity of purpose and performance; it is the secular equivalent of calling, suggesting a significant initiative by the individual without the complications of an inner voice. The word career also has another attribute not found in the other labels for what we do. It embraces a wider catalogue of life work. For example, a career might become a conscious repudiation of gainful employment altogether. An individual might adopt a life-style of creative drifting, a mode of existence in which deliberate indigence is coupled with the private search for new values.

No matter what our personal reaction might be to this option of dropping out, the educator, as well as the wider society, needs always to make room for such individuals; they represent the fallout of a society committed to a wide pluralism in life-styles. And this is the virtue of the term career. Unlike the other labels—most of them oriented to what one does during actual working hours—this term conveys a larger reach of considerations, somehow going beyond the context of services rendered and payment received. It pulls in a bigger picture, a fuller set of variables to ponder, and is for that reason a more valuable nomenclature for the educator's discussions regarding life work.

Shades of Marx

With the larger reach of the term career, we may be in a better position to examine the basic feelings we have toward work, as such, and to understand how we have rationalized those feelings into a systematic definition of work as a part, perhaps the most significant part, of our experience. For example, in earlier discussions regarding vocational training or education for work, there was a periodic appeal to a kind of ideological explanation for it all. The argument ran that work was not merely a survival mechanism but had something to do with a higher category of aspiration, with the human being's relationship to other human beings, and to his or her world. Out of the grubbiness of the class struggle, so said the Marxists, has emerged the metaphysical explanation we somehow have always been looking for: work is the prosaic name for humankind's reason for being! In one particularly illuminating passage in a work devoted to explaining Karl Marx's dialectical materialism and its relation to education, we hear the following:

> Labor is the very touchstone for man's self-realization, the medium of creating the world of his desire; and it is labor which should make him happy. Indeed, the essence of man is in his striving to achieve his desires. He is not provoked into learning and achieving by the pragmatic stimulus of an external threat. He labors to transform his world, to put his own mark on it (Cohen, 1955, p. 190).

In this Dionysian age of creature comforts and vast quantities of leisure time, it may be difficult to keep a straight face when somebody says labor should make us happy. But Marx may have been more right than he thought, and his argument can be shown to have manifestations at a much less sophisticated level of observation, namely, how individuals react to prolonged idleness. It is a fact that, for most of us, work is something we need. When it is withdrawn for any length of time, we miss it. Vacations may be getting longer, and hours may be getting shorter, but more often than not the released time is filled with more work. In some lines of activity, jobs develop a Parkinsonian crescendo of expectations, expanding by unnoticeable amounts the work thought necessary for their proper execution. Especially at the upper levels of the socio-economic spectrum in managerial and professional occupations, the evening briefcases are always full and the workload runs far beyond the 35- or 40-hour week.

Why do people work so hard and so much, even when they don't really need to? Why do they fear layoff, even though unemployment compensation is available? Why do they, at almost every level of income, dread retirement and the forced idleness which that condition represents? The answer may not lie merely in our precipitous readiness for boredom in a world full of stimulation but moreso in our desire to put our own mark on the world, to make it ours. Since work is the primary instrument for achieving this, most of us feel cut off from our experience when work is withdrawn. Our personalities continue in existence, our friends and neighbors remain, our relatives are still there, but things are not the same. There is a foreshortening of personal influence over our environment. Things get done without our knowledge. In small but significant ways, the world becomes transformed, neither with nor against our will, but merely beyond it. It's an eerie feeling, betraying a far deeper interest than we would like to admit in how our little sector of the world is to be managed.

So Marx may be right, for more reasons than he knew. Work is the primary dimension of our being, and as such it is central to our ego and what that ego wishes to implant in an otherwise indifferent natural order.

Look at it this way, choosing a career takes on a somewhat larger perspective. It becomes a choice of the mark we wish to make on our world. A career decision is not merely a matchup between abilities and outlooks on the one hand and some line of activity appropriate to them on the other; it becomes rather a selection of where best to exploit the possibilities for changing things along lines of one's personal desire. It is the choice of weapons and the determination of the arena in which our personal influence on the world can best be capitalized. The educator is therefore dealing with a third variable—not merely the student's aptitudes and interests, not merely the catalogue of occupational opportunities in the adult world, but something else both subtler and, in the end, more powerful—namely, the individual student's estimate of where her or his energies and talents can make the most difference.

The Puritan Work Ethic American Division

The question we should ask, however, is whether all this ideological argument is necessary. The Marxian thesis, some claim, is so much overblown metaphysical prattle, going far beyond the point necessary to explain the motivations of real people living in a real world. Why introduce lofty, cosmological rhetoric into what is essentially a prosaic, everyday phenomenon? The answer may lie in a line of explanation at once more modest and more plausible: the meaning we attach to work eventually takes on the coloration of the surrounding culture and its values. Whatever else it may be, work is the medium by which a society expresses itself in the world. As the anthropologists are fond of saying, when you are searching for the essence of a culture, don't trouble yourself over much with its geography, its symbols, its peculiar folkways, or the alleged temperament of its people. These are ancillary. Look instead at its work—its literature, its institutions, its technology. (As Calvin Coolidge observed, "America's business is business!") These are the ultimate measures of what the culture is all about. Thus, if work is the medium of cultural expression, then its role in our lives will inevitably be the product of what the wider culture expects.

This explanation turns out to be more compatible with American experience. It is doubtful that the American people, either consciously or subconsciously, have ever believed that their destiny was to transform the world in the Marxian sense. Instead, our Pilgrim origins, our pioneering beginnings, our frontier westering, and more recently our fanaticism with technology have all combined to produce in us what might be called the "achievement syndrome"; this syndrome lies much closer to the empirical real world of sheer adaptation than to some grand, political dialectic imagined for us by a nineteenth-century social philosopher.

The American people have always reveled in encountering their environment in a quasi-aggressive way. Unlike Asian societies, and even unlike most European peoples, we have found excitement and exhilaration in trying to figure out how to turn our surroundings to our own account. Like most human beings, we have been dissatisfied with what the natural order, untended, had to offer. But unlike others, we have not stood by consenting to its inadequacies; we have gone ahead and done something about them! Our response as a people has been to wrest some kind of control over our situation, not out of some transcendental urge to reshape creation, but simply to make life more comfortable, manageable, and interesting.

In an earlier day, this took the form of struggling against the uncertainties of an alien and unexplored continent. Our predecessors discovered that deliberate, well thought-out programs of environmental exploitation would eventually yield crops, houses, roads, and cities. Their simultaneous concern for human arrangements occasioned the buildup of our institutions—schools, churches, and governments.

More recently, our desire to control the environment has taken a scientific, mechanistic turn. We have created a vast technology, engineered not only to produce our supply of food, clothing, and shelter but designed also to run far beyond these basic needs to create completely new wants we never heard of—by now so firmly entrenched that we think their satisfaction is absolutely essential to the good life. The advertisers are in league with the manufacturers, and the entire economy is now devoted to the circular interdependence of want-creation and want-satisfaction, leading to more want-creation.

Looked at from this angle, work in America takes on a machismo quality. The producer, the money handler, the developer, the designer, the manager, the organizer of people and things become the new culture heroes. We have run beyond the Puritan notion that hard work builds character to the more purely American notion that hard work is the key to achievement! Achievement is now the American goddess. Work is therefore inexorably linked with the American character. Being task oriented, as they say, is the prime credential for the achiever; and achievement, per se, is the number one expectation which the American culture lays on every one of us.

Looked at in this light, career decision-making requires the rearrangement of elements so far examined. One's ultimate mark on the world is not the most important consideration. Neither is one's own set of preferences and interests. What comes forward as the decisive criterion is a career's promise of future success and achievement. The student looks at the problem and asks, In what career could I best satisfy society's demand that, whatever I do, I should rise to the top of that field?

In this strategy, there is a surrender to the demands of the culture; it is the supreme *other-directed* leitmotif of our social system that each individual is expected to succeed. But it is a surrender to a higher, or at least broader ethic—that of the world of work itself as defined in the American consciousness. Aspiration, drive, desire, application, perseverence, getting ahead, climbing to the top. . . . all those words that have lingered at the core of the American dream are summoned forth once more to set limits to the final choice.

An Existential Variation

It goes without saying that the counter culture advocates of the sixties and seventies have drawn our attention to the frailties of the preceding argument. There is a thinness of vision, a shallowness of definition, of the human spirit in the notion that our days should be devoted merely to impressing our fellow citizens with how much we can accomplish. Perhaps, they claim, a choice of career can be founded on something nearer the center of authentic personal living. We all may want, in a vague and undefined way, to make our mark on the world. And we all may have some ego need to achieve something that can be acknowledged and recognized by other people. But it still may be true that what is more evidently on display is not our work but ourselves. Some attention to this dimension is required.

Unfortunately, in much of the contemporary rhetoric on selfhood, there is an overkill of sentimentality regarding the presumed beauty of the inner person. There is also an overload of haziness and vagueness concerning just what it is we are talking about. For the purposes of this discussion, it is imperative to bring this notion down out of the air and into the context of real living. If this is possible, we may get some illumination on how this factor has its own influence over career selection and life definition.

The existentialists, following the Greeks, have a name for it. Jean-Paul Sartre speaks of "the human project," and he explains it in somewhat the following way: each human life is a slow accretion of experiences, responses to those experiences, and the outlooks and values which are generated by this dialectic. Each of us has a zero start, a point of origin for this enterprise, which presupposes nothing. Of course, it is true that each of us is born at a particular time, of a certain sex, of a particular set of parents, in a particular place. These are what he calls the "facticity" of our individual situation; they are given.

However, what is not given is our response to these predicates of our existing. We are the sole authors of the meaning we attach to these conditions of our being, and hence we are individually the sole authors of the responses we make to the fact of our existing. As the existentialists say, existence precedes essence, meaning that we wake up to our existing first and then define ourselves later. The activity of defining ourselves, of giving an essence, is the human project.

The existentialists lay a heavy load on us: each individual's human project is his or hers alone. Life, behavior, choices, the values on which one builds responses to one's situation—these are one's own origin. He or she is responsible for them. In one telling passage, Sartre reminds us that the individual is ultimately responsible even for his or her irresponsibility! We canot escape. Existing means choosing. And since there are no other agents requiring us to choose in this or that way, we must assume the full responsibility for the decisions we make and therefore for the kind of persons we turn out to be.

Of all our choices, it is obvious that the choice of life work is the most decisive in defining ourselves. It is almost the same thing. To choose a career, in the largest sense of this term, is to define who you are in the world. But from an existentialist perspective, the final criterion for this choice is not the mark one hopes to make on the world, nor the track record of achievement one hopes for, but simply the creation of a human life. It is the act of bringing into existence one, solitary, unique, unrepeatable instance of what it means to be a human being. Each of us is given one opportunity to define the word *human*. We define it with our lives.

As the central piece in this project, a career takes on the role of energy source and defining element in the individual's effort to make a personal statement about her or his existence. A career's first essential, therefore, is its power to provide the medium of expression for what an individual wants to say.

Therefore, work inexorably carries the ingredients for personal fulfillment. The individual, in private moments, is not thinking of marks he or she is going to make on the world, nor of achievements he or she intends to rack up on the scoreboard, but rather of where his or her own spirit can find the best release. Where can all the things I am and want to become find the fullest voice?

The child in elementary school or the adolescent in high school begins to sense the faint stirrings of this question and the inescapable obligation to deal with it in the career selection process. "What do you want to be when you grow up?" is not merely the make-talk, idle chatter of adults addressing young people. Its very frequency in our social intercourse suggests that the question lies close to the center of the growing-up process itself. Indeed, career choice *is* growing up! It is the method by which an individual slowly brings some definition to his or her life.

The Educator's Response

Without regard to which of the above three approaches to career selection seems most plausible, it is obvious that the educator's work is intimately tied up with the entire enterprise. The design of the curriculum, the selection of materials, the style of teaching, indeed, the entire ambience of the educational environment, contribute in some subtle but definite way to the manner in which a youngster addresses this concern. In an older pedagogy, it was thought safe to ignore the question of life work and to leave the decision to a later determination in the post-school years. Indeed, going to school was widely thought to be the best way to postpone the problem! The perennial student was the kid who just couldn't seem to grow up.

Nowadays, we are not so sure that delay and postponement is the best policy. Life is too complicated, the options too many. There is an urgency we have not felt before in bringing schooling and life into closer touch with one another—not in the class-trip-to-the-fire-station sense but in a generic locking together of what we teach and learn and what kind of growth and maturation we wish to generate in our students and in ourselves.

Career education is an exciting new way of probing that connection.

CAREER EDUCATION AS A JUSTIFICATION FOR SCHOOLING

Philip Lloyd Smith
Dr. Smith is associate professor of education at The Ohio State University and has written other articles on career education. This article was written in 1975.

It is hardly an exaggeration to say that career education represents an attempt to alter many present-day school practices, an effort advanced at a time when almost everyone interested in formal education is experiencing some degree of disenchantment with the school as an institution. Educators themselves are searching desperately for new ideas. For many, career education offers new hope. Proponents claim that it not only provides a new set of learning procedures but an educational ideal that is thought to justify those procedures. The argument offered here addresses the question whether career education is desirable, efficacious, and, most important of all, employs morally sound pedagogical techniques.

Career education is a rational alternative to existing school policy. Career education can be justified as an improvement over existing conceptions of schooling.

We have commonly recognized two types of benefits that can be derived from schooling. One kind has to do with changes in behavior, the mastery of certain skills, the acquisition of dispositions, the formation of beliefs and gains in understanding. Benefits of this kind involve qualitative changes in the human personality which, insofar as they are thought to be desirable in and of themselves, are said to be intrinsically worthwhile. They add to maturity as well as the nobility of the human spirit. Throughout history, the goals most closely associated with formal educational endeavor have been of this kind. At least as regards the rationale for schooling itself, other educational consequences traditionally have been considered subservient to character development and the training of the mind.

Even though schooling has usually been designed to provide these educational benefits, we all recognize that schooling often influences what Thomas F. Green has called a person's "life-chances" (Green 1971a). At least in our society, going to school has a bearing on a person's opportunities to share in available goods. Regardless of what is actually learned in school, indeed, whether anything is learned at all, simply having gone to school and preferably having graduated, has a certain instrumental value as far as attaining social and material advantage is concerned. Armed with the credentials of proper schooling, a person is in line for a better job, higher social status, increased earnings, and other such rewards not available to his or her unschooled peers. Although these consequences are surely beneficial to those who are schooled, they are not, however, educational in the above sense. In order to distinguish consequences of schooling that are not educationally beneficial from those which are, noneducational benefits will oppose benefits that have historically been regarded as educational (Pratte 1974).

The fact that schooling has noneducational benefits does not indicate a structural element in the schooling process. It represents instead the character of the social environment in which schools operate (Pratte 1974, p. 6). If we lived in a different social order, perhaps schooling would not provide such benefits. But we do, and undoubtedly it does. Over the years the belief that schooling adds to the life-chances of those who are schooled has provided a common motive to support our system of education. Notice that a distinction is drawn here between the rationale for supporting schooling and the motive for such support. The former has been put in terms of educational benefits, while the latter has been expressed as a desire for noneducational ends. The rationale for schooling has influenced its organization and structure, while the motive for defending formalized instruction is a fact independent of acknowledged teaching objectives. What this distinction points up is that words and deeds in the process of schooling have not always been intellectually consistent. They have sometimes served even to frustrate each other. Although both have given significance to schooling, each is deserving of different degrees of merit.

Almost everyone has been told at one time or another that access to the goods of society is contingent upon success in school. While the unqualified acceptance of this view has always made it something of a myth, it is not altogether without foundation. School achievement is still a fairly good predictor of success in post-school endeavors. Schooling shapes subsequent life-chances even though it might not be the force it was once believed to be. Surely, for many, schooling provides a means for upward social mobility, although admittedly not the most efficacious means. Most observers are quick to grant a connection between the level of school attainment and the probability of eventual fame and prosperity. Students are commonly exhorted to remain in school on the grounds that their material reward will be greater if they do (Pratte 1974, p. 21).

Educational critics are beginning to look with some skepticism, however, on glowing assertions about the noneducational advantages of schooling. And rightly so. Assertions of this type have not always served the interests of the school's clients. In our own country we have demanded school attendance on a large scale for well over 150 years and have sold it to the public by suggesting its necessity as a tool for noneducational gain. Students are required to spend considerable time in school and advised to spend even more. But the more schooling we have required or suggested the less schooling has served as a force in securing noneducational ends. The social and material advantages that are tied to schooling begin to disappear as more and more people are schooled (Pratte 1974, p. 22). Schooling is less a criterion for distinction as fewer people are without it. When schooling begins to lose its importance as a result of its near universal possession, supporters of schooling will frequently exert some sort of political pressure to raise the level of required or suggested schooling still further. Their hope is to reclaim the force of schooling in attainment of noneducational benefits. When this happens, the social and material advantages of schooling are associated with the next highest level of schooling. Richard Pratte has put the matter more parsimoniously:

> If everyone completed a given level of schooling, then the correlation between completing that level and any subsequent social/economic differences that may arise (income, occupational opportunity) would be reduced to zero. Under such conditions it can only be at some point beyond the ninth level that there can again exist any correlation between the level of schooling attained and any subsequent indicator of social standing or social mobility. And so pressure for more and more years of schooling will spiral upwards (Pratte 1974, p. 23).

Pratte brings out one more consequence of required or suggested schooling. The last groups to have access to schooling are almost always from the lower class. Such groups are very much in need of material amelioration. But when the "group of last entry," completes the utmost level of schooling, the principle of zero correlation sets in. Thus, those who are most in need of noneducational benefits, the group of last entry, are least likely to gain. What they were told was a sufficient condition for a better life turns out for them to be a necessary condition. Failure to receive adequate schooling proves increasingly more disastrous. At the same time, schooling becomes less important as a force in achieving noneducational ends. Conditions are ripe for a renewal of disenchantment with schools (Pratte 1974, p. 23).

In their effort to counter rising discontent with the schools, educators have discovered an alternative to increasing required or suggested time levels of attainment. They have found it possible to reconstruct the existing institutions and claim to have made a qualitative change in schooling procedures. Educators of our day have long since recognized that we cannot expect people to spend much more time in school than they already do, at least when their primary role in life is as a student. People want to get established and are not willing to defer cultural rewards much beyond young adulthood. Even where we are talking about availability of schooling and not schooling that is compulsory, the bulk of the population is subjected to social and economic pressures that make it practically impossible to increase the time they now spend in school. The promise of additional noneducational benefits can no longer be held out as carrots, for, simply, the rabbits are tired of running.

Recognizing this state of affairs, those who support career education will say that the process of schooling requires careful reexamination. Moreover, universal extension will not do. Rather than suggest or demand more schooling time, career education advocates have offered a plan which they say will mark a qualitative improvement in the practices of schools. Proponents of career education believe their scheme can alleviate disenchantment with schools and reinstate the public faith in the instrumental value of a formalized approach to learning. With their revitalized curriculum they believe they can get results that will be highly regarded by a practical-oriented society.

There appear to be grounds for questioning, however, whether or not any of these statements are true. Will improving the quality of education really have much effect on the capacity of those schooled to amass noneducational benefits? While supporters of career education almost always assume that it does, a recent study of this question concludes otherwise. Christopher Jencks has suggested rather strongly that the quality of schooling has little influence on life-chances (Jencks 1972). It is not what is learned in school but simply having gone to school that adds to the likelihood of success. We need to be skeptical of any claim based on the assumption that the quality of schooling has a significant bearing on noneducational concern.

But there is more on this point. Even if the opportunity for noneducational benefits were in direct relationship to the quality of schooling received, it is not obvious that schooling could be justified on the grounds of this relationship alone. Traditionally, at least, educational justifications have been based on educational standards. These standards, in turn, have contributed to the formation of an educational ideal which has value independently of its noneducational consequences. Understanding the history of culture, having the ability to communicate with others, and having a positive attitude toward particular social norms, for example, have been seen as worthwhile educational attainments independent of their importance in bringing about extrinsic rewards. While the noneducational benefits of schooling have sometimes been seen as necessary conditions for its justification, they have never been regarded as sufficient. If a system of quality schooling was effective as means for the attainment of noneducational benefits, this would not be enough to defend the system as ideal.

If career education is to be justified as a general system of education, as an educational ideal, and not simply as an aspect of a formalized educational program, then it cannot be defended solely on the ground of its noneducational benefits. To be justified as an educational ideal, career education must be shown to produce educational benefits as well.

Justifying the Career Education Movement

That career education is to be regarded as a proposal to implement a particular ideal is quite clear from the literature. As a movement, career education has grown out of the older movement for vocational training. Vocational training, at least for some students, was said to be necessary if they were to get the best possible education for *them* but it was never suggested that it was necessary for all students nor sufficient for any. Proponents of career education are more ambitious than their forebears. They seem to argue their scheme is both necessary and sufficient for anyone being educated.

Career education cannot be understood simply as a portion of the school's program nor as a separate field of study like vocational training (Hoyt et al. 1972, p. 6). The specific objective of successful career performance is converted into the primary aim of all education (ibid.). Career concerns are made a part of every student's course of study from the moment she or he enters school (ibid., p. 74). The emphasis on occupational information and skills is phased into every subject for every student, regardless of schooling level and academic interest or standing (ibid., p. 7). Any subject that cannot be shown to have significance for career concerns is deemed unworthy to teach (ibid., p. 74). Teaching itself is always centered around the problems of gaining employment and helping to assure that a worker is up to the task once a job is secured (ibid., p. 5). [Ed. Note: Hoyt has subsequently tempered these earlier views.]

The extreme formulation of these proposals makes them difficult to justify. It seems naive to deny that their implementation would create a good deal of artificiality in the school's curriculum. Most of what must be learned in life is not for the sake of getting a job but for the sake of leading a good and satisfying life. This sometimes involves occupational concerns, but not always and certainly not exclusively. Schools have traditionally been set up to concern themselves with the problem of leading a good and satisfying life. Only as a means to this end have they concerned themselves with the problem of getting a job. For this reason much of the school's curriculum has, up until now at least, had only an indirect relation to career concerns if, indeed, any relation at all.

A good and satisfying life is based, in part, on social participation in cultural and intellectual activities that are more inclusive than those found in the execution of most vocations. While in school, students ought to be able to engage in activities that increase their understanding of the world and develop skills and dispositions that make it possible to achieve a wide range of practical ends. Limiting school studies to career concerns makes it less likely, rather than more likely, that these objectives will be achieved. If we are to demand that school experience always be related to career performance when such connections do not always exist, we must admit to a certain amount of artificiality in the school's curriculum or else deny the appropriateness of much of what the schools have traditionally been established to achieve.

The concept of education can be viewed both as a product and a process. Sometimes education refers to the result, pointing to the educated person, for example. Alternatively, education can indicate the means toward an objective—when one is said to be receiving an education. In the former case, what one knows is all that counts, while in the latter, the manner by which one comes to know is of importance. When we discuss educational benefits, we are concerned with education in the sense of product; we are discussing the results of an education. When we are trying to decide whether or not a particular system of education is justified, surely we consider such outcomes and, also, the manner by which these results are achieved.

Any evaluation of this type always presupposes standards. The closer the system approaches these standards, both in terms of benefits and manner by which they are secured, the more defensible it is from a purely educational point of view. If the system considered is closer to the ideal than other available alternatives, then it is justified. And all other alternatives are not justified. The upshot of all this can be simply put: if career education is a better educational scheme than other available alternatives, then it must not only be capable of generating more educational benefits but must also be rated more highly in the way it brings these results about.

Means and Ends in Education

Educated individuals can be regarded as people with one or all of the following: (1) a justified true belief about themselves and the world; (2) skills and facilities that enable them to do what they believe they must in order to lead good and satisfying lives; and (3) humane attitudes or dispositions toward what they find in their experience, including, of course, their own thoughts, feelings, and behavior. All three of these characteristics can be regarded as knowledge of one form or another.

In the first case we say that educated people *know that* certain things are facts. What they know to be true they believe to be true and their beliefs are founded on evidence and argument. In the second case, educated people are said to *know how* to do certain things. Whereas in the first case knowledge was assumed to be propositional, in the second case it is performative and denotes some sort of behavioral capacity. In the third case, educated people *know to* do the proper thing at the proper time; they have a disposition to do what they know to be correct. Knowing to entails knowing how but goes one step beyond. Having a disposition to behave in a certain way includes not only the behavioral capacity to do it but also the tendency to do it as well. If a person knows to be punctual, for example, he or she not only knows how to be punctual but is punctual when necessary.

Any benefit that is truly educational, as opposed to noneducational, can be expressed in one or all of these three linguistic modes. If a person benefits educationally from schooling, he or she acquires knowledge that is either propositional, performative, and/or dispositional. If career education is to be regarded as educationally superior to alternative schemes, it must be shown to be the most efficacious road to knowledge. Clearly, career education proponents would be willing to make such a claim. These are, however, three reasons why critics have found their assertions somewhat bizarre. For one, there is little indication in the literature on career education that the acquisition of knowledge beyond that necessary to do a job is of significant educational value. But surely it is. The acquisition of knowledge has significance for education as long as it has a liberating effect on the mind. Most would agree that it has such an effect long after it loses significance for the concerns of gaining and holding employment. It is a serious criticism of career education to say that it fosters the acquisition of knowledge only so long as knowledge proves necessary in job related problems. If proponents of this scheme do not intend to delimit the range of educational benefits in this seemingly indefensible way and if instead they wish to acknowledge the importance of broadly based intellectual growth, they must demonstrate more clearly how their system can accommodate these concerns.

The second reason for skepticism is more sweeping than the first. Attempts that have so far been made to justify career education do not appear to be educational justifications at all. Arguments for career education are most often couched in terms of the noneducational benefits that are believed to accrue from its implementation. Since it is not obvious that any educational scheme can be so justified and since its justification would demand consideration of its educational consequences in any event, these attempts appear less than adequate. No one can expect to win over those who have doubts about the defensibility of career education unless there is a defense that amounts to more than reiteration of the assertion.

The third reason for doubt amounts to the denial that career education was ever designed primarily to benefit those being schooled. Critics who take such a view believe that career education was designed mainly to reinforce the existing social order, even at the cost of the common good. An accusation of this kind is undoubtedly unfair. Given the motivations of most career education supporters, it is not unlikely that those schooled by their means would be helped in many respects. Assuming this to be the case, it is still incumbent upon those who believe in the educational value of career education to show that exploitation is neither the motive force behind their efforts nor the inexorable consequence of their success.

Some Further Questions

One way for supporters of career education to demonstrate the educational value of the benefits that result from their scheme is to show that the manner by which these benefits are attained is itself educational. If a process has an end and is itself educational, the end will be educational also. More particularly, if the means that are used to bring about schooling benefits are both humane and intellectually expansive, then the benefits should be both humane and intellectually expansive.

Whether schooling objectives are aimed at shaping beliefs (propositional knowledge), or shaping behavior (performative knowledge), or both (dispositional knowledge), the manner in which they are realized can either hinder or aid the development of reflection and judgment. When a teacher informs students by simply telling them things, or when he or she influences their behavior by directing them, the manner employed is one of expediency. Here, the end is all that counts. If a teacher wants to instill certain beliefs, but nothing else, indoctrination may be more appropriate than instruction as a strategy for teaching. Likewise, if a teacher wants to influence behavior, but nothing else, he or she may find techniques of conditioning to be most effective. And where he or she intends to form particular dispositions but has no desire to convey the insight that provides understanding, persuasion may be superior to rational discourse. Whenever school functionaries are concerned with bringing about educational benefits but lack interest in means other than that of simple expediency, the school experience does not help students develop reflective thinking.

There are times when the means used in schooling are as crucial as the ends themselves. Means often represent objectives to be realized in their own right. In the standard educational situation, schooling must be conducted so as to respect the student as a person and to help her or him develop a capacity to think and judge independently. Here the manner of teaching represents an end over and above substantive teaching objectives. Instruction is designed to foster a student's potential for rational thought as well as to increase the scope of what she or he knows. Generally, we believe that students have a right to demand reasons from teachers. Their own explanations are to be taken seriously, and they are to be given an opportunity to come to their own conclusions. As a means of instruction, indoctrination is usually deemed unacceptable. We normally regard as inappropriate any approach to teaching that is concerned only with getting a student to believe what the teacher wants. If students are ever expected to accept what a teacher says, it is usually because we believe they have been given good reasons within their ability to grasp. But we almost always expect a teacher to reveal why as well as what when making assertions. And in so doing we expect the teacher to submit any claims to the rational criticisms of those being taught.

Even where the aim of teaching is performative knowledge, it is not normally enough simply to produce a capacity to act. We want teachers to justify the action in the eyes of the students. We want those who are schooled to see what they do as reasonable, if not compelling. And where the objective of schooling is to foster certain dispositions, teachers are expected to accompany their efforts with credible argument. The dispositions being taught must be seen as having a rational value. Israel Scheffler has expressed this same point by saying that the concept of teaching usually entails an obligation to acknowledge the *reason* of the pupils, i.e., their demand for and judgment of reason, even though such demands are not uniformly appropriate at every stage of the teaching interval (Scheffler 1960, pp. 57-58). Whenever the manner of teaching is designed to develop the ability to think, judge, and understand as well as to transmit knowledge as a direct educational benefit, we can speak of schooling as instilling reflection. The distinction between reflection and non-reflection should be clearly understood as limited to cognitive concerns.

Telling, by itself, like informing or mere lecturing, is not a sufficient condition for teaching to yield reflection. To do this, teaching must be more like a dialogue than a monologue. It is an activity that demands good judgment by students as well as teachers. Teachers must continually make judgments about such things as the consequences of their actions on others, the merits of their students' behavior, and the importance of the issues discussed. But as significant as these judgments are, they are no more crucial than the development of the same capacity in the students. Thomas F. Green has expressed this same point quite succinctly. He says that one of the activities inescapably involved in teaching is the exercise of the human capacity for judgment, and one of the pervasive goals of education must be the development of that capacity to its fullest extent (Green 1971a, p. 174). Schooling as an aid to reflection has an implied connection with evidence, grounds, and reasons. It is conducted as much for the sake of improving judgment as for increasing what is known. Forms of inquiry are, after all, the source of the subject matter we call educationally beneficial.

What manner of teaching is suggested by career education? The answer to this question is not easy to come by, but it is clearly important in evaluating the career education movement. Career education proponents sometimes claim to aid reflective thinking. But they rarely go beyond the bare assertion that they see the manner of teaching involved as important. They need to establish, if they can, that it is regarded as important in their scheme. It is regrettable that so much of the literature on a careers approach to schooling has to do with whether or not it brings about a sufficient number of noneducational benefits. If any educational scheme is to be truly justified, it must be shown to be more educationally profitable, in terms of both ends and means, than any available alternative. Perhaps career education cannot, in principle, be justified. Perhaps there is little room in this scheme for either educational benefit or what is usually regarded as the proper manner of teaching.

It is not yet clear, however, that either concern lies beyond the reach of career education. But it is up to those who believe in the movement, not its critics, to show that schooling of this type can foster the acquisition of knowledge and at the same time liberate the mind. Those who believe that career education represents the best type of schooling at our disposal would be well-advised to talk less of the work ethnic and its importance for social order and more about the educational value of relating school subject matter to practical interests (Hoyt et al. 1972, p. 14). The older vocational movement was frequently criticized either for ignoring or sometimes supporting an already corrupt and unjust society. Despite disclaimers to the contrary, one is provided with little assurance that the movement for career education would not produce similar effects. Asking students to step into an already existing job market without giving them an opportunity to evaluate the market itself is hardly fair. How can one defend educationally the claim that students should be "realistic and prepare for life as it is found upon graduation" (*Career Education* p. 8)? Where is the corresponding emphasis on developing a critical intelligence? An educational idea demands, among other things, an effort to give both the skill and the will to evaluate and change an unjust social order. John Dewey was only one of many to point out that a conception of education restricted exclusively to technical competency becomes a means of suppression rather than a means of desirable transformation (Dewey 1966, p. 319). Human beings are not simply human resources, nor do they represent solely an investment in human capital (Goldhammer and Taylor 1972, p. 111). Their potential to bring a high rate of economic return is hardly ever educationally relevant (ibid.).

Viewing education in terms like these makes it more, rather than less, difficult to see what is at stake in the educational enterprise. Education is not simply a means of making individuals contributing members of society. And a system of education which has demonstrated a capacity to contribute to economic growth and national well-being is not necessarily a desirable educational system (ibid.). Can an educational scheme designed to test economic and social ills free the mind from economic and social pressures? If the career approach to schooling is to be justified as an educational scheme, the answer to this question must be a resounding, Yes! And the plan in this approach must be shown to produce this effect.

A CRITICAL ANALYSIS OF CAREER EDUCATION

Carl J. Dolce

Dr. Dolce is dean of the School of Education at North Carolina State University. This article was written in 1975.

Career education is the most recent of a series of movements designed to change the curriculum in the schools of the United States. Following in the wake of progressive education and life adjustment education, the career education movement has developed quickly and has spread widely. This paper presents a critical analysis of the career education movement to date, and outlines some specific areas of concern.

One of the major criticisms of career education is that it was launched and implemented so rapidly that a steamroller effect occurred. When a major change in public policy in the United States is implemented without prior disciplined study and without serious public discussion, a widely espoused model of rational decision-making is violated. Career education is one in a series of major public educational policy decisions, which have been made without prior attempts to define the problems explicitly in the arena of public discourse, and which have been done without adequate consideration of the available alternatives, the consequences of those alternatives, and without a rational selection of those alternatives which optimize the costs and the benefits. The very process by which career education has been implemented has tended to obscure issues, to circumscribe discussion, and to create a new educational ideology based more on faith and hope rather than upon reason and evidence. If the proponents of career education are correct, then society will stand to benefit. However, if the proponents are incorrect, then resources will have been expended ineffectively, and, more seriously, individual students will have had less effective educational experiences than they could have obtained otherwise.

The certitude of advocacy has not been counterbalanced by the questioning of skepticism. The treatment of instructional problems via career education projects has proceeded on a massive scale with no prior validation, little specification of conditions, little testing of results, and with a faith in the goodness of the outcomes. Within six months of the January 1971 *Career Education Now* speech by Sidney P. Marland, Jr., then United States commissioner of education, career education efforts and expenditures by the Office of Education had increased significantly. In June 1971, Commissioner Marland, a skilled and able administrator, had persuaded the chief school officer of each state to commit that state's portion of $18 million in discretionary funds to career education (Marland 1974, pp. 10-11). Although the total sum was relatively small, as Commissioner Marland observed, "Money, however, even in small quantities—$180,999 on an average per state in this case—is a very powerful federal persuader," (ibid.). By 1972, $15 million had been allocated by the Office of Education to support career education models, and by 1973 the federal expenditure for career education had been increased to $43,242,000 (U. S. Department of Health, Education and Welfare 1974, p. A-7). To these minimum estimates of federal expenditures should be added the millions of dollars in expenditures by local and state education agencies.

Such expenditures of scarce resources occurred prior to the development of any systematic definition of career education and prior to public discussion and debate concerning the problems to be addressed or the alternatives available. Commissioner

Marland himself indicates that the first systematically expressed disagreements occurred in a small invitational meeting of the Board of Directors of the Council for Basic Education in October 1972 (Marland 1974, pp. 87-91). As Associate Commissioner Kenneth B. Hoyt has observed, significant changes occurred in Commissioner Marland's thinking about career education between the January 1971 speech and his November 1971 interview with *American Education.* This interview occurred after the meeting in which commitment was made by the chief state school officers (Magisos 1973, p. 15); one wonders to which concept the chiefs made a commitment.

Underestimation of the Complexities of Educational Reform

The leading proponents have seen career education as a vehicle for educational reform. Both Commissioner Marland and then Associate Commissioner (USOE) Hoyt viewed career education as a means of achieving a total reform of the educational system (Marland 1974, pp. xi-xii). Dr. Hoyt outlines explicitly the conditions which call for such reform (Bell and Hoyt 1974, pp. 7-8). There is little acknowledgment of earlier reform efforts, and there is little explicit analysis of why those reform attempts failed. Furthermore, there is little effort to demonstrate how career education will differ in substance from earlier reforms and how it will, in fact, accomplish the reforms it proposes. It is clear that massive infusions of resources alone have not achieved total reform as is evidenced by the history of the Elementary and Secondary Education Act. It is also clear that massive infusion of resources into professional development programs, even in connection with significant direct aid to school systems, has not achieved total reform as is evidenced by the history of the Education Professions Development Act. The total reform objective of career education seems to be founded more on hope than upon reason and evidence.

Even the attempt to destroy the distinctions among vocational, general, and academic curriculums is not based upon an analysis of the historical utility of these three types of curriculums. Historical utility, of course, does not necessarily indicate current validity. Successful efforts to induce change, however, will be based upon the development of alternatives rather than upon a homogenized approach which has not been demonstrated to meet the needs of all the students. There appears to be conceptual confusion between tracking, on the one hand, and necessary distinctions, on the other. Just as English and arithmetic are different subject areas, so are trade and industry courses different from biology courses. In much the same vein, vocational agriculture courses are different from distributive education courses. To overemphasize commonalities and to underemphasize differences invites a blandness which meets successfully no set of needs. One of the basic questions is how to develop a set of educational experiences which will meet the needs of those who require vocational training because of more immediate entry into the labor market, those who will continue into postsecondary education, and those who are undecided. Vocational education for all, a costly attempt which is advocated by some, appears to be as problematic a response as would be education aimed at college admission for all.

By aiming at total reform, career education asks that it be judged not only by more intelligent exploration of career opportunities but also by improvement in reading, arithmetic, written expression, oral expression, literary skills, and so forth. Within this framework, evaluation of career education projects must judge degrees of success or failure in improving academic skills and vocational skills as well as knowledge of career alternatives, in short, evaluation of the degree of success in meeting all the objectives of schooling. Commissioner Marland does not shy away from such a view (Council for Basic Education 1973, p. 3). Such an attempt is indeed ambitious, and the future course of events will indicate whether or not the ambitions were supported by realistic means.

Absence of a Clear Conceptual Framework

The most serious substantive issue in career education is the lack of an explicit conceptual framework. The absence of a clear conceptual framework for career education is not simply a matter of philosophical concern. There is also concern for the practical effects upon human beings who are involved in career education projects. When no boundaries are established for the concept, then any activity can be logically placed within the boundary of career education and no activity can be logically excluded.

In the absence of a prior explication, proponents have sought to have the best of two worlds. Desirable outcomes which are tangentially related to the concept can be claimed while any undesirable practices and outcomes can be disclaimed. If the undesirable practices did not affect directly the lives of human beings, such an approach would be the subject of interesting abstract argument. In the world of implementation, however, the objective, presumably, is not to win an argument but to benefit students and to avoid harm to students.

The failure to establish at least tentative boundaries and the apparent absence of consideration of possible consequences have resulted in at least some instances in which the career education activities do not appear to be either well-founded or in the best interests of students. One example is an interactive computer-based system designed to facilitate student exploration of occupational alternatives. This system has been used in connection with several career education projects. In the system are stored student data such as achievement and I.Q. test scores; the student is allowed to select for exploratory purposes an occupational cluster and a particular occupation within that cluster. In one demonstration of the system, a student with low I.Q. and achievement test scores selected for exploration the health occupations. When the student inquired more specifically of the computer information concerning *surgeon*, the computer flashed the message, "Aren't you shooting a little high? Select another occupation, please." When the student persisted in the attempt to explore the category *surgeon*, the computer flashed on the screen, "See your counselor."

This example indicates some possible undesirable results of failure to examine rigorously the consequences of activities in the light of an adequate theoretical framework. Misuse of student data, lack of understanding of the meaning of *exploration,* and an insensitivity to the student all combined to result in an unfortunate set of activities undertaken under the name of career education. These activities, in fact, seem to result in a situation which many proponents would regard as antithetical to desired objectives.

Pedestrian uses and misuses of test results are commonplace in far too many career education projects. In a number of such projects, the differential aptitude tests are administered, and the resulting career planning report is sent to the parents. Depending upon the individual scores, these reports contain such information as "It would seem highly desirable for you to think about other occupational areas more in line with your interests and which are better suited to your educational plans and abilities." The few lines of qualification in small print are in contrast to the large print of the *interpretation* of test results. One wonders about the effects of such malpractice on the life chances and career choice of some students.

A third example of a career education project might illustrate some of the problems resulting from an absence of prior rigorous examination of the concept. In this project, the teacher involved the students for nearly a year in a study of a nearby construction project. Arithmetic, English, science, and art lessons were based upon observed activities. The students appeared interested and highly motivated. The teacher received high praise for introducing this approach to the study of occupations in all aspects of the curriculum. Upon more thoughtful examination, however, it appeared evident that the exclusive focus of the learning activities for that time was upon blue collar jobs. Less visible professional jobs were not really considered. One might well wonder what the impact of the hidden curriculum of focusing on blue collar jobs might have on the less affluent. Will such a curriculum reinforce the existing tendency to enter such jobs without consideration of other alternatives or deny alternatives which many in our society regard more highly?

Thoughtful proponents of career education will immediately disclaim that such practices are representative or intended by the movement. However, such disclaimers are after the fact and do not alter the undesirable consequences upon students which have already occurred. The pronouncements about career education have not acknowledged the pitfalls prior to the fact. The absence of rigorous thinking about career education not only results in failure to specify the intended objectives and alternative means of attaining those objects, but the absence of such thinking also fails to guard against the probably more serious problem of unanticipated and unintended consequences of such activities. Of more concern is the fact that the task of pointing out excesses and abuses has been undertaken by the critics rather than by the proponents. Career education literature is notable for its absence of self-criticism. It would appear that the main objective is perceived by some to be a victory in an ideological battle rather than careful exploration of alternative ways to improve the quality of instruction for students.

Two contradictory strategies seem to have emerged in terms of establishing the boundaries of career education. Former Commissioner Marland apparently viewed career education as a means of unfreezing an unsatisfactory status quo in education. He has more recently observed, "Let us avoid constraining our prescriptive rules and stereotypes as to what career education is or must be" (Marland 1974, p. 20). Dr. Marland continues in that same paragraph with the view, "We are in *motion*—some say to a degree that has not been known before in generations of American educational history" (emphasis in the original). The implicit assumption is that motion per se is a positive value. However, motion or change can result in a situation less desirable than that condition which has been unfrozen. An educational future is too important to be allowed to develop as a result of happenstance. Associate Commissioner Hoyt feels, apparently, that there is a need for a more clear delineation of boundaries, and to this end he has developed a statement of rationale, assumptions, and a definition of career education (Bell and Hoyt 1974, pp. 7-9). Even in this statement the essentials of career education are not sufficiently delineated, and the cautions and prohibitions are not explicitly related to a meaningful, consistent framework.

In retrospect, the absence of a clear definition, when viewed in the context of attempts to develop four alternative models, appears to indicate a concentration upon delivery systems prior to specification of what was to have been delivered. The school-based, employer-based, home-community-based, and rural-residential-based models attempted to focus on means with insufficient attention to ends. There is virtually no discussion in the literature of the period which indicates any recognition of the possible relationships between ends and means. Ends, largely unspecified, seem to have been subordinate to means.

Some Conceptual Problems and Some Issues

The knowledge and evidence base upon which career education is founded appears to be inadequate to support such an ambitious understanding. Discussed briefly are some issues which require resolution if career education is to be successful.

● **Adequate reality.** Career education is based upon an implicit, static, theoretical model which does not appear to represent reality adequately. The stages of development are usually described as *awareness, exploration*, and *preparation*. At times these stages are subdivided by adding additional ones such as *orientation*. Presumably, these stages are intended to reflect the psychological development of the individual. What is unclear is the operational definition of these stages, or whether the stages occur in linear hierarchical fashion, such as awareness preceding exploration, or whether individuals are in the awareness phase in some areas while at the same time being in the preparation phase in other areas. It appears that individual development is not as neat as the career education model implies. The implications of superimposing such a model on the curriculum have yet to be explored. If preparation in some instances is a precursor to awareness and exploration, how is this to be handled in the instruction of students? Can there be simultaneous development of awareness and orientation? Is awareness at an early age the most effective approach? The essential point is that the stages of career education appear to have been set and accepted without intensive review of our knowledge base, without explication of assumptions, and without exploration of consequences. The fact remains that there is no consensus on how individuals arrive at career decisions, on which variables are operative, or at what stage these decisions are actually made. It is clear that vocational preferences for many students in the eighth or ninth grade or even in later schooling are neither realistic nor stable.

As Professor Donald Super indicated in a speech on 15 April 1975 at a Decisions Ahead conference sponsored by the University of Tennessee, career decisions might be more affected by such generalizable characteristics as acquisition of basic skills, motivation, and completion of certain courses than by a single set of occupational decisions at one point in time.

● **Systematic analyses.** The problems inherent in awareness and exploration phases, even if these are validly described phases, have not been addressed in a systematic way. It seems to be widely accepted that occupations are undergoing rapid transformation. If such rapid transformation exists, what does such a condition imply for awareness experiences for sixth, seventh, and eighth grade students, most of whom will not be ready to enter the work force for another six or more years? For those who will complete a baccalaureate program, the time lag could be ten or more years. A vast substantive study is needed concerning the effect of learning information which proves to be erroneous or outdated by the time the individual enters the work force. Job opportunities affect occupations and positions even more than interests and training. Of what is a student to be aware? That many jobs are available? The nature of such work? That different jobs pay different salaries?

Even more serious are the problems in student exploration of occupations in earlier years of schooling. The job prerequisites and job opportunities do, in fact, change in a relatively short span of time. Prior to the reduction of the aerospace workforce, it would have been difficult to present to students the more limited job opportunities which would exist prior to the completion of their education and training.

Although exploration is expounded as a necessary stage, there is little substantive discussion of the nature of exploration. It is apparent that each job cannot be explored by students and that somehow jobs must be categorized if they are to be approached intelligently. The fifteen occupational clusters, which are the most commonly used categories, are conceptually inadequate and do not fulfill the criteria applicable to valid classification systems. There are overlaps in the clusters; there are occupations which are common in several clusters; and the very definition of all the clusters is still under study. As late as June 1975, a special study was underway to clarify the marine sciences cluster. The effects upon students of inadequate clustering and categorization does not appear to be of great concern to career education advocates. Whether or not there are probable undesirable effects from such inadequate categorization should not remain an unasked question.

The change in jobs and occupations several times during the working life of many individuals has been well documented. Also well documented is that career patterns are not necessarily sequential in a hierarchy of positions. How the effects of these patterns should be reflected in an exploratory phase has not been determined.

Exploration activities in career education projects apparently are based upon the implicit assumption that exploration consists of viewing and experiencing several occupations. There seems to be little concern that the occupations chosen are representative in terms of skills required, social status, pay, job opportunities, etc. An implicit aspect of a rational exploration program is that the widest possible selection of alternatives be made available to students to explore. One pragmatic index of attempts to achieve representativeness would be to sample whether teachers in career education projects are sensitive to the need for representative alternatives and whether the teachers are knowledgeable about the structure of occupations, the nature of occupational clusters, and the requirements of various types of occupations and jobs. Preliminary study of teacher knowledge reveals great inadequacies.

The issues of required exploration, the questions of what constitutes a representative sample, and how to address this representative sample are seldom discussed. Given the differential impact of curricular experiences upon students of differing socio-economic backgrounds, the issues involved in exploration need to be addressed more directly.

• **Values and work.** Although career education is often defined as concerned with more than work, the almost exclusive attention in the world of implementation seems to be on the work world, with an emphasis upon jobs and occupations. Career education seems to be narrowing in concept to occupational education. The nonwork aspects of career education have received scant attention.

One consistent theme seems to be the dignity of work. While such a doctrine in the abstract might be valid, society does not, in fact, view all work as having dignity. To indoctrinate students to the contrary is to create a false image of society. The view of the lack of dignity of certain jobs is a societal problem and not an educational problem for school age students. When pressed, many of the exponents of the dignity of work concept reluctantly agree that for themselves and their children, certain jobs and occupations are not acceptable. If such is the case, the educational system is then being geared, without necessarily an intent to do so, to making acceptable among students that which is not acceptable in the larger society.

Furthermore, there seems to be the mistaken notion that work can be fulfilling and that education has failed if all work is not viewed as fulfilling. It would appear to be more realistic to concede that while work might be essential, it is not necessarily fulfilling. However, such a concession would then allow that work and work-related activities are only a part of life, and that other aspects need to revolve around occupations. Such a concession would, therefore, require a redefinition of career education and the role of career education in the curriculum. It might then be possible to allow that education can be a "consolatory activity," in the words of Mr. Clifton Fadiman (Council for Basic Education 1973, p. 21); that is, education can be the humanizing aspect in a world in which the work performed by many is dull and repetitive.

Such a concession would also be difficult to make by many current proponents because the implication is that work occupations are not necessarily the focal point of relevance for all students. While relevance might be achieved for some students, others might find relevance in poetry, music, abstract mathematics, or in any other area. The infusion approach could not be defended in terms of all students' needs, desires, and aspirations, and career education might then enter a more sophisticated and possibly more valid era.

The Current Momentum of Career Education

In addition to acting in the post World War II tradition of viewing public resources as relatively limitless, the career education movement has created its own momentum of vested interests. Career education had become institutionalized prior to the period of widespread public discussion and public exploration of alternatives. As the National Advisory Council on Vocational Education has noted, "Clearly the career education movement has powerful momentum" (National Advisory Council on Vocational Education 1974, p. 4). Then Associate Commissioner for Career Education, Kenneth B. Hoyt estimated that in 1974 career education activities of some nature were begun in approximately 5,000 of the 17,000 school districts in the United States (Hoyt 1975, p. 62). Commitment of resources and personal and professional effort tend to evoke psychological commitment. Psychological commitment tends to mitigate against the development of alternative problem definitions and alternative solutions.

The career education momentum is reinforced by continued leadership from the Office of Education, by congressional legislation in the Education Amendments of 1974 which specified the concept by name, and by the approximately 35 state boards of education which have adopted resolutions in support of career education. Clearly career education has become the "in" innovation. When innovations become in, commercial firms quite naturally seek to capitalize on such developments. Several large profit-making firms have developed and marketed extensively career education materials. Even the College Entrance Examination Board has developed studies, career education designed services, and research and development activities (Marland 1974, pp. 15-19). Also books which have only the loosest connection with career education now bear the title *Career Education* (for example, see Bolino 1973).

The growth of such psychological and material investments in an untested concept is not conducive to honest exploration of alternatives. Marland's sincere attitude in his chapter entitled "The Critics, Bless Them" (Marland 1974, pp. 107-128) is clearly not shared by the majority of proponents. Critics and skeptics are often dismissed as a few educational elitists, those who "refuse to recognize" (National Advisory Council on Vocational Education 1974, p. 4), or as defenders of the status quo. Given the nature of the human condition and given the acceptable methods of public policy determination in a republic, it would appear to have been more realistic to bless the critics prior to the investment of large sums of financial resources and the investment of large amounts of psychological capital.

For those who feel that they have arrived at the truth, criticism and discussion are needless and onerous activities. For those who are still seeking truth, criticism and discussion are welcome means of testing the validity of any idea. The present momentum of career education, which is a temporary source of its strength, might well prove to be the cause of its demise in the long run. The valid aspects of the movement, given such momentum and institutionalization, cannot be easily separated from those aspects which are invalid. Clearly, career education will not fade away tomorrow. Whether or not any vestiges remain after a decade remains to be seen.

It appears that more critical self-examination and study is needed if career education is to have a desirable long-range impact upon American education. Rather than continued effort to expand the number of career education programs and the number of students affected, greater effort should be given to the theoretical framework of career education and conceptual problems and issues which exist. The actual impact of career education programs upon human beings should be assessed more carefully, and such assessment should lead to revisions in concepts and practices which are congruent with more explicitly and carefully defined objectives.

REFERENCES

Bell, Terrell H. and Hoyt, Kenneth B. *Career Education: The USOE Perspective.* Columbus, Ohio: The Center for Vocational Education, 1974.

Bolino, August C. *Career Education Contributions to Economic Growth.* New York: Praeger Publishers, 1973.

Career Education. Washington, D.C.: U.S. Department of Health, Education, and Welfare, n.d.

Cohen, R. S. "On the Marxist Philosophy of Education." *Modern Philosophers and Education.* 54th Yearbook of the National Society for the Study of Education, 1955.

Council for Basic Education. *What Is Career Education? A Conversation with Sidney P. Marland, Jr. and James D. Koerner.* Washington: Occasional Papers No. 20, 1973.

Goldhammer, Keith, and Taylor, Robert E. *Career Education: Perspective and Promise.* Columbus, Ohio: Merrill, 1972.

Green, T. F. *The Activities of Teaching.* New York: McGraw-Hill, 1971.

Hoyt, Kenneth B. "An Introduction to Career Education." U.S. Department of Health, Education, and Welfare, 1975.

Hoyt, Kenneth B., et. al. *Career Education: What It Is and How to Do It.* Salt Lake City: Olympus, 1972.

Magisos, Joel H., (ed.), *Career Education.* Washington: The American Vocational Association, Inc., 1973.

Marland, Sidney P., Jr. *Career Education: Retrospect and Prospect.* Columbus, Ohio: The Center for Vocational Education, 1974.

National Advisory Council on Vocational Education, *Eighth Report,* September, 1974.

Pratte, R. "School and Purpose." Presidential Address of the Ohio Valley Philosophy of Education Society. Cincinnati: 15 November 1974.

Scheffler, I. *The Language of Education.* Springfield, Ill.: Thomas, 1960.

U. S. Department of Health, Education, and Welfare, Education Division, Office of Education. *Taxonomy and Profiles of Career Education,* Vol. 1, September, 1974.

Vocationalism and Humanism in Career Education

Career education and vocational education are often mistaken as the same thing. In reality, however, vocational education is a part of career education, but career education is more than vocational education. The confusion stems, in part, from a long-standing belief that vocationalism and humanism are two separate entities in our educational system. Also, since funding of career education was tied to that of vocational education in the first few years of its development, many educators linked the two. Although career education does contribute to vocational development of the individual, this is not its only objective. Career education contributes to the overall development of the individual, and, therefore, makes education more meaningful, including vocational education as well as the humanities.

This chapter consists of three articles which were written in 1975 at a time when the debate over the distinction between vocational education and career education was at its peak. Arthur G. Wirth's article sets the historical perspective; he reminds us that those who ignore history run the risk of repeating it. He points out that if career education and vocational education are to develop and have an impact on society and the individual learner we must resolve the conflict between vocationalism and humanism in both. Donald E. Super adds a psychological dimension to the argument and projects it in the future. Super draws heavily on his vocational development theories and research to illustrate his point. Like Super, Edwin L. Herr explores the psychological dimension.

THE HISTORICAL AND SOCIAL CONTEXT OF CAREER EDUCATION

Arthur G. Wirth

A recognized scholar in the areas of history and philosophy of education, Dr. Wirth is professor of education at Washington University in Missouri. Dr. Wirth has published several books and many articles relative to work and education. This article was written in 1975.

> The purpose of vocational education is to help a person secure a job, train him so he can hold it after he gets it, and assist him in advancing to a better job. . . . Vocational education must establish habits: habits of correct thinking and correct doing. . . . For its goals vocational education should go consistently to the world of economic activity (Charles A. Prosser 1949).
>
> The dominant vocation of all human beings at all times is living—intellectual and moral growth. In childhood and youth, with their relative freedom from economic stress, this fact is naked and unconcealed. To predetermine some future occupation for which education is to be a strict preparation is to injure the possibilities of present development and thereby to reduce the adequacy of preparation for a future right employment. . . . Such training may develop a skill in routine lines . . . . but it will be at the expense of those qualities of alert observation and coherent and ingenious planning which make an occupation intellectually rewarding. . . .
>
> The question of industrial education is fraught with consequences for the future of democracy. Its right development will do more to make public education truly democratic than any other one agency now under consideration. Its wrong treatment will as surely accentuate all undemocratic tendencies in our present situation, by fostering and strengthening class divisions in school and out (John Dewey 1916).

Career education's problem of self-definition is well-known. These quotations from early discussions on the role of the vocational aspects of education show that differences over definition are more than a contemporary frustration. Efforts to resolve them require more than semantic word play and more than discussions about pedagogical policies. The root causes of the ambiguities and contradictions in attempts at definition derive from unresolved conflicts among us about the life goals we wish to pursue under technological-corporate conditions.

It is my contention in this paper that major issues in the debate over vocationalism have been continuing ones. The contending positions were stated with stark clarity in the first round of debate (1900-1917) which culminated in the Smith-Hughes Act. By reviewing aspects of this early episode we may sharpen our perception of basic value conflicts—philosophical and political as well as educational. While not yielding the definitive answer to the question What is career education? this may make a contribution to understanding the complexity of the question.

There are two sets of promises in the American Dream: the promises of what Max Lerner called "America as a Business Civilization" and the promises of democratic equality, freedom, and participation. They interrelate at points but there are tensions between them. Both were represented in the debate over vocationalism at the opening of the progressive era.

Social Darwinists of the William Graham Sumner type enunciated the faith of the business ideology: society consists of isolated individuals of varying abilities and capacities. When left to pursue their self-advantage in rugged competition, they will bring forth the promise of ever-increasing, material plenty for all. From this wellspring flow all other goods—a home of one's own; education for the kids; support for religion, philanthropies, and the arts. Samuel Hayes in his comments on life in the United States in 1914 observed, "The American people subordinated religion, education, and politics to the process of creating wealth. Increasing production, employment, and income became the measure of community success, and personal riches the mark of individual achievement" (Hayes 1957, p. 12). Perceptive leaders who operated from these premises were aware that new corporate-technological-economic conditions had emerged. Critical contributions from American schooling would be required to meet the efficiency needs of the new system. The logic of social Darwinism for vocational education was quite clear. Vocationalism could clarify its purposes by giving unmistakable priority to meeting the hierarchical skill needs of the corporate economy and by instilling attitudes and training so each individual could move as high in the system as ability and qualities of character would permit.

But there were other forces in the progressive era with different kinds of concerns. They were represented by progressive "do-gooders" like the settlement house leaders working daily with the appalling problems of the teeming metropolises. They were concerned about the welfare of urban poor people, the disaffected attitudes toward schooling of their children, and whether democratic traditions and values could meaningfully be retained under new corporate-urban conditions.

Both groups had able spokespersons who could articulate clearly and forcefully the philosophical assumptions and rationales important to each. Social efficiency philosophers like David Snedden of Teachers College and Charles Prosser, the executive secretary of the National Society for the Promotion of Industrial Education and author of the Smith-Hughes Act, verbalized effectively and tirelessly the social Darwinist point of view. John Dewey adopted as his major philosophical concern the preoccupation of progressive reformers, articulated later by Paul Goodman as "whether or not our beautiful, libertarian, populist experiment is viable under modern conditions" (Goodman 1968, p. 274).

This paper aims to compare two philosophical models of vocationalism which grew from these two orientations in the progressive era.

The movement in the direction of adding a vocational component to American education had been under way for three or four decades before the turn of the century. The Civil War, like other major wars, had revolutionary consequences for American society. It generated the conditions for a new America marked by corporate industrialism and urbanism. The expansion of railways, heavy industries, mining, machine-centered agriculture, and business and government bureaucracies broke the mold of traditional ways of producing and distributing goods. Apprenticeship systems and on-the-job learning were no longer adequate for the new situation.

Before the war a bright young person might pick up principles and skills of engineering by working with those who were pushing through the railroads on the frontier. But as engine plants produced larger locomotives, as steel mills produced the components for heavier bridges and equipment, seat-of-the-pants training no longer sufficed. In retrospect we can see that the earliest innovations for formal technical training were designed to train leaders who could handle the complexities of science and industry. In 1860 there were perhaps only five schools of engineering. By 1880, as the shortage of engineers became painfully apparent, the number had increased to eighty-five. This development was accompanied by the creation of other professional schools in American universities—colleges of business administration, mining, agriculture and horticulture, forestry, veterinary medicine, and education. At lower levels commercial courses were introduced to train the white collar secretariat of the new corporations; for the workshops beginning efforts were made in industrial drawing, and the manual training movement was launched for pre-engineering in the high schools and for the cultivation of leadership within the labor force.

In spite of these moves only a tiny percentage of the population was involved. By the end of the nineties, a watershed decade, discontent about urban schooling was sharply on the rise. Interest groups as divergent as business and industry, organized labor, farm organizations, social workers, and women's rights groups began to call for some version of industrial education as an antidote to the sterility and ineffectiveness of the public schools. This broad move culminated in 1906 with the publication of the Douglas Commission's Report of the Massachusetts Commission on Industrial and Technical Education, and the founding of the National Society for the Promotion of Industrial Education (NSPIE).

But the tensions within progressive reform were quick to show themselves. Robert Wiebe has noted that:

> . . . By 1905 urban progressives were already separating along two paths. While one group used the language of the budget, boosterism, and social control, the other talked of economic justice, human opportunities, and rehabilitated democracy. Efficiency as economy diverged further and further from efficiency as social service (Wiebe 1967, p. 176).

On the subject of industrial education both groups were lamenting the waste in education. A closer look reveals that the social efficiency progressives were alarmed most by financial waste as they measured school output against efficiency criteria—the new rage of the era. The humanitarians were bothered about the human waste—those who left school while young entering into dead-end labor jobs and the irrelevance of classroom recitations. Thus Dewey in a chapter entitled "Waste in Education" charged that out-of-school experiences were not drawn on in classes and the recitations had little relevance for children when they fled at the end of the day. The schools, he said, were "isolated from life" (Dewey 1923).

Now we are ready to turn to how the two wings of urban progressivism saw the need for vocationalism in education.

The Social Efficiency Approach to Vocationalism

One of the groups most active in articulating the views of the business community was the National Association of Manufacturers (NAM). The association had formed as a result of the 1893 depression. Its members soon identified as the cause of their problems a serious overproduction which had accompanied frenzied post-Civil War industrial expansion. Catastrophe, they felt, would be their lot if they limited themselves to the demands of the domestic market. New opportunities lay overseas in Latin America and Asia. Their salvation lay in entering the international economic arena. As they ventured out, they found tough competition from aggressive German businesspeople. Soon they sent emissaries to Germany to assess the source of German advantage, which was the existence of a powerful set of carefully designed skill training programs. There were, for example, twenty-one different schools for the building trades alone; there were Werkmeisterschulen for supervisors and research-oriented Technische Hochschulen for engineers at the top. This finely graded set of training programs was neatly meshed to the hierarchical skill needs of the technological system. It was administered by practical people rather than fuzzy-minded educators.

Impressed by what they found in Germany the manufacturers set up their own NAM Committee on Industrial Education. Its chairperson, H. E. Miles, in 1911 reported a dismal contrast in American public education. His committee rolled out statistics of cost against performance of American schools and was dismayed at the low yield of school products. What, Miles asked, were the people getting for an outlay of $450 million and a school investment plant of $1 billion? Only 50% of children in school finished the sixth grade; one in three completed grammar school; and only one out of thirty finished high school. The problem, he said, was that the work of the schools rested on "theories instead of reality" (National Association of Manufacturers 1912). The schools, said Miles, offered a literary education which satisfied the one student in thirty who was abstract-minded. They were guilty of inexcusable neglect of the other twenty-nine.

Mile's committee became convinced that the German system not only offered a counter to the drift away from formal schooling by the nonliterary oriented students, but it also provided the German nation with a reliable labor force motivated by a positive work ethic. The words of a leading German philosopher of vocational education impressed the manufacturers:

> The first aim of education for those leaving the elementary school is training for trade efficiency, and joy and love of work. With these is connected the training of those elementary virtues which efficiency and love of work have in their train—conscientiousness, industry, perseverance, responsibility, self-restraint, and devotion to an active life (Simons 1966, p. 30).

What a difference such attitudes could make in American factories where, as Miles said, " . . . our factory children look upon a shop too much as upon a jail. There has developed among a considerable part of the adult factory workers a dislike, almost a hate, of work" (National Association of Manufacturers 1912, p. 154).

The association became convinced that American manufacturers could compete successfully in international markets only if the American school system introduced a set of separate vocational schools, guided by men of industry, patterned after the German model.

If America was to make such a radical innovation in its public school system new legislation and funding eventually would be required. The groundwork for that would have to be prepared by thoughtful and persuasive argumentation. Two educators within the vocational education movement, David Snedden and Charles Prosser, became prominent articulators of a social efficiency philosophy to support the German idea. David Snedden left a professorship at Teachers College, Columbia University, to become commissioner of education in 1909 under Governor Douglas in Massachusetts. He appointed his colleague, Charles Prosser, as his deputy to create and administer the new vocational programs. Snedden was a voluminous writer and was listed by Norman Woefel as one of the seventeen leaders in American education who were "molders of the American mind." He was the first editor of *The American Vocational Journal.*

Charles Prosser became executive secretary of the National Society for the Promotion of Industrial Education (NSPIE) in 1912 and had the organizational genius to bring about the coalition of groups which made possible the enactment of the Smith-Hughes Act. He was, in fact, the effective author of the act. He became director of the famous Dunwoody Institute of Vocational Training in Minneapolis and was the first executive director of the Federal Board of Vocational Education. In 1943 he was author of the Prosser Life-Adjustment Resolution which launched the ill-fated movement bearing that name.

The rationale they developed to support the technocratic model was marked by a conservative social philosophy, a methodology of specific training operations based on principles of stimulus-response psychology, e.g., a curriculum designed according to a job analysis of the needs of industry and by a preference for a separately administered set of vocational schools.

Snedden shared the basic faith of Herbert Spencer and the conservative social Darwinists that the emergence of scientific-corporate capitalism was the cosmic instrument for progress. He accepted the basic proposition of the manufacturers that what was good for business was good for America. In order to help more Americans enjoy progress, the task of education was to aid the economy to function as efficiently as possible.

Snedden worked from an assumption about the nature of social life which he borrowed from his sociology teacher Franklin Giddings:

> Society, like the material world . . . passes from homogeneity and indefiniteness of nonorganization to the heterogeneity and definiteness of organization. The process of selection is based upon the differences growing out of the unequal conditions of both heredity and nurture to which man is born. Inequality—physical, mental, and moral—is an inevitable characteristic of the social population (Giddings 1896, p. 9).

Snedden likened the good society to a winning "team group." A team was made stronger by specialization of functions. Some, like the officers on a submarine crew, would be trained to lead and coordinate; others would be trained for their special functions in the ranks (Snedden 1924, p. 554).

As Snedden saw it, scientific testing instruments combined with vocational guidance would make it possible for schools to do what Charles Eliot had suggested in 1907—differentiate children into programs according to their "probable destinies" based on heredity plus economic and social factors. The new junior high schools would perform the task of sorting students into differentiated courses: pre-vocational offerings in commercial subjects, industrial arts, and agricultural or household arts for those "who most incline to them or have need of them."

Frederick Fish, president of A. T. and T. and chairman of the Massachusetts Board of Education, was impressed by the vision of his commissioner of education and called on the schools to revise their values by providing training to meet "the practical needs of life" for "the rank and file."

The Snedden-Fish regime was prepared to act as well as talk. Snedden appointed his Teachers College colleague, Charles Prosser, to develop a system of vocational schools for the major industrial centers of the state.

By 1912, when Prosser became executive secretary of the National Society for the Promotion of Industrial Education, he had clarified his goal: to reject the impractical manual training of the general educators and replace it with "real vocational education." By this he meant training for useful employment—train the person to get a job, hold on to it, and be able to advance to a better job.

Prosser insisted that all of vocational content must be specific and that its source was to be found "in the experience of those who have mastered the occupation." A prototype of the plan favored by Prosser was established in the short unit courses which he developed while director of the Dunwoody Institute in Minneapolis. At the Dunwoody Institute, units were programmed in great detail to lead students step-by-step through the skill development cycle. Students punched in on time clocks, and instructors behaved like shop supervisors rather than public school teachers. A no-nonsense attitude prevailed. If students were not punctual, orderly, and efficient, they were asked to leave.

The Dunwoody style is recognizable in some of the features Prosser wrote into Smith-Hughes. Approved programs had to meet the criterion of "fitting for useful employment" persons over fourteen but under college age who were preparing for work on farms, in trades, in industrial pursuits, and the like. Federal funds were given only for support of vocational training classes. Funds for the training of teachers were restricted to those who "have had adequate vocational experience or contact in the line of work for which they are preparing."

Since his rationale excluded general educators from the management of vocational training, Prosser fought as long as possible for separately administered vocational education. In the final politicking prior to 1917, he had to make some concessions, but in the main he created a framework which permitted vocational programs to stand apart. The Smith-Hughes Act did establish a federal board for vocational education, separate from the U. S. Office of Education and responsible only to Congress. The seven member board consisted of the secretaries of labor, commerce, and agriculture and three citizens representing labor, agriculture, and manufacturing. The commissioner of education was added to allay the anxieties of the NEA.

Prosser was immediately appointed executive director of the federal board. In actuality, both the language of Smith-Hughes and the administrative style of Dr. Prosser assured that vocational education would function as a separate aspect of education within the states. The genius of Charles Prosser lay in his capacity to create well-tooled manpower training programs. Somewhere in a technological society that task must be done.

Progressive Reform and Dewey's Philosophy

The manufacturers were alert and vocal in their estimate of the kind of vocational training the schools should incorporate. The humanitarian wing of progressivism was by no means silent and had powerful spokespersons. In 1913, for example, at a joint meeting of the National Vocational Guidance Association (NVGA) and the NSPIE, a group of progressives led the NVGA to refuse the invitation of Charles Prosser to join that organization. The humanitarians were represented by speakers like Ida Tarbell, queen of the muckrakers, arguing for the inclusion of girls in industrial education; Owen R. Lovejoy, secretary of the National Child Labor Committee; and representatives of a Chicago reform group, such as George H. Mead and Frank Leavitt, of the University of Chicago, who joined John Dewey in opposing pressures to establish separate vocational schools.

Owen R. Lovejoy enunciated the point of view represented by this wing. Lovejoy told the convention that both industries and schools needed to be reformed before children could experience the "promise of America." He said that schools needed to introduce programs of vocational guidance which would "analyze our industries and train our youth to distinguish between a vocation and a job." He criticized the captains of industry who said, "Here are the jobs; what kind of children have you to offer?" Educators and guidance personnel must reverse the inquiry, said Lovejoy, and ask, "Here are your children; what kind of industry have you to offer?" (Lovejoy 1914, p. 13).

His position was supported by Frank Leavitt, who was to become the first president of NVGA. Leavitt said guidance workers needed to study industries from the point of view of whether they were good for children. Such studies, "if carried out in a comprehensive, purposeful, and scientific way, may force upon industry many modifications which will be good not only for the children but equally for the industry." Vocational guidance will not hesitate to make such demands just because an industry is rich and powerful, Leavitt added. "Why should we hesitate to lay hands on industry in the name of education, when we already laid hands on the school in the name of industry?" (Leavitt 1914, pp. 79-81).

While attending the 1913 convention John Dewey was at work on the thinking which would emerge in *Democracy and Education* in which he said, "At the present time the conflict of philosophical theories focuses in discussion of the proper place and function of vocational factors in education . . . significant differences in fundamental philosophical conceptions find their chief issue in connection with this point. . . . " (Dewey 1916, Chapter 23). It is worth noting that his most famous chapter on the vocational issue was not entitled "Vocational Education" but rather "Vocational Aspects in Education."

Dewey, who was eager to advocate vocational aspects in education as a pivotal instrument of school reform, encountered a major frustration in distinguishing his point of view from the version of vocational education as it was being put forth by Snedden and Prosser.

Snedden, Prosser, and Dewey were all critics of traditional schooling. On the surface there were points of agreement. They all condemned sterile, bookish education. Just below the surface, however, there were basic differences. Dewey was quite aware of the disagreements, but Snedden was hurt and bewildered when Dewey lashed out at him for his advocacy of separate vocational schools. Snedden expressed his sense of betrayal in a letter to *The New Republic* in which he said that those who had been seeking sound vocational education had become accustomed to opposition from the academic brethren. "But to find Dr. Dewey apparently giving aid and comfort to opponents of a broader, richer, and more effective program of education . . . is discouraging" (Snedden 1924, p. 40).

If Snedden expected Dewey to relent he was in for disappointment. Dewey replied sharply that his differences with Snedden were profoundly social and political as well as educational:

> The kind of vocational education in which I am interested is not one which will "adapt" workers to the existing industrial regime; I am not sufficiently in love with the regime for that. It seems to me that the business of all who would not be educational timeservers is to resist every move in this direction, and to strive for a kind of vocational education which will first alter the existing industrial system, and ultimately transform it (Dewey 1916, p. 42).

Furthermore, Dewey charged, Snedden had failed to meet the heart of his argument on pedagogical matters: "I argued that a separation of trade education and general education of youth has the inevitable tendency to make both kinds of training narrower and less significant than the schooling in which the traditional education is reorganized to utilize the subject matter—active, scientific, and social—of the present day environment" (ibid.).

Dewey's central concern was with the problems of persons and of democratic traditions in the technological society. He rejected the image of isolated individuals moved by the play of natural forces in the market place. He operated from the social psychology position of his colleague George H. Mead, with its self-other concept of personality. The self was seen as emerging from both the patterning of culture and the value choices of the individual. The premise held that if you wanted persons with qualities capable of sustaining democratic values, they had to be nourished in communities marked by such values. As Dewey saw it, people were beginning to repeat the rhetoric of democratic values while living in daily contradiction of them.

The task of overcoming the contradictions, as Dewey defined it, was to develop strategies for bringing qualities of the democratic ethos into institutions being transformed by science, technology, and corporatism. His general strategy was to seek means by which the qualities of mind required to reform institutions could be made available across the entire population.

In his design the schools were assigned a critical role: they could teach the hypothetical mode of thought required to handle complex problems; the schools themselves could be turned into communities where the young in living and learning would experience the life qualities exemplified in the creative work of scientists and artists. By spending the years of childhood and youth in such learning communities, the young might become the kind of people who could change institutional life-styles so they would serve to liberate persons rather than manipulate them as functionaries.

In *Democracy and Education* Dewey struggled to make clear his argument about how vocational aspects or occupations could become major instruments for general school reform.

> Both practically and philosophically the key to the present educational situation lies in a gradual reconstruction of school materials and methods so as to utilize various forms of intellectual and moral content . . . This educational reorganization cannot be accomplished by merely trying to give a technical preparation for industries and professions as they now operate, much less by merely reproducing industrial conditions in the school. The problem is not that of making the schools an adjunct to manufacturing and commerce, but of utilizing the factors of industry to make school life more active, more full of immediate meaning, more connected with out-of-school experience. The problem is not easy of solution. There is a standing danger that education will perpetuate the older traditions for a select few, and effect its adjustment to the newer economic conditions more or less on the basis of acquiescence in the untransformed, unrationalized, and unsocialized phases of our defective industrial regime. Put in concrete terms, there is danger that vocational education will be interpreted in theory and practice as trade education, as a means of securing technical efficiency in specialized future pursuits (Dewey 1916, pp. 369-370).

The key recommendation is to use occupations in a way to bring out their intellectual and moral content. We are promised that this innovation will make school life more active and more relevant to out-of-school experience and that schools so organized can influence mental dispositions in ways to help transform "our defective industrial regime."

The complexity of Dewey's position is indicated in the tortuous analysis he made of the related terms—occupations, vocations, callings—in *Democracy and Education*. On the one hand, Dewey spoke of occupations in referring to forms of work available to people in the new industrial era. In this case he described how work in industry and commerce was being transformed by scientific and technological factors.

> Industry has ceased to be essentially an empirical, rule-of-thumb procedure, handed down by custom. Its technique is now technological: that is to say, based upon machinery resulting from discoveries in mathematics, physics, chemistry, bacteriology, etc. . . . While the intellectual possibilities of industry have multiplied, industrial conditions tend to make industry, for the great masses, less of an educative resource than it was in the days of hand production for local markets. The burden of realizing the intellectual possibilities inherent in work is thus thrown back on the school (ibid., p. 367).

In practice, however, the schools were not seizing upon opportunities to draw on the intellectual possibilities of industry. Premature training for saleable skills neglected the liberalizing dimension of exploring things in terms of their broader meanings and of raising questions about human values. Public school trade training, because of its sharp focus on job skills, tended to create members of a permanent, subordinate working class. If denied access to liberalizing experiences, workers would not be prepared to help transform an unsatisfying industrialism into something more civilized.

In that same chapter, however, Dewey also used the terms occupation and vocation in ways which had nothing to do with earning a living. We must avoid, he said, using vocation or occupation to apply only to activities where tangible commodities are produced, or to imply that each person has only one vocation. In its broader definition, an occupation "is a continuous activity having a purpose." In this sense, it is something with which an individual is occupied; it is something in which he or she is interested and to which there is a commitment. Each individual, in this sense, has a variety of occupations, callings, or vocations. He or she may earn a living as a garment worker or an engineer. But he or she also may be a member of a family, may be active in community affairs and in political organizations, or may be passionately committed to playing the oboe. We tend, Dewey said, to name a person's vocation according to employment. "But we should not allow ourselves to be so subject to works as to ignore and virtually deny his other callings when it comes to the vocational phases of education" (ibid., p. 359).

Dewey employed a kind of accordion usage of the term occupation. In a constricted sense, Dewey used it to refer to specific jobs and concomitant training programs; more broadly, he used it in the sense of meaningful work from which intellectual, social, and moral significance would be extracted. Beyond paid employment, he used occupation to apply to activities where one's deepest personal purposes or interests were involved; and at its fullest extension he said "the dominant vocation of all human beings at all times is living—intellectual and moral growth" (ibid., p. 362).

His general point was that one's vocation, both in the sense of one's work and of one's central concerns, plays a critical role in self-fulfillment and continuing education.

> A calling is also of necessity an organizing principle for information and ideas, for knowledge and intellectual growth. It provides an axis which runs through an immense diversity of detail; it causes different experiences, facts, items of information to fall into order one with another. The lawyer, the physician, the laboratory investigator in some branch of chemistry, the parent, the citizen interested in his own locality, has a constant working stimulus to note and relate whatever has to do with his concern. He unconsciously, from the motivation of his occupation, reaches out for all relevant information, and holds to it (ibid.).

In this sense the schools had an important function in helping people find their vocations; although, in a genuinely humane community, all the other institutions would have this function too.

When Dewey was at the University of Chicago he created the Laboratory School where he put his ideas to work. Studies were organized around occupations such as weaving, gardening, cooking, and construction. Studies in the sciences, history, language, mathematics, and the arts were related to these activities. For example, children could get the feeling of how science and technology had affected such a basic process as the turning of raw wool into clothing by first trying the process by hand and then observing factory methods. They could study also what the social and human effects were when people moved from handicraft to corporate industrial modes of production. As students grew older, activities and studies could be extended to the out-of-school community; thus, Dewey developed an interest in the Gary Plan, where children combined science study with experiences in the school steam plant or in the steel mills of the town. Dewey was drawn, too, to the polytechnical education concepts in the USSR in the 1920s and the reforms of rural education in the escuelas de accion of the Mexican Revolution. Currently such programs as the New Jersey Technology for Children Project, the work of the Center for Technological Education in the San Francisco Bay Area, the Parkway Plan in Philadelphia, and the University Without Walls experiments contain features related to Dewey's rationale.

Finally, there was the valuational aspect. In *Individualism Old and New* and elsewhere he made his economic critique in which he argued that the single-minded pursuit of profit of a laissez-faire economy involved a tragic misuse of the power of science and technology (Dewey 1929). Children and young adults had to be educated so as to learn how to examine the consequences of technology. He stated the criterion they should learn to employ in an often-quoted statement in *Reconstruction in Philosophy:*

> All social institutions have a meaning, a purpose. That purpose is to set free and to develop the capacities of human individuals without respect to race, sex, class, or economic status. . . . (The) test of their value is the extent to which they educate every individual into the full stature of his possibility. Democracy has many meanings, but if it has a moral meaning, it is found in resolving that the supreme test of all political institutions and industrial arrangements shall be the contribution they make to the all-around growth of every member of society (Dewey 1950, p. 147).

The goal was to develop a populace who would take that criterion seriously and apply it to all institutions.

With a rationale like this Dewey joined those who resisted the pressures for a dual system in the vocational education movement. A general education, designed to promote industrial intelligence, would provide a genuine alternative to German dualism:

> Instead of trying to split schools into two kinds, one of a trade type for children whom it is assumed are to be employees and one of a liberal type for the children of the well-to-do, it will aim at such a reorganization of existing schools as will give all pupils a genuine respect for useful work, an ability to render service, and a contempt for social parasites whether they are called tramps or leaders of "society". . . . It will indeed make much of developing motor and manual skills, but not of a routine or automatic type. It will rather utilize active and manual pursuits as the means of developing constructive, inventive, and creative power of mind. It will select the materials and the technique of the trades not for the sake of producing skilled workers for hire in definite trades, but for the sake of

securing industrial intelligence—a knowledge of the conditions and processes of present manufacturing, transportation, and commerce so that the individual may be able to make his own choices and his own adjustments, and be master, so far as in him lies, of his own economic fate. It will be recognized that, for this purpose, a broad acquaintance with science and skill in the laboratory control of materials and processes is more important than skill in trade operations. It will remember that the future employee is a consumer as well as a producer, that the whole tendency of society, so far as it is intelligent and wholesome, is to an increase of the hours of leisure, and that an education which does nothing to enable individuals to consume wisely and to utilize leisure wisely is a fraud on democracy. So far as method is concerned, such a conception of industrial education will prize freedom more than docility; initiative more than automatic skill; insight and understanding more than capacity to recite lessons or to execute tasks under the direction of others (Dewey 1940, pp. 131-2).

As we approach the last years of the twentieth century a major challenge for all societies is to create life-styles which will overcome the divorce of technology from humanistic concerns. If we make it, educational reform and social renewal will go on together. The emergence of educational experiments aimed at providing humanizing experiences with technology will be one kind of sign. The flourishing of bland, well-engineered school efforts to serve narrow technocratic efficiency needs will be a counterindication. The inner conflict over which kind of society Americans want to create with the power of science and technology continues, only the stakes are getting higher.

CAREER EDUCATION AND CAREER GUIDANCE FOR THE LIFE SPAN AND FOR LIFE ROLES

Donald E. Super

Dr. Super is professor emeritus of psychology and education and research associate at the Institute for Psychological Research and School Experimentation, Teachers College, Columbia University. He is internationally known for his contributions to career development and guidance. This article was written in 1975.

Career education has many advocates and many critics. It has advocates because our educational programs are not perfect. Many young people are not challenged by the schools of today. We seek ways of improving things, and career education holds out an objective and a play of action. It has critics because it was promoted and funded while still a vague and ill-defined idea. Many programs were ill-conceived. Funds have been cut. Career education has too often been proposed as a panacea.

Advocates of vocational education have actually turned career education into occupational education. That these are really not the same would have been clear to both proponents and to funders had they known either the literature on vocational or career psychology or that on occupational sociology. They would have known that an occupation is what a person does to earn a living, while a career is the sequence of positions which constitute a person's work history. A career is operationally defined as the pre-occupational, occupational, and post-occupational positions which constitute the bulk of a life history. Occupational education teaches students about occupations and seeks to lead to an occupational choice; career education should teach about career development and help students to control the unfolding of their careers as changing sequences and combinations of roles in education, home, community, occupations, and leisure as they go through life.

Advocates of liberal education have, in contrast, sought to turn career education into education for life, for life in which work strangely figures little, if at all. That they have not often succeeded in doing this is perhaps due to the vigilance and initiative of vocational educators in recognizing when and how to get control of funds and to the funders, who have recognized that if career education failed to put some emphasis on occupations, it would fail to prepare students for the real world.

Counselors and psychologists interested in career development have been critical of both occupational and liberal arts approaches. They contend that career education and career guidance must deal with the lifelong processes of growth, exploration, establishment, maintenance, and decline, which constitute a career. It is not sufficient to help a person to understand him or herself, know the world of occupations, and make a suitable choice with plans for education, training, and eventual placement. People, occupations, and the economy change with time, and most people make significant changes of occupation during their working lives. Many occupations are "society-maintaining" rather than "ego-involving" (Havighurst 1964); self-fulfillment must often come from homemaking, civic, and leisure activities which provide outlets for aptitudes, interests, values, and needs. Career education and guidance must take these work-related aspects of life into account, for they are essentially part of the career.

A Theoretical Basis for Career Education and Guidance

Career education needs a sound theoretical basis. This is available in career development theory (Super 1957; Super and Bohn 1970b; Jordaan 1974a; Crites 1974). This is essentially a theory of life stages and developmental tasks, of career patterns, and of individual differences. These need to be considered before one can know what to expect of career education and career guidance.

Life Stages. The stages of a career are essentially those of development over the life span. These are the growth, exploratory, establishment, maintenance, and decline stages (Super 1957b). Each stage is characterized by the special importance of certain social expectations. For example, during the exploratory stage youths are expected to formulate occupational choices and during the establishment stage adults are expected to implement the choices and make places for themselves at work, in a home, and in a community. If a given task is well handled, coping with the next task is facilitated.

The *growth stage* is one of interaction between the child and the home, neighborhood, and school environment, resulting in the active development of some abilities, interests, and values and in the neglect and atrophy of other potentials which, given a certain glandular and neural makeup, might have become important. Relationships with people help or hinder development along certain lines; experiences with objects and then with ideas facilitate or discourage development along others. Boys have learned in our culture that they should be active and bold; girls have learned that they should be passive and sweet; and thus many boys develop mechanical aptitude, while girls tend to read and dance better than boys. Parents, teachers, and other adults provide role models. Concepts of self as boy or girl, as mechanic, or as potential ballet dancer emerge and are fostered or discouraged. Occupational preferences in this stage tend to reflect emotional needs more than aptitude or genuine interest, and they tend either to be fixated or to change fairly often.

The *exploratory stage* begins with adolescence, although exploration itself begins in infancy and continues throughout life as changing people and situations require reconnoitering.

Exploration involves trying out a variety of activities, roles, and situations. It may not be planned or goal-directed, but it may be undertaken specifically in order to find out more about aptitude for, or interest in, an occupation, a course of study, or career opportunity. It may be tentative at first, with increasing commitment. Jordaan (1963) and Super (1963a) have described vocational exploratory behavior in some detail, and Pritchard (1962), Rusalem (1954), Samler (1964), Prediger (1974), and Berglund (1974) have applied theory to practice. Poor exploration may be mere floundering, or even drifting, rather than systematic trial. Exploration results in the further development of abilities and interests. It confirms or contradicts the suitability of role models and of self-concepts. It aids in their clarification and it eventually makes possible their translation into occupational preferences and their implementation in paid employment.

The *establishment stage* usually begins in the mid-twenties, although some people drift, flounder, or explore for as many as ten years longer and some never achieve stable careers. With greater maturity, responsibilities, and experience men in their late twenties tend to find suitable employment or to compromise and settle for the best they can find; women of this age tend to devote full-time to homemaking, although some continue with double-track careers and many, often without having planned it, resume paid employment after a few years away from the labor market. From age 25 to age 45 the average American man changes jobs several times; stability is relative. Although this life stage begins several years after leaving school, it should be of vital concern to career education, as it is the stage into which school and college lead. How schools prepare for it has a great deal to do with how much drifting, floundering, and stagnating there is during the later school and early work years (Super, Kowalski, and Gotkin 1967).

The *maintenance stage* begins for most people at about age 45, although for many women the thirties involve re-exploration and a second establishment stage. Having settled into an occupation and often into a particular job, the individual is concerned with holding his or her own against younger people, keeping up with new developments, forging ahead by breaking new ground in his or her present, or in some related, field, or getting re-established in the labor force. It can be a period of fruition or of frustration, depending upon economic conditions and upon how well the developmental tasks of the earlier life stages have been handled. The maintenance stage may not seem to be important to a school's career education program, but some understanding of how what happens in the earlier stages of a career affects what happens in later years can be assumed to be important to getting and keeping control of a career.

The *decline stage* is one of changing and declining involvement in life in general and in occupations in particular. Although in some instances activity continues until death in the habitual roles at the usual pace and on the usual schedule, for most people there is a process of changing types of activities, pace of work, and hours or days of work. Those whose preretirement lives have involved occupational or avocational activities that are carried over into retirement, and thus preserve continuity of roles and of life, are happiest in retirement (Steer 1970). If this finding were somehow put to use in career education, it could result in the more satisfying pursuit of life roles throughout the life cycle.

Positions, Roles, and Tasks. As people go through each life stage, they are expected to occupy a number of different positions. Some positions are occupied in sequence, some alternately, some more or less simultaneously. Thus the positions of student, worker, and pensioner are generally occupied in sequence, but they may be occupied simultaneously.

There are at least ten major types of roles. In the approximate order in which these roles are dominant, they are:

1. child	4. spouse	7. citizen	10. patient
2. student	5. parent	8. "leisurer"	
3. worker	6. homemaker	9. annuitant	

The simultaneous and sequential nature of these roles, together with waxing and waning during the course of the life cycle, can be depicted as a rainbow in which the bands of color vary in width at any one cross section of the arc, and each individual's arc varies in width as it goes from left to right with the rainbow. Near the horizon representing birth, for example, there is just one band, one role, that of child. At the other end, if life continues into the eighties or nineties, there is often again just one band or role, that of patient in a comprehensive-care nursing home. But at the peak of the career and of the rainbow representing it there may be as many as eight major bands in a wide arc, for one person may play, more or less simultaneously, the roles of child to his aging parents, student in continuing education, worker in an occupation, spouse, parent, homemaker, citizen, and pursuer of leisure.

Occupying any position means that one assumes and is given a role and is expected to perform certain functions and act in certain ways. Occupying an executive position imposes the role of manager of the work of others and of performer of certain higher-level tasks, and in some corporations it means wearing conservative clothes and well-groomed hair. Holding a university professorship requires that one carry on research and write books and tell popular writers what they want to know about one's subject, but it permits one to wear tweeds, slacks, turtleneck sweaters, and loafers in the classroom and on lecture platforms.

At lower occupational levels also roles are prescribed rather rigidly in some occupations, more flexibly in others; for example, role-rigidity is typical of mass production assembly jobs on the one hand, and role-flexibility is typical of gardeners on the other hand. Roles shape people, and people shape roles, just as some people choose roles (e.g., lawyer) and others are cast in them (e.g., clerk in a family shoe store).

Theaters in Which Roles Are Played. Each role has a theater in which it is typically, but not uniquely, played. A child is still a child in grade school, with a teacher in loco parentis, and a mother is still a mother while at work if she has an emergency at home. The major theaters in which roles are played are:

1. home	3. school	5. retirement community or
2. community	4. work place	home

These theaters can of course be broken down into finer categories, the home having its kitchen, playroom, study, etc., and the community its service, recreational, welfare, health, and other facilities or little theaters.

Life Space. The varying multiple roles or bands of the life cycle's arc and the number of theaters in which roles are played depict the notions of life space and of life-style. The idea of life-styles is made concrete by the use made by the individual of the different types of theaters or life space, the number of roles that he or she plays, and the manner in which he or she plays them.

Career Patterns. The word career has two definitions. An incorrect definition is when used synonymously with *occupation,* for a person may engage in several occupations while in the pursuit of his or her career. The error arises because one of the definitions calls a career the continuous and progressive pursuit of one occupation. This is a middleclass definition based on the notions that one must always be climbing and that worthy occupations involve ladders that take one even higher. Some occupations are viewed as worthy of long-term engagement as careers because they provide opportunity for advancement. This is one of the important differences between machinists (who may advance to tool-and-die making and to being millwrights) and automobile assembly-line workers.

The psychological and sociological definition of a career is that of the sequence of positions occupied by a person during the course of a working and work-related life. This takes into account the facts that most people change occupations several times during their careers and that for many people occupational mobility is horizontal rather than vertical.

Careers have been found to include four patterns for men and seven for women. These are, for men, the conventional (some change, followed by stability); the stable (entry into an occupation after finishing training and remaining in it); the unstable (often called serial, alternating periods, which may be long and infrequent, of stability and change); and the multiple-trial (frequent change and short periods in any one occupation). For women, the conventional (homemaking after a period of paid work); the stable (either homemaking instead of paid work or it may mean paid work in only one occupation); the interrupted pattern (paid work, then homemaking, and again paid work); and the double-track career pattern (the simultaneous paid work and homemaking that is increasingly common today).

Continuous careers (the conventional and stable) are most common in the skilled, clerical, executive, and professional fields, or among the middle class (Miller and Form 1951); the discontinuous (unstable, multiple-trial, and interrupted) are common among men and women at the lower socio-economic levels, in the unskilled, semiskilled, and, to a lesser degree, clerical and sales fields.

Career education and guidance have typically been based on the assumption that most people pursue continuous, stable or conventional, careers. That this is not true of the majority of our population means that we have failed to meet the needs of the large numbers who pursue unstable, multiple-trial, and interrupted careers. Herein lies a fundamental and generally unasked question for counselors and career educators: what should education and guidance for discontinuity, for change both expected and unexpected, seek to accomplish, and of what should they consist?

What To Expect of Career Education

Plans. The first step in planning a program, or any other activity, is to establish its objectives. This is now such a commonplace that it may be well to point out that establishing objectives means, not to appoint a committee or to organize a workshop for the writing of long lists of high-sounding attributes and behaviors, but to make clear just what is to be accomplished. It is not altogether unfair to point out that, in creating the fad for listing behavioral objectives, we have achieved what the sorcerer's apprentice did when he started the water flowing: the lists keep pouring out and getting longer and longer. In reading program materials one sometimes gets the impression that, the more numerous the objectives listed, the more meritorious the proposal and the plan are expected to appear!

Specifying Objectives. It would be unwise to minimize the importance of clear statements of what a program is to accomplish, statements which begin at a general level and are followed by more specific attitudinal and behavioral objectives. Objectives need to be phrased in terms that make their attainment measurable. Generating the general statement should be a primary concern of the school administration, with appropriate expert help; developing the more specific objectives should be the primary concern of the director of career education and a team of curriculum specialists, counselors, career psychologists, classroom teachers, and evaluation experts.

This is another commonplace. In some programs the objectives have been developed ex post facto and largely by outside evaluators, as school systems have obtained funds for and started career education programs without having achieved clarity as to what the program was to accomplish. Generally the measurement people succeeded too well, and now the sorcerer's apprentice, having learned how to start words flowing, needs to learn how to stop them. Parsimonious statements of objectives are needed; how does one get them?

First, no one program should seek to achieve everything that a school should do. For instance, children may learn how to write better English in a career education program, but one might question whether this should be one of the objectives of such a program, for it is really a by-product. One should specify only the major objectives that are peculiar to the program, although it may be well to list anticipated by-products as such.

Secondly, not all desirable objectives are readily assessable, given the state of the art of measurement and the limited time available for administering tests and questionnaires and for collecting behavioral data from classrooms, resource centers, and the field. Therefore one should focus on the assessable objectives.

The general objectives of career education and career guidance are sixfold:

● To provide students with an understanding of the nature and sequence of life stages and of career stages, of the developmental tasks which characterize these stages, and of the changing major roles which people play (in sequence and simultaneously) in the various theaters or spheres of activity in the several stages.

● To help students develop realistic self-concepts, with esteem for themselves and others, as a basis for career decision.

● To develop in students a realistic and appreciative understanding of the world of work, with a broad perspective on opportunities and a specific focus on one or more clusters of occupations, together with knowledge of the educational and occupational pathways that lead to them and of the work ways of life that they involve.

● To help students know and appreciate the many avocational, domestic, and civic outlets for developed interests and abilities, outlets which in an automated society often supplement, complement, or even supplant paid work in making a satisfying life.

● To provide a basis for the making of sequential and increasingly specific career decisions in which self and occupational knowledge are synthesized for self-realization in work, in homemaking, in civic life, and in leisure, in ways which meet social as well as individual needs.

● To make these experiences available in ways appropriate to all students at each stage of their formal education.

Developing the Curriculum. A much debated and perhaps too quickly settled question in career education has been that of addition versus infusion. "Too quickly settled" because it has been viewed simplistically as an all-or-none matter, without recognizing that the best approach might involve the addition of some things and the infusing of others. Just what, where, and when must depend somewhat upon the personnel available and the other demands made upon the system.

When possible, infusion is desirable: it displaces nothing in the curriculum, and it minimizes the need for staff additions. The basic question is, What can be generally infused into or merged with regular classroom instruction, and under what conditions?

Infusion of career education material into classroom instruction appears to be frequently and rather well achieved in elementary schools. The curriculum has generally made use of life-situation material for the teaching of reading, writing, and arithmetic as well as for teaching citizenship, geography, and other social and scientific subjects. Teachers at that level have become skilled at using materials, activities, and other resources that serve as vehicles for skill instruction and as media for arousing subject matter interest. They have typically been open to help from subject matter specialists, knowing that they are not experts in everything. There is little pressure to teach any particular content, provided that the basic skills are mastered and general social and cultural orientation is accomplished.

Regular classroom instruction can be the vehicle, the teacher can be the intermediary, and the career education consultant can be the resource person. Some understanding of the nature of careers (the sequence of positions occupied during a lifetime as student, worker, and pensioner, with the varying demands that accompany each position) and of occupations (the variety that are theoretically and practically open, including their training, duties, rewards, and ways of life), can be provided in the teaching of social studies and of English. This is often done, but career education can help make it more systematic, more comprehensive, and more realistic. For example, elementary school children have long visited post offices and fire stations but have not so often observed a telephone operator at work with explanations of what she or he is doing and why; neither have they generally learned what lawyers do except in the poor sampling provided by television dramas; they have learned the use of arithmetic in shopping, but rarely have they learned how a navigator uses it in determining the location of a ship or an airplane.

In secondary schools infusion has generally not worked so well. It is the classical problem: subject matter emphasis in examinations and in teacher interest make career and occupational information more a distracting intrusion than an enriching infusion. Even when the information is as relevant as that on related occupations in a course on chemistry, it is still not the knowledge that college entrance exams cover; nor is it the information that the chemistry teacher feels she or he should be expected to know, even though summers are spent working in a chemical plant. Infusion does take place more readily in subjects such as English composition, with the assignment of career-relevant topics and literature depicting ways of life and work in various occupations, and history, with biographical data on key figures in political, cultural, economic, and social history. But this does not mean that English and social studies teachers exploit the career orientation and exploration possibilities of their subjects as consistently and effectively as they might. Neither does it mean that no effort should be made to help science teachers and others use their opportunities for occupational orientation better than they now do. A well-qualified and interested counselor can, given the mandate, develop a valued role as consultant to teachers on such matters, helping them to know and to make good use of materials, experiences, and people available through a resource center.

At all school levels infusion appears to work best when the responsibility for career education is clearly that of a well-qualified person in the central office, when there are career development specialists (most often counselors or guidance-trained vocational educators) in the larger schools to serve as consultants, and when the system has a well-organized and staffed career resource center with an outreach program into individual schools and into the community.

Addition, as contrasted with infusion, seems to play a more important part at the secondary level. Here it is essential to provide for activities and services which are beyond the realm of classroom teachers.

These may best be described as services of:

- Guided exploration.
- Synthesis of data.
- Individual application.

In guided exploration the counselor helps students to identify, plan, carry out, and evaluate sequences of experiences which help them better understand themselves and the opportunities which may be available to them. This is the essence of guidance. Students too often take courses simply because they are expected to or because the courses are interesting or they seem easy. Too often they join clubs because friends are doing it. They take jobs because they are available and fail to use other opportunities for experiences which might challenge or help them. They do not really understand their availability and their relevance. They need help from experts in human and social understanding who know the potential of school and community in putting resources to personal use. Take, for example, the boy who, during the summer after his junior year in high school, planned to return to summer camp as a counselor for the third year, when he might have planned to work in a nearby factory to learn whether or not mechanical engineering really appealed to him. (He did change plans thanks to a counselor's pointing out the need to try engineering before committing himself to it in college). Or, take Marjorie Miller, a senior who was spared a year or two of floundering in a technology institute because her counselor helped her see the need to explore and found the way to finance the means of doing so before she started specializing (Super 1957a). Or, finally, take the 36-year-old laundry assistant who wanted job security above all but who had not found it in the local leather-goods factory or in the laundry; whereas, in the nearby state hospital and in the post office job security was available.

In synthesis, students organize what they know about themselves and about opportunities. They generally do it better with professional help. A good deal of synthesizing, like a certain amount of planning, guiding, and evaluating of exploration, can be done in group guidance classes or meetings (Bennett 1964). But in both exploration-for-data and synthesis-of-data personal counseling is essential because of the individuality of needs and situations. Group discussion of what data to consider, of what facts mean, and of the interrelationships between sets of personal and social data, can help students to develop understanding and perspective. Discussion can include, for example, the influence of school grades and test scores on educational and occupational goals; the relevance to mechanical engineering of working in a factory; how much that seems irrelevant about an exploratory job can prove to be relevant if it helps to make new opportunities; and how the first two years of college can also serve as a trial period for such interests as biology and social sciences before making a definite choice of job-directed major.

Special contributions are made when competent counselors spend some time helping each individual student to consider the data on his or her own record, his or her unrecorded experience, and the trial and training opportunities that seem most appropriate for him or her. Knowledge can be acquired in groups but is made most meaningful when it is discussed personally at sufficient length with an informed person who can clarify feelings, help make connections, and pursue implications for action, not only in planning but in execution. It has been shown that computers can be given data and programs which enable them to supplement counselors in performing some of the functions of synthesizing personal and occupational data for career decision-making; students then make even more use of counselors in moving beyond synthesis to think things through and to formulate plans (Super 1970a).

Evaluation. In current theory and practice there are two kinds of progress-reporting or evaluation: formative and summative. The former is used to help shape and direct the development and carry out programs. The latter is essential to knowing whether or not programs have attained important objectives and if they merit continuation.

Formative Evaluation. Formative evaluation takes place at the end of important stages in the planning, carrying out, or support of a program or project; these are in some industries called phase reviews. They cause activities to be examined in the light of emerging defects when they may still be modified, but the milestones or phases that are established are too often dictated by budgetary calendars rather than by the nature of the project itself. What criteria should be used in doing these evaluations? They are well established in current usage!

Statements of objectives: how sound are the objectives in the light of career development theory? How valid are they for this program in this system? How clearly, parsimoniously, and operationally are they stated?

Methods: do they appear, in the light of prior experience, to be likely to attain the objectives? For example: Do they involve a combination of infusion into the regular curriculum and of added activities? Are both individual and group methods planned so that they supplement and support each other?

Resources: are materials, activities, and personnel to be used likely to produce the desired results? Are they organized and located in ways which make them likely to be well used? For example, are printed and graphic materials pitched at appropriate levels and to appropriate majority and minority groups? Are staff members properly trained for their work?

Processes: are the group and individual processes used in developing the resources and in putting the resources to use likely to produce the desired results? For example, is provision made for staff and community participation in development work, so that those who are to carry out the program feel the responsibility of authorship? Is the leadership style sufficiently democratic?

Summative Evaluation. Summative evaluation takes place at the end of a program, at the completion of a project or of a course. Ideally, it provides for short-term and long-term evaluation, the latter being done after enough time has elapsed to throw light on the enduring quality of the outcomes. It uses control as well as experimental groups, pre- and post-treatment data, so that the effects of the treatment may be clear. It uses numbers large enough so that tests of the statistical significance (the non-chance character) of the findings may be demonstrated.

There are essentially three types of evidence that are pertinent in evaluating the outcomes of career education programs. These are:

- Attitudes.
- Information.
- Behavior in life situations.

Attitudes provide partial evidence of vocational maturity, that is, of the stage reached in career development. They include planning ability and the use of resources helpful in vocational exploration and choice. People who plan ahead are aware of the decisions which they will be called upon to make; they think about the alternatives among which they will need to choose; and they are inclined to use resources such as counselors, alumni, and employed friends to find out more about careers that interest them. Such vocational maturity factors are measured by Crites' Career Maturity Inventory and the Career Development Inventory (Super 1974).

Information also provides a measure of vocational maturity, for it shows one result of planning ability, information being the result of a combination of interest, aptitude, and experience. Used as a before-and-after measure, information acquired and retained serves well as one index of the effectiveness of a career education program. Four types of information are relevant, depending upon the objectives of the program: (1) educational opportunities and requirements; (2) occupations; (3) decision-making principles; and (4) life stages. These, like the most relevant attitudes, are measured by Crites' and Super's tests.

Behavior in life situations is what interests us most. Career behavior begins early and ends late, and there are many such behaviors from which to choose. Which are relevant at a given stage of career development?

Having an occupational choice has often been used as an indicator of the success of career education and guidance programs (Super and Overstreet 1960). Occupational preferences mean little in eighth and ninth grades and little more in the later years of high school. Boys and girls who are exploring should be playing with a number of possibilities; consistency and realism of choice begin to have real meaning only in twelfth grade. To have them mean more at that time might be an appropriate objective for career education, as might agreement between occupational preferences (treated as clusters rather than as specific occupations even in twelfth grade) on the one hand and aptitudes and interests on the other.

Realism of reasons for changing positions as student and as worker during the first five to seven years after leaving high school, and gains or losses in career equity through position changes, are good longer-term measures of career behavior, as shown by work histories at the ages of 25 and 36 (Jordaan and Super 1974b). Other indices of drifting, floundering, stagnating, trial, instrumental, and stabilizing behavior have also proved valid.

Absentee, grade, and other such school reports have been used with success as indicators of changes in motivation through career education. However, as they are affected by many other factors, they should not be the only success criteria for career education.

Questions that should be asked in carrying out a review include the following:

The criteria: how conceptually adequate are the criteria for the outcomes? Do they make sense in the light of what we know about career development and in the light of the objectives of the program? For example, an elementary school program might be expected to increase the number and variety of occupations with which children are familiar, but not to give them an accurate picture of the work of people in all the major fields of work. A program for seniors might be expected to result in an increase in the number of students with plans, including one or more alternatives, for their first year or two after high school, with projections of possibilities beyond that time, but not to result in definitive and stable occupational choices.

The measures: how reliable and valid are the indicators of outcomes which are to be used or have been used? These questions have been made familiar to us in connection with tests and inventories, but they have to be asked also about attendance records, grades, teachers' and counselors' ratings, employers' evaluations, etc. Some of the attributes and behaviors on which we would like to have data are not reliably measured, and some that seem reliable and that look good have not been proved to measure what they appear to measure. The judgment of experts who know the facts as shown by the relevant research is needed here.

Conclusion

Career education has been described by some in terms which make it seem synonymous with education itself. Others seem to view it as the panacea which will cure all the ills of education. Still others would have it mean vocational education, occupational education, or liberal education. It cannot be all of these, nor is it truly any one of them. It should be education which helps people to look ahead, to consider possible adult roles and ways of life, to understand and develop tentative plans for alternative paths that may lead to one or another sequence of positions that are likely to make possible satisfaction with the major life roles of worker, citizen, and homemaker. How well defined career education and career guidance are in a given school system depends on the kind of intellectual leadership that the specialists, who help individuals achieve self-fulfillment, exert in support of administrators, who are willing to act but who need proposals and programs.

CAREER EDUCATION: SOME PERSPECTIVES ON VALIDITY AND CONTENT

Edwin L. Herr
Dr. Herr is professor and head of the Division of Counseling and Educational Psychology at Pennsylvania State University. Nationally recognized for his contributions to educational guidance, counseling, and career education, Dr. Herr is presently serving as president of the National Vocational Guidance Association. This article was written in 1975.

Since 1971, career education has made considerable impact on the educational mentality of America. Critics have damned its implications for a new vocationalism, have called its concept of education utilitarian, and have accused it of misassumptions and oversights (Nash and Agne 1973). Others have suggested that career education must respond to some fundamental issues about schooling and work if it is to have a permanent place in the American educational structure (Morris 1973). Its proponents continue to argue the merits of the goals subsumed by the term career education, whether these be career awareness, employability, individual choice, educational understanding, or some other composite term seen to be necessary for an effective life under the current social and economic conditions in America.

Depending upon who the spokesperson is, the goals stated for career education tend to describe a continuum of emphases with employability on one end, self-understanding at the other, and such goals as educational meaningfulness somewhere in the middle. In fact most career education projects have attempted to create interactive conditions so that all of these goals can be met in some fashion, although certain emphases are likely to be seen as dominant depending upon existing resources, educational level at which the project operates, biases of the project director, and other factors.

Before career education approaches solidify in either their rhetoric or practice, it seems useful to examine briefly the validity of the underlying conditions to which career education responds and to ask the question, How do current educational programs already meet needs to which career education responds? Such an analysis offers the potential to spur self-conscious attention among career education advocates to the underpinnings and to the shaping of career education emphases as well as to the linkages which can be forged with other educational movements. While many issues or conditions giving impetus to career education could be considered, only two such matters will be addressed here. They include the following assertions:

● Too many students fail to see meaningful relationships between what they are asked to learn in school and what they will do when they leave the educational system.

● Too many persons leave our educational system at both the secondary and collegiate levels unequipped with self-understanding and career decision-making skills.

Educational Meaning

In a society which has become increasingly concerned with psychological issues and self-identity, it is to be expected that attention would focus upon whether students see meaningful relations between what they are asked to learn and what they will do with such learning later in life. The sheer quantity of life and occupational alternatives from which a person can choose in this society places an historically unparalleled psychological burden upon the individual. When such constraints as state-defined manpower quotas, sex differences, or caste restrictions are neutralized in their restrictive effects upon choice, the psychological burden upon the individual to choose with purpose and in terms of self-definition is intensified.

Indeed, the philosophical principles which underlie national values give impetus and credibility to individual attempts to find meaning and purpose in life. The insistent clamor by the mass media, some aspects of education and religion, and other social stimuli make it necessary for each person to answer questions such as, Who am I? What do I want to give to life or get from it? This causes the individual to believe that one who is without answers is without purpose and a sense of self. During the search for answers people frequently become alienated or place upon education labels like "meaningless" or "irrelevant" if the relationship between their learning and their questions is not direct and clear.

The question of the meaningfulness of education has probably been energized most intensely by college students, although the matter is not confined there. Sandeen has reported that in relation to the meaning of a bachelor's degree, "Purely academic efforts seem, to increasing numbers of students, largely unrelated to the really important questions of life. Many students evidently have decided that, if any meaning is to be found, it must be done apart from the actual structure of the college" (Sandeen 1968). Lefkowitz found similar results from conducting random interviews with some 300 students from over 50 colleges and universities in the eastern U. S. In particular, his finding was that "over two-thirds of the students interviewed stated that college education, or what was being presented to them, was not worth the effort" (Lefkowitz 1973).

With respect to the high school, Ralph Tyler has stated that:

> We currently fail to educate approximately one-third of the youth enrolled in high school. . . . They are concerned with becoming independent adults, getting jobs, marrying, gaining status with their peers, and helping to solve the ills of the world. They perceive little or no connection between the educational content of the school and their own concerns.
> It is a rare school today that helps the student deal with the personal, social, economic, and moral problems which confront him . . . (Tyler 1970, pp. 478-481).

Edward Martin has suggested that one can expect a certain amount of discontent about courses simply as a function of the sparring between the young and old. However, he contends that:

> . . . other complaints, involving boredom and confusion, are more serious and often go unspoken: Why are we studying this? Why is it important? Often we do not treat these questions seriously enough, or we fail to explain sufficiently our answers. This adds to the confusion. The main complaint of twelve- and thirteen-year-olds is not the irrelevance of their studies: it is rather that they are not let into the secret of the importance of what we ask them to study (Martin 1971, pp. 1087-1103).

The lack of balance or meaningfulness (i.e., relevance) in current forms of education is echoed by other observers. Robert Lathrop has observed that " . . . the programs that exist in most schools are so out of balance with the total needs of youth that other aspects of the child's life (nonacademic) are given only token attention or are ignored completely" (Lathrop 1974, p. 200). Using Project TALENT data, John Flanagan reported that in 1970, only 61% of the girls and 51% of the boys in the sample answered "well" or "very well" to the question: "How well do your school courses meet your needs?" (Flanagan 1973).

Self-understanding and Career Decision-making Skills

A part of meaningfulness or relevance in education has to do with its attention to self-understanding and individual decision-making. While these outcomes have long been embodied in educational philosophies, they have typically been treated as though they were by-products of something else rather than behaviors which could be addressed directly. However, many current perspectives on education support the need for direct attention to be given to self-understanding, career decision-making skills and their corollaries.

Garbin, Salomone, Jackson, and Ballweg analyzed worker adjustment problems of youth and concluded that youthful employees often fail at their jobs, not because they lack technical competence, but because of the absence of skills relating to the nontechnical complex—getting along with others, being punctual and responsible. (Garbin et al. 1970).

In essence, the research of Garbin et al. demonstrated that "the basic difficulty of many youths is not that of finding a job, but in keeping one . . ." More specifically, their research showed that in their sample of 642 young workers the most difficult things that had to be learned were: technological (46.7%); interpersonal (19.2%); personal (14.8%); and organizational (4.3%). A related study reported survey findings which suggest that the maladjustment of secondary students to the work place may be more related to poor interpersonal skills than to inadequate technical skills (Garbin et al. 1967). Other reviews of literature (Garbin, Jackson, and Campbell 1968; Stogdill 1966) tend to support the above conclusions. Similarly, Reubens' research indicates that basic literacy and good work habits may be more important for employment than occupational skills per se (Reubens 1974).

Implicit in observations about problems with interpersonal skills and other psychological adjustments in work is the need for each student to come to terms with a variety of personal questions and with clarifying the self-concept. Hoffman, in discussing self-understanding for productive living, has observed that "the questions teachers should be encouraging students to ask are, 'Who am I?' 'What influences me?' and 'How can I control the influences upon me?' Once these answers are found, or at least sought, the most neglected area of education will take its place as the most important" (Hoffman 1973, p. 76). Livingston has viewed the matter in the following perspective: "One reason university graduates have had so much difficulty making the transition from academic life to the world of work is that they have failed to develop in school the self-identities needed to enable them to make firm career commitments" (Livingston 1970).

Self-understanding has been found to have important implications not only in the transition from school to work but also from secondary school to further education or within the secondary school itself. For example, Sievert has reported that shop achievement is related to self-concept and occupational subject matter (Sievert 1972). O'Hara has demonstrated that the self-concept relates not only to occupational choice but to high school achievement as well, and that the importance of these relationships increases from the ninth to twelfth grades (O'Hara 1966). The implication of such a correlation is that students who persist in school are those who can find meaning in what they are learning or can see its necessity in relation to what they want to do; those who do not find such a condition in school drop out. These relationships apparently function even earlier than the ninth grade. R. L. Williams and S. Cole report that measures of the self-concept at the sixth grade are significantly and positively related to the child's conception of school, social status at school, emotional adjustment, mental ability, reading achievement, and mathematical achievement (Williams and Cole 1968). J. A. Oakland, too, has reported relationships between levels of high school achievement, responsibility, and planning (Oakland 1969). Eugene Nadler and Gilbert Krulee found compatibility between personal needs and the objective features of school situations to be major factors in higher grade point average (Nadler and Krulee 1961).

E. L. Herr, Richard Warner, and John Swisher, in summarizing existing research, reported that at the secondary school level there are relationships among self-concepts, achievement levels, and perceptions of environmental expectations (Herr, Warner, and Swisher 1970). In a related study, James Hansen and Herr found that chronically truant students thought they were receiving more pressure to compete academically, to go to college, to plan and structure, to look and act properly, and to engage in heterosexual activities than did a control group of students not chronically truant (Hansen and Herr 1966). Apparently, the chronically truant either did not understand the reasons for these environmental demands, the environmental demands were antithetical to their personal needs, or they had not achieved ways of coping with them which were successful or rewarded in the high school they attended. Thus, they chose to escape from these demands through truancy.

While many more studies could be cited, the point should be adequately made that the development of self-knowledge and understanding is an important element in academic and vocational achievement and in making a choice. The research of Roger Tierney and Al Herman, among others, indicates that many students do not have the skill to make realistic self-estimates and that such a skill apparently is not being developed by schools (Tierney and Herman 1973). Sheldon Roen has argued persuasively that only through "education for choosing" will individuals become more competent choosers (Roen 1967a and 1967b). The rise of the affective education, values clarification, and psychological education movements over the last few years are testimonies to these deficits in American education.

The Convergence of Career Education and Psychological Education

One of the points which has not yet been discussed at any length in professional literature is the potential meshing of career education, deliberate psychological education, affective education, and/or values clarification precisely at this point of promoting self-understanding. Each of these movements advocates that schools should give more attention to the psychological/personal development of students (as compared with primary or sole reliance on cognitive/intellectual skills). Personal development in these contexts emphasizes the importance of helping students achieve the attitudes, behaviors, skills, and self-understanding which are essential to attainment of an adequate level of personal competence. More specifically, personal competence is typically seen in these models as including the acquisition by adolescents of the aesthetic, ethical, philosophical, career, organizational, and interpersonal understandings and skills which are essential to self-identity, problem solving, and decision-making.

Table 2-A compares current emphases in career education and psychological education (combining values clarification, affective education, deliberate psychological education) to illustrate points of congruity and difference (Herr 1975, pp. 1-4).

Career education and the various approaches combined here under the term psychological education share many common goals although their descriptive language and emphases differ somewhat. For example, approaches to both career and to psychological education stress the importance to student development of self-understanding, planning, and problem-solving and decision-making skills. Career education is likely to advocate casting these against possible educational and work alternatives while psychological education would likely cast them in terms of interpersonal relations or moral and ethical reasoning. While psychological education approaches would probably give a central place to values clarification, career education would probably see values clarification as only one of the aspects of acquiring self-understanding as the evaluative base for making educational and career choices.

Both career education and psychological education express concern for modifying the school climate or its organizational structure. Career education approaches frequently stress the need for increased educational options which respond to a wider range of human

TABLE 2-A.
Comparison of Current Emphases in Career Education
and Psychological Education

Career Education	Psychological Education
• Efforts to end the curriculum separation between general and vocational education.	• Ways to have schools attend specifically to the emotional development of students.
• Processes of insuring that persons leaving the formal educational structure have employable job skills.	• Processes by which students can acquire such attributes as self-respect, conscientiousness, concern for others, a sense of justice.
• Programs to facilitate individual choice making so that occupational preparation and acquisition of basic academic skills can be coordinated with developing individual preference.	• Programs to teach students values processing and values clarification.
• Modifications in curricula to make them more career relevant by incorporating concepts from career development research and theory (e.g., self-awareness, knowledge of educational and career alternatives, analysis of life-style options).	• Curricula designed to focus on the psychology of interpersonal relations, marriage, parenting and child development, psychological coping skills, and ethical reasoning.
• Models of articulating the contributions of elementary, middle, and secondary schools to a system of explicit student attitudes and behaviors pertinent to decision making, educational/career planning, and the acquisition of work skills.	• Efforts to develop organizational structures by which students can analyze, interpret, and make decisions about social problems.
• The primary construct in career development is the development and implementation of the self-concept.	• Emotional development, including values education, precedes sequentially through various stages of competency.
• The possession of job skills as well as planning and decision-making skills provides personal dignity and a sense of power to affect the future.	• Opportunities in education for students to interpret current emotional experiences lay the base for the personal development of value commitments and emotional structures which transfer to the future.
• Career development can be described in terms of learning tasks and educational objectives which are important at each educational level.	• Students need to acquire ways of organizing and understanding experience as well as ways of planning and organizing activity in relation to such areas as self-understanding, personal identity and autonomy, interpersonal communication, and ethical reasoning.

talents than those primarily verbal and abstract. Further, such approaches would probably contend that schools do not provide sufficient opportunities for choice, nor do they value education for choice. Thus, insufficient attention is paid to helping students link their present learning to future educational alternatives or to the ways such learning is applied in various work alternatives. Psychological educational approaches would probably make observations complementary to those of career education while stressing opportunities for emotional experiences through the performing arts, improvisation, situational dilemmas, and direct involvement in life outside the school, e.g., community service.

In sum, career education and psychological education share concerns for educational structures and processes which stimulate personal development beyond that which is purely academic or intellectual in substance.

Career Education Content: Some Implications

If career education is to provide perspective on oneself and on the relevance of one's education, then the content of career education must be considered. The following represents several implications.

First, as the educational and social conditions to which career education responds are analyzed and found to deserve attention, it is likely that current definitions of academic skills or educational outcomes will undergo change. Obviously, the definition of such skills or outcomes depends upon what criterion of educational effectiveness you use—work success, productive citizenship, personal competence, lifelong learning, informal consumership. Robert Darcy, for example, has indicated that the basic skills related to work success include: communication skills, computational skills, manual dexterity or motor skills, and group organization and human relations skills. It is his position that employability, productivity, and earning power are enhanced by verbal skills (reading, writing, speaking), mathematics, manual skills, and the ability to work effectively with other people (Darcy 1969).

James Coleman has argued that there are several basic skills which should be provided by the educational system before a student becomes eighteen years of age. They include:

- Intellectual skills
- Skills of some occupation that may be filled by a secondary school graduate
- Decision-making skills
- General physical and mechanical skills
- Bureaucratic and organizational skills
- Skills for the care of dependent persons
- Emergency skills
- Verbal communication skills in argumentation and debate (Coleman 1972).

Marland has contended that interpersonal and organizational understanding are "survival skills" without which one simply cannot exist in a modern nation-state (Marland 1972). Similarly, E. Gross has contended that preparation for work life involves:

- Preparation for life in an organization involving authority, security quests, impersonality, routine, conflict, mobility, and demotion.
- Preparation for a set of role relationships.
- Preparation for a level of consumption involving a certain style of life.

• Preparation for an occupational career, involving changes in the nature of job and different types of jobs, depending on the position in the life cycle (Gross 1967).

While other pertinent examples of skills considered by experts to be relevant to the needs of students in today's world could be cited, these are sufficient to draw some implications for career education. First, career education could give impetus to the educational system's recognition that basic academic skills necessary in today's society include more than reading, writing, and communication but extend to interpersonal skills and organizational understanding as well. A second potential response of career education to enhancing educational meaningfulness would be to provide a context in which students can acquire basic academic skills in less abstract ways than now seem to be the norm. Tying such skill acquisition to concrete problems in living would be one alternative in this regard. Third, career education can contribute to the meaningfulness of basic academic skill acquisition by direct effort to acquaint students with the link between basic academic skills and their application in educational and career alternatives.

Second, extending the suggestions for educational meaningfulness further, career education content can also be informed by a variety of research findings. For example, Gribbons and Lohnes in examining the concept of readiness for vocational planning reported the importance of a number of factors which can be related to understanding, acting upon the meaning of what one is learning, and the relationship of these to the future. Among the variables listed were:

VARIABLE I. FACTORS IN CURRICULUM CHOICE
Awareness of relevant factors, including one's abilities, interests, and values and their relation to curriculum choice; relationships between curricula choice and occupational choice.
VARIABLE II. FACTORS IN OCCUPATIONAL CHOICE
Awareness of relevant factors, including abilities, interests, values; educational requirements for choice; accuracy of description of occupation.
VARIABLE VI. INTERESTS
Awareness of interests and their relation to occupational choices.
VARIABLE VII. VALUES
Awareness of values and their relation to occupational choices (Gribbons and Lohnes 1968).

Similarly, Super, Starishevsky, Matlin, and Jordaan have indicated that among the twelve behaviors and attitudes which underlie or foster vocational preference in adolescence are included:

• Use of resources—principally a set of instrumental behaviors by which one copes with exploration whether it is focused on self-understanding or occupational description; this element is present in relationship to a large number of persons or objects: parents, counselors, teachers, materials, part-time jobs.

• Awareness of factors to consider in formulating a vocational preference—this involves knowledge of the possible bases for preference—whether intellectual requirements, relationship between interests and appropriate outlets, need for alternatives, or availability of outlets for different self-characteristics, i.e., security, prestige.

• Differentiation of interests and values.

• Awareness of present-future relationships—this factor is concerned with coming to terms with the interrelationship between present activities and intermediate or ultimate vocational activities: for example, understanding educational avenues and their requirements as these provide access to different fields or levels of occupational activity.

• Planning for the preferred occupation—the focus here is on decisions as to what to do and how to do it (Super et al. 1963b).

These examples are only a few of the many concepts that can be incorporated into career education approaches to enhance student understanding of the meaningfulness of education. Extended lists of other possibilities can be found elsewhere (Herr and Cramer 1972b; Herr 1972a). The basic point is that educational experiences created to help students make use of such examples as those cited from Gribbons and Lohnes and from Super represent ways of translating educational meaningfulness from an abstraction into concrete behaviors. In a sense, these implications for career education content also speak to the "so what" questions—Why am I taking this course? What good is it? Why is this subject matter important?—which for many students underline, in practical terms, the relevance or meaningfulness of education.

Third, inherent in the implications above is a concern for self-understanding. More specifically, however, career education activities provide a vehicle to help students understand the sense of power and purpose which being an informed and effective choicemaker represents. Such understanding can flow from helping students acquire the knowledge of personal characteristics and the processes by which such knowledge allows one to evaluate possible life alternatives and identify information which is personally relevant from that which is not. Pertinent to career education efforts in this regard is a range of possible content.

For example, D. H. Blocher has contended that self-understanding would include knowledge of the social roles an individual is likely to play, opportunities available for the expression of individual characteristics in regard to such areas as leadership, creative or original contributions, helping relationships, coping behaviors, and consequences of these in relation to different role expectations (Blocher 1966). Other examples of promoting self-understanding would include direct efforts to assist students in acquiring decision-making skills, considering and developing specific personal responsibility behaviors, learning problem-solving or planning skills, and processing and clarifying personal values. Finally, career education will need to continue to stimulate educators of all types to accept the fact that education can no longer confine its goals to the development of technical or academic skills. Rather, increased efforts must be devoted to assisting students to grow in the values, attitudes, and understandings which permit them to choose and use technical skills within a larger personal plan of commitment.

REFERENCES

Bennett, M. E. "Strategies of Vocational Guidance in Groups." In *Man in a World at Work*, Borow, H., ed. Boston: Houghton-Mifflin, 1964.

Berglund, B. W. "Career Planning: The Use of Sequential Evaluated Experience." In *Vocational Guidance and Human Development*, Herr, E. L., ed. Boston: Houghton-Mifflin, 1974.

Blocher, D. H. "Wanted: A Science of Human Effectiveness." *Personnel and Guidance Journal* 44 (1966): 729-733.

Coleman, James A. "How Do the Young Become Adults." *Review of Educational Research* 42 (Fall 1972).

Crites, J. O. "Career Development Processes." In *Vocational Guidance and Human Development,* Herr, E. L., ed. Boston: Houghton-Mifflin, 1974.

Darcy, Robert L. "Manpower in a Changing Curriculum." *American Vocational Journal* 44 (March 1969): 57-60.

Dewey, John. *Democracy and Education.* New York: MacMillan, 1916.

Dewey, John. *Individualism Old and New.* New York: Putnam, 1929.

Dewey, John. "Learning to Earn." In *Education Today.* New York: Putnam, 1940.

Dewey, John. *Reconstruction in Philosophy.* New York: The American Library, 1950.

Dewey, John. *School and Society.* Chicago: University of Chicago Press, 1923.

Flanagan, John C. "Education: How and For What." *The American Psychologist* (July 1973): 551-556.

Garbin, A. P.; Campbell, R. E.; Jackson, Dorothy P.; and Feldman, R. *Problems in the Transition from High School to Work as Perceived by Vocational Educators.* Columbus, Ohio: Center for Vocational and Technical Education, Ohio State University, 1967.

Garbin, A. P.; Jackson, Dorothy P.; and Campbell, R. E. *Worker Adjustment: Youth in Transition from School to Work: An Annotated Bibliography of Recent Literature.* Columbus, Ohio: Center for Vocational and Technical Education, Ohio State University, 1968.

Garbin, A. P.; Salomone, J. J.; Jackson, Dorothy P.; and Ballweg, J. A. *Worker Adjustment: Problems of Youth in Transition from High School to Work.* Columbus, Ohio: Center for Vocational and Technical Education, Ohio State University, 1970.

Giddings, Franklin. *Principles of Sociology.* New York: MacMillan, 1896.

Goodman, Paul. *People or Personnel* and *Like a Conquered Province.* New York: Vintage Books, 1968.

Gribbons, W., and Lohnes, P. *Emerging Careers.* New York: Teachers College Press, 1968.

Gross, E. "A Sociological Approach to the Analysis of Preparation for Work Life." *Personnel and Guidance Journal* 45 (1967): 416-423.

Hansen, James, and Herr, Edwin L. "School Truancy and Environmental Press." *The School Counselor* (November 1966).

Havighurst, R. J. "Youth in Exploration and Man Emergent." In *Man in a World at Work,* Borow, H., ed. Boston: Houghton-Mifflin, 1964.

Hayes, Samuel. *The Response to Industrialism.* Chicago: University of Chicago Press, 1957.

Herr, Edwin L. "Career Education and Psychological Education." *SRA Guidance Newsletter* (March/April 1975): 1-4.

Herr, Edwin L. "Contributions of Career Development to Career Education." *Journal of Industrial Teacher Education* 9 (Spring 1972a): 5-14.

Herr, Edwin L., and Cramer, S. H. *Vocational Guidance and Career Development in the Schools: Toward a Systems Approach.* Boston: Houghton-Mifflin, 1972b.

Herr, Edwin L.; Warner, Richard W., Jr.; and Swisher, John D. "Perspectives on High School Environments." *Peabody Journal of Education* 48 (October 1970): 56-62.

Hoffman, D. "Teaching Self-Understanding for Productive Living." *NASSP Bulletin* 57 (1973): 74-79.

Jordaan, J. P. Exploratory Behavior. In *Career Development: Self-Concept Theory,* Super, D. E., et al. New York: College Entrance Examination Board, 1963.

Jordaan, J. P. "Life Stages as Organizing Modes of Career Development." In *Vocational Guidance and Human Development,* Herr, E. L. ed. Boston: Houghton-Mifflin, 1974a.

Jordaan, J. P., and Super, D. E. "The Prediction of Early Adult Vocational Behavior." In *Life History Research in Psychopathology,* Ricks, D. F.; Thomas, A.; and Roff, M. eds. Minneapolis: University of Minnesota Press, 1974b.

Lathrop, Robert L. "The American Educational Structure." In *Vocational Guidance and Human Development,* Herr, Edwin L., ed. Boston: Houghton-Mifflin, 1974.

Leavitt, Frank M. "How Shall We Study the Industries for the Purposes of Vocational Guidance?" U. S. Bureau of Education, Bulletin no. 14. Washington: Government Printing Office, 1914.

Lefkowitz, L. J. "Our Newly Developing Wastelands: The American Colleges." *Intellect* 101 (1973): 371-376.

Livingston, J. S. "The Troubled Transition: Why College and University Graduates Have Difficulty Developing Careers in Business." *Journal of College Placement* 30 (1970): 34-41.

Lovejoy, Owen R. "Vocational Guidance and Child Labor." U. S. Bureau of Education, Bulletin no. 14. Washington: Government Printing Office, 1914.

Marland, Sidney P., Jr. "Career Education 300 Days Later." *American Vocational Journal* 47 (February 1972): 2.

Martin, Edward C. "Reflections on the Early Adolescent in School." *Daedalus* 100 (Fall 1971): 1087-1103.

Miller, D. C., and Form, W. H. *Industrial Sociology.* New York: Harper and Row, 1951.

Morris, John E. "Issues in Career Education." *Clearinghouse* 48 (September 1973): 32-36.

Nadler, Eugene B., and Krulee, Gilbert K. "Personality Factors Among Science and Technology Freshmen." *Journal of Educational Psychology* 52 (October 1961): 223-231.

Nash, Robert J., and Agne, Russell M. "A Case of Misplaced Relevance." *Journal of Teacher Education* 24 (Summer 1973): 87-92.

National Association of Manufacturers, *Proceedings,* 1912.

New Republic, The. 3 (15 May 1915).

Oakland, J. A. "Measurement of Personality Correlates of Academic Achievement in High School Students." *Journal of Counseling Psychology* 16 (1969): 452-457.

O'Hara, R. P. "Vocational Self-Concepts and High School Achievement." *Vocational Guidance Quarterly* 15 (1966): 106-112.

Prediger, D. J. "The Role of Assessment in Career Guidance." In *Vocational Guidance and Human Development,* Herr, E. L., ed. Boston: Houghton-Mifflin, 1974.

Pritchard, D. H. "The Occupational Exploration Process." *Personnel and Guidance Journal* 40 (1962): 674-680.

Prosser, Charles A., and Quigley, Thomas H. *Vocational Education in a Democracy.* Chicago: American Technical Society, 1949.

Reubens, Beatrice G. "Vocational Education: Performance and Potential." *Manpower* 6 (1974): 23-30.

Roen, Sheldon R. "Behavioral Studies as a Curriculum Subject." *The Record* 68 (April 1967): 541-550.

Roen, Sheldon R. "Teaching Program in the Behavioral Sciences." In *Emergent Approaches to Mental Health Programs,* Cowen, Emory L., et al., eds. New York: Appleton-Century-Crofts, 1967b.

Rusalem, H. "New Insights on the Role of Occupational Information in Counseling." *Journal of Counseling Psychology* 1 (1954): 84-88.

Samler, J. "Occupational Exploration in Counseling." In *Man in a World at Work,* Borow, H., ed. Boston: Houghton-Mifflin, 1964.

Sandeen, C. A. "The Meaning of a Bachelor's Degree." *School and Society* 96 (1968): 101-102.

Sievert, Norman W. "The Role of the Self-concept in Determining an Adolescent's Occupational Choice." *Journal of Industrial Teacher Education* 9 (Spring 1972): 47-53.

Simons, Diane. *George Kerschensteiner.* London: Methuen, 1966.

Snedden, David. "Education for a World of Teamplayers and Teamworkers." *School and Society* 20 (1 November 1924).

Steer, R. A. "The Relationship Between Satisfaction with Retirement and Similarity of Self-rating for Post-occupation and Present Activity in Educators." Unpublished doctoral dissertation. New York: Teachers College, Columbia University, 1970.

Stogdill, R. M. "Psychological Job Adjustment." In *Guidance in Vocational Education,* Campbell, R. E. Columbus, Ohio: Center for Vocational and Technical Education, Ohio State University, 1966.

Super, D. E. ed. *Computer-assisted Counseling.* New York: Teachers College Press, 1970a.

Super, D. E. "The Definition and Measurement of Early Career Behavior." *Personnel and Guidance Journal* 41 (1963a): 775-779.

Super, D. E. "Education and the Nature of Occupations and Careers." *Teachers College Record* 58 (1957a): 301-309.

Super, D. E., ed. *Measuring Vocational Maturity for Counseling and Evaluation.* Washington: American Psychological Association, 1974.

Super, D. E. *The Psychology of Careers.* New York: Harper and Row, 1957b.

Super, D. E., and Bohn, M. J., Jr. *Occupational Psychology.* Monterey, Calif.: Brodes/Cole, 1970b.

Super, D. E., and Overstreet, P. L. *The Vocational Maturity of Ninth Grade Boys.* New York: Teachers College Press, 1960.

Super, D. E.; Starishevsky, R.; Matlin, R.; and Jordaan, J. P. *Career Development: Self-concept Theory.* New York: College Entrance Examination Board, 1963b.

Super, D. E.; Kowalski, R. S.; and Gotkin, E. H. *Floundering and Trial After High School.* New York: Teachers College, Columbia University (mimeo), 1967.

Tierney, Roger, and Herman, Al. "Self-estimate Ability in Adolescence." *Journal of Counseling Psychology* 20 (1973): 298-302.

Tyler, Ralph. "Schools Headed for the Seventies." In *Needs of Elementary and Secondary Education for the Seventies.* General Subcommittee on Education of the Committee on Education and Labor, House of Representatives. Washington: Government Printing Office, 1970.

Wiebe, Robert. *The Search for Order.* New York: Hill and Wang, 1967.

Williams, R. L., and Cole, S. "Self-concept and School Adjustment." *Personnel and Guidance Journal* 46 (1968): 478-481.

CHAPTER	
3	

Legislation Affecting Career Education

In most cases, enactment of federal legislation is a response to a specific social need or problem. Thus, legislation regarding career education is a response to the need for educational reform. Federal and state initiatives are intended to stimulate local educational change. Several federal measures in particular, Public Law 92-318, Public Law 94-482, and H.R. 7/Public Law 95-207, have spearheaded legislative change.

The three articles comprising this chapter discuss the legal aspects of career education from its early beginnings to the enactment of the Career Education Act (P.L. 95-207) in 1977. Sidney P. Marland, Jr. traces the legal evolution up to P.L. 92-318. He believes that the legal foundations of career education were provided in this way, and that career education has evolved out of a vocational education measure. Elinor Water delineates the involvement of women and the benefits they may derive from career education. Thomas J. Sweeney and Marie C. Shafe present an interesting account of legislation affecting career education as it related to counseling. They especially emphasize the implications of P.L. 94-482.

CAREER EDUCATION: RETROSPECT AND PROSPECT

Sidney P. Marland, Jr.

Dr. Marland served as United States commissioner of education from 1970 to 1972. During that time he was instrumental in the development and implementation of landmark legislation for career education. From 1972 to 1973 he served as the nation's first statutory assistant secretary of education in the Department of Health, Education, and Welfare, and from 1973 to 1978 was president of the College Entrance Examination Board. This speech was delivered in 1974.

Elliot Richardson when serving as Secretary of HEW used to say, "Where I stand depends upon where I sit." The place where I sit today is the College Board, from which vantage point I will treat two themes: the laws relating to vocational and career education, and the responses now being shaped in the College Board to relate to this increasing educational priority. The College Board is an association of 2300 schools, colleges, universities, and state systems, serving several million students a year from middle school to adult education. The message of this paper is to view vocational and career education, both in nature and practice, in retrospect and prospect, from the vantage point of the College Board, and to examine the processes now in motion in that venerable institution so long identified as the fearsome gatekeeper of academe.

By odd coincidence, never remotely imagining myself a member of the College Board staff, to say nothing of being its president, I served as a member of the Board-sponsored Commission on Tests back in 1967. At that time, the commission was conducting a detailed investigation of the Board's role in American education and making a series of suggestions and recommendations about how that role should change. My own particular concern then—as now—was to restore to education a balance between academic and occupational values. This was a time when attitudes toward vocational education had, in my view, reached an all-time low.

In a special paper written for the commission I urged "that an institution be created that would give to vocational-technical study (at secondary and post-secondary levels) the same level of respect and prestige that the liberal arts studies now have, and would recognize (human) excellence in areas that are now limited primarily to intellectual (excellence)."

My brief continued: "This is not an easy task in a society whose values have so brightly illuminated the virtues of higher education. This proposal is not intended to diminish the importance of the present academic program. On the contrary, it seeks to elevate the arts of the world of work to the level of the liberal arts as socially desirable goals for (all) students."

It is interesting to look back upon the work of that independent commission, charged with giving external counsel to the vast College Board, and to weigh its influence today. The commission asked for *symmetry*, between the individual learner and the institution. It asked for a redress of the dominant power of colleges and universities over students, whether aspiring candidates or enrolled learners. Not surprisingly, James Coleman was a prime mover in that commission—and only a few years later, in 1973, we find him declaring in "Youth: Transition to Adulthood:"

As the labor of children has become unnecessary to society, the school has been extended for them. With every decade the length of schooling has increased, until a thoughtful person must ask whether society can conceive of no other way for youth to come into adulthood. If schooling (as it is) were a complete environment, the answer would properly be that no amount of school is too much, and increased schooling for the young is the best way for the young to spend their increased leisure, and society its increased wealth. . . . But schooling, as we know it, is not a complete environment, giving all the necessary opportunities for becoming adult (Coleman 1973).

We were both asking for more balance between formal learning and experience in conventional work. Coleman, the scholar, and I, the practitioner, had reached the same position by different roads.

Coleman continues:

The absorption of adolescent time by the school has contributed greatly to the dominance of the *student* role among the many roles that a young person might have. The delaying of work until after the completion of schooling gives the adolescent no place in the work force (ibid.).

One may wonder whether there is not a dichotomy, indeed, an internal contradiction, when in the same breath one speaks of the College Board and career education. But if one is concerned about young people in this last quarter century of the 1900's one cannot escape the relatedness.

One of the earliest members of the College Board, in the first decade of this century, was Harvard, along with a dozen other men's and women's colleges and universities of high prestige. Indeed, the esteemed President Elliot took the trouble to travel from Cambridge to Trenton to plead eloquently before a meeting of the Association of Colleges and Secondary Schools of the Middle States and Maryland for adoption of the resolution establishing the CEEB. Harvard, however, notwithstanding its academic reputation, had its origin as a school dedicated to the development of vocations. As Steve Bailey reminds us, during Harvard's first 100 years, 75% of its graduates, as intended, entered the ministry.

This is to say again that career education is not an invention of the present decade. The harmonizing of occupational development with academic learning is not, as some declare, a passing fad. It is time, however, that we bring system and order, curricular strength, and philosophical unity to a condition that has been ad hoc, unsystematic, and not consciously and deliberately responsive to the lifetime needs of the learner.

Since the earliest days, our country has given high priority to providing education for the people and to making it useful. *The primary aim of these first colleges in the 17th and 18th centuries was not necessarily to increase the continental stock of cultivated people, but rather to supply its particular region with knowledgeable ministers, lawyers, doctors, merchants, and political leaders.* These colleges tended to be at the very center of each colony's affairs and to involve the partnership of academic and lay community leaders with great regularity. Again, career education's call for increasing this partnership is not new.

Through the years, as private and public educational institutions spread in the colonies and along the frontiers, the functional—or vocational—role of education remained strong, as witness the important passage of the Morrill (Land Grant College) Act in 1862 at a turning point in our history, in the midst of a war which at once divided and in many ways united the nation and its resources. Fundamental to this monumental legislation was the recognition of the academic and practical needs of the people, changing higher education dramatically, and putting it in the midst of the agricultural and industrial affairs of the nation, and adding new respectability and purpose to the place of vocation in post-secondary education in America. *The two complementary threads, academic and occupational, were articulated and wedded by the philosophy of the Morrill Act which set in place our great land grant university structure.*

If we attempt to trace the source of divorcement between the academic and vocational threads that make up our educational history, I must count the Smith-Hughes Act (1916) as one of those instruments of divisiveness. I will not labor the point, but for all its great contributions, and self-evident worth, Smith-Hughes and its subsequent generations of federal law have, regrettably, legalized the divorce of vocation from academe. We seek now, and with some evidence of effect, a beginning toward reconciliation.

By the mid '60s, Congress began slowly and tentatively to ameliorate the sharp divisions imposed by Smith-Hughes. The Vocational Education Act of 1963 (U.S. Congress), which became operational only in 1965, continued the support of agricultural subjects, home economics, distributive education, and other traditional crafts, but gave new impetus to work-study programs, residential schools, area vocational programs and, happily, to *general education as it could be tied to specific needs in vocational education.* This was a step toward a breakthrough in the historic separation of academic and vocational education.

After two years' evaluation of this law by the Advisory Council on Vocational Education, Congress accepted some major recommendations for amendment and put them into effect in 1968. These changes provided many of the major dimensions for career education:

- National and state advisory councils
- Research and training with emphasis on development of career programs
- Cooperative and work-study programs
- Focus on curriculum development and exemplary (model) programs

And then came the Educational Amendments of 1972. Much of this historic legislation has already impacted heavily and constructively on American education. But one feature of this law remains closeted in the Executive and Congress, unnoticed, unfunded, and scorned. Let me read you a passage or two—as we now, in 1975, ponder the renewal and reform of the Vocational Education statutes and at the same time examine more closely today the unfolding message of career education's philosophy.

Public Law 92-318 (92nd Congress, June 23, 1972)
Part B, Occupational Education
For the purpose of carrying out this part, there are hereby authorized to be appropriated $100,000,000 for the fiscal year ending June 30, 1973, $250,000,000 for the fiscal year ending June 30, 1974, and $500,000,000 for the fiscal year ending June 30, 1975.

(page 81)

The Secretary shall—
(1) provide for the administration by the Commissioner of Education of grants to the States authorized by this part;
(2) assure that manpower needs in subprofessional occupations in education, health, rehabilitation, and community and welfare services are adequately considered in the development of programs under this part;

(3) promote and encourage the coordinations of programs developed under this part with those supported under this part with those supported under Part A of this title, the Vocational Education Act of 1963, the Manpower Development and Training Act of 1962, title I of the Economic Opportunity Act of 1964, the Public Health Service Act, and related activities administered by various departments and agencies of the Federal Government; and

(4) provide for the continuous assessment of needs in occupational education and for the continuous evaluation of programs supported under the authority of this part and of related provisions of law.

The Commissioner shall—

(1) coordinate all programs administered by the Commissioner which specifically relate to the provisions of this part so as to provide the maximum practicable support for the objectives of this part;

(2) promote and encourage occupational preparation, counseling and guidance, and job placement or placement in post-secondary occupational education programs as a responsibility of elementary and secondary schools;

(3) utilize research and demonstration programs administered by him to assist in the development of new and improved instructional methods and technology for education and in the design and testing of models of schools or school systems which place occupational education on an equal footing with academic education;

(4) assure that the Education Professions Development Act and similar programs of general application will be so administered as to provide a degree of support for vocational, technical, and occupational education commensurate with national needs and more nearly representative of the relative size of the population to be served; and

(5) develop and disseminate accurate information on the status of occupational education in all parts of the Nation, at all levels of education, and in all types of institutions, together with information on occupational opportunities available to persons of all ages.

(page 82)

Planning activities initiated under clause (2) of subsection (a) shall include—

(A) an assessment of the existing capabilities and facilities for the provision of post-secondary occupational education, together with existing needs and projected needs for such education in all parts of the State;

(B) thorough consideration of the most effective means of utilizing all existing institutions within the State capable of providing the kinds of programs assisted under this part, including (but not limited to) both private and public community and junior colleges, area vocational schools, accredited private proprietary institutions, technical institutes, manpower skill centers, branch institutions of State colleges or universities, and public and private colleges and universities;

(C) the development of an administrative procedure which provides reasonable promise for resolving differences between vocational educators, community and junior college educators, college and university educators, elementary and secondary educators, and other interested groups with respect to the administration of the program authorized under this part; and

(D) the development of a long-range strategy for infusing occupational education (including general orientation counseling and guidance, and placement either in a job or in post-secondary occupational programs) into elementary and secondary schools on an equal footing with traditional academic education, to the end that every child who leaves secondary school is prepared either to enter productive employment or to undertake additional education at the post-secondary level, but without being forced prematurely to make an irrevocable commitment to a particular educational or occupational choice; . . .

(pages 83 & 84)

(a) There is hereby established in the United States Office of Education a Bureau of Occupational and Adult Education hereinafter referred to as the Bureau, which shall be responsible for the administration of this title, the Vocational Education Act of 1963, including parts C and I thereof, the Adult Education Act, functions of the Office of Education relating to manpower training and development, functions of the Office relating to vocational, technical, and occupational training in community and junior colleges, and any other Act vesting authority in the Commissioner for vocational, occupational, adult and continuing education and for those portions of any legislation for career education which are relevant to the purposes of other Acts administered by the Bureau.

It seems to me that this largely unfulfilled document of law leaves very little unsaid on the subject of career education. One of its principal architects, that giant of educational vision in the Congress, Albert Quie, has said that indeed the statute might well have been called the Career Education Act. Unlike its historic forebears in federal law, this law deals with all levels of education and is freed from the constraints imposed in the Vocational Education Act and its subparts to deal with secondary schools. It embraces all learning, including academic learning, putting aside the historic divorcement noted earlier. It carries respectable budgetary authorizations at the half-billion dollar level; and it rightly assigns major creative authority and initiative to the states. It calls heavily upon the lay community for counsel. It is, in my judgment, a sound base for the advancement of career education by any name. It is the instrument, which has so far eluded us, for reforming our schools and colleges.

Those who see career education as a threat to vocational education (and I believe their numbers are diminishing) should first confront this statute. It sustains the state vocational advisory councils and authorizes new funds of its own, rather than divert vocational education funds from the traditional laws and programs. Those vocational educators who have thought deeply about career education have acclaimed it the best thing that has happened to vocational education in 53 years. I happen to agree. And I think it is time to put aside the legalized divorce and, as we reach out for renewal of the laws, to have the wisdom, creativity, and common sense to put the two together. The combined level of authorized funding would exceed a billion dollars—which is sufficient as a starter to make truly significant differences in schools and colleges and, especially, in the lives of our students.

The extended thread of career education law which found its place in the Amendments of 1974 gives further substance to the federal role and, for the first time, establishes the name and gives purpose to the concept. While this statute is nearly submerged in a cluster of miscellany under Part C of the 1974 Amendments, it does for the first time offer, along with the *name*, career education, a modest budget for the Office of Education to encourage continued planning and development activities in the states. Yet the 1974 law might well have been included as an extension of the Occupational Education feature of the 1972 law, and both might well embrace the anticipated extensions of the Vocational Education Act. So long as our laws imply a separation of academic learning from occupational development, we will fall short of the ideals which career education addresses. We will as a society, I regret to say, continue to scorn vocational education as "something different."

The law which established NIE (also in the 1972 Amendments) gave a tandem impetus to career education as the singular specific program mandate in the total authorization. Ideally, the federal role, sensitively managed, can and should take two broad responsibilities under this collection of law: (1) research and development, including evaluation and conceptual discipline and model building under NIE; and, (2) combined funding support of all occupationally related education by OE, at all levels of teaching, without the strings and trappings of legislated programs that have gathered bits and pieces of categorical federal control and constraint for over a half century.

Turning now to the College Board, I would see it as a mirror reflecting, as it should, the evolving laws and practices in the schools and colleges, especially over recent years and with the future.

Coinciding with the beginnings of the great surge in college enrollments in the decade of the 1960s, the College Board began slowly to change and expand the relatively narrow focus of its basic admissions testing program to include more services and information for both younger and older students. The style and coverage of the board's national directory of colleges and universities (the *College Handbook*) were altered to include more and better information about the rapidly growing number of member institutions. The new and relatively inexpensive Preliminary Scholastic Aptitude Test was begun in 1959-60 to provide high school students with earlier guidance information. Later, the PSAT was combined with the National Merit Scholarship Qualifying Test to help reduce multiple testing in the secondary schools. In the same decade, two new College Board programs were established, both representing important departures from the historic role of testing for selective admissions. The first, the College-Level Examination Program was designed for the emerging and as yet undefined population of nontraditional students, typically adults, and was based on the theory of offering academic credit for what a student had learned, no matter how or where the student had learned it. After a slow start in the middle-1960s, CLEP caught on and by the early 1970s had begun to reach extensive national audiences of adults and of younger students, with an estimated 100,000 candidates in the 1975-76 year.

Equally important, the College Board developed and introduced another program of tests and measures aimed primarily at serving the two-year colleges and their students. The Comparative Guidance and Placement Program (CGP) represented another move away from selective testing and offered a new dimension of measuring skills, aptitudes, and abilities in career fields.

As I have suggested earlier, the Commission on Tests, an independent group of scholars, administrators, and researchers, worked from 1967 to 1970 to produce its two-volume report bearing on suggested changes in the direction and emphasis of the College Board's work. As a result of this report the board did introduce additional new activities and modifications in existing programs designed to extend and diversify the information flow for students of all ages. It also introduced new services to aid colleges and state education agencies in their management and long-range planning work.

Among these developments, the Student Descriptive Questionnaire (SDQ), has proved especially useful to students and to institutions, since it provides valuable additional information about a student's abilities, interests, and plans, including career aspirations.

Also during the past five years, the College Board has developed another non-testing service that has been increasingly valuable to institutions of higher education in a period of relatively stable enrollment. The Student Search Service is a computer-based operation that can be tailored to meet each institution's needs and specific requirements in a given year. This service endeavors to match institutions and candidates, with the initiative resting upon the student.

However, probably the most important development of the 1970s affecting career education has been that of the Decision-Making Program and its related services. Originally focusing on younger students at perhaps the junior high level, the program and its concepts have now been extended to include secondary students at every level as well as adults in many walks of life. The reception of our course of study in Decision-Making in schools and education agencies throughout the country has been gratifying. Plans are now under way to offer additional dimensions of this program to aid teachers and counselors who want to relate decision-making to the career education curriculums.

Within the past year, the College Board has taken two additional and integral steps toward becoming a significant force in career development during the remainder of this decade and, perhaps, on into the 1980s. During my short time at the College Board I have come to respect and value the power and influence of this voluntary organization of schools and colleges to affect education and society in a positive way. I would not underestimate at this point the need for such voluntary groups and agencies, as distinct from government, to act with vigor and dispatch to help institutions, students, and their mentors to move in directions that will bring about basic changes in educational thinking and planning—reform if you will—in career development as an essential component of all educations.

The first development to which I allude consists of a state-level study of career education being conducted by the board, and now in the final stages of its ten-month duration. Supported by a grant from the National Institute of Education, this project involves reviewing and analyzing many existing state career education models and strategies for coordinating and implementing career education programs in states throughout the country.

Those conducting the study are exploring a number of barriers to full implemetation of career education at the state level, such as those which impede the transfer of students from school systems to other learning situations; unnecessarily require the certification and credentialization of individuals for particular careers; segregate federal, state, local, and private funds intended to finance the education and training of individuals at all age levels; divide academic and vocational curricula in schools.

The anticipated outcomes of the project include a listing of existing effective career education linkage systems in states, an identification and analysis of the most critical linkage areas, models of career education delivery systems, and approaches for successful implementation of such systems, including recommendations for legislation.

Through cooperation from the several states, and a broadly representative advisory committee, this linkage study has progressed most favorably in the last several months.

We have in the course of this study come to realize how very important the role of the several states is in the advancement of this reform. We have come to appreciate the importance of the federal role as a source of developmental and technical assistance and the need for this leadership to continue. We see career education nearly ready for significant federal funding following the research and development stage. We have come to believe that career education is, at present, best and most widely installed at the elementary level; less so at the secondary; significantly less so at the post-secondary level, except for community colleges.

The College Board, consistent with its by-laws which call for it to facilitate the guidance and counseling function of schools and colleges, is attempting to come to grips with a concrete service to the process of career education. Under the NIE grant we have, as noted earlier, studied numerous institutions across the country to identify good linkages between schools and the workplace. Among those investigated and illuminated for emulation are the University of Cincinnati, where the Career Dynamics Center has built upon the strong cooperative education program dating back to 1906. Mandatory work experience in a number of occupational fields at Cincinnati expresses the career education theme at the post-secondary level.

Another activity which we have examined and described for emulation is the State Department of Education in Florida, where state law has brought local school boards into formal companionship with the Florida State Employment Service to facilitate and systematize job placement and follow-up after high school.

The list of worthy sites where career education is finding a prominent place is nearly endless. Just a few weeks ago, another of the founding members of the College Board, New York University, published its statement of goals for the next five years. Developed by a task force of faculty, administration, alumni and students, engaging literally hundreds of participants, the goals statement placed career development on an equal level of institutional priority with increased academic excellence. The statement declared "an intensified responsibility for helping students relate their academic interests to practical career opportunities." The statement embraced the needs of the nontraditional and adult learner, charging the university with responsibilities "to meet the needs of new groups seeking higher education, including increased numbers of people planning total career changes."

These patterns of institutional reform in process are the forces which push the College Board to find its enlarged place in the service of education, including career education.

At the elementary and secondary level we are engaged in designing new career education services for six states and have joined in a consortium for experimental and developmental trial, utilizing the background and tools of the familiar SAT, PSAT/NMSQT, Achievement Tests, and Advanced Placement as foundations for new designs and instruments for facilitating the reality of career education as a state responsibility. The states involved are Ohio, New Jersey, Minnesota, Louisiana, Georgia, and Maryland. All of these states have launched major programs in career education to prepare students for living and working in society. Along with the participants, the College Board has demonstrated willingness to invest significant sums of money for research and development of services and materials in a cooperative exploration of ways to measure basic career competencies—those generalized skills and attitudes that all students should acquire before they leave high school.

Without exception, the first priority that these six states established for new and improved service to career education was specific curriculum material and faculty training in decision-making for career development. The College Board is now in the process of developing improved decision-making materials, designing teacher education workshops, and formulating new assessment instruments that will endeavor to serve counselors for *all* students, not solely those seeking higher education.

The College Board's close companion, Educational Testing Service, is also at work on fundamental research and development activities which bear directly upon career education, and which may find their way into the Board's services over time. SIGI, a system of computerized guidance services for reinforcing the counselor with many occupations related facts and values, is now in advanced field test status. A new program at ETS called

CAEL (Cooperative Assessment of Experiential Learning) is just what its name implies—a system for helping colleges and universities recognize important and measurable external experiences that can be equated responsibly with college credit. This is clearly in the career education spectrum of recognizing the worth of work as well as study. There are now 160 participating institutions involved with ETS in this experiment.

In summary, let me offer some recommendations to those of us who see the potential of a major reform in American education, and who have a hand in its implementation:

• Let us set aside the narrow and self-serving differences over turf and power. There is ample room for vocational education to flourish as never before and, indeed, be in the vanguard of the career education movement along with academic leaders and enlightened administrators. Let the teachers of academic subjects, the defenders of the liberal arts at all levels, welcome the specialists in vocational and occupational development as respected equals.

• Let us, at long last, welcome the community—labor, business, and industry—into the totality of education. They are willing, and we desperately need them, not at arm's length but as full partners.

• Let us give vigorous and unstinting support to the federal agencies, NIE and OE in particular, as they endeavor to harmonize the necessarily parallel thrusts of research and development on the one hand and operational financial support and technical assistance on the other. To accept the leadership of the federal arm is not a submission to federal control.

• Let us avoid depending on our prescriptive rules and stereotypes as to what career education is or must be. Let teachers and professors themselves help to invent it in their respective spheres of influence. For, like a poem or a painting, it can be different things to different people depending upon the beholder. *We are in motion*—some say to a degree that has not been known before in generations of American educational history. Let there be no high priests who claim to know all the answers about career education. Rather, as in all worthy social enterprises that have advanced our people, let those who must be the implementers, including the students, be the leaders in their individual ways. It is quite possible that at this point in this movement for reform the leadership is not limited to the conventional or traditional places of influence. It is quite possible at this moment that the discerning and demanding student, especially in high schools and colleges, is the principal power source for better education for all.

WHAT DO WOMEN WANT? AND HOW CAN LEGISLATION HELP?

Elinor Waters, Brian Dates, and Jane Goodman
All three authors are on the staff of the Continuum Center for Adult Counseling and Leadership Training at Oakland University. Dr. Waters is director of the center and from 1975 to 1977 served as national chairperson of the Commission on the Occupational Status of Women of the National Vocational Guidance Association. This article was written in 1977.

Full equality in the world of work will come when work is recognized as an integral part of the lives of women as well as of men, and when job opportunities, both real and perceived, do not differ on the basis of sex. In that, perhaps utopian, future, career education for all can be uniform. At this time, however, women need special counseling interventions and affirmative action in hiring, promoting, and equalization of pay.

In this article we shall briefly discuss the career development and counseling needs of women at various ages as well as some of the programs which have been developed to meet these needs. We shall then describe the current status of legislation relating to career education for women and make suggestion for its implementation.

While most theorists agree that a developmental approach to career education is best for everyone, it is essential when we are talking about women. Sex stereotyped perceptions of "appropriate" occupations have appeared in children as early as kindergarten (Schlossberg and Goodman 1972); therefore, activities designed to reduce bias must begin at least that early. Indeed, we would like to suggest that an effective intervention process would need to start with parents of preschoolers, or even expectant parents! In addition, since the influences toward conformity are so strong in society, it seems any unidimensional approach is doomed to, at best, token success. An effective plan must be multifaceted and addressed to the needs of parents, children, adult clients, counselors, teachers, and employers.

Data on the current status of women in the market place is particularly discouraging to the extent that while gains have been made, women are not proportionately represented in most occupational areas (U.S. Department of Labor 1975a). In many ways, women are not doing as well as they were in 1950. In 1950, when women represented only 28% of the civilian labor force, they held 40% of the professional positions. By 1974, women constituted 39% of the labor force, and still only 40% of the professional positions. During that period, women increased their representation in the technical worker category by 3.5%. However, this was offset by a decrease in the percentage of women in managerial and administrative positions. Decreases also occurred in the percentages of women employed as sales people, operatives, and service workers. The large gain in overall percentage of women in the work force was due primarily to an increase in the number of women in clerical positions—a whopping 9.3%. Some progress has been made by women entering skilled crafts, and further progress may be stimulated by two articles in a publication of the Department of Labor entitled *Womanpower*. "How to Succeed in a Journeyman's World" describes the movement of women into the skilled crafts. "In the Manner of Rosie the Riveter" tells how Employment and Training Administration (formerly Manpower Administration) programs are preparing women for nontraditional fields that offer higher pay and increased advancement opportunities (U.S. Department of Labor 1975b).

Women have fared equally badly in the educational arena. Although the percentage of women in college has increased from 7% to 20% since 1950, fewer women are college graduates than men, and women are underrepresented in postgraduate study. Perhaps the most discouraging data deal with the widening of the earnings gap between women and men. In 1950, women employed full-time year-round earned 65% of the salaries of men similarly employed. By 1973, that figure had dropped to 57%, a measurable 8% widening of the gap. These statistics deal with women in general. For special subgroups, such as minority women, displaced homemakers, and poorly educated or older women, the situation may be even more acute.

The Need for Early Career Development

These statistics underline the need for affirmative action programs which begin well before the employment phase via a developmental career guidance or career education approach.

Much of the recent literature has endorsed this concept (Crites 1976; Holland 1971; Schlossberg 1975; Veroff and Feld 1965). Briefly this approach holds that career development occurs as educational and vocational pursuits interact with other life pursuits, and that this process continues throughout life. Furthermore, the nature of guidance or career education for one's improved career development should not be viewed as a static, tradition-based set of related services that simply assist individual choices. A career guidance or education program must consider present and future needs, desires, and expectations of its clientele, as well as those of the society.

In total, then, the posture that we recommend for career development programs is one which emphasizes the developmental aspect of career choice rather than a simple "one-shot" attempt to fill jobs. Such a developmental approach would minimize the effect of practices which have kept women at the lower levels of the job ladder. These ad hoc practices have forced or steered women into jobs which they initially felt were interim or "insurance" endeavors. Twenty years later many women find themselves still in these interim positions—with no chance for advancement or change.

To return to the effects of a developmental approach on women, we suggest that initial attempts to counteract sex stereotyping of careers be made at the inception of a child's formal education, if not before. In addition, if all life experiences are to be thought of as influencing or interacting with vocational choice, it cannot be simply career education which is aimed in this direction, but all educational efforts. In working toward these goals the workbook, *Today's Changing Roles: An Approach to NonSexist Teaching*, published by the National Education Association, may be helpful (Educational Challenges, Inc. 1974). The contents are organized progressively for elementary, intermediate, and secondary students so that all grade levels can be included. Materials can be incorporated into mathematics, English, and social science classes to provide an overall educational approach to counteract sex stereotyping and bias.

At the intermediate or middle school level, girls are often ahead of boys in thinking of and making some initial career decisions. Since this is a teachable moment for many girls, career development seems especially appropriate at this stage.

At the secondary level, a number of unbiased guidance programs have been developed. The College Entrance Examinations Board's *Deciding* program provides help in decision-making, a key element in life planning, and may be used in classroom situations. The Center for Vocational Education at Ohio State University has developed a curriculum unit, *"Planning Ahead for the World of Work,"* for female secondary school students. A study on the effect of this unit (Vetter, Brown, and Stehney 1975) demonstrated decreased sex stereotyping among students exposed to the curriculum, particularly in their attitudes toward work after having children.

At the college and adult levels, *How To Decide, A Guide for Women* (Scholz 1975) is a helpful resource. In addition, Oakland University's Continuum Center for Adult Counseling and Leadership Training offers career development programs which help women and men who are contemplating changing careers or reentry into the work force (Goodman, Walworth, and Waters 1975). A workbook, *Directions for Change* (Walworth and Goodman 1975), is used in the Continuum Center's programs and may be helpful for other adult groups.

Finally, since work occupies such an important place in our society, the leaving of it also needs to be dealt with through pre-retirement counseling. W. Hunter and T. Collins have some valuable suggestions in this area (Hunter 1976; Collins 1970). In working with older adults, the peer counseling model may be particularly effective.

In order for programs like those mentioned above to be implemented effectively, pre-service and in-service training must be provided for teachers, administrators, counselors, and other career specialists. A vehicle for doing so is provided by Birk's module, *Providing Life/Career Planning for Women and Girls* (Birk 1977).

Three monographs published by the National Vocational Guidance Association—*Counseling Girls and Women Over the Life Span* (Matthews et al. 1972), *Facilitating Career Development for Girls and Women* (NVGA 1975), and *Planning Ahead with Girls and Women: Strategies for Action* (NVGA 1978), all contain useful methods and approaches to eliminating sex bias and stereotyping while enhancing the delivery of career-related services to women.

The University of Georgia Center for Continuing Education has developed "A Statewide Program for Counselors of Women" (1977), designed to improve the competency of personnel who come from a wide variety of job settings and who counsel women.

Current Legislation on the Future of Women's Careers

With the foregoing concerns and program types enumerated, let us examine the current legislation which may have impact on the future of women's careers. Public Laws 94-167, 94-482, and P.L. 95-207, the House of Representative's Elementary and Secondary Education Act of 1977, will be highlighted. Clearly our discussion is based on information available at a particular moment. Because of the speed with which new legislation is introduced and the need for monitoring at both the initial and authorization stages in a bill's life, we suggest that readers keep up to date with one of the many legislative reports. The *WEAL Washington Report*, published by the Women's Equity Action League is particularly relevant to women's issues, as is the newsletter, *Women and Work*, published by the U. S. Department of Labor.

Briefly, Public Law 94-167 mandates the holding of state women's meetings and a National Women's Conference concerning the barriers which face women, and P.L. 95-207 authorizes new funding for career education in elementary and secondary schools. Public Law 94-482 (Education Amendments of 1976 to extend the Higher Education Act of 1965) contains twenty-three sections pertaining to vocational guidance, counseling, and education for women.

Effectiveness of these laws in overcoming sex bias in employment and sex stereotyping of careers will rest largely on the interpretation given them by agents responsible for their implementation. Depending on how they are applied, these laws could prove either valuable in enhancing the occupational status of women or stultifying.

In many ways, these three pieces of legislation are interrelated. The findings which emerge from the hearings authorized under P.L. 94-167 should be communicated to state and local districts responsible for carrying out the mandates of P.L. 94-482 and P.L. 95-207. We hope that appropriate means for communication will be found.

In order for these laws to be maximally effective, it is important that career education programs focus around a carefully sequenced developmental approach. It is equally important that career education programs teach people the processes of decision-making. Once this skill is mastered, people will know how to gather information about themselves and the world of work, and to assess this information in terms of their values. They will then be able to set priorities, develop alternative plans of action, and begin implementation. Such a process is applicable to work, leisure, and life planning. The fact that most people now, voluntarily or involuntarily, make major career shifts during their working lives is another argument for the importance of the developmental process approach to career education.

Although sequencing and a process-oriented approach are desirable components of any career education program, they are crucial for women's programs. Timing is particularly important because women's receptivity to thinking, not only about careers in general but also about nontraditional careers in particular, is greater in earlier years and may diminish during adolescence. Learning process skills is of special relevance for women because their career patterns are more often discontinuous than those of men.

A major caution regarding P.L. 95-207 is that nowhere in the law is there mention of the need to reduce sex bias or stereotyping. Without such provisions, programs teaching boys that careers are for implementing one's self-concept and girls that careers are for "pin-money" or as "insurance" employment could conceivably be funded.

P. L. 94-482 is far better in this regard. Apparently recognizing the already existing gap between the sexes as concerns career opportunities, it clearly encourages unbiased practices for elementary, secondary, and post-secondary career counseling, and indeed, funds such things as child care so that women may enter and complete career education programs. It also makes provisions for in-service training to help teachers and guidance personnel learn ways of identifying and overcoming sex biases. We would hope that as part of the developmental approach, provisions for mid-life and retirement counseling would be made to help those women who are facing those particular life passages.

Our hope is that P.L. 95-207 might be redesigned or amended with emphasis on unbiased practices thus eliminating the need for remedial action at the post-secondary level, as outlined in P.L. 94-482.

In sum, we are endorsing the developmental approach to career guidance and programs which have been designed to promote it. As regards the three pieces of legislation, we must be more cautious. Results of meetings funded under P.L. 94-167 could hold great import in the area of women's career concerns if the spirit of the lawmakers is well intentioned rather than tokenistic.

Secondly, we suggest that more language specifically addressed to the career needs of young women would assure that P.L. 95-207 does not support the status quo, but instead takes steps toward elimination of sexist barriers. Finally, we believe that P.L. 94-482 holds much hope for overcoming sex biases if the approach taken is a developmental, process-oriented one. Thus, while we laud the intent, the promise, and the potential of these three pieces of legislation, we must at this point remain cautiously optimistic.

LEGISLATION AND COUNSELORS:
DO YOU SEE THE PENDULUM SWING?

Thomas J. Sweeney and Marie C. Shafe

Dr. Sweeney is a professor in the School of Applied Behavioral Sciences and Educational Leadership at Ohio University and has acted as a consultant for educators in industry programs.

Dr. Shafe is acting dean of education at Rollins College in Florida. Her professional areas of emphasis are guidance and counseling and career education and she serves as consultant in career education to schools in several states. This article was written in 1977.

The proverbial pendulum is swinging toward counseling and guidance services once again. Federal legislation, recently passed or under consideration, will make the National Defense Education Act of 1958 insignificant by comparison. The Education Amendments of 1976 (Public Law 94-482) have that capability already if fully funded. There are some substantial differences between the resources and expectations of the 1950s and the 1960s and those of the present time.

In 1958, Congress responded to what they perceived as an external threat to our national posture as a world power. Today the congress seems more attuned to the domestic needs of our citizenry, now and in the future. NDEA funds originally were intended to identify and guide the gifted young person into technical fields useful in the national effort. Today the legislation speaks to the career and life needs of people of all ages.

Guidance and counseling was very much a fledgling profession in 1958. Clearly, NDEA funds provided an impetus for the counseling profession, which the Johnson years for a "Great Society" expanded into counseling services outside of the schools, employment or rehabilitation offices. Now, once again, federal funds may provide a thrust and scope which propels the counselor into a vital and demanding role.

Unlike the earlier years, however, we have, as a profession, both experience and greater resources. With the funding comes greater expectations and closer scrutiny. The present era can be summed up in one word—accountability. It is with us today and it will be all the more significant in future legislative reviews. Preparation and delivery of services by the teaching and counseling professions will also be called to account.

The purpose of this article is three-fold:

• To provide some indices of direction for professional responses to legislation from the literature.

• To highlight significant aspects of recently passed or proposed legislation.

• To suggest implications for counselor preparation and delivery of counseling services.

Indices for Change

Responding to the extensive pressure for educational accountability exerted by public and special interest groups as well as legislators, the National Center for Education

Statistics (NCES) conducted a canvass of state education agencies in all 50 states and the District of Columbia (Goor 1976). The study reported a movement toward "the development of performance-based standards of educational attainment." According to NCES, "the intent of this movement is to provide an educational program that enables all pupils to master, at a minimum, certain fundamental skills at a specified level of attainment." The skills are categorized in two groups, *basic* (or *cognitive*) and *life*—those skills needed to perform daily life tasks. NCES found twenty-four states in the planning and developmental stages of a program of performance-based education (PBE) in both basic and life skills at the elementary and/or secondary level. Five states had operational programs. PBE program aspects are such activities as performance-based standards for teachers, out-of-school learning opportunities, alternatives for measuring competencies, and setting new promotion or graduation standards that are performance-based rather than courses- or time-based. There is evidence to suggest that counselor preparation, credentialing, and delivery of services also are being influenced by this trend.

Closely aligned with the performance-based, accountability issue is the expectation that education must address both the cognitive and affective needs of students. This denotes the necessity for more integrated teacher and counselor preparation through pre- and in-service activities. This imperative is no more clearly seen than in career development. Career development, according to the National Vocational Guidance Association-American Vocational Association position paper on career development, refers to "the total constellation of psychological, sociological, educational, physical, economic, and chance factors that combine to shape the career of any given individual" (NVGA-AVA 1973). These associations call for teachers to provide group guidance experiences and help students increase their understanding of their own interests, capabilities, and expectations with the assistance of guidance personnel.

The Center for Vocational Education proposed a two-dimensional model for guidance: (I) Problem-Need-Resource Identification and (II) Problem Resolution (Drier 1976). The implementation of this systematic model must have the active participation of classroom teachers and other school personnel. The first dimension includes such components as career development group, assessment of staff competency needs and individual student needs, and planning. Community relations and involvement, classroom-based guidance, placement, and evaluation are some of the aspects of the second dimension. This model, too, points toward a comprehensive delivery systems approach to guidance services interfacing with academic discipline offerings.

Further evidence for a renewal and change of counselor preparation has been provided by the Commission on Counselor Preparation for Career Development/Career Education sponsored by the Association for Counselor Education and Supervision (ACES 1976). The commission recommended that counselor preparation should "train counselors for collaborative relationships with other educators," as well as impart skills for development of guidance-based career education programs. Additionally, the commission recommended that counselor preparation programs emphasize career development training for counselors to deliver comprehensive career guidance to all persons. Included in the training should be skills in organizational development and the change process whereby counselors could more effectively implement career development programs and activities in schools and agencies. The commission further set forth fifteen counselor competencies it believed to be essential for delivery of comprehensive career guidance services.

The North Central Association for Accreditation of Schools and Colleges recently conducted a two-year study of 1,280 administrators, counselors, and teachers to determine the future directions of counseling and guidance (Gibson 1976). Gibson found that considerably more emphasis will be placed upon career guidance and consultation with teachers, other educators, and parents. The study participants believed counselors of the future should be active and skillful as change agents, consultants, affective education specialists; and decidedly skillful in needs assessment, accountability, and working with all age groups including adults, as well as developing and implementing career guidance and career education activities. The study pointed toward significant changes needed in counselor preparation programs.

These statements and studies suggested that:

• Performance-based preparation strategies which can demonstrate their effectiveness in better teaching and counseling services are being required.

• Preparation for life is requiring teaching and guidance activities which address not only the cognitive and affective development of our youth but the continuing renewal of all persons who choose to exercise their right to career and life planning assistance.

• Counselors, counselor educators, and counselor supervisors must remain responsive to and anticipate the changes taking place within the community as well as in the educational enterprise.

Highlights of Recent Legislation

The breadth and complexity of the legislation passed or under consideration defy a simple summary. At best we can only highlight representative proposals which illustrate the tone and direction of federal legislation. The Education Amendments of 1976 (P.L. 94-482) are particularly relevant. First, they have been passed into law but continue to need support for full funding and careful guidance in their implementation, and second, their complexity requires careful study by major segments of the teaching and counseling professions.

A new perspective in teacher and counselor preparation is required in order to respond to the Education Amendments of 1976. Through this law, the commissioner of education is authorized to provide for " . . . institutes, workshops, and seminars . . . to improve professional guidance qualifications of teachers and counselors . . . " The act was passed " . . . to represent a consistent, integrated, and coordinated approach for meeting needs and delivering comprehensive services and programs." This legislation further suggests the need for specific criteria and standards of proficiency and accountability for services and programs.

The amendments direct the commissioner to approve funding for vocational education leadership development programs only if " . . . a comprehensive program in vocational education with adequate supporting services and disciplines such as educational administration, guidance and counseling, research and curriculum development" is evidenced. The implication, therefore, calls for an integrated, collaborative approach in training.

More specifically, areas within P.L. 94-482 which directly apply to counselor preparation and supervision programs are outlined below.

Teacher Training Centers (Title I, Part E): create a major departure from traditional university-based education. Local school systems will be charged with responsibility to improve teaching skills of local personnel. Field-based training utilizing programmed materials, video feedback, and performance-based criteria will no doubt follow the trend of recent years.

Counseling supervisors have a unique opportunity to extend their activity into teacher renewal as never before. Counselors as consultants to teachers, parents, and other school personnel will be well within reason if we respond to the teacher needs for developing the communication, group, encouragement, and discipline skills which they desire.

Training for Higher Education Personnel (Title I, Section 151): provides institutions of higher education with a charge to prepare teachers, including guidance and counseling, administrative, or other education specialists with pre-service or in-service training who either (1) are themselves from cultural or educational backgrounds which have hindered such individuals in achieving success in the field of education or (2) are preparing to serve in educational programs designed to meet the special needs of students from such backgrounds.

Life-Long Learning (Title I, Section 132): designates a thrust for developing the potential of all persons including improvement of their personal well-being, upgrading their workplace skills and preparing them to participate in the civic, cultural, and political life of the nation. The particular needs of older and retired persons must be addressed. Parenting and related family and personal development needs are to be among those for which services are provided.

Students from Disadvantaged Backgrounds (Title I, Part D): provides a means for training higher education staff leadership personnel who will specialize in improving the delivery of services to students from disadvantaged backgrounds.

Educational Information Centers (Title I, Part D): sources of service include counseling and guidance to all individuals in a geographical area no greater than that which will afford reasonable access to the services of the center. Its purpose is to maximize the individual's access to information concerning training, retraining, financial aid, and job placement.

Consumer and Homemaking Education (Title II, Section 202): addresses the need for greater concern for child development and guidance, family education, and consumer wisdom. The implications of this section make possible services to depressed areas, correctional institutions, and health care facilities.

Vocational Guidance (Title II, Section 134): requires initiation, implementation, and improvement of high-quality vocational guidance and counseling programs and activities; provides for vocational resource centers to meet the special needs of out-of-school individuals including those seeking second careers, those entering the job market late in life, those coming from economically depressed areas, early retirees, and the handicapped; provides funding for guidance counselors to obtain experience in business and industry, the professions, and other occupations which will better enable them to carry out their duties; specifically requires training to acquaint counselors with: (1) the changing work patterns of women, (2) ways of overcoming sex stereotyping, and (3) ways of assisting girls and women in selecting careers; and also provides counseling for youth offenders and adults in correctional institutions.

Vocational Education Personnel Training (Title II, Section 333): includes training and retraining for counseling and guidance personnel to meet the special needs of persons with limited English-speaking ability.

Career Education and Career Development (Title III, Section 334): provides for the planning of career education and career development programs for all age groups. A very significant section, it also includes the training and retraining of persons, i.e., teachers, counselors, administrators, and other educators, to develop and implement the conceptual program planned.

Guidance and Counseling (Title III, Section 335): authorizes the commissioner to make grants which would (1) increase and improve preparation of guidance and counseling practitioners, (2) provide adequate information regarding guidance and counseling as a profession, (3) fund institutes, workshops, and seminars designed to improve the professional guidance qualifications of counselors and teachers, and (4) train supervisory and technical personnel to be employed in guidance and counseling agencies and systems.

Another significant law, sponsored primarily by Congressman Carl Perkins of Kentucky, is P.L. 95-207, Elementary and Secondary Career Education Act of 1977. This law provides pre-service and in-service training of educators for infusing career education concepts and approaches in classrooms as well as developing and implementing career guidance, counseling, and placement and follow-up services, utilizing counselors, teachers, parents and community resource personnel. Teachers, counselors, and administrators are to be given help in developing career education programs.

P.L. 95-207 is the major boost career education and career guidance have needed. The law provides for the hiring, training, and retraining of career education personnel within local and state education agencies. Development and application of adequate certification standards for these career education coordinators and other personnel are essential. Statewide needs assessments, evaluation studies, and leadership conferences are anticipated and will provide funds for collaborative efforts by educational agencies with government, business/labor/industrial/professional organizations. These can become a vehicle for adequate delivery of comprehensive career education and career guidance services. Not only is the need so amply recognized, the funds for servicing the needs of the public are covered within the law. The establishment and operation of career education resource centers to be utilized by students and the general public are viewed as an opportunity to implement a comprehensive services delivery system for all ages. P.L. 95-207, like P.L. 94-482, affords educators the opportunity to be resourceful, innovative, and nontraditional.

Additional bills with which counseling and guidance personnel need to concern themselves include:

● S.3869: establishes youth community services which would include job counseling, guidance, and placement and would provide funds for training counseling personnel and for the improvement of counselor training programs.

● S.170: (Title I, Part D) offers occupational and career counseling programs and services for special population youth as well as training grants for counseling and placement personnel.

● S.3849: (Title III, Part B) provides for innovation in pre-service and in-service in the field of guidance and counseling.

● A variety of bills apply to youth employment, placement, and counseling. These include: H.R. 20, H.R. 30, H.R. 121, S. 1, Title II, S. 20, S. 249, S. 1242, and S. 427.

● H.R. 1118 provides for support services to older Americans.

● Provisions for counseling services are indicated in S. 794, the Juvenile Delinquency in the Schools Act of 1977.

Implications for Training and Retraining

The potential for a quantum leap in both training and delivery of counseling services is clearly within the realm of possibility. For new legislation to be meaningful, however, will require an uncommon response from educators. Trainers and practitioners will alternately change roles, for each has something to learn from the other. Common goals will transcend age, work classification, or other categories of status.

Institutional education, as we have known it, will be transformed into a process which touches virtually every person throughout life. Technology will both complement and confuse the efforts of educators. At times, methods such as cognitive mapping of learner styles will provide departures from traditional teaching modes. Evaluating life experiences for comparability to more formal educational training will challenge even some of the most liberal academicians.

The thrust for more responsive services to minorities, the elderly, the disadvantaged, and others holds portent of better services for all. To help make this possible, we must use the new and proposed legislation as opportunities to be creative and accountable. Let's look at some possible ways that hold promise:

● Implicit in all of the above provisions is a strong mandate for planning, research, and evaluation. The legislation provides for both national and state plans and coordination. Too often in the past, counseling personnel have not appreciated the significance of participation in such activity. It is imperative that such not be the case now or in the future. State guidance supervisors, counselor educators, and personnel in rehabilitation, employment security, corrections, community service, mental health, and school counseling must join their counterparts in schools, business, industry, and government to develop mandated, comprehensive, five-year state plans. Collaboration on national priorities by these groups is equally important.

● The counselor competencies and recommendations developed by the Association for Counselor Education and Supervision (ACES) Commission on Career Education and Career Development and the position statement by the American Vocational Association and National Vocational Guidance Association need close examination as to how they may be actively implemented through pre-service and in-service training rather than stored as "silent resources." Both have significant implications for accreditation of training programs, certification, and licensure requirements, training strategies, and negotiated job descriptions for professionals and paraprofessionals.

● Counselor preparation programs must conduct a critical assessment of current training modes, program strategies, and delivery systems to outline specific, accountability-based programs which meet the changing needs, skills, and competencies projected. Professional associations such as ACES should encourage and collaborate with such efforts, particularly as they relate to accreditation of training programs.

● Competency-based training, assessment, and certification are well under way in a few states but require much refinement (Kennedy 1976; Shoemaker and Splitter 1976). Similarly, licensure efforts often refer to the desirability of competency rather than degree requirements per se. The tendency of licensure legislation to be exclusionary in implementation would be moderated by well-designed, valid, and reliable assessment tools.

• Innovativeness in training and retraining of counselor trainers and supervisors should be a prime consideration. Examples of this may include: practitioners collaborating in the design of seminar/workshop experiences for renewal of college professorships; counselor educators providing career counseling services to employees within business/industrial/professional settings in exchange for learning/work experience sites for training and retraining of counselor trainees; or professional associations designing instructional workshops on improved methods of teaching for trainers and supervisors (Cromier and Cromier 1976).

• University trainers of teachers, counselors, and other specialists have an opportunity to develop joint proposals for interfacing field experience and university training with areas of specialty. Both on-campus and off-campus training can be integrated to provide students with realistic working relationships long before graduation.

• The philosophical and operational orientation of trainers, supervisors, and practitioners must shift to encompass not only the young, the entry-level school trainee, the middle class, English-speaking, or daytime working, school-year recipient of services. The senior author has supported the cause of counselors in licensure and for a national counselors register because there are great numbers of persons who need our services (Sweeney and Sturdevant 1974; Sweeney and Witmer 1977b; Sweeney 1977a). The great majority do not require mental health services, per se. They do require easy access to free or low-cost counseling and guidance related to careers, parenting, decision-making, and related areas. Vocational educators are logical allies to the kinds of services this vast population requires.

• More direct services for and attention to parents, the needs of women, the handicapped, older citizens, and disadvantaged bilingual Americans will require greater attention to recruiting trainers, supervisors, and trainees who are uniquely qualified through personal identification or experience to assist populations such as these.

• Finally, we must identify and use indices of change, of improvement, and of outcomes which demonstrate the effectiveness of our services. As employment and rehabilitation personnel have known for many years, not all services can or should be cost-effective analyzed. Those that can be measured by outcomes or change should be identified and used in reports, testimony, and evaluations.

Summary

The responses to new and pending legislation are both hopeful and challenging. With support from the joint efforts of those of us in vocational education, higher education, public schools, local and state government, as well as professional associations, the legislators will fund the activities which we are competent to provide. The passage of P.L. 94-482 is more than wishful thinking; it is a hopeful sign of more service opportunities to follow.

The challenge lies in not only doing what needs to be done but in doing it well. Experience reveals that in the absence of clear goals, well-planned activities, adequate resources, and substantive evaluative data, good intentions run astray under legislative scrutiny. Only a few years ago, some persons were predicting the demise of counselors and of counseling as a profession. Evidently the legislators are prepared to see it otherwise. The pendulum is swinging toward counseling and guidance as important, collaborative services to many people. We must respond again with out best effort and the knowledge which we have gained through our experiences since 1958.

REFERENCES

ACES. Position paper of the Commission on Counselor Preparation for Career Development/Career Education. Washington: Association for Counselor Education and Supervision, April 1976.

Birk, J. *Providing Life/Career Planning for Women and Girls.* College Park: University of Maryland, 1977.

Coleman, James S., et al. *Youth: Transition to Adulthood.* Report on Youth of the President's Advisory Committee. Chicago: University of Chicago Press, 1974.

Collins, T. *The Complete Guide to Retirement.* Englewood Cliffs, N.J.: Prentice Hall, 1970.

Crites, I. O. "Career Counseling: A Comprehensive Approach." *The Counseling Psychologist* 6 (1976): 2-11.

Cromier, L. S., and Cromier, W. H. "Developing and Implementing Self-instructional Modules for Counselor Training." *Counselor Education and Supervision* 16 (1976): 37-45.

Drier, H. N. *Programs of Career Guidance, Counseling, Placement, Follow-up, and Follow-through: A Futures Perspective.* Columbus, Ohio: Center for Vocational Education, 1976.

Educational Challenges, Inc. *Today's Changing Roles: An Approach to Non-sexist Teaching.* Washington: The National Foundation for the Improvement of Education, 1974.

Gibson, R. L. *Future Directions for School Guidance.* North Central Association for Accreditation of Colleges and Schools, June 1976.

Goodman, J. S.; Walworth, S. A; and Waters, E. B. "Down With the Maintenance Stage: Career Development for Adults." *Impact* 3 (1975): 44-51.

Goor, J.; Tomlinson, T.; and Schroeder, A. *State-wide Developments in Performance-based Education: A Survey of State Education Agencies.* Washington: National Center for Education Statistics, 1976.

Holland, I. L. "A Theory-ridden, Computerless, Impersonal Vocational Guidance System." *Journal of Vocational Behavior* 1 (1971): 167-176.

Hunter, W. *Preparation for Retirement.* Ann Arbor, Mich.: Institute for Gerontology, 1976.

Kennedy, D. A. "Some Impressions of Competency-based Training Programs." *Counselor Education and Supervision* 15 (1976): 244-250.

Matthews, E.; Feingold, N.; Weary, B.; Berry, J; and Tyler, L. *Counseling Girls and Women Over the Life-span.* Monograph. Washington: National Vocational Guidance Association, 1972.

National Vocational Guidance Association—American Vocational Association. Position paper on career development. Washington: NVGA-AVA, 1973.

National Vocational Guidance Association. *Facilitating Career Development for Girls and Women.* Washington: NVGA, 1975.

National Vocational Guidance Association. *Planning Ahead with Girls and Women: Strategies for Action.* Washington: NVGA, 1978.

Schlossberg, N. K. "Career Development in Adults." *American Vocational Journal* (1975): 38-40.

Schlossberg, N. K. and Goodman, J. S. "A Woman's Place: Children's Sex Stereotyping of Occupations." *Vocational Guidance Quarterly* 20 (1972): 266-270.

Scholz, N.; Prince, J.; and Miller, G. *How to Decide. A Guide for Women.* New York: College Entrance Examination Board, 1975.

Shoemaker, J. T., and Splitter, J. L. "A Competency-based Model for Counselor Certification." *Counselor Education and Supervision* 15 (1976): 267-275.

Sweeney, T. J. "Message to the Association." *Counselor Education and Supervision* 16 (1977a): 164-165.

Sweeney, T. J., and Sturdevant, A. D. "Licensure in the Helping Professions: Anatomy of an Issue." *Personnel and Guidance Journal* 52 (1974): 575-581.

Sweeney, T. J., and Witmer, J. M. "Who Says You're a Counselor?" *Personnel and Guidance Journal* (1977b).

University of Georgia Center for Continuing Education. *A Statewide Program To Improve the Competency of Occupational Personnel Who Function as Counselors of Adult Women.* Athens: University of Georgia, 1977.

U.S. Department of Labor. *1975 Handbook on Women Workers.* Bulletin 297. Washington: Employment Standards Administration, 1975a.

U.S. Department of Labor. *Womanpower.* Washington: Employment and Training Administration, 1975b.

U.S. Department of Labor. *Women and Work.* Washington: Office of the Secretary, n.d.

Veroff, I., and Feld, S. *Motives and Rules.* Unpublished manuscript. Ann Arbor: University of Michigan, 1965.

Vetter, L.; Brown, A. J.; and Stehney, B. J. *Women in the Work Force: Follow-up Study of Curriculum Materials.* Columbus, Ohio: Center for Vocational Education, 1975.

Walworth, S. A., and Goodman, J. S. *Directions for Change.* Rochester, Mich.: Oakland University, Continuum Center, 1975.

Women's Equity Action League (WEAL). *WEAL Washington Report.* Washington: National Press Building, n.d.

Organization and Administration of Career Education

The administration of career education at all levels is probably the most important factor in its full implementation. By definition, career education embraces all aspects of education and some aspects of career choice which lie outside the formal educational structure, i.e., in labor, business, and industry, etc. As a result, no one group alone can administer career education effectively. It will require the cooperation and active involvement of many individuals and specialists both within education and without.

Administration at the national level is accomplished through the Office of Career Education which is under the Assistant Secretary for Elementary and Secondary Education in the Department of Education. At the state level it has been administered usually by a coordinator in charge of career education. Most of the problems, however, arise at the local level where career education activities are administered by school officials who may or may not be entirely familiar with career education or who may or may not be supportive. For career education to flourish at the local level requires the most imaginative administrative system possible, including specialists as well as lay people from the community. The administration of career education must be accomplished at the local level in such a way that it permits and encourages integration of the school and the local community.

The three articles in this chapter were written in 1977 at a time when the administration of career education at all levels was most uncertain. Kenneth B. Hoyt presents an accurate account of the federal administration of career education before the passage of P.L. 95-207, a law which delineated the present structure at the federal and state levels. Nancy M. Pinson presents an objective view of state reform as related to the administration of career education. Evelyn L. Hausmann and Gary Green provide survey data which indicate the "state of the art" of local administrative approaches as they were practiced in the summer of 1977.

ADMINISTRATION OF CAREER EDUCATION: FEDERAL PERSPECTIVES

Kenneth B. Hoyt

Author of six books and numerous articles on career education, Kenneth B. Hoyt is the most prolific writer in the field. Since 1974 he has served as director of the Office of Career Education, Office of Education, Department of Health, Education, and Welfare (now Department of Education). Dr. Hoyt was also professor of counselor education at the University of Maryland. This article was written in 1977.

From a federal perspective, the executive branch of government is charged with administering laws enacted by the Congress. It is only within the parameters of such laws that administration takes place at the federal level. It is accomplished through development and application of rules and regulations, derived from the language of the legislation, and designed to provide guidelines to recipients of federal funds.

Within the federal bureaucracy, administration takes place at both an internal and an external level. At the internal level, multiple administrative decisions are made with reference to such matters as reporting channels, number of staff assigned to a given operation, physical facilities, short- and long-term budget-making and accounting procedures, developing and gaining approval of rules and regulations, and office expense fund allocation. The administration, in making such decisions, must do so in accordance with existing laws. The bureaucratic skills involved in influencing such decisions for any given unit of government are crucial in determining that unit's effectiveness in external administration. Within the Office of Education's Office of Career Education, internal administration is handled, operationally, by the deputy director.

At the external level, federal administration takes place in terms of relationships with the general public—including those who are direct recipients of federal funds. This, too, must follow the law. The Office of Career Education (OCE) was established as a separate unit within the Office of Education (OE) by Section 406, P.L. 93-380, the Education Amendments of 1974. That law specified that the director must report directly to the commissioner of education. Further, that law established the National Advisory Council for Career Education (NACCE), established guidelines for appointments of its voting and nonvoting members, and charged the NACCE with advising the secretary of health, education, and welfare, the commissioner of education, and the director of the National Institute of Education (NIE).

The OCE was directed by P.L. 93-380 to: (1) assess the current status of career education, (2) further refine the career education concept, (3) demonstrate the best methods and procedures in career education, and (4) communicate an understanding of career education to the general public. This article is an attempt to describe how the OCE administers these four basic functions. First it seems important to describe relationships between the OCE, the NACCE, and the Education and Work Task Force of NIE—the three parts of the federal government most obviously concerned with career education.

OCE, NACCE, and NIE Relationships

It would be easy, but inefficient, to assign completely discrete domains to OCE, NACCE, and NIE with respect to career education. Rather than succumb to this form of bureaucratic "turfsmanship," these three entities have elected to operate in an atmosphere of mutual helpfulness. They have not worried about whether or not any overlap of functions has occurred. Here, both the basic legal functions and examples of overlap will be presented.

The NACCE is basically charged with giving advice. It has given such advice to the Congress, to the secretary of HEW, and to the commissioner of education. It is also free to provide advice to OCE and to the Education and Work Task Force of NIE. As an advisory body, the NACCE, of course, does not exert any administrative control or operational responsibilities for the actions of those it advises. For example, it is in no way involved in the grant or contract award procedures carried out by OCE or by NIE. It does not approve—or disapprove—any official rules and regulations of government agencies. It has its own annual budget allocated to it by the commissioner of education but receives no funds from Congress appropriated for use by OCE or by NIE.

This, of course, is not to say that the NACCE is without power or influence. For example, it is perfectly free to develop, either independently or through contract, policy and conceptual papers on career education. A number of such commissioned papers have been contracted for and published by the NACCE. The NACCE has the authority, if it chooses to use it, to develop its own definition of career education. To date, it has chosen to endorse and accept OCE's definition of career education, but it is under no obligation to do so. The influence of the NACCE is clearly seen in the form of career education legislation currently under consideration in the Congress. Both the oral and written testimony of the NACCE are clearly evident in the wording of that legislation. Policy advice given to the federal government by the NACCE receives careful consideration and is often influential in administrative decisions.

The Education and Work Task Force of NIE, headed by Dr. Corrine Rieder, is basically charged with research, product development, and dissemination functions in career education. Many examples of NIE's good efforts exist. In the area of basic research, for example, NIE has been responsible for sponsoring research aimed at contrasting the effectiveness of the original four OE models for career education. In product development, NIE's sponsorship of projects leading to packaged materials designed for use in reducing occupational sex stereotyping is one example of many product development efforts. As a dissemination agency, NIE's contractual relationship with the ERIC Clearinghouse on Career Education is an obvious example of effort in this area. In all three ways—basic research, product development, and dissemination—NIE's Education and Work Task Force is making valuable contributions to career education.

Like the NACCE, NIE's Education and Work Task Force is also free to engage in conceptual efforts in career education. For example, NIE has its own definition of career education, and NIE staff persons have been very active in writing and publishing conceptual statements regarding career education. They have, in addition, sponsored conferences, seminars, and workshops of various kinds where basic conceptual and operational issues facing career education are identified and discussed.

Relationships between OCE and NIE have been cordial and cooperative in nature. For example, NIE professional staff have served on OCE project proposal review teams, and vice versa. The NIE was a cooperating agency in the commissioner's National Conference on Career Education and, in addition, provided the funds required to publish the official proceedings of that conference. Suggestions made by OCE for needed product development efforts in career education have been sought and used by NIE's Education and Work Task Force. In all these ways and others, NIE and OCE staff members have worked together as professional colleagues. Still, in a strict administrative sense, neither of these organizations directs or controls the operations of the other. The NIE does not suggest to OCE the kinds of demonstration projects to be funded, and OCE does not direct NIE to engage in one kind of research as opposed to another. Both OCE, as part of OE, and NIE activities are coordinated by the office of the assistant secretary for education and the office of the secretary of HEW. Thus, the OCE and NIE's Education and Work Task Force enjoy a professional partnership but, administratively, operate independently of each other.

The remainder of this article will concentrate attention on the three primary functions of OCE, namely, (1) developing, (2) demonstrating, and (3) communicating the concept of career education. As part of this discussion, OCE relationships with other agencies of the federal government will be used as illustrative examples.

Administrative Actions Related to Developing the Career Education Concept

At the time the Congress passed P.L. 93-380 establishing the Office of Career Education in the OE, there was no official OE definition of career education. One of the clear mandates given to OCE by the Congress was to engage in a national dialogue aimed at clarifying and refining the meaning of career education. This has been regarded by OCE, since its establishment in 1974, as a major and continuing task. Here, the basic administrative procedures utilized in carrying out this congressional assignment will be described.

First, it was recognized that the career education concept is one that is evolving primarily at the local community level, not in the research labs of universities nor in the organizational labyrinth of the federal government; thus, OCE determined that the prime source of input in developing a national consensus on the meaning of career education must be career education practitioners. As a preliminary step, the director of OCE wrote a career education concept paper and presented it to a national meeting of state coordinators of career education for criticism and suggestion. The network of state coordinators of career education (employed in various state departments of education) were then asked to nominate to OCE the five to ten most outstanding local education agency career education coordinators in each state. In a series of 20 two-day miniconferences, the preliminary version of the OCE career education concept paper was discussed and critiqued by participants. Two additional miniconferences were then held involving persons identified as leading career education conceptualizers in the nation. They, too, critiqued the OCE preliminary concept paper and made suggestions for its revision.

Based on this national network of local career education coordinators, state coordinators of career education, and leading career education conceptualizers, the final version of the OCE concept paper, entitled "An Introduction to Career Education: A Policy Paper of the U. S. Office of Education," was sent to the government printing office in the fall of 1974 and was published in 1975. That paper provided the first official OE definition of career education. The definition was purposely stated in broad consensus terms in language that both allowed and encouraged states and local communities to devise more specific definitions for themselves.

Second, an immediate effort was launched beginning in the fall of 1975 to organize a system for gaining national input and suggestions for revising the OE career education policy paper in ways that reflect the evolving nature of career education. Organizationally, this was accomplished through asking the state coordinators of career education and the approximately 275 participants in the 1974 miniconferences to nominate persons from various categories to attend a set of 1975-76 miniconferences. A total of 27 miniconferences were conducted during the 1975-76 school year, each involving 12 participants for an intensive two-day meeting with the director of the Office of Career Education. Persons nominated for participation in these miniconferences were expert practitioners in the area for which they were nominated. All of these 1975-76 miniconferences concentrated attention at the K-12 level, with some devoted to various kinds of "actors" in career education and others devoted to the topic of how to provide the best career education for special segments of the K-12 student population. Names of these 27 miniconferences included, to mention only a few:

"K-3 Classroom Teachers and Career Education"
"School Counselors and Career Education"
"Parents and Career Education"
"The Business/Labor/Industrial Community and Career Education"
"Career Education for Minority and Low-Income Students"
"Career Education for Handicapped Persons"
"Career Education for Gifted and Talented Persons"

Third, the miniconference method for use in carrying out this congressional mandate was continued during the 1976-77 academic year with 19 additional miniconferences. The first 10 of these were devoted to particular kinds of post-secondary education settings and bore such titles as:

"Career Education in the Community College Setting"
"Career Education in Non-Public Colleges and Universities"
"Career Education and Adult/Recurrent/Continuing Education"
"Career Education and the All Volunteer Armed Forces"

As with previous miniconferences, participants were nominated by a combination of state coordinators of career education and former miniconference participants because they were actively engaged in career education in the particular setting for which they were nominated. A second set of nine miniconferences were devoted to professional education associations and involved four representatives from each of three such associations in each miniconference. This set, of course, was designed to gain input regarding ways members of various professional education associations were viewing career education.

The total effort, over a three-year period, resulted in input from more than 800 career education experts from all 50 states in 68 miniconferences. The director, OCE, personally conducted each of these miniconferences and took the notes of the discussion. The basic organizational method used was an "outside-in" rather than an "inside-out" approach. That is, the OCE elected to concentrate attention on gaining reports of practices, concerns, and advice from practitioners in the field rather than attempting to take the OCE policy paper to the field and simply distribute it.

As a result of this effort, the OE policy paper is now badly in need of revision. Participants in the 68 miniconferences provided sufficient input, in terms of both ideas and experiences, so as to make it mandatory that the OE policy paper on career education be completely rewritten. That task may be completed prior to the time this article appears in print. Once this has been done, the process of seeking continuing national dialogue—and so the basis for still further revision—will begin again.

Administrative Actions Related to Demonstrating Career Education

Provisions of P.L. 93-380 clearly called for OCE to enage in activities designed to demonstrate the best methods and procedures in career education. While it was clear from the law that the major effort here must be devoted to the K-12 level of education, it was also clear that small beginnings could be made on demonstrating career education in additional settings.

The primary organizational approach utilized in carrying out this congressional mandate has been that of grants and contracts. Six major grant categories were established by OCE. They are the demonstration of:

- incremental improvement efforts, K-12 level
- career education for special segments of the population
- career education in special settings
- training and retraining in career education
- communication methods for career education
- state plans for career education

Within the federal government structure, both the categories in which grants are to be made and the tentative amounts planned for each category must be approved by the commissioner of education and by the office of the secretary, HEW. The justification necessary to obtain such approval must be written both from the standpoint of congressional mandate and the needs of the field. Once such approval is secured, along with approval of rules and regulations pertaining to this process, the official notice to invite grant proposals in each category is printed in the *Federal Register.* While not required by either law or regulation, the OCE has established a practice of sending copies of the *Federal Register* announcement to all state coordinators of career education and encouraging them to make sure all career education practitioners in their states are aware of them.

The *Federal Register* announcement includes the date by which grant applications must be received in OE's Application Control Center. Between the time of this announcement and its closing date, formal grant application materials are mailed by OCE to any person or organization requesting them, and a record is made of all such mailings. These materials include complete instructions for making a grant application and, in addition, list the criteria (and the number of points assigned to each) by which each proposal will be judged.

Within OCE, lists of prospective panel readers are made in three categories: (1) local K-12 career education practitioners; (2) state coordinators of career education; and (3) college/university career education experts. These lists are compiled from OCE miniconference participants, personal knowledge of OCE staff members, and nominations received from persons in the field. Panels of reviewers are established as soon as possible after the grant application deadline with the number of such panels for each category determined by the number of proposals received in each category. Each panel consists of three persons, one from each of the three lists described above, plus one or more federal employees with expertise in the area but employed outside of OCE. Each review panel is chaired by an OCE staff member, but that staff member has no vote.

Each proposal is read and scored independently by each voting panel member. Final point scores for each proposal are obtained by adding the individual point scores and dividing by the number of voting members on the panel. When more proposals are received in a given category than can be read carefully by one panel, multiple panels are established along with a super panel whose members are given only the top proposals as rated by earlier panels in that category. When all scores have been assigned, proposals received in each category are listed in their order of rank and recommended by OCE for funding, in that order, until funds for that category are exhausted. These OCE lists are then sent to OE's Office of Contracts and Grants where staff members there attempt to negotiate final grant arrangements, including suggested budget cuts, with each organization or institution recommended for funding.

Thus, administratively, grant awards, like the conceptual effort described earlier, is effectively controlled by outsiders, not by federal employees. This is assured by having a majority of panel members for each panel being nongovernment employees.

Each year, a small number of contracts, as opposed to grants, are also negotiated. These contracts represent special efforts to follow a particular congressional mandate and/or to clarify further a particular portion of the career education concept. For example, during 1977-78, one contract was let for purposes of applying a common evaluation process across a number of operating career education efforts so that OCE could better meet the congressional mandate of specifying the best methods and procedures in career education. A second 1977-78 contract allowed OCE to demonstrate two different approaches to career education in the college/university setting as recommended by miniconference participants during the 1976-77 miniconferences. As with the grant procedure, panels of reviewers, a majority of whose members are employed outside the federal government, read and make recommendations with reference to each application received.

Administrative Actions Related to Communicating the Career Education Concept

The OCE is properly viewed as contributing to, rather than controlling, the meaning of career education. The goal has been to accumulate the widest diversity in points of view from the widest possible range of people concerned with career education, and to communicate the knowledge gained through this kind of activity to the widest possible variety of audiences. By doing so, it is hoped that individual career education practitioners and conceptualizers will be aided in their attempts to derive an acceptable meaning of career education for themselves. In no way is the OCE view of career education intended to be any kind of ultimate truth. Rather, OCE communications are more correctly pictured as attempts to communicate consensus statements. Obviously, no one would pretend that, because a particular point of view appears to be held by many persons, it is necessarily better than a different point of view held by a single person.

Within HEW's Division of Education, OCE publications receive wide distribution. Individual parts of the division, such as The Fund for the Improvement of Postsecondary Education (FIPSE), NIE, and the various OE bureaus, are free to accept or reject the OCE policy publications. Similarly, OCE views on career education are communicated, usually on request, to other government agencies which, to date, have included the Departments of Labor, Commerce, Defense, and Agriculture. The OCE concern has been one of making sure the knowledge gained by OCE is available to other parts of government concerned with career education. It is, in no way, aimed at directing or controlling their activities in this area. As a result, some parts of government have followed OCE conceptual views of career education closely, while others have varied considerably in their interpretation of the concept.

A serious communication effort has been launched by OCE aimed at the various national organizations and associations whose members might be expected to be interested and/or active in career education. This includes a wide variety of professional education associations, organizations representing business and industry, organized labor, and community service organizations having national headquarters aimed at communicating with local chapters. Both input into formulating the career education concept and knowledge gained by OCE in its conceptual efforts have been involved here. The collaborative nature of career education has made this a necessarily important area of communication.

Continuing attempts at maintaining two-way communications have been established with the state coordinators of career education in the 50 state departments of education. This group has provided a great deal of valuable consultative advice to OCE and, as a usual practice, is the one group to which OCE findings are first communicated. Similarly, conscious and conscientious attempts are made to maintain two-way communication with all prior participants in the OCE sponsored miniconferences described earlier.

The primary communications vehicles utilized by OCE have been papers and monographs officially cleared through OE's Office of Public Affairs. More than 40 papers and more than 20 OCE monographs have been published in the last three years. None of these carry copyright restrictions and persons receiving them are free to reproduce them for use by others if they choose to do so. A second communications vehicle used by OCE has been the presentation of speeches to audiences throughout the nation. Reactions to those speeches have been taken as indicators of the degree to which the OCE concept of career education finds acceptance.

Finally, the OCE has maintained a strong and serious communication effort through the media of written correspondence, telephone calls, and visits with persons in the OCE offices. Several hundred telephone calls and letters are answered each year. These have resulted in the collecting of several thousand examples of career education materials developed by local career education practitioners. These are stored in an OCE career education resource center and made available for use by OCE visitors from throughout the nation.

Concluding Remarks

The federal role in career education is catalytic but not controlling in nature. The strength the federal effort brings to career education is the perspective that can be gained by continually seeking a national, rather than a state or local, view of career education. That strength is properly utilized only if those who possess it recognize that the price one must pay for gaining perspective is a marked loss in competence to function as a career education practitioner. That is, the federal strength comes from the inputs voluntarily given by others at the national, state, and local levels. The key words are listening, sharing, and communication. So long as these remain the primary words in the federal effort, that effort can play a useful and important role in the evolution of the total career education effort.

THE ADMINISTRATION AND MANAGEMENT OF CAREER EDUCATION WITHIN STATE AGENCIES

Nancy M. Pinson
A nationally known career education consultant, Dr. Pinson has co-authored Career Education and the Elementary School Teacher *with Kenneth B. Hoyt. Currently she is working with Edwin Herr in investigating a policy study in guidance and counseling. This article was written in 1977.*

The state education agency's unique responsibilities for planning, facilitating, and certifying educational programs for elementary and secondary schools have not typically included initiating or backing a new educational thrust. Historically, this task has fallen to the learned societies, professional associations, and with increasing regularity, the United States Office of Education.

In the past, innovations generating from these bodies were viewed by the state agency as presenting the options either to serve as the unquestioning conduit of that innovation or to reject it on the grounds of its inappropriateness for its schools.

Career education was not the first innovation to cause a variation in this state response pattern, but the probable reasons for that variation warrant comment. First, career education was obviously appealing to state bureaucracies in terms of its ready-made and vocal lay constituency; the typical taxpayer and board member could hardly have been more supportive. Second, it offered a new sheen to the agency image by providing a unifying theme around which favored and/or established programs could be refreshed and perpetuated. Third, agency staff members could be redeployed, rejuvenated, and in some cases, hired—as a result of agency commitment to provide state leadership. Most remarkable, the nonexistence in the early 1970s of earmarked money from either federal or state coffers did not prove to be a significant deterrent to state activity in career education.

Looking back over this period of more than five years, one is struck by the continual use of the term *activity* in early but unpublished reports of a given state's first involvement with career education. A marked acceleration was observed in both the pace and flexibility with which business as usual was conducted. Teamwork took on new meaning when state personnel willingly assumed extra duties; state personnel crossed traditional lines to assure the transformation of an idea into concrete practice. In essence, the state agency was behaving as if it had pulled the coup of the decade. Hadn't it succeeded in stealing the idea of career education from under the noses of its then mute conceptualizers at the federal level? Having done so it could modify the early concepts of career education, with relatively little interference, to approach that form which would best suit its own needs and purposes.

The State Education Agency and Career Education

In the beginning, career education and the state education agency should logically have been natural enemies. The state, after all, has an admirable record of intelligently resisting any federal encroachments on its responsibility for the education of its citizens. So much conspired against acceptance of the rhetoric of a commissioner in 1971. Witness the statements published that same year by the Council of Chief State School Officers (CCSSO) prior to the official advent of career education:

Federal priorities and categorical aid appear to be determined more by pressure and emotion than on the basis of a more scientific needs assessment.

The federal goverment should assist the states in educational endeavors, but should not require uniformity among them through regulations or other techniques affecting (their) eligibility to receive federal funds.

The state is the final and responsible agent for acceptable levels of quality programs within its boundaries (Council of Chief State School Officers 1971, p. 9-12).

How did the CCSSO, and earlier how did some of its member states, reconcile their excitement about career education with these inarguable principles of statehood? To seek the answer to this question by reviewing the vast literature on career education's emergence and growth would be superfluous (see Herr 1976) and probably fruitless. It is, however, worthy of note that, excluding individual state publications which now number in the hundreds, only a few documents (Herr 1976; Jesser 1976; Crawford and Jesser 1975; Hayas 1976; Hansen 1976; McLaughlin 1976; Pinson 1975; Smoker 1974; Clary 1973) have spoken at any length on this generalized agency response. But even these publications find agreement among authors on only one state agency variable—that career education was, and still is, a pervasive but basically impersonal presence in most state agencies.

Interestingly, these writers and dozens of others seem to prefer to list numbers when they write about agencies in general—quantifying personnel, board resolution, enacted legislation, and so forth—at that bureaucratic level. Only when they describe school district activity in those same states does their narrative assume qualitative aspects. It is then that the writer begins to rhapsodize. Flesh and blood, trial and error, people and events can now be enthusiastically described. The state agency, all this while, does not help its sterile image in the career education press by turning out austere compilations of flowcharts, conceptual models, guidelines, and fail-safe goals and objectives. Nowhere in these documents do we find a hint of human impress or a clue to the kinds of people who are struggling, succeeding, or failing at career education in a bureaucracy which must necessarily give equal attention to many other priorities and needs.

The question remains. To what can we attribute the remarkable, if unrecorded, accomplishments of involved state agencies in keeping the career education presence alive? A number of educated hunches come to mind:

• Most state education agencies (SEAs) have scrupulously avoided affiliating career education with any one discipline. It was not to be a new curriculum section; therefore, it did not run the risk of competing with the agency's established programs or priorities.

• Most SEAs have been comfortable for more than a decade with the heritage of staffing or funding for federal programs. The transition from exemplary activity in career development (as authorized in Part D, VEA as amended in 1968) to a new allegiance, career education, posed a lesser ethical dilemma to the state bureaucrat than it did to the understandably outraged career development chronologist/theoretician in the counselor education ranks.

• Most SEAs have employed a low-profile approach to selling career education. This has usually involved in-service efforts with eager local practitioners as opposed to a possibly futile staff development push within the agency itself. The assignment of this task to guidance trained or oriented staff by most SEAs illustrates a generally held agency belief that these individuals are less likely to incur wrath in those with whom they work.

• Most SEAs have enjoyed the initially warm reception and positive support for career education provided by their Divisions of Vocational Education.

• Most SEAs have benefited from the voluntary career education enlistments of certain "temporarily down at the enrollment" disciplines (foreign languages and the arts, for example). Adult education and industrial arts, on the other hand, appear to find in career education a certain quixotic relief from their exclusively vocational alliances.

• Most SEAs have been quick to recognize that the well-publicized needs of special groups, whether they be girls and women, minorities, the handicapped, disadvantaged, or gifted, permit them to suggest that career education could provide a partial satisfaction of these needs.

Perhaps the best hunch comes from the leader characterizations so ably, if chauvinistically, drawn by Michael Maccoby. He may come closer to the answer to our question in his description of a new kind of corporate leader, the gamesman, than we may now be willing to admit. The gamesman, as contrasted with the craftsman, the jungle fighter, and the company man, loves change and wants to influence its course (Maccoby 1977, p. 39). It is tempting to hypothesize an institutional analogy here with career education—one which suggests that the degree to which the state agency is still making noises and doing something about career education is probably related to how many staff people of this sort, both male and female, have been—and still are—involved.

One could also apply Maccoby's characterizations to the evolution of the present-day career education bureaucrat who has been involved at the agency level since the beginning. He or she may well have begun as the lone jungle fighter, lived through the craft stage of polishing the concept lovingly, entered and was accepted by the company, to finally become a winner by virtue of being associated with a popular cause long enough to build a credit reserve.

State agencies seeking or finding answers to these and other questions dealing with alternative reasons for the apparent durability of career education within their own ranks are not mentioned in the literature. Perhaps they should be. Unfortunately, reporting on career education leadership variability is to celebrate deviancy in the EA's administration and delivery of one educational thrust, a treatment which might become contagious. (One would suspect that, given the ground rules associated with the present detente in career education, healthy agency contentiousness about its practice has been effectively silenced in favor of generating impersonal platitudes about its timeliness and fit.) The truth is that, while its protagonists at the state level can be lumped together in the conviction that career education, in some guise, is vital to the reform of education, their actual points of view about the medium of the message are so diverse that some coordinators still refuse to sit down together. A not altogether negative state of affairs, as it may turn out.

The Council of Chief State School Officers (CCSSO) has defused much of this dissension in the ranks by publicizing, albeit internally, individual state achievements. Perhaps more than any other group, they have established an intimacy among states on this topic, which has preserved the image of cohesion, if not always the fact. No state agency would now willingly disassociate itself or its assigned staff from a hubris which frequently and glowingly reports its own gains in board resolution, policy statements, legislative mandate, plan development and task force appointments, distinguished advisory groups, governor's conferences, curriculum guides, community coalitions, needs assessments, learner outcomes, or any combination of these and other accomplishments. Yet even the CCSSO's warm advocacy of the state agency's effort in career education has a limited effect. Neither it nor the states have been equipped or disposed to respond to the criticisms expressed by the General Accounting Office report, e.g., the dearth of hard data on career education's effect upon its beneficiaries, or of any real evidence of its impact on teacher and counselor education programs (U. S. Government Accounting Office 1976).

If isolated progress has been made in these areas, most states are unwilling to take credit for these advances for two reasons: (1) they are usually the result of locally and independently conducted research and (2) they are all too often the unplanned and unhappy consequence of human chemistry at work. While it is true that these advances may be aired for the first (and possibly last) time in front of congressional committees, the typical state agency is far more concerned with what it describes as the demonstration, beyond all reasonable doubt, that the SEA's role in career education should be standardized to the degree necessary to achieve a ready response to these and other criticisms.

The picture of the state agency beating a dignified retreat when faced with these absolutes is relatively new. Fingers have been burned once too often by their well-intentioned incursions into the territories of local agencies and other state boards to forget the lessons learned. Restraint is now the name of the game. So go the lessons as we SEA types watch each other tremble on the brink of a denouement which would add career education to the long list of brave ventures which received the kiss of death through agency packaging. (No matter that the creators of some of these ventures have scuttled into some distant woodwork, to be held forever blameless.) Our rationalization is that the monopolistic look of "no overlap, predictability, and uniformity" is less to be prized than the given idea's reliability, adaptability, and capacity for molding itself to individual circumstance. The state agency really still believes it can have it both ways. On the one hand, it welcomes federal policymaking in education if it is limited and restricted to a resource role, when on the other, it continues to delude itself with the belief that this time it will be different, that career education will not assume the controlling characteristics common to all social welfare legislation enacted since 1958.

To the states, the most worrisome aspect of a federal theory of career education policymaking is the assumption that federally led discussion, leading to national agreement on long-term objectives, will assure state consensus on means. They are convinced that the price of reporting such consensus, at its very least, will be vagueness and at its highest, major discomfort or disaffection. Agency personnel would much prefer to defend their belief that agreement in general need not mean agreement in particular, that negotiation and renegotiation are benchmarks of state policymakers, and that their administration of career education would be of little consequence to their schools if it did not involve continuous redefinition of objectives as well as means. How much of this seeming intransigence is due to simple human fatigue, or to what is perceived by the states as an insuperable accumulation of federal directives in education, is anybody's guess. It is within the realm of possibility that a state agency might even fire a few salvos of independence at the Office of Career Education. It is also possible that the same state agency will quickly revert to its well-learned posture of deference.

Epilog

During the preparation of this article, a national event and a personal event combined to reinforce my bias toward state autonomy in career education. The House passed H.R. 7 (now P.L. 95-207) with a resounding majority, auguring well for a cleaner bill when combined with the Senate version. Should its final provisions be funded by some future appropriations subcommittee, certain state agency personnel will be finally and irrevocably the custodians of its resources, its accountability, and its appearance in the schools.

Virtually on the heels of this landmark occasion in the career education chronology, I was forced, by the simple circumstance of moving my desk, to sort through pounds of related correspondence and memorabilia which had accumulated since 1969. It was all there. A vivid reconstruction of the time when states and their agency personnel were happily caught up in the polemics of the "new" thrust. Bureaucrat squared off against bureaucrat in subjective, if not personalized, battle with career education the cause to be attacked or defended. Good deeds in its name proliferated, and crass commercialism and standardization had yet to rear their heads. Nostalgia, yes, but are we ready to accept what we thought we wanted for so long? Are we equipped to deal with the loneliness that characterizes the end of any struggle?

Even when we recognize that the comfortable chaos that defined our earlier career education behavior could not have continued indefinitely if this reform was to achieve its broad purposes, we as individuals tend to cling to the last vestiges of debate. In the absence of any other excuse, we will argue that the present pendulum swing of career education to a desirable uniformity of management and delivery may well presage a measurable loss of the necessary ardor to get the job done. It all comes down to the need of both agency and individual to recapture some of that early sense of mission, without surrendering the rational accumulation of data and experience. That need, expressed with increasing frequency by agency colleagues across the country, is the single most impressive support for the conviction that it is a hollow reform that does not enrich and celebrate its practitioners as well as its beneficiaries.

The state agency, in the last analysis, is only as effective as the sum of its motivated and valued personnel. As career education moves into a stage which will be characterized in every state and territory by its easily duplicated and standardized components, it should be our task to assure that a celebration of involved individuals and agencies who are unique and unconforming will be viewed as an even greater achievement.

AN EXAMINATION AND ANALYSIS OF CAREER EDUCATION ADMINISTRATIVE ARRANGEMENTS AT THE LOCAL LEVEL

Evelyn L. Hausmann and Gary Green

Dr. Hausmann is associate professor of home economics education at Kansas State University and directs workshops in vocational education.

An associate professor of occupational education at Kansas State University, Dr. Green has helped develop career guidance centers and the Kansas Institute for Career Development. He has authored a book on career education and serves as a consultant. This article was written in 1977.

Local administration of career education is almost an open issue. There are no official national guidelines regarding this matter, and there are very few state guidelines. The state plans for career education should offer some concrete directions. However, until these plans are in effect, local districts must either wait until official guides come out or set up their own administrative arrangements. Thus, local administrators have been forced to decide, both financially and operationally, what priority career education will assume within their districts. This specific problem has led to very diverse local administrative arrangements in career education.

Local administration includes all those persons who have the assigned responsibility and authority to direct or influence the actions of subordinates in the local educational structure (Proehl 1973, p. 203). The administrative structure of a school system, while varying from district to district, has a number of supervisory levels which include the superintendent, the administrators of individual schools, and the curriculum and subject matter specialists. Each level has its respective depth and breadth of direct involvement and its degree of specificity. However, the ultimate responsibility for directing the implementation of a careers curriculum in the local system lies with the superintendent. How this person chooses to delegate his or her authority and responsibility is a matter of personal choice based upon whatever criterion he or she uses to make such judgments.

This paper examines and analyzes the kinds of local administrative arrangements which have been developed by individual school districts in the state of Kansas. Kansas does not, at this writing, have an official state plan to indicate the direction local administration of career education must take. Therefore, the following arrangements have evolved from the various conditions and circumstances within districts. One can assume that these are relatively common situations and that an examination of the resulting systems might be of some value to other districts involved in developing their own administrative strategies.

Types of Administrative Arrangements

School Superintendent. In this type of arrangement the school superintendent retains the full authority for planning, organizing, and implementing the program of career education activities within a district. Generally speaking, there is no formalized career education plan. This type of administrative arrangement originated because of several factors, two of which are: (1) the school was small, rural, and restricted by staff, size of community, and financial resources, and (2) the administrator had a strong personal commitment to career education or assumed it was financially or politically expedient to get involved in career education. Within this model (Fig. 4-1) the superintendent is responsible for communicating career education to his or her subordinates and associates. Not only will he or she be in contact with school principals, but he or she will be directly involved with faculty and support staff. In this model it is usually the superintendent who makes the initial contact with the community. This activity occurs as a result of personal presentations or cooperating with teachers in preparing worthwhile career education public relations activities.

The planning and coordinating of this type of administrative arrangement basically involves a three-step process. The method of operation is initiated by the superintendent of the local school district who informs the principals, counselors, and teachers of the general objectives and structure of the program. This procedure is then followed by an orientation and training session conducted by a state department of education specialist or an outside

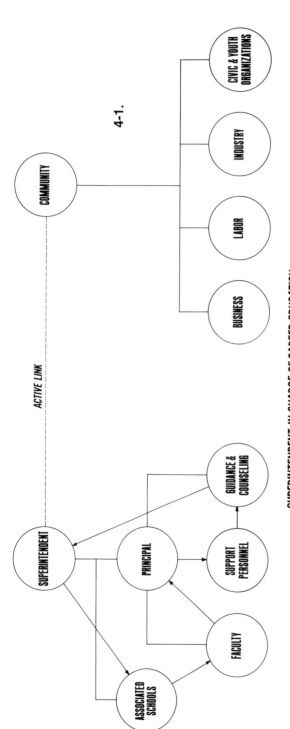

SUPERINTENDENT IN CHARGE OF CAREER EDUCATION

FULL-TIME CAREER EDUCATION COORDINATOR

consultant. The third step in the process might involve the development of curriculum guidelines, the procurement of career education information, and a plan for infusing the world of work material and information into the classroom. These activities are usually divided between the faculty and the administration. The degree of teacher interest and teacher acceptance is often a result of the superintendent's recommendations and enthusiastic initiative in coordinating all of these activities.

Full-time Coordinator. This type of administrative arrangement provides for full-time employment of a staff person whose responsibility it is to organize, assist with curriculum development, disseminate information and materials, and to act as a coordinator for developing and implementing a district-wide career education plan (Fig. 4-2). The full-time coordinator has the primary task of coordinating the total school activities as well as developing active community involvement. The full-time coordinator usually works through the local administration in developing faculty planning sessions and in-service workshops. Other activities include working closely with individual teachers in developing classroom projects, developing and selecting career education materials, and serving as a liaison between the teachers and resource persons in the community.

In most cases, full-time career education coordinators are employed by large school districts, and career education activities are planned and implemented for several schools, grades K-12. Funding for this type of arrangement requires a commitment on the part of the district's administration for both the coordinator's salary, the development of resource materials, and for in-service training for teachers.

Part-time Coordinator. The part-time career education coordinator is already employed by the school district and is required to divide his/her time between career education and some other job such as counseling or teaching. There are many similarities between the tasks of the part-time and full-time coordinators. Both are responsible for providing career education resource information and curriculum materials for the teaching and/or counseling staff within a local district. They also help develop in-service activities for teachers and make the necessary contacts in the community with business and industry, labor, and parents. He/she may work with only one school but, in some cases, the part-time coordinator plans and conducts activities with several schools and is responsible to a single principal. Generally, the part-time coordinator (Fig. 4-3), has the responsibility of facilitating the activities of teachers, building administrators, support staff, and guidance and counseling personnel. In most cases they have direct and active contact with the business, labor, and industrial community, but in some cases individual teachers arrange for field trips and guest speakers.

It appears that many of the part-time coordinators were employed as full-time specialists when career education was new and in need of a great deal of planning and implementation. After a school district had successfully implemented career education, these persons were assigned other responsibilities. Many of these people are now located in medium-size schools in which career education is funded solely by the district, and they are devoting approximately one-half of their time to locating career education resource materials and encouraging faculty participation.

School Resource Person. A school resource person is employed full time within the district and has been asked by a principal or superintendent to display and/or disseminate career education materials in conjunction with her/his present job. The resource person has no responsibilities as far as developing, implementing, or providing in-service education

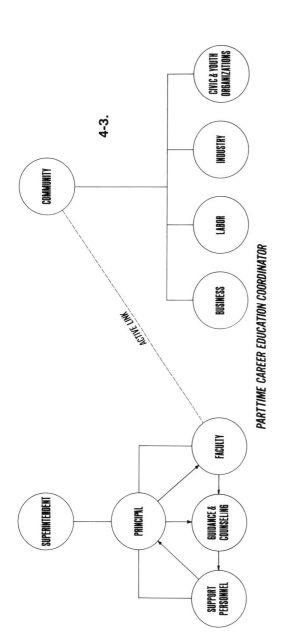

PARTTIME CAREER EDUCATION COORDINATOR

4-3.

ACTIVE LINK

SUPERINTENDENT

PRINCIPAL

FACULTY

GUIDANCE & COUNSELING

SUPPORT PERSONNEL

COMMUNITY

BUSINESS

LABOR

INDUSTRY

CIVIC & YOUTH ORGANIZATIONS

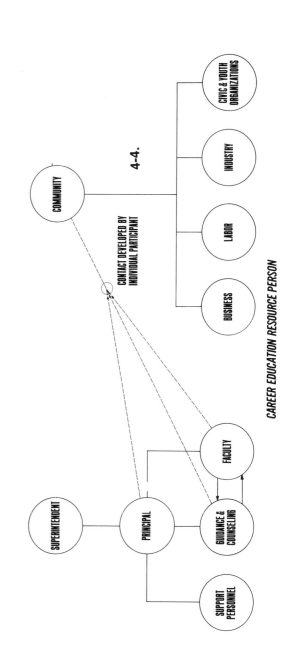

CAREER EDUCATION RESOURCE PERSON

4-4.

CONTACT DEVELOPED BY INDIVIDUAL PARTICIPANT

SUPERINTENDENT

PRINCIPAL

FACULTY

GUIDANCE & COUNSELING

SUPPORT PERSONNEL

COMMUNITY

BUSINESS

LABOR

INDUSTRY

CIVIC & YOUTH ORGANIZATIONS

with reference to career education. He or she is often interested and committed to career education. This person has a full-time appointment as a teacher, librarian, counselor, or curriculum specialist. It has been noted that the administration will usually assign the resource procurement duties to a librarian or counselor when a volunteer is not present. Under this arrangement, the school district seldom has a plan for curriculum development, in-service education, and/or community involvement. Occasionally, in-service activities are recommended by the superintendent and could consist of after-school sessions conducted by a career education specialist from the state department of education or by an outside consultant. Basically, the career education activities of the resource person are limited to the faculty. Primarily, the activity involves gathering materials and communicating the what and how (Fig. 4-4). The link between school and the world of work occurs as a result of participation by administrators, guidance and counseling personnel, and faculty. This type of arrangement usually does not provide for in-service follow-up.

Basically, the responsibilities of the career education resource person involve: (1) designating and ordering appropriate classroom education materials, i.e.,film, curriculum guides, commercial materials, etc., (2) stockpiling these materials and developing a means of communicating to teachers/students where they can obtain these materials, and (3) displaying and forwarding these career education materials to interested faculty and students within a specified school.

In this type of arrangement, the resource person has little contact with the administration and, in most cases, receives no funding to support the activities. The career education resource person may rely heavily on the state department of education specialists, teachers, and interested community members for materials and activities appropriate for classroom use. This type of administrative arrangement is primarily a dissemination function.

Career Education Facilitator. A career education facilitator and his/her staff are employed cooperatively by two or more school districts to provide both instruction and information to faculty and students. The facilitator is usually located in a regional education center and is responsible for implementing career education activities in numerous schools and may conduct activities in one or more counties. In many cases, the facilitator will have a staff consisting of two to five persons. These individuals will have various responsibilities ranging from curriculum development to in-service training. Their functions might include: (1) organizing and teaching in-service classes, (2) individual school curriculum development, (3) recommending career education materials and resources, (4) making contacts with business, labor, and industry, and (5) working with interested and motivated faculty members who serve as contacts in the schools. One faculty member in each school usually accepts the responsibility of distributing materials and communicating the needs of the teachers to the regional facilitator. The facilitator develops a working relationship with teachers and they in turn make individual contact with business, labor, and industry (Fig. 4-5). Funding for this type of arrangement is a cooperative effort on the part of participating schools. Supervision of the career education facilitator is limited and usually comes from the director of the regional center.

Other Administrative Arrangements. In isolated cases, a school system may employ a lay person to provide help in procuring and disseminating career education information. This person is usually a noneducator and a resident of the community who is interested in the career options of students. Examples of persons who have been employed to organize this

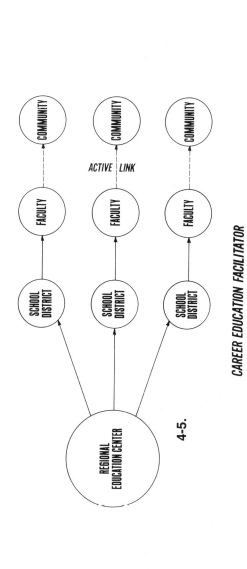

4-5.

CAREER EDUCATION FACILITATOR

ACTIVE LINK

4-6.

LAY PERSON MODEL

activity are retired business persons, retired military personnel, and homemakers. This arrangement often evolves when funds are not available to employ a full- or part-time coordinator from the teaching ranks. It seems to have great potential. As outlined in Fig. 4-6, the lay person, upon receiving administrative approval, works mainly with teachers and guidance and counseling personnel.

Evaluation of the Effectiveness of Select Career Education Administrative Arrangements

A survey instrument was developed to secure data from administrators, guidance personnel, and secondary and elementary teachers. The questions on the survey instrument dealt with specific career education concepts in an attempt to measure the degree to which the participants perceived their own school district's success in integrating career education. The six categories around which the questions were developed are initiation, awareness, implementation, community involvement, student reaction, and general evaluation.

Three to six statements were developed to describe each of the six categories. The statements were written in a positive form. The mean scores for each category, as well as the total score of all categories, were statistically treated to provide an indication of the respondent's acceptance or rejection of a particular administrative arrangement. Table 4-A is an example of those included in the survey instrument.

The sample population consisted of 350 public school (K-12) personnel in Kansas. Two school systems were identified which represented each administrative arrangement—a total of ten schools. A sample was drawn by selecting every fifth name from the

TABLE 4-A. Survey Instrument Examples			Definitely true	True most of time	In between	False most of time	Definitely false
Initiation	Item 5	I approve of the system our district uses to plan and carry out our career education program.	1	2	3	4	5
Awareness	Item 12	Most teachers in our district have a reasonably accurate understanding of the philosophy and objectives of career education.	1	2	3	4	5
Evaluation	Item 30	I believe our career education program has made the educational experience more meaningful to most students.	1	2	3	4	5

TABLE 4-B.
Two-Way Analysis of Variance Among Five Administrative
Arrangements and Four Educational Groups

Source	DF	Sum of squares	Mean squares	F-ratio
A Administrative arrangement	4	5.35	1.33	4.8*
B Groups of educators	3	3.66	1.22	4.4*
A × B	12	10.73	.89	3.2*
Residual	245	67.75	.28	
Totals	264	87.49		
P < .05				

school system's master rosters until 350 names were obtained. The sample consisted of administrators and personnel from guidance and counseling and secondary and elementary education. There was no follow-up mailing. The total return was 265 (76%).

In order to estimate the reliability of the instrument, a coefficient alpha was completed. Reliability was .90.

Analysis of Data. A two-way analysis of variance was completed on the total mean scores, using five administrative arrangements and four educational groups as factors. Since all cell sizes were unequal, a best squares analysis of variance was used. F-ratios that were significant at the .05 level were obtained for both main effects and the interaction (Table 4-B).

Results. The Fisher Least Significant Difference (LSD) test was used to ascertain significant differences among the means. The results were as follows:

Group 1: It appears that elementary teachers prefer the facilitator type of administrative arrangement over others although the full-time coordinator as an administrative arrangement was an extremely close second, with the superintendent as an administrative arrangement rated low.

Group 2: Secondary teachers appear to prefer the resource person administrative arrangement. Although full-time and part-time coordinators were in the upper half of the mean scores, the secondary teachers have not been completely sold on career education as an integrated part of all curriculum. They may prefer sending their students to a resource person rather than assuming the responsibility.

Group 3: The full-time coordinator appears to be preferred by guidance personnel. Guidance personnel usually have a large number of responsibilities that are not directly related to guidance, and they prefer an arrangement that assumes the career education responsibility. The resource person and the superintendent arrangements ranked rather low with the guidance and counseling group.

Group 4: There was no significant difference between the four arrangements from the administrators' point of view. This may be accounted for by the fact that the administrative group provided the smallest sample and administrators reacted to their own arrangements.

Also, administrators may be more familiar with the various arrangements and are able to perceive the advantages or disadvantages of each group.

Summary and Implications of Findings. The purpose of this study was to evaluate the perceived effectiveness of career education administrative arrangements in Kansas. The study was designed to elicit educators' attitudes toward various plans used to implement career education within their own schools or districts as well as their attitudes toward the success or failure of these plans. Although the research did not hypothesize a specific administrative arrangement as meeting the objective, there are some implications that can be drawn from the analysis of data.

The participating educational groups did not all prefer the same type of administrative arrangement. Although there is only a limited indication of difference, the mean scores were high enough in three of the four groups to indicate a trend. Generally, the administrative arrangements of full-time and part-time coordinators were very acceptable. The full-time coordinator ranks reasonably high in all four groups, while the part-time coordinator and the facilitator are in the top half of the mean scores. It appears that the superintendent as initiator and manager is the least favorable arrangement, as it ranked low.

In light of these findings, further research to explore why different groups of educational personnel react differently to different career education administrative arrangements may be needed. However, the models and the reactions to them have illustrated both the multiple ways local leadership use to conduct career education as well as the lack of clarity about which arrangement is preferred.

REFERENCES

Clary, Joseph R. "Statewide Effort To Implement Career Education." In *Career Education.* The Third Yearbook of the American Vocational Association, Magisos, Joel, ed. Washington: American Vocational Association, 1973.

Council of Chief State School Officers. *State and Federal Relationships in Education.* Washington: Council of Chief State School Officers, 1971.

Crawford, Robert L., and Jesser, David L. *The Status and Progress of Career Education.* Washington: Council of Chief State School Officers, 1975.

Hansen, Kenneth. *Synthesizing Work and Schooling: The Roles of Community and Society.* Report No. 91. Denver: Education Commission of the States, 1976.

Hayas, Denise K. *Career and Vocational Education: 1975 State Activity.* Report No. 89. Denver: Education Commission of the States, 1976.

Herr, Edwin L. *The Emerging History of Career Education: A Summary View.* Washington: National Advisory Council of Career Education, 1976.

Jesser, David L., et al. *Career Education: A Priority of the Chief State School Officers.* Salt Lake City: Olympus, 1976.

Maccoby, Michael. *The Gamesman.* (As reviewed by Paul Roazen in *The Saturday Review,* 22 January 1977) New York: Simon and Schuster, 1976.

McLaughlin, Donald H. *Career Education in the Public Schools 1974-1975: A National Survey.* Palo Alto, Calif.: American Institutes for Research, 1976.

Pinson, Nancy M. *Career Education: A Professional Introspection.* Washington: Council of Chief State School Officers, 1975.

Proehl, Carl W. *"Administering Career Education."* In *The Third Yearbook of the American Vocational Association,* Magisos, Joel H., ed. Washington: American Vocational Association, 1973.

Smoker, David. *Career Education: Current Trends in School Policies and Programs.* Arlington: National School Public Relations Assoc., 1974.

U. S. Government Accounting Office. *Career Education: Status and Needed Improvements.* Washington: USGAO, Manpower and Welfare Division, 1976.

Business, Industry, and Labor Views of Career Education

Career education, unlike education in the main, must rely heavily on the support of business, industry, and labor for its full implementation. Those involved in managing career education programs must be well acquainted with what is available in the local community that can be utilized by the school, and they must establish a dialogue with those segments of the community which offer this support.

Since its beginning, career education has been encouraged by business and industry. Labor, however, has not been as supportive, and after almost ten years still has reservations. Some labor leaders believe that career education programs will place students in business and industry replacing workers already there. This is a misunderstanding of the basic purpose and goals of career education.

Chapter 5 consists of six articles written in 1978 by leaders in business, industry, and labor, who were asked to express their views. Lee Hamilton and Charles Heatherly attempt to establish a basis for support by industry and business of education in general and of career education in particular. Gene Hensley explicates some of the problems associated with increased interaction between business and industry and career education. William McKnight gives an account of the roles of business in career education and provides some insights into how business can assist further in bridging the gap. Eugenia Kemble provides a picture of labor's position as taken by The American Federation of Teachers and discusses the resolutions passed by that organization in 1976 in support of career education. Carroll M. Hutton offers a view of career education strategies as seen by UAW and explains the initial hostilities felt by organized labor. Sidney P. Marland, Jr.'s article is an update and traces some of the problems and prospects relative to the cooperation of labor, industry, and business.

BUSINESS AND INDUSTRY PROSPECTIVES ON CAREER EDUCATION

Lee Hamilton and Charles Heatherly

Lee Hamilton is assistant vice president and deputy to the senior vice president of the National Association of Manufacturers. He assists with policy development and maintains liaison with members of Congress on issues of concern to industry.

Charles Heatherly is director of education for the National Federation of Independent Business, a member of the board of directors of the National Association for Industry-Education Cooperation, and past member of the National Advisory Council for Career Education. This article was written in 1978.

Career education is widely understood to encourage, indeed to require, business and industry participation which goes beyond the traditional roles assigned by educational theory and practice. Because of the innovative relationships called for by career education reformers, both business and education have developed some misunderstandings that need to be removed so that future progress in career education can be assured.

The difficulty of effective communication is illustrated in the story of the businessman who went out in his new boat for the first time, only to find after he was far out to sea that he had a leak. He turned to his ship-to-shore radio and frantically called, "Mayday! Mayday!" The Coast Guard responded quickly and said, "We hear your Mayday. What's your position?" The businessman hesitated for a moment and then said, "I'm executive vice-president of the First National Bank, and please hurry!"

American business and industry have been concerned with education for well over a century. The American economy expanded very rapidly after the Civil War, and the need for skilled workers expanded apace. Yet, in 1870, no public or private school on the secondary level offered any industrial skill training, so industry established its own programs. The apprenticeship systems that suited a nation of farmers and entrepreneurs could not meet the needs of industrial expansion. Nevertheless, noninstitutionalized training continued to be the principal route to business careers well into the twentieth century.

By 1916 it was estimated that over 60,000 boys were enrolled in industry-sponsored training programs. The National Association of Corporation Schools, organized in 1913, had 150 members when it merged with the American Management Association in 1922. Even today, most of the larger and many medium-sized companies carry on some type of classroom educational activity, either wholly within the corporate environment and staffed by their own personnel or in cooperation with college- or university-provided expertise.

By the 1920s it had become obvious that business and industry could not meet its manpower and management needs solely through in-house training programs. An advanced industrial nation needs professional and managerial talent of many kinds. New technology changed some jobs and created others. The integration of traditional learning with practical skills became more important. Hence came the need for a partnership with the schools and a mutual understanding of the respective needs and roles of education and industry.

A modern, integrated economy creates an interdependence among the sectors of the business system—manufacturing, banking, retailing, etc. This development affected the character of small businesses: their educational needs changed and, hence, their relationship to the schools. Today, small business people are as deeply concerned with education as are the executives at larger corporations.

Obviously, many changes have taken place in the nation over the years. Change, however, has been accompanied by distrust and suspicion in many quarters. A step toward reducing this problem is taken when educational institutions and business firms are viewed as having complementary, not antagonistic, roles. In schools, more than any other place, public and private resources can be mixed to promote both public and private (individual) goals. For such a mixture to prove fruitful, however, all participants—educators, businesses, students, and parents—must understand the interests of the others and the particular resources that each group brings to the educational process.

Because of the changes just mentioned, business firms have a keen interest in the direction and quality of American education. Their interest, however, goes much deeper, as the reasons that follow will show.

Reasons Why Businesses Support Education

The first reason can be called corporate citizenship. Many business people and the firms they represent want to be involved in education programs. They consider their work with schools as one means of discharging a community service responsibility, just as they contribute to the Community Chest or United Fund.

Secondly, business firms are financial contributors to the educational system. Nationwide, the average share of local real estate property taxes contributed by business and industry is about 40%. In some communities it can run up to 80%. Local taxes are a significant business cost, and business people are naturally interested in getting the best possible return on their education tax dollars. Business people are oriented toward efficiency, productivity, and the achievement of goals. They tend to look upon schools as service establishments that ought to be run efficiently while maintaining a certain level of quality control.

A third reason for the link between business and education is industry's need to have a reliable and continuing supply of well-educated individuals entering the labor market as potential employees. The cost of recruitment, selection, and training is lower when a basic education has been provided by the schools to all citizens and specialized training provided to adequate numbers of entry-level personnel in professional and technical fields.

In addition, most business people believe that the industry or trade which they represent (engineering, marketing, financial management, retail selling, etc.) can provide young people with careers that are personally and financially rewarding. They believe that careers in business offer as much challenge, fulfillment, and public benefit as careers in government, medicine, or other callings commonly considered more ideal.

The outcome of education, i.e., the worker, also concerns the business community. Moreover, the worker is a growing concern of all who understand the relationship between economic productivity and our national prosperity in general. This relationship is not something that can be modified or repealed by the wishful thinking of academic theorists who would prefer to de-emphasize the role of work and equip students only for their roles as consumers, philosophers, social activists, or critics. The role of productive work remains the cornerstone of social progress and human happiness.

This fact is all the more important in the light of increasing competition in the world market. American business and industry must compete for both raw materials and markets for finished products. If we continue to lose ground in this world market, all Americans will be affected. The ability to adapt to changing markets and technologies requires technical proficiencies as well as analytic and communication skills. Career education must live up to its commitments to fulfill these needs.

A fourth reason is the students' need to know about the business system and the economic principles through which it operates. A knowledge of basic economic principles is as essential today as grammar or mathematics and should be so recognized in the basic curriculum required by school authorities. This education in economics is vital to the fulfillment of the student's citizenship role. It is just as vital as knowledge of the powers of Congress or the means of calculating square roots.

The interests of the business community may be self-evident in regard to the curriculum of economics, but two points should be stressed:

• The less the institutional framework of our society is accepted by the majority of the citizens—not just the elite—and the more our institutions are subjected to unfounded criticism or excessive expectations, the more likely these institutions are to break down, leading, over the long run, to a growth of government intervention and control throughout society. This applies to all institutions, not merely the business system.

• If the economy of a free society is to perform properly, citizens must generally accept its institutional framework. Once confidence and general acceptance are undermined or lost, a major political emergency is the likely result.

A vicious circle seems to be already in operation in our system. As the free market is weakened, people tend to look to government to find a solution. This dependence is then used as an argument for more government regulations, more comprehensive planning of the economy. This further weakens the economy, and the cycle begins again. This is the story of the British economy, where the government—whether Labor or Conservative—was unable to retreat from previous interventions and found itself in a whirlpool of accelerating demands and unfulfilled promises.

To the business person (and others who have studied the matter), the relationship between economic freedom and other freedoms is direct and inescapable. As freedom of enterprise and of economic choice is constricted, other freedoms also suffer, including academic freedom. The more jobs that are tied to the political process through subsidies, contract regulations, commissions, transfer payments, and direct services, the greater the political intervention and manipulation of private decisions of citizens in every institutional framework—job, family, recreation, travel, etc. There is no escaping the dependency cycle once a majority of citizens come to see their economic well-being as tied to political decisions rather than their personal efforts and achievements in the marketplace.

To say that the business system is efficient, productive, and, hence, important to our material well-being is true but is only part of the story—perhaps the less important part over the long run. The importance of the free economy in providing the economic framework for the expression of larger human values and creativity is of equal significance. A free society utilizing a free economy is the only social arrangement whereby the ideals of equality and excellence can be balanced and become mutually supportive. The ideal of excellence, in the American heritage and throughout the western world, is an ideal of individual achievement, not of enforced mediocrity. An environment of economic freedom is the indispensable foundation for the survival and growth of that spirit of achievement in all areas of human endeavor.

These are not all the reasons supporting a role for business involvement with the schools. However, a recognition of these interests and motivating factors will provide both educators and business people with at least a fertile soil for the nourishment of good ideas and worthwhile innovation in the pursuit of increased business-education cooperation.

The Limits of Career Education

The overall success of the nation's schools is a matter of great pride to most Americans. No society, past or present, has devoted as great a percentage of its total resources to formal schooling. No society has made schooling so widely accessible and available. It is this historic success of the nation's schools which makes their present failures so glaring—and so unacceptable. In this regard, business and schools have much in common. In each case, the critic's role is enhanced because of past achievements.

Notwithstanding the historic record of public education, the nation's schools are today caught in a pincer movement. The taxpayer demands that the schools prove their effectiveness. On the other side, the student demands a curriculum that is relevant to immediate interests and future needs. In this setting, and by the hopes of groups with different perceptions of the problem, career education emerged as a reform movement aimed at infusing relevance throughout the curriculum.

From the beginning, there has been a flap over its definition, or, as some charged, its lack of definition. It's not an academic discipline like philosophy, history, or mathematics and, hence, has no general theory—at least not yet. It is often perceived more as a coalition of reformers, each with a different prescription for the schools' problems but marching together under the banner of career education. It is "more than vocational education" but is not "general education." It is "a concept not a program," yet it requires programmatic efforts to achieve its goals. All in all, after several years of official support from the U.S. Office of Education (USOE) and numerous attempts at definition, its precise meaning and relationship to other reform concepts are unclear.

The first step toward clearing the air in this matter of definitions may be to recognize and accept the limits of career education: it is not a panacea for all that ails modern education. It won't necessarily pacify the unruly child nor keep school from being boring for some students. It may not reduce vandalism in school or absenteeism. Nor is it guaranteed to make all work enjoyable and creative. Finally, we must add, it will not cure unemployment or even reduce it substantially. (It may affect the structure of unemployment if teenage youth are enabled to enter the permanent labor force via cooperative work experience programs and liberalized union apprenticeship rules).

The Work Market

Both work and learning are hard: they take time, energy, and discipline. But as William Faulkner said of work, "There is nothing else, really, you can do for eight hours a day that will give you satisfaction."

The parameters of career education were laid out by Kenneth Hoyt (1975) in the USOE policy statement on career education. In this statement, the focus of career education is on the concept of work. He defined work in a manner that distinguishes it from ordinary labor or physical exertion. Work is "a conscious effort. . . aimed at producing socially acceptable benefits for oneself and others." It includes both work for wages or salaries and work for charitable or altruistic reasons (Hoyt 1975).

J. R. Rossi, in an unpublished essay written for the American Institute for Research, Palo Alto, has differentiated career education from vocational education through the vital role of choice and planning:

> The making of a career decision. . . becomes the crucial aspect of an individual's ability to transform labor into work and to become the person he wants to be as a result of working. Career refers, in this sense, to one's projection of what one will be as the result of the activities in which one engages. The world of work can thus be interpreted not only as a socially predefined world one enters, but also as the world one creates through the process of self-definition and self-actualization (Rossi 1976, p. 46).

Reading these two passages by Hoyt and Rossi, we can readily see how far the philosophy of career education has traveled from the world of vocational education and manpower training. Career education encompasses occupational training and skill development, but also much more. It insists on the role of rational choice and planning in the career development of the individual. It suggests that education should do more than impart particular skills and subject-area expertise, basic though these functions may be. Education should also enable the student to choose rationally from available career alternatives.

This concept does not suggest that career options are infinite or that everyone can be guaranteed an equal opportunity to succeed in any specific occupation, whether doctor, engineer, or gourmet chef. It does suggest that a person's options are expanded in direct proportion to (a) self-knowledge; (b) knowledge of the world, including its economic, political, cultural, and technological values; and (c) capacity for relating her or his resources/skills to the needs of others. In this view, labor market is an obsolete concept: *work market* is a more accurate and useful term for the interaction of human talents, needs, and resources within the framework of a free society that places its highest value on individual freedom and self-expression.

The work market includes all purposeful human activity. It is value neutral in the sense that it does not tell people what purposes are worthwhile or what kind of work is most fulfilling. This will, of necessity, be left to the judgment of individuals. Nor does the work market reward all work equally or even through a uniform value system, such as money. Some work provides only psychic rewards rather than monetary rewards, but most work provides a mixture of both. It is a disorganized and even chaotic market, indeed, and any attempt to homogenize all work so that it can be parceled out in units and shared equally by all members of society is naive and dangerous.

Work and the Liberal Arts

We have discussed work at some length to elaborate on Hoyt's distinction between career education as "preparation for work," and vocational education as "preparation for a job, through the acquisition of job-specific skills." A specific job is certainly part of one's lifework, but preparation for a specific job is not all that is necessary for preparation for work. Work is purposeful, productive, and may include monetary compensation, but whatever the rewards or incentives that attract a particular person to work, one's preparation for work involves far more than the learning of a specialized skill. It also involves preparation for making decisions and choices about which skills to acquire, which skills to develop to what extent, and for what purposes. It involves development of self-knowledge, self-confidence, and an awareness of one's limitations as well as one's potential. It means the harnessing of the boundless energy and yearnings of childhood and adolescence into productive channels for present and future happiness.

Educators or others who think such reforms would emasculate the liberal arts by draining off students from universities to private sector employment display both an ignorance of the origin of the liberal arts and an elitist contempt for the judgment of ordinary people. The liberal arts do, indeed, point the student toward an eternal dialogue on the great questions of human existence: What is justice? What is truth? How are these questions posed in human literature, art, history, and politics? When Socrates engaged his fellow citizens in dialogue on these questions, the dialogue was framed by shared experiences of a very concrete nature—experiences in war, in politics, in love and friendship, in commerce and trade, and in the religious practices of Athenians. They were not pulled out of ancient texts or discussed with inexperienced adolescents. Socrates' questions derived from the incompleteness of experience, i.e., the incompleteness of sensate experience, the satisfaction of the appetites and organic needs of man.

In brief, the utility of the philosophic enterprise depends not simply on the asking of questions but moreso on the context of personal experience which renders the questions necessary and meaningful. The liberal arts, then, can be pursued throughout life and without a formal curriculum, but the most salient point is that they are more profitably pursued when the student has sufficient experience of the world to render his or her reflections and inquiries meaningful.

To say that career education belittles the liberal arts or distracts students from true education betrays a misreading of the intent of career education and an overly rigid and historical notion of the role of the liberal arts. However, career education does reject the kind of liberal arts curriculum that suggests that a student should master a certain number of academic disciplines before entering the world of productive employment. Such advice is a sure formula for alienation and wasted years of study.

The philosophy of career education assumes that American society is open and dynamic enough to accommodate the immense range of ambitions, hopes, and values found on any university campus—with the sole exception of the overt revolutionary who would destroy the imperfect freedom of human institutions for the utopian dream of the perfect society. Revolutionaries judge societies according to standards created by their own ideologies, not by the societies they condemn. How can any society live up to expectations derived from a social contract never signed? A society is justly accountable to the promises and standards acknowledged in its founding and its traditions, and by those standards, American society has to be judged rather successful.

There Is Much To Be Done

A dean at a business school on the west coast recently remarked that several years of research and reflection on his own experiences in the business world had revealed a startling fact: the one skill most often correlated to success in the business world was not a specialized knowledge of the subject, such as accounting, law, sales, or marketing. It was, simply, skill at written communications. This should not come as a surprise to anyone. But it should awaken business leaders to the importance of career education and the inadequacy of job-specific skills as the goal of education.

Business leaders as much as educators need to reexamine priorities and practices. If career education is to achieve the reforms envisioned for American education, business leaders will have to study its meaning and implications more carefully and join a genuinely collaborative effort at all levels of education. A beginning has been made, but there is much work to be done.

PROBLEMS AND POSSIBILITIES OF INCREASED INTERACTION AMONG BUSINESS, INDUSTRY, AND EDUCATION

Gene Hensley

Dr. Hensley is director of the Career Education Project for the Education Commission of the States in Denver. He has also acted as consultant to USOE programs. This article was written in 1978.

For several years career education has attracted the attention of educators; political decision makers; leaders in business, industry, and labor; and the general public. It has not been a casual interest. The notion that career education constitutes a natural and sound objective of education is shared by many persons regardless of political affiliation, educational philosophy, or nature of employment. At the state level, for example, career education has continued to receive support from a wide cross section of policymakers. The Council of Chief State School Officers has passed a series of positive resolutions; the Education Commission of the States has indicated its support through resolutions and programmatic activities; the National Association of State Boards of Education has recognized the importance of career education by adopting supportive policy statements. In addition, a majority of state education agencies has appointed full-time career education coordinators to assist local districts in implementing their programs. At the same time, federal support for career education has been significant for more than seven years. There currently exists strong federal legislation, and even more comprehensive legislation is pending. There has been a National Advisory Council for Career Education since 1974, and there are a number of federal assistance programs that provide support to states and local districts for exemplary programs, innovative ideas, and career-related services. Among nongovernmental groups there is also strong interest: the National Education Association; the National Youth Organizations; the United States Chamber of Commerce; and the National Urban Coalition.

These forms of interest and support are strong indicators of the growing acceptance among educators, policymakers, and others of educational reform that infuses career concepts into schooling from kindergarten through post-secondary study, aiming to ensure that educational outcomes will be satisfying and productive for students, professionals, and employers. Like other innovations however, career education has taken its lumps. There have been problems with definitions. Many persons still have difficulty differentiating between career education and vocational education. Millions of lay persons remain confused about career education or have yet to hear of it. Some write it off as another proposed education panacea without substance. But many would agree that there now exists a new case for strengthening the relationship between education and work. There is clearly widespread recognition of the importance of combining educational experience with work experience, and there is renewed interest in collaborative efforts between education, business, and industry that will make education more relevant.

On this most would agree: the time is long overdue for communities and states to bring education and work together in an effort to make career education a major component of education. A discussion paper published for the Education Commission of the States in 1976 noted that:

> . . .all too many students look forward neither to school nor to work. Partly because they have seldom experienced making real choices. . .and partly because they feel that the deck is stacked against them and that they have no clear choices available, they often feel trapped or lost. With infrequent chances to practice or experience making decisions of real consequences and with little or no training in developing decision-making skills, they drift aimlessly, evidencing alienation and bitterness with respect to both school and work.

> . . .The community often lacks any sense of purpose or power to bring about changes needed in either the school structure or the work structure. Both are frequently seen, perhaps without reasons but often with mistrust, . . .as self-serving, unapproachable bureaucracies in league against both parents and children. "The school doesn't teach my kid what he needs to get a job, and the world of work doesn't have a place for him anyhow." But what can parents . . especially a poor person or minority, do about it? Rarely does anyone ask their advice or even inquire into their feelings (ECS Report No. 91, 1976).

Motivation for increasing the cooperation between education, business, and industry is frequently tied to specific issues such as the school dropout problem or perceived discrepancies between the requirements of employers and the quality of education. Fundamental, however, are issues related to the changing meaning of work and the high rate of unemployment. While it is doubtful that education alone should be held totally accountable for the unemployment problems of youth, these problems must be faced by all who want increased educational cooperation among business, industry, and education. As the teenage labor force continues to increase, the number of adolescents who are looking for work continues to outpace this nation's ability to provide employment. Most persons probably know this, whether or not they have read or analyzed recent unemployment statistics.

Even more significant is the fact that there have been major changes in the meaning of work. Research has shown, for example, that college seniors do, in fact, hold positive attitudes toward work, but they perceive work as more than earning money, gaining status, or simply serving as an expedient means to an end. Work, as they perceive it, must be satisfying and beneficial to others and cannot be separated from other elements of a person's life. Students see themselves as different from their parents; they hold different attitudes about work, and they differ markedly in their perceptions as to what work is all about. Social class, ethnicity, and sex differences are also important when planning for increased cooperation among business, industry, and education. Work is not an isolated experience. It is an integral part of life. There is clearly a role for career education to play in improving the educational preparation of Americans for productive and fulfilling lives, but how is the concept to be implemented?

Issues in Strengthening Collaborative Efforts

Despite the growing interest in career education at the federal, state, and local levels, this important concept is not likely to be implemented fully without increased participation of business and industry. When states and local districts have actively sought support of business and industry for career education, they have moved far ahead of those that have not. The first steps in initiating increased cooperation have not always been taken by educators. Business and industry have often discovered career education to be a saleable product but have lacked buyers in the education community. This situation points to one of the major issues in strengthening the participation of business and industry in career education. Who should take the lead?

In the final analysis it may matter little who leads in the initial planning efforts, but the long-standing separation of education and work has contributed to the continuation of bad habits by both educators and leaders in business. Educators feel more comfortable with other educators. Business persons talk to their own kind. Government leaders talk to their peers. The interaction of these institutionalized groups is not widespread. Each waits, often impatiently, for the other to act. Finally, when an educator, legislator, board member, business person or other takes the problem in hand, positive things begin to happen. One does not have to be directly involved to be a catalyst. The key to addressing these communication issues centers on the importance of one person or group initiating a conversation, developing a dialogue, and settling down to a series of planned and structured discussions. Certainly, all parties must have some idea about what they want to accomplish. Proposed levels of collaborative activities must be established beforehand to determine what outcomes are possible before serious discussions begin.

Another continuing issue is whether the interests of education, business, and industry are compatible. Are individual and group motives compatible? Can they be reconciled? Fundamental to resolving such issues is a recognition that individuals and institutions often initiate actions because of their own interests. Whatever the circumstances, all interests must be served. Such situations are not new for education—or for business and industry. They are political. They frequently involve negotiations and compromises and a clear understanding of the overriding public interest. In such cases objectives will not be achieved without a delineation of differences, alternative courses of action, and variables that may strengthen or inhibit cooperative efforts.

There is also the question of whether existing education programs can be coordinated with the opportunities that now exist for work. Education systems tend to separate education and training from many of the realities of earning a living. Involved are subquestions of finance, public versus private education, the traditional role of post-secondary education, new solutions versus long-term approaches to solving problems, as well as bias that is sometimes ignored by those who seek educational reform.

Important also are such questions as these: Who is responsible? Is career education a federal responsibility, a state responsibility, or a uniquely local issue? Clearly, both federal and state governments have important roles to play. Work opportunities, laws related to employment, certification requirements, and other factors must be considered. What is the relative impact that state, federal, and private programs have on infusing curriculum with principles of work and on resolving the continuous separation of work and education? Is career education cost beneficial? Are present programs programmatically effective at state and local levels? Can the cost for effective programs be translated into outcomes that are defensible? These are difficult questions to answer at the present time, but they must be addressed.

Some educators feel that collaborative efforts among leaders in business, industry, and education will lead to external control of schooling. Closely related to this issue is the notion that increased cooperation will lead to a pattern of abdicating responsibility for the curriculum of education to nonprofessional outsiders. From the beginning, career education advocates have recognized the necessity of close relationships between the communities of work and education.

While there are many dimensions to this issue, we must recognize that education is a political enterprise; that both educators and noneducators must be involved in it; and that noneducators are accustomed to making educational decisions.

Potential Barriers to Increased Interaction

Potential barriers to increased industry-education cooperation vary from region to region depending on a host of economic, legal, demographic, and geographic factors (e.g., wealth and population characteristics, state laws and regulations, rural/urban differences, and even transportation factors). Even with these widespread differences, however, it is possible to identify several common problems or barriers that deserve careful study:

• **The participation of business and industry in state and local career education efforts is frequently not sought in the beginning.** Since business and industry are important members of the career education process and are an integral part of the political processes in education, they must participate in the development of policies and laws. It is unlikely that members of business and industry can develop strong commitments, reach consensus on the goals of career education, and fully cooperate with states and local districts if participation is not invited and encouraged through all phases of policy development—long before programs are ready for implementation.

• **Certification and credentialing.** Although this problem is not limited to career education (reciprocity of certification, for example, is a major problem for states in all areas of education), it has special significance for career education. Many persons in business look forward to participating in pre-service and in-service programs for teachers but face hurdles when placed on special assignments in public schools. Rigidly drawn standards limit the scope and frequency of these collaborative efforts.

• **Identifying career prospects.** Career education advocates can cite numerous instances when students were prepared for occupations that no longer existed; when the requirements specified in job descriptions bore little if any resemblance to the task of the position; and the demand for personnel was so unevenly distributed geographically that the demand for workers was virtually impossible to establish. More and better information is needed concerning career prospects if career education programs are to be replicated and if the cooperative efforts of business, industry, and education are to be expanded to facilitate regional and educational cooperation.

• **Competencies perceived by business or industry for a working life are often unclear to students, teachers, and others in the education community.** The notion that career education represents a response to a call for educational reform is far reaching and implies that educational reform is not all that is needed. Social, political, and economic reforms are equally necessary. Right now the goals and objectives of institutions differ. Business and industry are profit centered and cannot be expected to be otherwise. Education is unaccustomed to thinking in these terms and sometimes finds it uncomfortable to relate dollars to outcomes. Educators balk at the idea that their roles should be limited to training workers to fit a mold prescribed by forces outside education, including business and industry.

- **Security, safety, and insurance-related problems.** A number of companies have pointed out that for security reasons visits by outsiders must be restricted. Some industries would have to develop elaborate security arrangements if students and teachers were to be brought into plants on a regular basis. Further, some industries are particularly concerned about safety and should be. Work in many plants is dangerous, and safety can be a serious problem for persons (especially children) unfamiliar with shop routines and practices. Some industries cannot safely conduct large tours or must limit visits to secondary school age or older groups. Insurance problems also constitute a real barrier. For example, a number of business and industry representatives have indicated that school field trip insurance does not relieve the company of the liability in the event of injury to students. Also, insurance problems can occur when part-time student employees are injured.

- **Continuity of communications between the schools and business and industry.** Frequently mentioned by persons in business and industry is the importance of a continuing relationship between schools, business, and industry. The changing roles and responsibilities inside both systems, including the promotion and reassignment of personnel and the continuous reorganization of administrative units, work against the continuity that is essential if formalized and long-term relations between local districts and business are to be maintained.

- **Time and money.** Time and money are important considerations for both industry and education. Funding for career-related activities that involve the cooperation of business or industry cannot always be obtained by the schools. At the same time, many small businesses and companies willing to participate in the proposed programs may not have financial resources that can be allocated. Time, which can easily be translated as money, can be even more important. Serving on an educational advisory board, participating in industry or school seminars, supervising interns, or conducting tours all require that considerable time be allocated by schools and industries. Both have been guilty of reserving time and space for activities most directly related to immediate payoffs.

- **Inertia and the gap between the requirements of business or industry and the program objectives of schools.** This problem, as expressed by career education advocates both in education and industry, has at least two dimensions. First, many key decision makers in education, business, and industry remain unconvinced that educational linkages are important. In some cases, there is the expressed idea that *our way* is the right way and *their way* is the wrong way. In short, there is significant resistance to institutional change. For example, those who do not view careers as a logical and desirable goal of education are not receptive to efforts outside the academic community to establish cooperative relations that involve the larger community. In much the same theme, leaders in industry or business whose involvement in education has been limited to programs with their own personnel can be extremely resistant to a perceived invasion by educators. Second, school priorities, methods of instruction, and training equipment do not necessarily compliment the requirements of business or industry. Just as industry is not always willing to provide information, seminars, and tours to keep school personnel abreast of new techniques and skill requirements, educators sometimes are unwilling to leave classrooms and administrative assignments to observe production procedures, to study expected performance factors, or to view the latest in technology.

Increasing the Participation of Business and Industry in Career Education

Restoring the unity of school and work is a major objective of career education. It is a goal shared by many leaders in business, industry, and education. Many career education advocates would agree that education and the business/industry community are not well acquainted. Whether career education can maintain its momentum in the years ahead will, in the author's opinion, depend to a great extent on the continued acceptance and increased participation in career education efforts at both policy and implementation levels by the larger community, including business and industry. After several years of efforts to increase collaborative activities, basic questions remain unanswered. In some states, collaborative efforts of education and industry have been going on for several years, and many problems have been resolved. In others, major successes are not so apparent. In some local school districts, corporations and businesses have initiated cooperative programs which have resulted in highly successful partnerships. In others the linking of school and work must be accomplished incrementally, on a one-to-one basis.

A number of business and education organizations have initiated efforts to develop broad-based and sustained collaborative efforts to address problems that involve decision-making at both the policy and implementation levels. For example, the National Association of Manufacturers has supported the development of industry-education councils to bring all the educational resources within the community together to address the collaboration of industry and education. Basic to this concept is the idea that communications between industry and education can be strengthened when there are means for coordinating action and when plans for action can be mutually agreed upon and addressed. Activities of the council include instruction and curriculum development, career guidance, materials and service functions, and education and general management study and assessment. The National Association of Manufacturers has also taken a strong position in support of the appointment of persons at federal, state, and local levels of government and education to coordinate and encourage formal cooperation between business, industry, and education.

In another important effort, the National Association for Industry-Education Cooperation was created to mobilize the resources of industry to assist schools in developing programs relevant to the needs of industry. Emphasis is on improved communications between education and industry. It also sponsors community workshops and has published a placement service training manual to assist state departments of education and local agencies in developing job placement services programs. Along the same lines, the Chamber of Commerce of the United States has supported efforts to encourage increased education and business-education cooperation. For example, in 1973 this group sponsored a national conference on career education that resulted in a number of proposals for strengthening cooperation in the implementation of career education.

If increased participation of business and industry in career education programs is to continue, there are major changes that must occur. First, an improved legal basis for career education programs must be developed. As a preliminary step, attention must be given to the nature and extent of participation of business and industry in career education policy development and program implementation in each state.

Even more fundamentally, schools, business, and industry must seek consensus on the goals of education. A productive alliance between education and business must necessarily involve the participation of labor, parents, and other formal and informal groups. The total community is not likely to agree upon everything, but it can reach agreement on general purposes and priorities for action. While the schools should probably take the lead in developing a working consensus, this does not rule out the possibility that members of the business and industry community could set the stage for preliminary conversations and decision making.

In order for all this to come about, attitudinal changes within and among educational institutions must occur. Schools must no longer view themselves as merely educational institutions but must accept a greater role as social institutions. This broadened self-image portrays the essence of a career education concept wherein career education is infused into, not added onto, the curriculum. Within this framework, career education supports the goals of all education. It is an opportunity that is based in reality, and made necessary by reality. (Education, after all, is a human-service enterprise that is linked to the real world—the world that recognizes work as an integral part of living and surviving.)

State and federal laws must be examined. Laws that prohibit or complicate the cooperation of business, industry, and education must be altered. Many laws introduced in the past impede or prohibit industry-education cooperation; these must be studied and evaluated in terms of current curriculum goals, the high level of unemployment, and the renewed effort of education, industry, and labor to cooperate in the implementation of career education.

The role of the states in the implementation process deserves more stress than it has received in the past. The federal commitment to career education ideas is well known, but the states, which have the major responsibility for education, hold the key to the full implementation. Federal support has been substantial and will probably increase. However, when one considers the importance of potential state support for career education as compared to the commitment of the federal government, one can conclude that the success or failure of career education is in the hands of state leaders. State support and responsibility for education far exceeds that of the federal government; without a strong commitment at the state level, no education movement can survive. States will need help, as will the local districts; it will be the state and local linkages of business, industry, and education that will ensure the implementation of career education. Political and educational linkages within each state and among states must be strengthened to carry this out. Alternative approaches to the particular characteristics of each state need to be identified. Strategies for developing working partnerships among the various levels of policymaking in state government, business, and industry should be studied, with the ultimate goal of combining resources.

Above all, however, business and industry must be brought into the picture at an early stage. In fact, no institution of the community will stand for a minor role in this effort. Their roles must not begin after policy has been determined.

At another level, the career education movement could be the key to bringing about greater regional and national cooperation among states. Solutions to current problems related to certification and credentialing call for cooperation among the states in developing approaches. At the same time, better comprehensive data on business/industry/education cooperation must be available. Currently, there are hundreds of articles and reports that address numerous state and local issues, but much of this information is scattered, poorly catalogued, and not tailored to the needs of groups requiring different types of information.

Publicity is needed. The number-one problem in implementing mandated education legislation at the state level has to do with interpreting outcomes to the community. It may be trite to say that improved communications are essential, but the truth is that bad publicity or the lack of any publicity at all continues to hamper the implementation of career education. Career education is different from past efforts at educational reform. It did not originate with a particular design and proceed through a series of predictable activities calculated to sell a new idea. It has no national organization to serve as an advocacy group. It cuts across all levels of education and is dependent upon the support of many who assume various roles and responsibilities in our society. It is a strong movement, but it is not likely to survive without vigorous and persistent leadership. Consensus among decision-makers is a fundamental requirement, and a solid alliance between business, industry, and education is essential to its success.

BRIDGING ANOTHER GAP: BETWEEN BUSINESS AND EDUCATION

William McKnight, Jr.
Mr. McKnight is a publisher of educational textbooks and is currently serving as chairman of the State of Illinois Private Industry Council for Balance of State in the planning, implementing, and administration of CETA-Title VII. This article was written in 1978.

According to several recent surveys, inflation appears to be the number one worry of many American citizens. The President, Congress, labor leaders, business people—all address themselves to the problem of controlling inflation. What does inflation have to do with career education? What possible effect can career education have on the effort to control inflation? According to many business people, quite a bit! This conclusion is drawn as one reads and hears about business leaders attributing much of the cause of inflation to a decline in productivity, which, in turn, is partly caused by the on-the-job attitudes and behaviors of some of their employees.

Commonly cited on-the-job behavior problems include: lack of concern for craftsmanship; an inability to get along with co-workers and customers; and high levels of Friday and Monday absenteeism. These behaviors, which combine to reduce productivity, are symptoms which are in no small part attributable to a society that does not consider employability an educational goal. Couple these behaviors with generally negative attitudes toward work itself and the potential loss of productivity becomes truly alarming.

Redirecting Education
These circumstances should prompt business-oriented people to urge a redirection of educational investment in ways that will give a much greater emphasis to (1) education for

employment and (2) a better understanding of free market economics and business practice. Extensive unemployment among the 18- to 25-year-old population, generally negative attitudes toward work, and poorly developed reading and communication skills among many of the young unemployed point out that too many are failing to attain some very important educational objectives. Shouldn't we be asking why?

Several years ago former Congressman Roman Pucinski, in his book *The Courage to Change,* pointed to these same deficiencies in education. Pucinski stated: "Its content. . . too often has no immediate relationship to the adult world they (students) will face" (Pucinski and Hirsh 1971, pp. 6-7). At about the same time, then U. S. Commissioner of Education, Dr. Sidney Marland, Jr., proposed the establishment of career education as a national priority, describing this as a concept that says three things: (1) that career education will be a part of the curriculum for all students, not just some; (2) that it will continue throughout a youngster's stay in school, from first grade through senior high school and beyond, if he or she so elects; and (3) that every student leaving school will possess the skills necessary for a start at making a livelihood, even if the student leaves before completing high school (Marland 1971, p. 25). We then witnessed a flurry within educational circles to refocus academic subjects to include related occupational information; to provide a continuous and systematic guidance, counseling, and placement service; and to develop new curriculum materials based upon a number of occupational clusters. It was a good start.

Between 1970 and 1975 there was much meaningful research in human growth and career development. This helped identify factors that facilitate or impede a student's development of aspirations and plans of action that lead to a satisfying placement in the labor market and to the development of individual identity. In this period of time, there transpired some immediate curriculum change. It enhanced the implementation of career development concepts or at least broadened the curriculum in ways that gave emphasis not only to mastery of content but also to those processes so important to career development—occupational decision-making and self-understanding.

Career Education as Basic Education

Since 1975 the back-to-basics movement has seemed to dull some of the early enthusiasm for implementing career development concepts, even though educators and business people alike recognize that values and attitudes toward work are as much a part of the basics of our American heritage as are the three R's. Certainly readin', 'ritin', and 'rithmetic are vitally important to preparation for a satisfying and productive life. The current back-to-basics thrust is most appropriate. Just as essential, however, is preparation to apply skills, occupationally, in the most effective way possible. There is no sensible reasoning that says one emphasis must be submerged by the other.

The 1980s will surely be the time to give full attention to career education. We must realize that this emphasis can enable students to understand better the relationships between subjects offered and the real world of work. Unfortunately, some students view education as a series of unrelated self-contained courses. Career education, however, can help weld education into a unified experience.

Career education up to now seems to have been everybody's business and, consequently, nobody's business or responsibility. It has even appeared as a threat to some in the educational structure, even in its simplest but probably least desired application, described as infusion. This seemingly new relationship of work to subject matter is generally strange. It is not even discussed much in texts or teacher's guides. To the traditionalist, it can be construed as taking valuable time and focus from the acquisition of tool skills.

It is time to get the act together. Career education should be ready for a time-place-subject focus. It appears that an agreement is approaching on the two areas of skills and/or processes at the secondary school level—self-understanding and (career) decision-making. Whether a move toward a course or inserted units becomes formalized, the teaching/learning materials and methods are rapidly becoming available in highly refined and effective forms. Educators must accept these tools, thus taking on the responsibility of providing all youth with information on careers and the skills needed to select, prepare, and enter a career field.

Business Support and Leadership

To attain acceptance, in whatever the form of its implementation, career education must have support and leadership from many individuals, groups, and organizations beyond the school. In the private sector, the business community in particular can make tremendously important inputs; however, this can happen only if school people open the way and if individual representatives of labor and industry will take the time and the initiative to assist the career development phase of their local educational program.

Any business-oriented person, and especially those who have at some time expressed criticism of their schools' effort to prepare young people for the world of work, should feel the obligation to visit their schools. They should talk with administrators and teachers to know for certain what is being done and to help define what might be done to make that program even more effective. Only in this way can there be an effective, cooperative effort toward:

● Providing an understanding of personal interests, aptitudes, abilities, and skills as they relate to furthering the student's career and educational goals.

● Developing an understanding of the broad range of occupations; the organization of industry; and the methods of production, distribution, and services.

● Establishing attitudes and value judgments regarding worth and function of the individual and the world of work.

● Providing classroom activity relevant to the world of work.

● Providing adequate and up-to-date skill development and technical knowledge commensurate with the level of education the student pursues.

Career Awareness and Orientation

Looking back, acceptance of career education concepts across the country has been happening, albeit slowly. As long ago as the early 1960s, there was a thrust to change vocational education's emphasis to focus upon the people who need the skills rather than upon the occupations that need skilled people. Prior to passage of the 1968 amendments to the 1963 Vocational Education Act, the Advisory Council on Vocational Education brought attention to a career development concept that even then was emerging. They said that "orientation and assistance in vocational choice may often be more valid determinants of employment success, and therefore more profitable uses of educational funds, than specific skill training" (Advisory Council on Vocational Education 1968, p. 49). This suggestion in no way downgrades the value of, and need for, job skill courses. In the past ten years we have seen vast improvement in both course selection and course offerings in an expanded vocational program.

Vocational education is constantly adjusting to the ever changing employment needs of our society, but some weaknesses have remained. One such weakness is the lack of wholehearted support (meaning funding) for pre-vocational courses. In junior high school industrial arts and home economics courses, for example, all students should be given opportunity to explore occupational areas and clusters before they are asked to choose high school subjects (thereby, making vocational decisions). Similarly, all elementary students should be involved in the kind of systematic activity that would teach fundamental principles and concepts about the market system, business and industry, and the nature and role of work in our society. This might lead them into more meaningful occupational explorations when they reach the junior high school program. It has become abundantly clear that if vocational supervisors must fund this type of pre-vocational course by withdrawing vocational funding support from existing skill development courses at grade ten and above, it just will not happen. Additional legislative authorization and appropriations, either state or federal, directed toward orientation and assistance in making vocational choices, as identified by the Advisory Council ten years ago, is probably the only way this will happen.

Need for Implementation Funds

Millions of dollars have been appropriated by Congress for research and development of more effective curriculum and instructional materials that will help teachers attain career education goals. What seems not to be understood very clearly is that past experience demonstrates there will be no truly widespread implementation of these new program concepts, however good they may be and however wanted by local school districts, until state and/or federal funding is made available for teacher preparation and to purchase materials and equipment to get these programs started. It is the relatively high start-up cost of education programs that is the deterrent, not continuing cost. A great amount of time and federal money has been directed toward inventing more and more wheels, while too little has been appropriated to get those wheels rolling.

Most business people realize and understand that change comes about more slowly in education than in business. The tempo, however, can improve if new thoughts and outside experiences are provided by lay persons who care enough about the school program to want to do more than just criticize or remain apathetic; yet too seldom are such working partnerships realized. Educators assume business people are too busy. Business people assume educators will think they just want to meddle if they step forward without invitation. It is a gap that can and should be bridged.

Roles for Business

There are many ways the business community can assist schools in their attempts to make career education an important part of the continuing education process. A few such ways would be:

● **Help obtain supporting legislation.** School boards and administrative personnel can certainly use the business community's leverage in directing attention of legislators toward realization of the economic benefits that eventually accrue from a viable career education emphasis. Lacking funding support from state legislatures, local schools having tight budgets are hard pressed in trying to implement and/or expand a career development program in the middle school or junior high school. State support is essential.

The state of Arizona provides an excellent example of what can happen when business, labor, and the professions join educators in a combined effort to let legislative representatives know what career education can mean to the welfare of citizens of the state. Starting with a $2 million appropriation in 1972, and increasing to a top funding for career education of $4.8 million in 1975, Arizona legislators have appropriated a total of $19 million in five years for such implementing necessities as teacher retraining, acquisition of career-oriented instructional materials, and like essentials. This combined emphasis was not all money directed. In one recent year (1976), 6,552 guest speakers visited classrooms to share knowledge and information about the world of work. The entire range of career families was represented by these speakers.

All of this happened because an enlightened business-industry group helped spark action, working closely with Superintendent Carolyn Warner, Arizona Department of Education, and her staff, to keep legislators fully informed about both need and outcomes. The Arizona effort formula was simple. They first agreed upon what was wanted as a community (education, business, labor, professions). Then they set about informing legislators. They did not promise anything career education could not deliver, lower unemployment, for example. They did point out career development concepts that have worked, like cooperative education and work-study. They made it a point to indoctrinate all lobbyists on career education's objectives, helping them see what the payoff can be to their specific interests. They developed a corps of friends of career education among persons who are around the legislature. They simply told the career education story where it counts. They now distribute quarterly and annual reports to legislators, detailing what is happening.

Until more funding is directed into the school program below grade ten for implementation of career exploration courses, whether it comes from state appropriations as in Arizona or from federal sources, very little career education will interweave classroom activity at these strategic levels of instruction. This level of funding cannot be achieved without support from business, labor, and the professions—eventual beneficiaries of career education.

● **Recognize and fully support cooperative education opportunity.** A very effective way the business community can aid and abet career education is to participate wholeheartedly in cooperative education. In many regions of the country, cooperative education has become the fastest growing phase of the career development emphasis. Cooperative education bridges the gap between school and work for many young people. There are many patterns, but most typical is the program that enables the student to spend half days in school and half days on the job. Such features as a job interview, relationships with fellow workers, adjusting to supervisory discipline, and the experience of live work for compensation make for a valuable experience not available through the textbook or typical classroom activity. Other types of cooperative education involve short-term (paid and unpaid) employment as well as opportunity for observation. Work experience unrelated to the school program also produces educational outcomes that may be individually meaningful for future career roles.

In cooperative education, the school's responsibilities to the student have been discharged partially through a daily world of work class experience of one period. Besides individual tutoring or assistance in unique job-related information and/or skills, these classes have provided group instruction in the business of living as an adult in America. The content commonly includes working together skills, interpersonal relationships, personal budgeting, banking services, borrowing money, insurance, social security, laws of the work place, consumer skills, and taxes. The significance of this listing is its uniqueness to cooperative education—the specific preparation of young people with the skills of living in contemporary society while they acquire earning skills.

● **Provide employment experience or business orientation for local teachers.** In-service programs of varying duration, organized and sponsored jointly by business agencies, like the Chamber of Commerce, that work with school administrators, provide a series of experiences which will acquaint employer representatives with the school program and will enable classroom teachers to understand better the research, finance, marketing, distribution, personnel, and administrative functions of a business organization. Planned discussion sessions and visits to businesses within the community over an extended period of time accomplish this. Planned tours and actual employment of teachers in the summer vacation period are other techniques which the business community can use to enlighten school people about the employment milieu.

● **Support the school's guidance, placement, and follow-up services.** This type of cooperative effort can assist in maintaining data banks: on jobs available; on job openings; on youth and adults who wish to be employed or reemployed; and on aids for the design of new programs and improvement of existing programs that changing employment opportunity may impose. For years college and university admissions personnel—the *employing* institutions—have devoted countless hours to work with school guidance people in pursuit of the college-bound, high school graduates. It makes good sense for managers of business enterprises to be just as concerned about the work-bound graduate.

● **Speak out about business and tell it like it is.** What business people can do, perhaps better than school people can do alone, is help young people gain a proper understanding of the importance of their attitude toward work. Young people sometimes reject the system only because they do not understand it. As Peter Drucker has suggested, these criticisms by youth actually obscure their real concerns with the burden of decision among so many avenues of opportunity open to them. Drucker states: "The society of organizations forces the individual to ask of himself: 'Who am I? What do I want to be? What do I put into life, and what do I want to get out of it?' " (Drucker 1968, p. 248). Those within the system who provide these many avenues of opportunity should provide students with factually helpful answers.

Summary

Business has important inputs to offer young people as they learn about themselves as well as the what and why of our free economy. The formal career education program provides the ideal forum for this kind of discussion.

Business and industry have every reason to become deeply involved in education—and especially career education. Business people should want to respond to the alarming statistic that in any one year about two million young people leave formal education lacking skills adequate to enter the labor market at a level commensurate with their academic and intellectual promise. Many leave with no marketable skills whatever. Such fruitless effort wastes education dollars. There is an even greater loss in the lack of confidence and self-esteem and in the feeling of alienation these young people have as so many of them drift toward becoming future statistics in unemployment, welfare, and sometimes even crime.

This situation should stir desire within each of us to do something constructive personally to change such statistics. One giant step would be to make career education a part of the school curriculum for all students throughout their academic experience. There should be a particularly strong emphasis on that phase of career development that helps them explore occupational opportunity early enough so that there is time to make studied choices of skill courses based upon known facts about occupations, personal interests, and aptitudes—a la Sidney Marland's initial concept.

Earlier in this century most students knew why they were in school and where they were headed. As school populations have increased and our technologically based society has become more sophisticated, many of those who pass through the formalized educational experiences we provide today seem more alien to the workaday world than were students several decades ago. For these persons, education may have become a goal for its own sake or perhaps for the easy living it is thought to assure. Others pass through and exit with nothing happening it seems—not skill acquisition, college preparation, or job competence. Society's problems, control of inflation among them, are now making it apparent that an understanding of the world of work, systematically preparing for entry at levels appropriate to one's talents and aspirations, and developing appreciation for the work ethic are important societal goals. That is why career education must be made an integral part of the educational system—a program of instruction formulated specifically to facilitate the process of career development.

POSSIBILITIES AND SHORTCOMINGS IN CAREER EDUCATION

Eugenia Kemble

Eugenia Kemble is special assistant to the president of the American Federation of Teachers (AFT) and is responsible for program development and policy on early childhood education, education for the handicapped, career education and school finance. This article was written in 1978.

How education relates to preparation for work has been a topic of long-standing concern to educators. The latest wave of interest in this complex issue began in 1970 when Sidney Marland, Jr., then commissioner of education, coined the term career education. Since then, policy initiatives having to do with education's role in preparing young people for work have broadened to include work-study programs and even the youth training programs supported by the billion dollar Youth Employment and Demonstration Projects Act. This law has added an education-and-work dimension to the Comprehensive Employment and Training Programs administered by the Labor Department.

The real issue, no matter what the terminology, is where should formal education stop and work begin? What is really best for young people in terms of their long-range preparation for life—a life that in our rapidly changing economy may require holding several jobs? Our concern is that career education, and all of the other work-oriented education programs based on a similar set of assumptions, continue to be grounded in a full education in basic academic subjects. Whatever it is that career education contributes to a child's education ought indeed to be a real addition and not detract from academic preparation.

This is not to say that teaching students more about careers is not necessary. The more we examine how much high school students know about the world of work and careers, the more we see how poorly informed they are. The most recent evidence of this comes from a study done for the National Assessment of Educational Progress. While the data collection for this study was done before large numbers of career education programs were put into operation, its results undoubtedly continue to be significant. Of the sample examined, only 35% of the 17-year-olds had talked to a school counselor about their career plans. Although 70% could name at least one skill or ability that would be needed for the job of their choice, only 49% were able to name two or more.

Despite these glaring shortcomings, guidance services are all too often the first to be cut in a budget crisis or to be pared to the bone when a school bond issue goes down. The American Federation of Teachers (AFT) estimates that our secondary schools now have on the average only about half the guidance counselors they really need. Even given guidance services, there is much more career information and direct exposure to the real work life that could be offered by our schools. Students need to know occupational projections related to careers they might pursue. They need to know the specific skills required by any job. They need to know about the role and function of labor unions and what they can expect from union membership. Some students need to see the relationship of occupational skills to academic skills before they will be motivated to learn to read, write, and compute.

Insofar as career education is aimed at meeting these needs, the American Federation of Teachers views it as an educational benefit that will add tremendously to the services schools provide. Obviously our support for an emphasis of this sort involves making hard choices. Explaining these choices leads to a discussion of some of the problems career education has posed thus far.

Running through all the reports and rhetoric on career education is the idea that high unemployment among youth is somehow related to inadequate educational preparation—that schools are not providing each student with a saleable skill after high school. The logic of this argument then moves on to suggest that the real burden for high youth unemployment falls on the schools and that if only the schools had the right, relevant program, all high school graduates would immediately find a place in the labor force.

This line of thinking, leading to the creation of new career education programs, places an unfair burden on the schools for unemployment problems they did not create. Students who are attracted to such programs on this basis will be disastrously misled into thinking that training in a saleable skill will assure them a job. This has never been career education's interest or claim. Skills won't sell unless there is a market for them. In fact, students who short-circuit general education in search of occupational training will find themselves lining up for jobs behind those with more education whether the job market is open or tight. In short, youth employment is more a matter of economic policy than it is educational policy, and although students may benefit from some exposure to job skills, they should not be lured into thinking that this is a good substitute for basic grounding in academic skills. Career education programs that involve the substitution of on-site or hands-on experience for basic academic subjects may seriously shortchange students in their search for qualifications that will enable them to compete in the job market.

There are two other troublesome rationales used by career education advocates. One is the cynical idea that the labor force as well as the ranks of the unemployed, are increasingly over-educated and that, correspondingly, too much education is a bad thing. It is hardly surprising that this idea, as well as the popularity of career education programs based on it, has taken hold during a period when unemployment is disastrously high. Whatever the problems of credentialed degree holders in finding jobs that match their qualifications, they are still in a better competitive position than those with less education. There may be legitimate questions as to whether the job payoff is worth the cost, but then, job payoffs are not the only payoffs to consider. Education is not just for the purpose of job qualification, and its benefits should never be viewed exclusively in those terms.

A second concern with the thinking behind career education thus far is the romance many of its supporters seem to be having with work place experience. According to reports received from AFT members, it seems apparent that most career education programs afford students exposure to primarily low-level jobs—as waitresses, clerks, auto mechanics, busboys, and the like. We hope educators will encourage states to support career education efforts that afford exposure to a broader range of career possibilities. Otherwise career education programs will be subject to the criticism that they encourage tracking and have the affect of narrowing rather than broadening the educational experience and the career aspirations of students.

The AFT also has more specific concerns relating to the career education thrust of the past administration. The employer-based career education model developed by Sidney Marland, Jr., and the Work Experience and Career Exploration Program funded by the Department of Labor contained elements to which the AFT and the AFL-CIO strongly objected. No career education programs should encourage the violation of child labor laws, allow for the payment of subminimum wages, compromise health or safety laws related to work, or allow for the displacement of adult workers by students.

One major educational phenomenon of the past two years that must be brought into this discussion is the reported decline of standardized achievement test scores among our public school population. A number of highly respected studies have reported on this development, though none have come up with definitive explanations. One of the most important of these, *Achievement Test Score Decline: Do We Need to Worry?* by Annegret Harnischfeger and David E. Wiley, speculates on the possibility that a part of the cause for decline comes from shifts in the curriculum. "The strongest explanatory power seems to come from curricular changes. Our gross data indicate a considerable enrollment decline in academic courses. Secondary pupils have been taking fewer courses in general English and mathematics. But also enrollment in typical college preparatory courses, such as algebra, first year foreign language, and physics, is decreasing," they say (Harnischfeger and Wiley 1975).

Although there is no evidence to indicate specifically or conclusively that career education programs are even partly responsible for this, it seems more than simple coincidence that emphasis on career education as well as other nontraditional curricular areas is rising while achievement test scores are falling.

Assuming that tests are measuring what we want them to measure, and assuming that English and math should and will continue to be basic elements in any solid curriculum, we think that policymakers should address themselves to the very real question of whether career education programs supplement or substitute for basic curriculum. More specifically, financial pressures on education budgets are causing cutbacks in regular school programs, while career education programs conducted at the work place with little or no cost to the school system are offered in their places.

Another major concern relates to the governance of public education. One of the ideas that has been popularized of late is the notion that career education, which involves a closer relationship between business and the schools could be better supervised by education and work councils. The AFT has been seriously concerned with the possibility that new structures for implementing career education programs may, in fact, allow the private sector to take on some of the responsibility of education. Any look at the nature of business involvement in these programs can't help but raise the suspicion that what business might really want from career education is public subsidy for its own training programs.

Problems like the ones presented here have been documented by a number of AFT locals and state federations. Their responses to a survey dramatize the problems as well as some of the positive aspects of career education:

> The programs pull students away from academic classes during the regular day. . . . There is poor supervision of both students and program. . . . Our school board is on the bandwagon. Other required courses for graduation have been dropped. . . . but career education and work experience have not been cut. . . . There is only one counselor for every 300 students; they are terribly overworked. . . . Funds have been channeled away from the regular program. Students see it as easy credit for pay while other classes such as languages, science, history, and English are cut and can't fill their enrollments. . . . Students can graduate very early because of work experience. . . . We are suspicious because of the board's reactions and emphasis on this while they are cutting regular programs. There is much resentment.

From Illinois:

> The program is beautifully conceived and beautifully presented on paper. . . . The implementation is totally missing. . . . Career education in Illinois exists only on paper and in brochures . . .

From Florida:

> To my knowledge the student goes to class for three class periods where he is taught math and English. Then he works for the second half of the day.

From California:

> In their junior and senior years, students can earn a maximum of 2 credits a year by working at least 10 hours a week. These credits are in place of credits that would otherwise be earned in a classroom. . . . I know there are violations of child labor laws and inadequate enforcement which affects students working in nonsupervised jobs.

From New Jersey:

> Strengths of the program are: low class/teacher ratios and the provision of guidance services; the value of experience in the world of work; the making of more realistic career selection; and the availability of experienced teachers. Weaknesses include: the fact that there is no coordination among programs and that there is no one person in charge of these programs. The central administration lacks knowledge in this area. . . . At the middle school level students are given full credit as a major subject(s) for work in this area. At the high school level students may earn 15 credits per year toward their graduation requirement.

From Texas:

> Usually the work is menial and unrelated to any particular field of study (students serve as waitresses, dime store clerks, busboys, etc.) . . . in elementary programs career education was given priority over reading, history, and music.

From New Hampshire:

> We lack the number of guidance counselors needed for the students . . . one vocational guidance position was created in the past year but more than one is needed for a 3,000-pupil high school.

From Maryland:

> The shortened day for work study has eliminated teaching positions and possibly lowered academic standards. A student cannot participate in a class without being present.

These descriptions, when coupled with the legitimate issues and concerns that have been raised by the AFL-CIO, have led the AFT to make a number of recommendations with regard to career education programs. At its 1976 convention, the AFT passed a resolution urging its state federations and locals to participate in the development of these programs using the following guidelines.

● Expanded guidance and counseling services must be provided to all students. Career education programs which offer additional guidance—which expand upon the basic curriculum and which are aimed at career awareness—should be supported. Teachers may wish to use job resource persons in these programs, but such persons should be chosen by the teacher and be under his or her supervision. Nonprofessionals should not be used in professional roles. Such programs should include accurate treatment of the role of labor unions and should deal with unions as well as employers in making job placements. In fact, such placement services should be expanded.

● Alternative programs which have a career orientation may be provided for students who cannot function in, or who do not obtain benefit from, regular school programs. While some of these may involve work experience, they must be carefully constructed so that they are clearly the responsibility of the public school system and are aimed at broadening rather than narrowing youth's educational experience.

● Where career education programs involve any kind of experience at the job site, they should be tried only in industries where there is full employment and where no adult workers will be displaced. These programs must supplement a basic education and not act as a substitute for it.

● The AFT will resist the creation of programs which involve watering down child labor laws, providing for subminimum wages, lowering the school-leaving age, or weakening health and safety laws related to work.

● The AFT strongly opposes career education programs that involve turning over some of the responsibility for public education to the private sector. Cooperative education and work community councils should in no way undermine the authority of publicly elected or appointed school boards. The AFT opposes voucher plans that would subject both education and its consumers to the whims and prejudices of the marketplace.

In addition to the guidelines, there were a number of specific proposals recommended by the convention delegates. These were based on a belief that the most hopeful career education programs have not yet been tried:

● Job training programs which build upon a basic education by combining further academic experiences with on-the-job experiences should be expanded. These might include internship programs for teachers, career ladder programs for paraprofessionals and others, as well as apprenticeship programs.

• More information should be presented on job availability, occupational projections, job access, etc. Information which is available should be compiled and disseminated in some useful form.

• Adult education programs must be expanded. Such programs should service all adult educational needs whether they be for job training or retraining or for personal enrichment. They may take the form of worker sabbaticals, paid educational leave, deferred educational opportunity, and the like. Programs that provide workers with recognized credentials should be available to them. Programs now offered by institutions of higher education that provide for career training should not be cut simply because they are expensive.

• Restrictions against the use of public schools by adults must be re-examined. Special programs which allow adults to return to school to complete a high school program should be implemented.

Although the American Federation of Teachers has been skeptical about career education up until now, we still have hopes that positive changes which would redirect the program could make it an important addition to the work of schools. The Elementary and Secondary Career Education Act of 1977, which authorized over $400 million over a period of four years for career education programs, could provide the basis for this redirection. Much will depend on how local educators decide to use these funds, however, since the law is very general and unrestrictive. If those who develop career education programs could make sure that their thrust does not amount to the replacement of academic subjects with work experience, and if their commitment to expanding guidance and counseling services could be strengthened, career education would get more enthusiastic support from the American Federation of Teachers.

CAREER EDUCATION STRATEGIES: A U.A.W. VIEW

Carroll M. Hutton
Carroll Hutton is director of the education department of UAW. He has also served with the AFL-CIO and is a member of the National Task Force on Career Education. This article was written in 1978.

Introduction

Organized labor's role in the evolving career education movement has developed greatly in recent years. Reviewing the steps in this development will lead to a better understanding of labor's current position. It is hoped that better understanding will be the development of an improved working relationship between labor unions and career education advocates.

Overview

Career education can and should be considered as one of the methods to promote constructive changes in our educational system; however, the concept cannot be extended to operational and implementation strategies unless those strategies have the active support of a broad cross section of our mixed and complex society. Thus, organized labor must be recognized as a segment of that cross section. Those who might argue against this recognition should be reminded that union membership in the United States now exceeds 20 million persons. Multiplying this number by the average family size yields a total of over 80 million persons who are directly linked to labor unions.

Prior to the passage of the Career Education Incentive Act (Public Law 95-207), there was active support for the legislation from community leaders and from many of the so-called special interest groups. Some of those special interest groups have widely divergent, and even adversary, relationships in their backgrounds; yet they rallied and made their wishes known to our lawmakers.

That type of broad-based community support would not have been possible if any of the powerful and outspoken segments of our society had actively opposed career education. The voice of organized labor, along with other voices, was heard loud and clear during the lobbying efforts which preceded passage of the Career Education Incentive Act. Positive legislative support for the Career Education Incentive Act was achieved despite mixed feelings within the ranks of organized labor.

Initial Hostilities Toward Career Education from Organized Labor

From the time Dr. Sidney Marland, Jr., first coined the term career education in 1970, the views of organized labor were largely ignored. To support that contention, a person need only review Dr. Marland's book, *Career Education, A Proposal for Reform.* Some 22 pages in that book reflect the views of business and industry, but positions of organized labor are dealt with only superficially. That relationship has changed under the leadership of Dr. Kenneth Hoyt, the present director of the U.S. Office of Career Education. Dr. Marland's handling of labor unions seemed to reflect the commonly inherent bias of administrative or management philosophies, as they relate to labor unions. While this bias was not consistent in all areas during the evolvement of the career education concept, it was prevalent at the federal level during the early years. In many cases labor unions were invited to participate in developing career education after policy formulation had already begun. This reflects the classical, yet archaic, labor-management relationship: first come management decisions and then labor union concurrence or opposition to those decisions. Put another way, this philosophy is an extension of the view that management teams are supposed to be the moving parties, and labor union representatives only have the right to grieve or defend against adverse impact of management's action.

Labor unions, with some justification, had strong suspicions that this philosophy prevailed during career education's early formative years. With little exception during those years, there was only minimal opportunity provided for organized labor to put forth its views about career education.

Even today, labor union activity with career education is far from ideal. Lack of direct representation from organized labor on the National Advisory Council for Career Education (NACCE) is an example of a gnawing and festering aggravation to labor unions. Despite the documented fact that organized labor has made major contributions to our public education system, the acceptance of labor unions in all phases of career education policymaking still leaves much to be desired.

Examples of Positive and Constructive Working Relationships Between Career Education and Labor Unions

Fortunately, some unions in certain areas have had an opportunity to participate. Experiences of the United Rubber Workers (URW) in Akron, Ohio, and the United Automobile, Aerospace, and Agricultural Implement Workers of America (UAW) in Michigan, are two such examples. Akron, Ohio, is the location of a substantial part of the membership of the United Rubber Workers. Because of this, their potential strength as an influential partner in career education was recognized. The recognition was belated but, nonetheless, it did occur. Since 1975, their relationship with local education has resulted in cooperative exploratory and planning activity, thereby producing URW sponsorship of in-service training sessions for classroom teachers. Other correlating activity is also taking place. The constructive relationship between the URW and local educators in Akron, Ohio, may well be a model for others to follow, build, and improve upon.

In 1974, Michigan passed a career education law which established the Michigan Career Education Advisory Commission. The statute clearly provided for participation on the commission from the broad community, including organized labor. The commission membership has representation from the American Federation of Labor-Congress of Industrial Organizations (AFL-CIO), United Auto Workers (UAW), Michigan Federation of Teachers (MFT), and the Michigan Educational Association (MEA).

Many constructive efforts have come from this Michigan commission. As a by-product of the commission's activity with career education in Michigan, the UAW issued a policy statement in January of 1976, endorsing the commission's career education philosophy and expressing a willingness to work with educators and others toward its successful implementation.

Although the Akron accomplishments have not been specifically duplicated, the relationship between educators and labor unions in Michigan has a solid foundation. Cooperative implementation strategies can be freely developed from this solid foundation.

Looking Ahead

Several significant activities have taken place which should give impetus to organized labor's participation with career education. The career education mini-conference for labor union representatives, conducted by the U. S. Office of Career Education, reviewed and explored policies and practices of organized labor as they would apply to career education. Problem areas were discussed. Conferees reinforced positions taken by labor unions in opposition to changing child labor laws or diluting minimum wage standards under the guise of furthering career education. Organized labor will continue to oppose such efforts and any other activity which jeopardizes the job security of the existing work force. The belief was again expressed by labor union representatives who attended the conference that viable, legal alternatives can be developed which would achieve the goals of career education. Rather than spend time discussing conflict areas, the view was expressed at the conference that positive and agreeable activity should be explored, with the objective of developing programmatic strategies. Strong deterrents to student hands-on activities have also surfaced. These are the current health and safety laws, restrictions imposed by worker's compensation laws, and the increased risk of public liability lawsuits. Local education agencies (LEAs) placed themselves in great jeopardy without knowledgeable administration and supervision of student field trips to work sites. A conference conclusion suggested that LEAs should contact central state labor bodies before embarking into the no-man's-land of student hands-on activities.

During the exchange of views and experiences with Dr. Hoyt at the mini-conference, several examples of cooperative activities between labor unions and education were discussed. In addition to the experiences of the United Rubber Workers and the United Auto Workers, other conferees cited examples such as significant assistance to LEAs in obtaining CETA funds for certain career education activities, the providing of classrooms with resource persons, and access to occupational information.

Labor union representatives, either in direct contact with LEAs or through advisory committee structures, need to lend assistance with:

- Establishment of goals for career education at federal, state, and local levels.
- Identification of desirable performance indications or learning objectives for students.
- Participation with in-service training sessions or workshops.
- Recruitment of a cadre of resource personnel from organized labor who can supplement guidance activities.
- Expansion of cooperative and distributive educational programs.
- Development of alternatives to full-scale student hands-on activities.

Conclusion

Recent policies, statements, and positions taken by organized labor have, with little exception, supported career education. Their current positions are consistent with their aggressive historical support for improvement in public education. Views of labor unions have not begun and ended with applicability only to their own members. Rather, they reflect sympathy for problems of poor people, minorities, and other educationally disadvantaged segments of our society.

Hostilities displayed by labor unions during career education's formative years were caused by the frustrations of exclusion from policymaking. They were reacting to policy which did not include their concerns. They were reacting to decisions made for them by groups outside the labor movement. In areas where organized labor was included from the beginning with policymaking decisions, labor unions have participated in community partnership arrangements which have led to cooperative activity. This has included lobbying for career education legislation and funding.

Unions are cognizant of the tangible benefits that implementation of career education should produce. Improving student performance in areas of career development, as well as academic and vocational skills, is a welcome and refreshing change to some of the current educational objectives. As long as the career education movement stays on this track and provides for input from organized labor, it can expect support from labor unions and, in particular, the UAW.

CAREER EDUCATION UPDATE

Sidney P. Marland, Jr.
Dr. Marland served as United States commissioner of education from 1970 to 1972. During that time he was instrumental in the development and implementation of landmark legislation for career education. From 1972 to 1973 he served as the nation's first statutory assistant secretary of education in the Department of Health, Education, and Welfare, and from 1973 to 1978 was president of the College Entrance Examination Board. The following speech was delivered at the Commissioner's National Conference on Career Education in 1976.

We are gathered today around a single idea that has brought us together in common purpose. That idea is career education. It is not a new idea. It was not a new idea in 1971. It has been an underlying concept of civilized people's self-development since the beginning. That is, *growing up to work.* But somehow, over the generations, education had come to mean schooling—and learning had come to mean something that happens only in schools and colleges—and growing up to work was something that happened *outside* schools and colleges, and never the twain should meet. Career education's message was, and remains, a sincere call for reform that says the two are rightly inseparable, that work is not mean or repulsive, and that education has a very essential part to play at all grades and for all ages in helping people ready themselves for work—intellectually, socially, economically, emotionally, and spiritually. The reform applies to the schools and colleges, but it also asks for reform in those other places that contribute so much to the education of our people *outside* the classrooms. It asks for new commitments from business, labor and industry, from governments at federal, state and local levels. It asks for a larger order of humaneness from the American people altogether as they attempt to enlighten the lives of others, especially the young, through better education—not only that which happens in schools and colleges.

Let us talk first about work itself as a proper component of education. Work has been related to education by official definition from the United States Commissioner of Education and by the esteemed chief governmental officer in career education, Dr. Kenneth B. Hoyt, whose imaginativeness and intellectual leadership have been heavily invested in this conference. That statement reads as follows: *Career education is the totality of experiences through which one learns about and prepares to engage in work as part of his or her way of living.* You will note the phrase "totality of experiences." That does not mean the experiences that happen from 9 to 3 in classrooms alone or, indeed, solely in the laboratories and libraries of our universities. But I make bold to say that the primary responsibility for orchestrating what Hoyt calls "the totality of experiences" resides in the formal education structure. Somebody has to be in charge of education, and I do not think it ought to be industry or labor or business or "the feds" or City Hall. It is a function of teachers and professors, school administrators and trustees, and state education departments. If there is to be a larger place for those other parts of our society—and I hold there must be—the *initiative* for bringing them together rests with the educators. (I will come back to that challenge.)

One of the first goals of the career education philosophy is to make the idea of work understandable—even by the very young in our elementary schools. Oscar Wilde once quipped, "Work is the curse of the drinking class!" Not so. Work is something that all of us do, whether for profit, for psychic fulfillment, for leisure fun, or through compassion and care for others. But work we do, or we are vegetables. All kinds of work are to be honored, from the honest and necessary ministrations of the cobbler and the window cleaner to the awesome skills of the computer analyst and the surgeon. Work, career education teaches, is good, necessary, and joyful. And people—young people especially—ought to know much more about it in its thousands of different modes and know much more about themselves, their aptitudes and their competencies of work. Elliot Richardson, of numerous distinctions and cabinet posts, in pleading for their engagement in career education, recently told a meeting of industrial leaders assembled by the Department of Commerce: "There is no satisfaction in life that equals that of work well done. Of all the things that satisfy human cravings work is the largest. You cannot eat eight hours a day; you cannot love eight hours a day; you cannot fish eight hours a day (not every day unless that is your livelihood). Work is a satisfaction that no one else can give you—and no one can take away." A recent penetrating (and saddening) analysis of the current economic woes of Great Britain made recently by the *New York Times* contained, I believe, some important insights into work, labor, and society. Class distinctions, based in part on occupation and career, permeate the faltering economy in England. Many of the brightest young men and women go to Oxford or Cambridge and from there into teaching, the foreign office, science, and finance, but rarely into corporations, manufacturing, services or sales. "Trade isn't something a gentleman does," one writer notes. "It's a matter of the dirty class and the clean class," says a professor. "This is the oldest class division the world has known." I would be the last in the world to oversimplify a complex situation like the one in Britain, but I would suggest that the nub of our problem is that, for whatever reasons, we in this country have stratified and separated work and seek to isolate work from learning and labor from the liberal arts. Schools and colleges, with the collaboration—not merely the cooperation—of business, labor, industry, and government are now, here at this place, dealing with that proposition. It is changing education in America.

Business

Let us look at business first. There are at least three good reasons under the self-interest category that make sense for business to be a major collaborator in the career education enterprise:

- You help develop better manpower for your own operational needs.
- You create an improved environment for your own work force and facilities by reducing unemployment, welfare, and their related social evils.
- You improve the purchasing power of the consumer to buy your goods and services.

These are fairly straightforward, honest and respectable reasons for joining in this education effort. But there is another reason that does not relate solely to business's bottom line, and it is the best reason of all—there is a new sense of *selfless social concern* on the part of business to make a better and fuller life for all people. Enlightened leaders in business and industry have begun to take an active part in the education of our people, not merely as taxpayers, but as working companions to teachers and professors. This kind of teamwork is becoming more commonplace and this attitude has been lucidly and powerfully expressed by the U. S. Chamber of Commerce in its 1975 publication entitled *Career Education: What It Is and Why We Need It.*

Irving Shapiro, chairman and executive officer of Dupont, stated recently, "While we as a nation are concerned about the continuing high level of unemployment, we are more concerned when we realize that half of the unemployed are under age 20. These young people do not know about jobs and do not have the skills for jobs. The solution in finding more jobs must come from the *private sector,* not government. It is bad enough that the government already employs one out of every six workers." Mr. Shapiro was pleading for a larger commitment from business to confront this enormous chasm in our present state of affairs. That chasm cannot contain much longer the flood of social unrest and human frustration that derives from 20% youth unemployment and double that for minorities. I believe that business—large business—is ready to join hands with educators in creating an educational environment that will provide real work experience as a part of the educational system and will ameliorate the disjuncture between manpower needs and developed people.

I am among those who maintain that work experience is a legitimate part of the curriculum for every high school student; that such experience should be viewed as a laboratory course of equal value with chemistry, biology, or physical education; that we should shake off the chains and rituals of a six-hour school day, or a five-day week, or a 180-day year in viewing the work-laboratory curriculum. As a legitimate part of the curriculum, the learner would not be paid. The business enterprise should be reimbursed for its modest, out-of-pocket costs by the schools to make clear that a variety of legitimate experiences are assured and that the business does not have to justify getting "its money's worth" from an entry level employee on the payroll doing repetitive tasks.

This does not preclude the appropriateness of cooperative work programs for pay, for work-study arrangements, or for paid apprenticeship training. These and other opportunities for earning while learning would *follow* the work laboratory requirement which could be fulfilled during any of the high school years. How does this relationship between the schools and the work place take form? There can be a multitude of forms, deriving from the initiative and creativity of the parties. One example: Three or four years ago the Security Pacific Bank in San Francisco went to the superintendent of schools and asked, "What can we do to help?" The superintendent replied, "Can you provide 12 places for unpaid real-work experience in your bank for high school students interested in careers in banking?" Today there are 400 California students in Security Pacific Banks across the state. Under supervision they first spend a 30-hour period in exploring numerous banking functions. They then are offered the option of a 90-hour period on one or two specific jobs, again without pay, in what I have called the work laboratory. The schools award five academic credits for this laboratory learning. The bank is happy, finding that many students choose careers in banking. The schools are happy. The students are happy. This model, in one form or another, is being carried out in a number of businesses. I propose that every business, large and small, can find high satisfaction, good public relations, and excellent cost benefits from such a program for every student passing through our secondary schools, public and private, for whatever period of days or hours that the parties determine.

The academic work of the student in history, mathematics, English composition, and science, in the presence of sensitive teachers is made compatible with the banking experience.

Labor

Now let us look for a moment at organized labor in its relationship to career education. The picture is less clear. There are those who say organized labor is opposed to career education. Not so, in my judgment. Organized labor, over the centuries—and I include the esteemed guilds of 15th Century England as historic forebears to our American labor system—were practicing career education long before the Smith-Hughes Act of 1917, for which American labor was a prime mover. Since its beginning, the labor movement in America has been a champion of education for all—long before that idea was fashionable.

But if labor appears, in the eyes of some, to resist career education, there is good reason. The conventional alliance between business and education, which I have cited, has tended to by-pass labor. Labor in America chooses not to be by-passed. Labor is also very sophisticated in the realities of the statistics of unemployment. When Mr. Shapiro of Dupont rightly and responsibly deplores the statistics reflecting unemployment of the young, labor, quite appropriately, can say, yes, that is a problem, but we are concerned about unemployment among the old and the not so old—the rank and file who are the labor movement. Any educational reform, any *change* in our system that threatens them is wrong. Students must not be exploited at low pay to displace mature workers, even in the name of career education.

I do not see displacement of workers by learners. I do see the historic role of labor rallying again to education, including the career education concept, so long as labor is a part of the design and not a victim of the co-opting process after the design is formulated.

In Bridgeport, Connecticut, last year, at the initiative of Bridgeport's Central Labor Council, an extraordinary alliance was fashioned with the Bridgeport Chamber of Commerce to institute the Vocational Exploration Program, VEP as it is called, clearly a career education concept. This was *labor's* initiative, as a responsible social act. Charles Bradford, executive director of the National AFL-CIO Human Resources Development Institute in Washington reports, "Organized labor is giving full support to this concept. But we recognize some problems. Management does not fully understand career education nor does it fully understand labor's place in it. If you want labor's support at the local level, bring labor in at the very start through the Central Labor Council or the local plant bargaining unit. We of AFL-CIO have 18 cities now in the Vocational Exploration Program following the Bridgeport model."

Since the days of the ancient craft guilds, labor has been concerned about education. There is no reason to doubt its concern now, and for the very same reasons that concern business: a sustaining body of developed labor manpower, a good living environment for the members, a growing market for the goods and services which labor produces.

Back in 1971 we asked labor's judgment on the career education idea. We did follow the rule of engaging labor's participation at the start. At that time we were encouraged by such thoughtful labor personalities as Walter Davis of AFL-CIO, and Gus Tyler, assistant president of the Ladies' Garment Workers Union. Mr. Tyler, writing in 1973 stated, "The turn to career education is a positive act, a move to restore balance. It recognizes that . . . life still is real and earnest, that physical sweat is no stigma, that there's work—much hard work—to be done, and that an educational system must recognize this overriding and eternal imperative."

Career education, writes Tyler, "can be a way to bring American education back to its senses and to prove to a nation that has grown skeptical about the value of schooling that education still is a *sine qua non* for an enriched life in a free society." Subsequent reinforcement came from Mr. Nelson Jack Edwards, vice president of the United Auto Workers, and from the extraordinary example set by union leaders in the General Motors policy statement of a year ago.

Yes, labor has been in the profession of developing the young for work for a long time. The apprenticeship system not only taught woolcarders, and chimney sweeps, and barrel makers to practice their trades. They taught the young the responsibilities and joys, the satisfactions and dignity of work well done. And they taught the essential academic skills of communicating and calculating to accompany the craft.

If there is reluctance on the part of organized labor in some quarters to join in this reform—which not only calls for reform of business and industry and education, but reform of labor itself—it is very probable that labor has not been sought out on an equal footing from the start to share in finding the solutions.

Industry

It always gives me a little problem to separate business from industry, and labor from industry. In a simplistic way, I see industry as often having a larger sphere of community or national influence, and I see it as different from business only in its role as a producer of goods and services in companionship with labor. Oversimple as that may be, I used the California bank as an example of business. Let me use General Motors or the Bell System as an example of industry as we look for reality in the career education complex.

Last year General Motors, after thorough deliberation and negotiation with its unions, adopted a corporate nationwide policy, starting with the earnest commitment of the chairman of the board, Mr. Thomas A. Murphy.

Under the title, *General Motors and Career Education,* Mr. Murphy's policy statement declares, "General Motor's support of quality education includes the concept of career education in America's schools and colleges by direct action." The policy then goes on to specify what that means operationally and to fix the responsibility for the implementation of the policy on every appropriate line officer, including plant manager, throughout the country. This was not an act of public relations rhetoric. It was an industry-wide policy thoughtfully designed and studiously weighed with union leaders before adoption.

Started in Warren, Ohio, as an experiment, the program now moved to 101 of the 110 General Motors plants and installations where career education coordinators on the company payroll are now in place to work with schools, labor, and the community in pursuit of the career education goals. In 40 of the plants, in-plant experience is being provided for students as well as teachers and counselors. And the program has been in effect for only a year.

Many other illustrations from industry—not the least of which is the Bell System—can be pointed out: Western Electric, General Electric, Chrysler, Chance Vought, and many corporations in the insurance industry such as New York's Life and Equitable.

Any single one of these topics—business, labor, industry, government, citizens at large, and school people—could command the time I have and more. Hence I must touch only the highlights in this overhasty review, neglecting many features.

Government

The recent history of federal legislation on career education is strong and shows signs of becoming stronger through the authorities of the Office of Education for general funding and the National Institute of Education for continued creative activities in research and development of the work/education theme. In 1972, Congress passed a law authored by Congressman Quie of Minnesota. The law, the Education Amendments of 1972, included Title X of Part B entitled, "Occupational Education Programs," which while never funded, addresses and supports virtually all of the theory, philosophy, and implementing measures of career education. This was the start.

By 1974, nine states had passed specific laws prescribing career education; others had encouraged the concept through the budget process. Other states are now weighing such legislation. Twenty-eight states have established full-time career education staffs. Forty-two have adopted affirmative policy statements on career education.

Back in Congress in 1974, the Education Amendments for the first time directly established career education with a modest first stage authorization of $10 million for experimentation and demonstration. This 1974 law established the Office of Career Education in USOE and created a National Advisory Council for Career Education with specific charges to keep Congress informed of progress.

A few weeks ago, the conference committee of the house and senate, before adjourning, passed further legislation reaffirming career education, extending its scope beyond elementary and secondary education to include schools and colleges, and doubling the authorizations for funding—still in the experimental-demonstration mode. The president signed this bill, the Education Amendments of 1976, just a few days before Congress adjourned.

And now, when Congress returns from its electoral adventures, there will be the very substantial Perkins Bill, probably to be entitled the Career Education Act of 1977. Congressman Carl Perkins has stated that he expects to hold hearings very promptly and seek early passage of this legislation. In introducing the bill last December, Congressman Perkins declared:

> The prime reason I introduced that bill is to encourage greater federal assistance for state and local school districts in implementing career education programs.
>
> My second reason in introducing the bill is to help clarify the distinction between career education and vocational education. If the concept of career education has any validity—and I believe it does—it ought to be adopted as part of the regular curriculum by school districts . . .

State and federal legislation and the support of Congress and state legislatures are good, but one does not reform education by acts of law. Reform happens in schools and colleges, and in business, labor and industry when the people in charge, including the teachers, decide it *should* happen—and not until. Legislation gives encouragement, some financial support, and government authority to stimulate change. But it does not *in education* produce change. That happens only when the classroom door closes and the teacher and students change. They cannot do it alone, no matter how committed they may be, and I am not speaking of money. Small sums, yes. But career education does not necessarily add on new programs and services and new large costs. It changes what is already there. Fifteen to twenty dollars a student—or 1% of student cost—is a fair sum for installing career education. Some school systems heavily engaged in career education have found they can do the job for as little as $2 per student to meet the new costs of increased counseling services, faculty development, and instructional materials.

Education

What about academic benefits deriving from this reform? Career education relates to all levels of education and infuses occupational relatedness to the curriculum—*all* curriculums. And there is very strong evidence now emerging from evaluations that demonstrates the favorable gains in academic achievements by students in career education. Reading scores are higher; mathematics scores are higher. Not only have these beneficial results been measured in inner cities with disadvantaged children, but in the favored suburbs. Prince George's County, Maryland; the schools of Miami, Florida; Lincoln County, West Virginia; the high schools of Philadelphia are examples where measured gains in reading and mathematics have been demonstrated convincingly under the career education concept. I could cite many school systems where the evidence tells us that newly motivated young people learn better, when they relate the curriculum to their personal destiny, when they feel they have some control over it.

But I say again, the reform of education will not happen unless it starts in the schools. No matter how willing business and labor and industry may be to join hands with teachers, counselors, administrators, and boards of education, the schools must take the initiative. Like the superintendent and the bank president in San Francisco, somebody had to say, "How can we help?" or "Can you help us?" And then, once the help is offered, the schools must learn the complex and demanding task of coordinating the enormous new and willing powers of the community, not simply as advisors, taxpayers, and consultants but as full partners in the enterprise. These are the "boundless resources" of Willard Wirtz's vision. This means risk-taking with shared authority which is unfamiliar to the conventional system of education. But the times call for risk-taking if we are to restore the public trust in our schools and colleges which has never been so dismal as it is today.

The Public

So we come full circle to the people at large and the students themselves, students of all ages. They do expect more from education than we are now offering. I know of no way except through career education to respond to this call for something better than we are now providing. Over the past four years the Gallup Poll has cited the rising expectations on the part of the people for relating work to education.

In 1972, with no prompting or word cues, 40% of the people named *preparation for work* as the prime object of education. A year later, with options displayed by the poll, over 90% agreed that the schools should "give more emphasis to study of trades, professions, and business to help students decide on their careers." Gallup observed, "Few proposals (in the art of polling) received such overwhelming approval." Today, the recently released results of the 1976 Gallup Poll sustain this expressed demand from our people placing in the minds of the people development for work as the biggest priority of the schools.

Students in college, equally concerned about their future work circumstances, are asking the faculties for more occupational realism. This demand must not yield to the pragmatic and, I hope, transient preoccupations with jobs. For college is much more than job-readying. The high place of the liberal arts as the custodian of the underlying values and wisdom of a developed people is threatened by this expectation. The colleges must respond with a new harmony, sustaining the high place of the liberal arts in our society and relating these essential learnings usefully to the occupational expectations of the learner. It is not a question of *either* liberal arts *or* occupational development; it must be both. That is the essence of career education.

Dr. Theodore DeBary, provost of Columbia University, has cogently described the situation: "A liberal education is viewed as consisting equally of general education and specialized (occupational) training, the two complementing one another from the freshman year of college to even the level of postdoctoral training."

Dr. Glen S. Dumke, chancellor of the California State College system, also urges postsecondary career education in a statement calling for "a foundation of liberal education and, based upon that, a specialized program enabling the student to fit himself or herself into the economy or society in a practical way." Many other colleges and universities are taking similar policy measures prompted, at least in part, by student expectations.

At whatever level of education, the liberalizing power of the arts and humanities were never so essential to the growth and intellectual development of our people. Vocationalism must not take over.

The brief sketches of career education's impact upon business, labor, industry, educators, the public at large, and *primarily* students suggest a success story. Viewed over time, we have come a long way, but we have much *farther* to go. The survey of career education mandated by Congress in 1974 was completed in early 1976 by American Institutes for Research. The report declares, by extrapolation of its large sample, that 60% of the school systems in America are making at least limited efforts toward establishing career education, declaring that the concept is rated as "important" or "absolutely essential." Almost 57% of the school districts are providing faculty development for some faculty members in career education. Twenty percent of the teachers in our schools are engaged in in-service staff development in career education. Yet only 3% of the districts may be described as meeting all of the criteria of the survey, as truly conducting a comprehensive career education program. When one translates these numbers, three percent of some 17,000 districts, it comes to 500 systems with career education now in place and 60% asserting career education is important or essential and taking steps toward its installation. This comes to 10,200 districts out of 17,000. These are impressive numbers for a concept which has moved into place in four or five years, when we consider the immensity, diversity, autonomy, and individuality of our system of education and its historically staid traditions. There has probably never in our educational history been such enormous movement toward a central concept of reform over such a brief span of time.

But we have truly only begun. Let me in closing cite some of the items of unfinished business of career education. A study entitled, "Bridging the Gap," published last year by the College Board, identified a number of these issues. But I offer these personal judgments as imperatives for the continued reform of education:

• More systematic teacher education, in-service and pre-service, at all levels, especially in infusing the traditional academic curriculum content with occupational realism.

• Engagement of the community, together with business, labor, and industry in formulating and implementing new policies and procedures. Educators must learn to give up some of their traditional territorial claims if there is to be genuine community involvement in providing work-site learning experiences for the young.

• Counselors at high school and college levels, so central to career development, must be freed of their paper shuffling chores to engage deeply in the work of career counseling, and many of them must refresh themselves in business, labor, and industry to equip themselves more fully for the task of helping all young people make decisions about their futures. Human aspirations, self-understanding, and decision-making about life's choices are at the heart of this issue, and these are the domain of counselors.

• We must as a nation greatly improve our methods of forecasting manpower needs so as to avoid the dreadful waste and frustrations deriving from over-supply and under-supply in occupations such as we have experienced in teaching and some of the technologies.

- We must move from the experimental-demonstration to the operational-installation mode. The legislation intended for hearings when Congress reconvenes will give this issue momentum and money, and all concerned should get behind it.

- We must stop implying that career education will solve all our social problems such as unemployment, drug abuse, declining test scores, crime, and environmental abuse. Career education does address these deep problems. But it cannot solve them alone. We must also make clear again and again that career education is not vocational education.

- We must resolve the hindrances of obsolete laws and agreements that prevent young people from working, that limit the days or hours of school, that place unreasonable burdens of liability on cooperating businesses offering work sites for the students, and that give excessive emphasis to the credentialing of teachers and counselors and limiting the usefulness of talented volunteers.

- We must assess the outcomes of career education and document the evidence that, where career education has been systematically installed the academic growth of young people, including those in college, improves dramatically with intrinsic motivation deriving from the learner's own reasoned application to the learning task. Most of us have been too busy implementing career education to take the pains to document for others the measurable gains.

- We must stop talking about worker alienation and get to the root of the matter through education and the work place. We must try to make work desirable and joyful, to make clear to our society that *good* work of whatever calling is to be honored—a task for all involved including government, industry, business, labor, and education.

- Finally, we must find the chemistry that will unite the enormous power for good that exists among the parts, including business, labor, industry, government, the concerned public, the student, and the educators. The initiative must come from educators. The other parts do not aspire to a take-over of education. But I believe they are ready to join forces. To fashion the new social structure for helping people grow up to work, school leaders must resist cloistering learning from the world of work. Reform is a dangerous word to too many school and college people. But our society, which ultimately we all must serve, asks for reform. We cannot sit still in this storm of public discontent toward education.

In conclusion, to set in place the new and larger function that I ask our private sector, including labor, to comprehend, I quote from a leader of business and industry, Donald MacNaughton, chairman and chief executive officer of the Prudential Insurance Company. He speaks for corporations:

> We must re-focus our view of the corporation and start thinking of it as a socio-economic institution rather than as an economic institution which has some incidental social responsibilities. . . .
>
> The socio-economic concept of business is not a passing fad which will be joining the long list of management ideas which, over the years, go up like skyrockets and tend to come down just as quickly. . . . If this happens, it will be one of the worst mistakes American business has ever made, because I am convinced that what is involved here is, in fact, a matter of survival.

There were many six years ago, who noted archly that career education was a passing fad and, like its many predecessors, it, too, would pass. This meeting today is ardent witness to their error. But if, over the next five to ten years, we do our work well, there will no longer be a need to speak of career education. We will speak again of education, for it will have changed.

REFERENCES

Advisory Council on Vocational Education. "Vocational Education: The Bridge Between Man and His Work." Notes and working papers concerning the administration of programs authorized under Vocational Education Act of 1963, Public Law 88-210, as amended; printed for the use of the Committee on Labor and Public Welfare. Washington: Government Printing Office, March 1968.

Drucker, P. *The Age of Discontinuity.* New York: Harper and Row, 1968.

Education Commission of the States. *Synthesizing Work and Schooling: The Role of Community and Society.* Denver: September 1976.

Harnischfeger, Annegret, and Wiley, David E. *Achievement Test Score Decline: Do We Need To Worry?* Chicago: CEMREL, 1975.

Hoyt, Kenneth B. *An Introduction to Career Education: A Policy Paper of the U.S. Office of Education.* Washington: Government Printing Office, 1975.

Marland, Sidney P., Jr. *Career Education, A Proposal for Reform.* New York: McGraw-Hill Book Co., 1974.

Marland, Sidney P., Jr. "On Career Education." *American Education 7* (1971): 25-28.

Pucinski, Roman C., and Hirsch, S. P. *The Courage To Change: New Directions for Career Education.* Englewood Cliffs, N. J.: Prentice-Hall, 1971.

Rossi, J. R. "Philosophical Analysis of Career Education and Development of a Taxonomy for Career Education Activities." Unpublished technical paper. Palo Alto, Calif.: American Institutes for Research, May 1976.

CHAPTER	# Career Education in the Elementary School
6	

Career education can be seen as a life-long process, starting prior to formal schooling and continuing after. For this reason it is as viable a process at the elementary school level as at the secondary and postsecondary levels.

A case is often made, and rightly so, that if career education is to have a real impact on our educational system, it should be emphasized at the elementary level because it can reach more learners at that level than at any other. In addition, at this early stage it can help in forming desirable attitudes and values which may assist the individual throughout life. Implementing career education at the elementary level, however, presents challenging problems that many traditional educators may not be willing to face.

This chapter consists of four articles written in 1975 and addressing career education at the elementary level. Mary-Margaret Scobey provides some insights on the significance of career education at this level, outlines its goals, and suggests ways of implementing it. Esther E. Mathews discusses the self-concept and its implications for instruction in career education, whereas Betty J. Stevenson provides valuable suggestions for objectives. Kenneth Hoyt presents an interesting account of the implications of evaluation of career education instruction at the elementary level.

SUSTAINING THE FOLLOWERS IN ELEMENTARY EDUCATION

Mary-Margaret Scobey

Professor emeritus at San Francisco State University since 1972, Mary-Margaret Scobey is perhaps best known for her book on elementary vocational education, Teaching Children About Technology. *This article was written in 1975.*

Many so-called innovations appear in varying stages of development in elementary schools. We find open education, team teaching, multilevel grouping, and other strategies. There are the new math, linguistics, and variations of reading, social sciences, life sciences, and art as modifications of the traditional curriculum areas. The optimists may call these new developments blessings, while the pessimists consider them afflictions. During the past twenty years, however, we have witnessed a positive upgrading of schooling as the innovations in teaching strategies merge with modifications of curriculum content.

Change, we know, takes place sporadically and irregularly. It is not a gradual, smooth transition. In every educational innovation, theoretical ideas take hold in random fashion and emerge as applied programs that may vary from fanatical extremes to only slight alterations of the traditional format.

There is a diagram that may be used to illustrate the growth of an idea. It shows how innovations are integrated into the educational system. The *agriculture curve* is merely the curve of normal distribution, with special labels for each section of it. It was first used by agriculturists to help explain the stages through which a new agricultural process is accepted and used (Fig. 6-1).

At the left end of the curve, we find the *innovators,* or those people who conceive and introduce a new idea. These are the experimenters, creators, and stimulators. Next, we find a slightly larger group of *early users,* or those people who grasp an idea, move it ahead, begin to develop a concept, and give it the first practical application. The largest group in the center of the curve are the *followers,* or those who have been convinced that an idea will work; they have seen enough of it in action to give it a try. They work to improve the concept

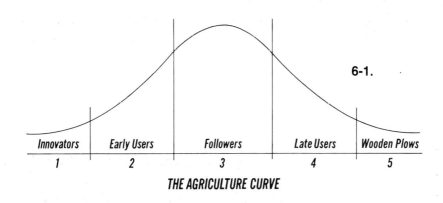

6-1.

THE AGRICULTURE CURVE

and organize it so that the results may be satisfactorily measured. The smaller group near the right end of the curve, the *late users,* are those who are tagging along because the movement has been proved and the consensus is acceptance; the guidelines are firm and clear. At the far right, the final small group is termed *wooden plows* because these people are so inhibited by habit and tradition that they accept, achieve, or put into practice little or nothing that is new.

How does career education fit into this scheme? The concept is here. It is beginning to take hold. Certainly the first impetus came from the U.S. Office of Education and from a small group of innovators who presented the idea and provided enough stimulation for beginning interest. Early users were those who accepted the idea and established formal programs, generally in the form of temporary projects financed by state or national agencies. Included in the group of early users are such agencies as educational regional laboratories and professional consultant firms. The early users have developed a demonstrable concept and proved its viability. They have identified ways to develop career education and have proved that it works. They have provided sample objectives, curricula, instructional materials, and methods of evaluation.

We are now apparently at the rising curve of the followers, because we find many elementary schools across the country either with carefully organized programs or with individual teachers struggling to implement the concept. Give these followers support, nurture them a bit, and the group will continue to grow, stimulating the late users to move. We simply won't worry about the wooden plows.

Important at this point, then, is help for teachers so that the increasing number of followers can achieve instructional success. How might this be accomplished? First let us consider the problem of social change in which career education is emerging. Then let's take a look at career education and its innovative implications. Finally, an analysis of the concept as it has developed in the elementary school will give us some final guidelines for sustaining the followers.

CAREER EDUCATION AND THE SOCIAL NEED

Social and cultural change is often frustrating. Yet educational trends will show us that in the United States schooling has always reflected the needs and desires of the people, even though at times the struggle to change has been long and difficult.

First, schools taught reading so that religion could be pursued. At periods of war, nationalistic and patriotic emphases were made. We have established nursery schools to accommodate working mothers; we have developed adult education to meet the needs of mature people who desire supplementary education for recreational or occupational purposes. We have opened higher education to both sexes and, through city colleges and an increasing number of scholarships, made it possible for most competent students to receive a college education.

Currently, minority groups ask for equal opportunity; the poor plead for satisfactory employment. Today's recession further emphasizes the need for young people to have adequate preparation for work. We need to revitalize efforts to assure achievement of economic security in a world where technology changes rapidly and the work related to it may be modified quickly or become obsolete.

Here is an example. In 1973 *Newsweek* pointed out: "The demise of *Life* and other picture-oriented, general-interest magazines during the past several years has made things tough indeed for photojournalists." *Newsweek* goes on to quote professional photographer Tony Wolff, whose work appeared in both *Look* and *Life:* "Ten years ago, if you asked a kid what he wanted to be, he might have answered: 'A *Life* photographer.' What's he going to say now? 'I hope I'll get an exhibit at the Museum of Modern Art,' or 'I want to take pictures of my friends'?" The day of the photo essay appears to have passed, and this means photographers must seek new ways to sell their skills.

Job obsolescence is not the only difficulty. Federal Reserve Board Chairman Arthur F. Burns lists six problems the United States must solve to have lasting prosperity. The fourth problem he states is shrinking gains in productivity, or shrinking output per man hour. He says there are two reasons for this: (1) industry has not had the incentives needed to invest enough in new plants and equipment or in advanced research, and (2) the unfavorable change in attitude of the labor force and some laxity in management show that workers are well trained but that they work with less energy, and absenteeism grows.

Perhaps the greatest challenge to educators lies in these two factors: the change or obsolescence of jobs and the attitudes of both workers and management. How is this best handled at the elementary school, where years are ahead of the young child before he or she will enter the labor force? Do we need to develop attitudes toward work that will help the young worker find satisfactions in it, appreciating all levels of labor? How can we include the ingredient of change in knowledge and skills needed for an unknown job in future years? Is all-around knowledge and flexibility of understanding the answer? Can we teach willingness to accept and anticipate change?

Compounding the teacher's responsibilities is the fact that technological modifications mean keeping up with the changes, maintaining current knowledge of technological processes and the jobs related to them. It is also a problem just to keep in mind the rules and regulations governing the work of our public officials!

Regarding the demands of current social needs, Downs sums up the situation well:

> The impact of industry and technology on our society's goals and values has caused our nation to reconsider the role of education. We are fast realizing that a society like ours, in which individuals are expected to enter the labor force and produce the goods and services needed, can no longer tolerate an educational system that largely ignores the world of work if it intends to accept the responsibilities of space-age youth. Since a person's work role does not limit his preparation in society, but provides a foundation on which to build his life, then a comprehensive career education is a fundamental necessity for all who aspire to a productive, contributing, and satisfying role in this technically oriented culture (Downs 1973, p. 1).

It is to this end that many elementary schools have developed what are sometimes called innovative programs of career education.

Career Education an Innovation?

Innovation is something which is newly introduced, some kind of change. What is considered new or recent is actually a matter of relative judgment. An educational innovation, therefore, may be considered some modification of recent origin which changes established systems of school organization and structure, content areas, teaching strategies, instructional materials, or any combination of these. In this sense, career education is an innovation because Sidney Marland, Jr., presented career education in 1971 as a design to establish a new base for learning. Today we see much evidence that career education programs have utilized and merged other new ideas in educational practice and also added a different, exciting, practical dimension to content. In most cases, the influence is a positive one.

The basic idea behind career education, however, has been a concern of educators the world over for a long time. The following works of innovators have relevance for the elementary school: Bacon (1561-1626) advocated that the components of daily life be the center of study, rather than past action; Locke (1632-1704) believed in empirical learning related to experience and the environment; Rousseau (1712-1778) suggested that the best teacher is experience in life activities; Pestalozzi (1712-1778) developed a curriculum around the workaday world; John Dewey (1859-1952) urged learning related to the real world:

> . . . . (We need) to make each one of our schools an embryonic community life, active with types of occupations that reflect the life of the larger society, and permeated throughout with the spirit of art, history, and science. When the school introduces and trains each child of society into memberships within such a little community, saturating him with the spirit of service, and providing him with the instruments of effective self-direction, we shall have the deepest and best guarantee of a larger society that is worthy, lovely, and harmonious (Dewey 1900, p. 40).

The second *Yearbook of the National Society for the Scientific Study of Education* (1903) presented a curriculum design suggesting both occupations and historical studies for each grade. Bonser and Mossman (1923) pleaded for the curriculum changes which would provide for the individuality of the child and content related to the work of life. James Conant in *Slums and Suburbs* pointed out that children of a technological and urban society need educational experiences preparing them for subsequent employment (Conant 1961). Jerome Bruner stated: "I cannot escape the conclusion that the first order of business in the transformation of our mode of educating is to revolutionize and revivify the idea of vocation or occupation" (Bruner 1973, p. 23).

Of more immediate mention, Dr. William D. Rohwer, Jr., of the University of California at Berkeley, outlined what the *St. Petersburg Times* (Florida) on February 19, 1975, called a revolutionary proposal. Rohwer suggested that:

> In elementary schools students would be free to work on any projects they desired, including traditional subject areas or even topics of their own choosing such as computer programming or the lore of professional baseball. . . . In general, the elementary school curriculum would be designed to afford children repeated experiences of what work is like and what success in school is.

Analysis of the beliefs of this long list of educational innovators proves that (1) work activities and life have concerned educators for centuries and are apparently gaining impetus today, and (2) general education could become more practical, more stimulating, and more humane if the study of work efforts were an integral part of the curriculum.

We can agree that the career education concept is not new. Yet, the term itself is relatively new. Career education has surely brought about changes in schooling. It has often changed attitudes of learners toward formerly traditional aspects of education. It has given administrators and teachers a different approach for improving instruction. It has changed curriculum emphases and helped to unify and centralize the separate subjects. Yes, influence is most evident. You decide whether or not career education is an innovation!

Career Education Defined

Career education is focused on the learner's career. Here diverse interpretations arise. Narrowly defined, career may mean the series of jobs an individual holds during the productive years of his or her adult life. Increasing numbers of authorities hold the broader perception that a person's career includes all of life's activities—those related to educational, social, and recreational, as well as economic purposes. Both views tend to agree that career education attempts to help young people achieve a satisfactory place in society and a happy and productive work life. They also agree that career education must be sensitive to a life and environment that constantly change.

"Is this so very different," some ask, "from what conscientious educators have always expected?"

Today's goal, career educators answer, is to make all areas of the curriculum relevant to work and integrate them to a meaningful whole. But as Louise J. Keller said, "It is easier to conceptualize career education than to implement the concepts of career education" (Keller 1974, p. 40).

When in 1970 the career education idea was first introduced, there was shock and surprise among some elementary school educators. Teach vocational education to children? Pick a career for a six-year-old? Prepare a youngster for a lifelong occupational career? Add another subject to the curriculum?

In reality, and as most of these elementary educators found out upon reflection, the character of the elementary school curriculum and instructional organization is particularly conducive to the kind of integration the career innovators wanted. The central theme suggested merely placed an emphasis upon bits and pieces of curriculum previously offered. The problem was to analyze the content of career education so that it would be adequate for the needs, interests, and abilities of young children.

James I. Briggs Jr., director of the Center for Career Planning and Placement at Georgetown University, Washington, D.C., said in 1975 in an interview with representatives of *US News and World Report:*

> . . . A lot of the how-to-find-a-job advice that's given today, . . . is fruitless until the individual (college) student has a strong knowledge base. He needs to know about himself and about the world of work, so that he can say: "These are my goals, and here is how I plan to reach them, step by step." This sort of self-knowledge and self-confidence often is far more important than the external economic situation in determining success in getting a job.

Most career education programs in elementary schools seek to achieve the beginning of Briggs' goal by concentrating upon awareness: awareness of self (both intellectual and manipulative abilities); awareness of social relationships and the individual's role in them; and awareness of the environment and the contributions work has made to it. The purpose is to build a positive and accurate self-concept, understand differences between people, develop attitudes valuing the dignity of all work, and quite properly, gather a smattering of information about the many kinds of work available.

It is evident that career education draws its leadership from both vocational education and industrial arts. Terminology, however, tends to emphasize occupations as related to work and careers. We hear about *occupational preparation, occupational development,* and *occupational information programs.* When relating these terms to the elementary school, one must remember that *occupation* may mean the learner's current work effort and activity, or the developmental tasks in progress. It can also mean awareness of and beginning level orientation to the ways in which people organize work efforts to offer goods and services to a society. And again, we emphasize that young children are not only developing positive attitudes and values, but they are also relating this to themselves—their intellectual and physical involvement, their particular preferences. Implementation of career education in this way is not preparation for a specific occupational career. Rather it is an orientation to the world of work, awareness of self as a worker, and appreciation for the industry of people.

Goals of Career Education in the Elementary School

A single learning experience or a series of related activities may contribute to the achievement of one or more of the following goals:

● Understanding of the self: the roles one plays, interaction with people and the environment; the many settings of life—home neighborhood, community; preferences, weaknesses, talents, abilities; personal development; discovery of personal needs, interests, skills.

● Insight into self as a worker now and as a prospective adult worker; anticipation of possible career goals; career consciousness.

● Awareness of the multiplicity of career goals; how goals may change with time and experience.

● Understanding that one's career is an integration of all dimensions of one's life.

● Acquaintance with and beginning comprehension of the broad occupational fields, the vast range of jobs.

● Orientation to the changing character of work and the job market.

● Development of attitudes toward the dignity of work and the satisfactions derived from it; what work is and how people value it; the value of work to the individual and to the society; the relation of schooling to work.

● Development of some simple basic tool skills.

● Familiarity with a sampling of simple industrial processes and production.

● Experience with industry and workers in it; interaction with workers of social agencies.

● Understanding of interdependency, cooperation in occupational endeavor.

● Interpretation of our industrial-technical culture at an appropriate level.

● Development of leisure-time preferences.

● Knowledge of the differences between goods and services.

● Identification of the different environments for work.

Achievement of the above goals will not be easy. Every one of them, to an appropriate depth level, most likely will not be attained. The teacher who conscientiously tries to achieve most of them will have to demonstrate:

● An open mind.

● Ability to take advantage of ordinary teaching situations to emphasize the career concept.

● Sensitivity to points of view which emphasize careers, industry, and technology.

- Desire to constantly increase her or his own knowledge—become familiar with the work arenas in the community, visit places of work.
- Willingness to seek assistance from others: members of the community, special teachers, consultants in industrial and vocational education.
- Ability to select teaching objectives after a careful study of priorities.

Implementing Career Education in the Elementary School

Younger children, of course, deal with the simpler aspects of the above goals. They develop simple skills with tools; they learn simple social amenities; and they try many kinds of activities and learn to understand their own successes and failures. They also become familiar with the workers of the immediate environment, appropriate to their own limited life-space.

Then, as learners grow older, they develop scholastic skills and begin to appreciate the ways in which these skills help all people in their daily life and also how these skills are utilized in more sophisticated forms by certain workers. It takes the boredom out of the three Rs. The teaching of arithmetic could include its relationship to the computer and the multiple occupations in the field of computerization. Children develop language skills and become conscious of their fundamental need by all mankind and how those same skills are utilized by workers in the several media of communication.

In addition, pupils learn through performance-based activities. They learn some of the details of construction and manufacture, experiment with some of the processes, manipulate some of the tools and machines, and develop an understanding of the interdependency of many kinds of workers to produce an item and maintain it. They become familiar with governmental and social agencies, the need for them, the ways in which they operate, the services they render, and the fabric of various jobs making all this possible. Not only do students learn of the great diversity of work, the responsibilities of jobs, and their contributions to society, but they also learn something about the educational and experimental requirements necessary for the job and how one rises in the hierarchy of occupational responsibility.

Within the established elementary school curriculum, there are unlimited ways a teacher may help children understand the occupational implications of ordinary school work. The teacher can also help each child think about work in relation to his or her own preferences and abilities.

Most elementary school career education programs are carried out in the regular classroom by the teacher who has a career orientation or by the teaching team that has established some guidelines for cooperative development of the career education theme. Special consultants in career education, industrial arts, or vocational education frequently lend valuable technical assistance.

The separate disciplines of the curriculum, especially the social studies, are enhanced and enriched by the career education emphasis. Passive, verbal activities characterizing traditional education are decreased and experiences using the active, multisensory, multimedia approach are increased. Children enter upon firsthand, concrete experiences of the hands-on variety. These are supplemented by the more verbal but active situations in which people are interviewed, demonstrations are observed, and roles are simulated in dramatic form. Individuals and small groups plan, execute, and evaluate tasks related to the study. Research includes reading, querying, observing, collecting, experimenting, and reviewing many kinds of audio and visual materials. Career education, then, utilizes all the best methods of instruction, but lends a practical, interesting, and relevant focus to enrich the total educational experience for young children.

Teachers who provide such a rich program and the educational leaders who work with those teachers will find that possible educational experiences are unlimited. Some guidelines may therefore be helpful in the selection of the most effective learning activities.

How then can we sustain and help the followers? Perhaps the first task is to ascertain that the basic purpose and intent of the career education concept is clarified so that goals may be realistically stated and understood. Teachers will need to be sensitive to career education and the ways in which it can emerge in daily classroom work. Tools and materials need to be procured and adequately disseminated. Guidelines, developed cooperatively, that include objectives, suggested classroom activities, and resources will also make acceptance of the program easier. Furthermore, the development of community support and cooperation is not to be forgotten—it can make or break a program. Perhaps the best way to assure success is to evaluate the program in operation regularly and to analyze other programs so that one may learn from the experience of others.

CAREER EDUCATION AND THE SELF-CONCEPT

Esther Matthews

Dr. Matthews is professor of education at the University of Oregon at Eugene. In 1974-75 she was president of the National Vocational Guidance Association. This article was written in 1975.

The relationship between career education and the child's self-concept, as it develops during elementary school, is receiving increasing attention. It is almost taken for granted that understanding and implementing the self-concept lie at the heart of vocational development. However, the linkages between the self-concept, career education, and vocational development remain unclear or at least not universally understood as they apply to practice.

Further problems are exemplified by the necessity for establishing a philosophical base and a theoretical structure to support and sustain career education. The present career education goals and their evaluation are not providing a philosophical and theoretical structure. The imperative demands of society and the financial support for career education have also produced action in need of re-evaluation in terms of the individual human being served.

The objectives of this article are: (1) to discuss the centrality of the self-concept through viewing the work of E. Erikson and Donald Super; (2) to review career education goals of the elementary school; (3) to summarize Severinson's initial attempt to provide a philosophical and theoretical base for career education; (4) to summarize a few broad frameworks for applying theory to the elementary school; (5) to present an important applied research method for use in implementing vocational development in the elementary school; and (6) to discuss the humanization of career education through the contribution of A. Combs.

The Centrality of the Self-Concept

Theoretical and applied knowledge of the self-concept is central to an understanding of career education and vocational development at any life stage. During the elementary school years, our focus here, self-concept insights can radically optimize the human development of children. Lack of knowledge or insensitive application can stunt and distort the evolution of mind and personality.

Erikson's Early Life Stages. The elementary school career education person can profit from repeated study of the work of Erikson. His broad frame of reference for the entire life cycle reminds us that life is a process incapable of sharp segmentation. Stages merge into one another. Stage resolutions are never complete but recur in subsequent parts of our lives (Erikson 1959).

Erikson divided life into eight stages from infancy through adulthood. He posed a distinctive task for comparative resolution at each stage. The tasks were expressed in positive and negative terms along a continuum. He maintained that in order to move toward the next growth stage the individual needed to resolve reasonably each stage's specific task.

Here we will be looking only at the periods of life that elementary school children have experienced. The nature of the tasks is clearly based upon the self-concept of the individual. The elementary school children have experienced some resolution of these stages and tasks: infancy, trust vs. mistrust; early childhood, autonomy vs. shame and doubt; play age, initiative vs. guilt; school age, industry vs. inferiority.

It is clear that trust, autonomy, initiative, and industry are highly productive translations of the self-concept that have deep significance for career education and for vocational development. Study of these factors would indicate that each one exemplifies an expansion of basic trust in the self and in the trustworthiness of supporting adults.

Career education persons can analyze their own program and practices in relationship to how well or poorly the self-concept of each individual child is enhanced or restricted. The analysis would focus particularly on the availability to each child of reasonable and appropriate opportunities for choice instead of being continually directed; for independence rather than dependence; for inner self-direction in contrast to external direction; and for decision-making rather than submission.

In order to implement a career education program consistent with self-concept theory, we also need to be thoroughly familiar with the contributions of Super.

Super's View of the Self-concept. For over two decades Super has directed part of his research toward defining, clarifying, and elaborating the role of the self-concept in vocational psychology. Much of his later work has derived from a key statement within his initial theory of vocational development:

> . . . the process of vocational development is essentially that of developing and implementing a self-concept: it is a compromise process in which the self-concept is a product of the interaction of inherited aptitudes, neural and endocrine makeup, opportunity to play various roles, and evaluations of the extent to which the results of role playing meet with the approval of superiors and fellows (Super 1953, p. 190).

In 1963 Super defined the elements of a self-concept theory of vocational development and clarified a language and structure of the self-concept. According to him, the elements of a self-concept theory of vocational development include the processes of formation, translation, and implementation. The formation of the self-concept begins in infancy and extends throughout the course of life. There are discernible aspects in the evolving formation of the self-concept: exploration, self-differentiation, identification, role playing, and reality testing (Super 1963). It is apparent that these concepts have found their place in well-developed career education programs.

The translation of the self-concept into occupational terms proceeds through identification, experience, and awareness. Sometimes the translation proceeds bit by bit, as when success in a school subject leads to taking advanced courses and later on preparing for a related occupation.

Super feels that the implementation of actualization of self-concepts results from the training and education that enables one to move into a place in the world of work.

Super's contribution to our knowledge of the self-concept is important for practitioners in several ways. The educator is reminded of the complexity of the self-concept system, the many layers of meaning and the qualitative differentiations provided by the terms defined below. An expanded knowledge of self-concept theory could also result in the vivid translation of the recognition of each child's individuality into all aspects of the curriculum and its derivative experiences (ibid.).

Some of the important terms in order of complexity as defined by Super are:

Self-percept
Primary self-percept: unmodified or raw impression of an aspect of the self.
Secondary self-percept: simple self-concept which has come to function as a percept.

Self-concept
Simple self-concept: organized, related percepts with accrued meaning.
Complex self-concept: abstraction from and generalization of simple self-concepts, generally organized in a role framework.

Self-concept System
The constellation, more or less well organized, of all of the self-concepts.

Vocational Self-concept
The constellation of self-attributes considered by the individual to be vocationally relevant, whether or not they have been translated into a vocational preference (ibid., p. 19).

Concentrated study of these definitions moves one far beyond the view of a unitary self-concept, toward a realization of the intricate nature of identity.

The next important stage of Super's thinking relates to the dimensions and metadimensions of the self-concept. Dimensions of the self-concept refer to those traits and characteristics which people attribute to others and to themselves. We are all acquainted with long lists of characteristics like this. Super adds that we must also become familiar with the dimensions of the dimensions—or the metadimensions—of self-concepts. He considers distinctions between self-concepts and self-concept systems to be of fundamental importance. The distinctive characteristic of the metadimensions (listed below) is that they can all be used to describe characteristics of any single dimension of self-concepts. He says, for example:

> It is possible to assess the amount of self-esteem associated with any one trait (I am anxious and heartily wish I were not), the degree of clarity characterizing any one trait (I am sort of friendly), or the abstraction of a self-description (I like being with people) (Super 1963, p. 25).

METADIMENSIONS OF SELF-CONCEPTS
AND SELF-CONCEPT SYSTEMS

Self-concepts	Self-concept systems
Self-esteem	Structure
Clarity	Scope
Abstraction	Harmony
Refinement	Flexibility
Certainty	Idiosyncrasy
Stability	Regnancy
Realism	

(Ibid., p. 24)

It would probably take a career educator or a vocational counselor many years to absorb and apply this perspective to her or his work; yet the increased quality in the understanding of, and service to, human life make the effort worthwhile. Understanding and applying these insights would also lead to more qualitative and differentiated perceptions of individuals. At present gross generalizations may be made that can lead to extreme inaccuracies of observation. In turn, inaccuracies can result in distorted judgments and low-level decisions. Definitively stated goals can lessen this problem in career education at the elementary school level.

Career Education Goals for the Elementary School

One comprehensive view of the goals of career education is supplied by the National Standard Career Education Model—Kindergarten Through Adult (1972). Grades K-6 are heavily dominated by the concept of career awareness. In grades 4-6, career orientation and career explorations are emphasized. Goal statements are entered for every grade level. These goal statements are derived from the following general categories: appreciations and attitudes; self-awareness; decision making; educational awareness; career awareness; economic awareness; skill awareness, beginning competence; and employability skills.

Underneath these eight goal divisions there are fifty-six entries for K-6 only. Many subgoals are broad and general and almost all are extremely difficult to translate directly into curriculum experiences for young children. Some examples will help to explain the translations needed to the actual lives of children—Grade 2, "relate basic skill development to life roles within the community;" Grade 5, "understand the impact of career clusters on life-styles."

The usefulness of the complex chart of career education goals lies mainly in the ingenuity of the applications derived. The dangers lie in the objectivity of such models, resulting in their use in mechanical, predetermined activities placed onto children (for their own good!). Another grave difficulty is the tendency to use such systems on a group basis without due recognition of the wide spectrum of individual differences within every group.

Increasing numbers of career education people are aware of the need to specify a theoretical and philosophical base for career education. Furthermore, there is a growing sense of the importance of individualized and developmental approaches to career education.

Severinson's Individual Developmental Approach to Career Guidance

Severinson has proposed an Individual Developmental Approach to Career Guidance (IDACG) which helps in the translation of goals to activities. He has begun to suggest a

163

philosophical base and a theoretical framework. Guidelines for implementation and for evaluation are also provided with emphasis, however, upon the secondary school (Severinson 1973).

The philosophical base for Severinson's IDACG is borrowed from Beck (1963), by way of Blocher (1966). Blocher's existential, developmental philosophy is expressed in the following statements:

• The individual is responsible for his own actions. He has a measure of choice and must make these choices for himself.

• Man must regard his fellow men as objects of value, as part of his concern. Since his fellow men are part of him, he must apply this concern to all of society.

• Man exists in a world of reality. The relationship of man to his world is a threatening one, for much of what he encounters he cannot change.

• A meaningful life must remove as much threat from reality as possible, both physical and psychological. The goal is to free man from threat so that his optimum development can be obtained.

• Every person has his own heredity and has had experiences unique to himself. He can thus be expected to behave differently from others whose experiences are different.

• Man behaves in terms of his own subjective view of reality, not according to some externally defined objective reality. Behavior is able to be judged only in terms of personal values or external roles.

• Man cannot be classified as good or evil by nature. These terms may apply to goals, objectives, or patterns of behavior. They have no meaning when applied to man himself.

• Man reacts as a total organism to any situation. He cannot react intellectually or emotionally to the exclusion of the other. When man attempts to compartmentalize himself on such a basis, he becomes anxious and less free to develop in an integrated way (ibid., p. 19).

Career education people or counselors can readily analyze their practice in terms of these statements. What proportion of educators are willing to accept an existential, developmental philosophy as a base for practice is, however, not yet known.

Severinson's next difficult task of developing a theoretical base from Blocher's philosophy seems insufficiently advanced to warrant summarization (Severinson 1973). Some of the reasons for this conclusion include: (1) the complexity of the task; (2) the dependence chiefly upon Super's early valuable work (Super 1953 and 1957) and the exclusion of his later and critical contribution to our knowledge of the self-concept (Super 1963); and (3) the absence of attention to the work of other theorists (Roe 1964; Tiedeman et al. 1963; Hershenson 1968; Tyler 1959).

The value of Severinson's work may lie in calling attention to the necessity for an individual, developmental approach to career guidance and for the eventual evolution of an integrated base in philosophy and theory. Explicit and well understood, such a base lends itself to practical application.

Applications to Practice. Many educators are already familiar with the important graded series of materials by Limbacher under the general title of *Dimensions of Personality* (Limbacher 1970). At each grade level a major developmental theme is highlighted. For example, at the sixth grade level the theme is *becoming myself*. In every instance the student is involved in a discovery-type, decision-making experience. Everyday incidents are used as a thought and feeling focus for discussion. Open-ended incidents are provided to stimulate consideration outside of school. Parents are encouraged to read the materials and discuss them with their children.

The materials weave together the values and understandings related to the whole process of evolving a self-concept. Pictures, cartoons, and incidents at the sixth grade level include *finding my feelings; my physical growth; my emotional, social, and intellectual growth;* plus a heartening *I'm still growing* emphasis!

One of the thought-provoking "Peanuts" cartoons by Charles Schultz is called "The Meaning of Growth." Lucy asks Charlie Brown: "How's the birdhouse coming along, Charlie Brown?" He replies: "Well, I'm a lousy carpenter, I can't nail straight, I can't saw straight, and I always split the wood. I'm nervous, I lack confidence, I'm stupid, I have poor taste and absolutely no sense of design. So, all things considered, it's coming along OK!" (Limbacher 1970, p. 194)

I guess Charlie Brown's career education person was not too immersed in the self-concept literature!

One caution is in order for those considering Limbacher's materials. They need to be pre-read to eliminate instances of vocational sex-role stereotyping. This can be done by any sensitive person—in fact, there may be revisions underway to correct the occasional sex bias. The series provides a humane and lively base for assisting students to understand, develop, and expand their self-concept systems.

Other authors, Sylvester and Matthews (1972), have suggested the use of a simple four-question framework as a base for elementary school career guidance and vocational development. The questions are: What am I like? How am I changing? What will I be like? How will I affect others and how will they affect me? This seemingly simple model can be developed to a high level of complexity and richness by utilizing the ingenuity and creativity of children and adults in school or home.

An Applied Research Method

An interesting research method for use in implementing vocational development in the elementary school is found in Fulton's research. Her instrument has real promise for curriculum application and is an interesting research method which involves and excites children (Fulton 1973).

Fulton developed an instrument called the Career Concepts Inventory (CCI). The purpose of the CCI was to investigate how children (preschool through grade five—from suburban, rural, and urban locations) perceive selected characteristics of the world of work.

Fulton felt the need for developing this instrument after her review of the research indicated that: (1) most theories of vocational development have paid little attention to the individual prior to junior high school; (2) no instrument was available to measure the vocational development at or prior to elementary school; (3) occupational information available to elementary school children is frequently limited, inaccurate, or obsolete; (4) the formation of vocational attitudes and values begins early in life and seems closely related to vocational choice; (5) since young children begin making occupational choices, and important prevocational decisions often have to be made by the junior high student, preparation for making these decisions is necessary at the elementary school level; and (6) with the increasing emphasis on vocational development at the elementary school level, the lack of developmental research (prior to junior high level) in the vocational domain is a serious problem for program developers (ibid., p. 88).

The CCI consists of seven sections, each investigating a different aspect of vocational development: initial interview, occupational listing, occupational absurdities, vocational vocabulary, and occupational ranking.

Fulton's whole approach seems to be highly promising with respect to sensitivity to individuality and awareness of developmental understandings. Children most likely become involved and excited during the process of the CCI experiences. They must surely gain a sense of self and a feeling of growing competence as their opinions and knowledge are sought out. The introduction of the humor of absurdities will also delight children. The lack of right-wrong answers and the absence of competitive aspects are also encouraging. Not having seen the instrument, I cannot judge whether or not sex-role stereotyping is present, but I would hope that the recent nature of the work would insure the absence of stereotyping of any variety.

One ultimate aim of career education is to prepare learners for more satisfactory human existence. Educators, then, should be conscious of the humanization of career education.

Humanization of Career Education

The ASCD Yearbook for 1970, *To Nurture Humaneness,* edited by Scobey and Graham (1970) offers a much needed balance to the abstract, generalized material found within many fields of education, including career education.

One contributor, Combs (1970), considers the human dimension to be an educational imperative. He feels that we have made a fetish of objectivity and that we have come to venerate objectivity as part of our mores. The result is clear—a devaluation of the human being. We have forgotten that learning has always had two phases: (1) the acquisition of new knowledge and experience and (2) the discovery of its meaning. In order to respect this condition of life, according to Combs, we must shift our attention from self to learner: "We have to be less concerned with what we do and much more concerned with what happens in the hearts and minds of those we do things to" (ibid., p. 176). The growing emphasis upon humanistic education has already "brought us an understanding of the self-concept, new concepts of human potential and self-actualization, new insights into motivation and learning."

How can the educator draw upon the work of some of the author's contributions? A reader might sort out the work of the contributors and create an integrated and individualized synthesis of the theory, philosophy, and applications suggested here.

For example, Erikson provides a distinctive framework for viewing life as a series of stages posing developmental tasks. All aspects of the elementary curriculum (including career exploration and awareness) may be viewed through their contribution to establishing trust, autonomy, initiative, and industry in young children.

The work of Super can also be directly applied to the individual child. A teacher might experiment with his terms and definitions in an attempt to capture, at a depth level, the complexity of one child. Gradually, viewing every child in multidimensional terms would become a habit.

The individualization of each child's development could then be easily sifted through Severinson's philosophic translation of Bech by Blocher. The educator would be moved to ask questions such as: "How much responsibility do I encourage in each child? How did I demonstrate that I value each child? In what ways can I diminish threat?"

The contributions of other authors are clearly and directly related to daily practice in the classroom—the thought and feeling emphasis of Limbacher; the key questions raised by Sylvester and Matthews; and the utilization of the instrument developed by Fulton.

Finally, the contribution of Combs lends a humanistic perspective to the entire education process. As we study models, systems, and practices, we need to realize that they are distant approximations of human reality. The humanization of career education is the next giant step forward. Career education as a purposive and constellating force has made a significant contribution in triggering the national conscience into aiming to provide a better education for all people. The challenge now is to develop a consistent philosophical and theoretical base, to relate theory to practice, and to infuse knowledge with humane understanding.

DEVELOPING AND ACHIEVING INSTRUCTIONAL GOALS IN CAREER EDUCATION

Betty J. Stevenson
Betty Stevenson is a teacher in Oquawka, Illinois and has been involved with the State Advisory Council on Adult, Vocational and Technical Education and the Regional Manpower Committee. This article was written in 1975.

Career education programs are planned at the elementary level to provide children with experiences to help them grow in knowledge and understanding about themselves, others, and the world of work. The general goals of such programs are to develop in pupils favorable concepts, values, and attitudes. The elementary level is not too early for the child to understand that people work to produce goods and services and to develop such values and attitudes as: I want to be a courteous person; I want to do a job well; and I can do a job well.

The premise that career education can achieve stated goals early in the life of the child is well-supported. Atherton and Mumphrey (1969, p. 39) write, "The preparation for a career begins with life itself." The very young child is interested in the things she or he experiences within the environment. Children imitate. Their play is their work as they act out life's role. The child may be a doctor because of a visit to a doctor's office or because he or she has received the gift of a doctor's kit.

Herr and Cramer cite the recommendations of the 1968 National Advisory Council's general report, *Vocational Education: The Bridge Between Man and His Work,* which says that the curriculum in elementary school should contain occupational preparation based upon a realistic view of the world of work. The curriculum becomes more complex as children grow older by including a more detailed, sophisticated study of the production and distribution of goods and services. Concepts of economic and industrial systems should increase in complexity as the student progresses through the program (Herr and Cramer 1972).

Dr. Sidney Marland, Jr. views career education as a continuous process of learning. He feels that the public schools should provide experiences that will develop world-of-work concepts for the young child. The middle school student needs to explore vocational possibilities, and at the secondary level students need training for job entry or for further formal training. Marland has charged the schools with grave responsibility.

In accepting this challenge, educators are committed to meet the needs of the children they serve. To ascertain planned goals, it is necessary to take a dimensional view of the forces of home and community that influence the preschool child and of the influences that will continue to be exerted upon the child during his or her years in school.

Though formal education begins at the kindergarten level, children have formed ideas about their environment before school entry. Johnny Joe, age four, learns about neighborhoods, about building houses, and forms other occupation-related ideas. Johnny Joe tells his grandmother that he must finish his work before he can go to bed. He must water Mommy's flowers, or the flowers will die.

"The primary school years (K-3, or age 5-9) are not the beginning, as many teachers seem to believe" (Cross 1974, p. 129). Children come to school with a ready-made set of values formed through interacting for approximately five years with a family, with peers, with a local neighborhood, and with the wider community through television, radio, and books. The child's experiences color his or her attitudes about parents, about community people, and about school. Children react to their environment as they have experienced it. Educators will agree with Cross that the child's ability to relate to others will be influenced by the degree to which people in the child's home environment value education, appreciate the worth and dignity of teachers, accept without prejudice people different in color or creed, and believe in the dignity and honor of the working person. Attitudes and values become habits.

Thus, the ultimate task and goal of the school are to receive each child as a unique person with varying capabilities and, within the span of twelve years, to nurture these children into comparatively mature individuals, equipped with entry level skills for the occupational world. Career education is a common denominator that can unify the efforts of the school, of the home, and of the community to educate toward this goal.

The Division of Vocational and Technical Education, State of Illinois, proposes the following:

> Career education can unify the entire educational plan through progressive learning experiences based on the developmental level of the students . . . . Occupational Information Program activities should help a student to develop an awareness of the dignity in work and the useful functions performed by workers; become aware of a larger number of occupations; develop a realistic self-concept of abilities and limitations as related to the world-of-work; learn about occupational opportunities through exploration. From a broad base of information a student develops an awareness of his career preferences, elects a program related to his career interests, and eventually narrows his educational program to accomplish his career goal (Division of Vocational and Technical Education, pp. 1-3).

Career education at the elementary level does not involve career choosing. Rather, the child becomes more perceptive of a wide range of work roles and develops related concepts, values, and attitudes about the world of work. The child achieves no concrete idea of what she or he will be, but if given opportunities for varied experiences pertaining to the world of work, the child will be better equipped later to perform the developmental task of career choosing. She or he may be able to attain a higher level of vocational development. Super (1957) writes that vocational choice is a continuous process rather than a single event.

Establishing a Career Education Program

Career education cannot be effected without work. Educators who firmly believe in the value of career education must initiate ways and means to plan goals and implement programs. Much groundwork has already been done in this area. One of the early steps toward planning and implementing a program is deciding upon a major emphasis to meet the needs of the students at each grade level. Then within this major emphasis ideas must be organized in scope and sequence, and materials must be selected. Sequential, organized, and coordinated programs are the most effective.

Step 1: Established need. From the beginning, new career education programs must be supported by the board of education, the administration, the guidance personnel, the teachers, and the people in the community. School personnel must be cognizant of occupational information concepts. Teachers must accept career education as important enough to allocate time and energy for planning and for activating the plans. Bailey and Stadt (1973) write that teachers must internalize some type of theoretical position relative to career development. Teachers without a theoretical orientation will find it difficult to select from among the many available types of curriculum materials or to integrate such materials into an organized program of instruction. Because career education concepts may be unfamiliar, ideas at first may seem nebulous to the teachers and to other people involved. There may be a reluctance to include more subject matter into what seems to be an already crowded curriculum. A supportive board of education and an administration whose educational philosophy places importance upon the career education program will provide planning time during workshops and give extra secretarial assistance as needed. A well-planned workshop, including discussion and audiovisual presentation of materials, will orient the staff to the program, and a visit to a good demonstration center to view a program is worthwhile.

Advisory councils composed of community people and school personnel can facilitate change by conducting local surveys to assess the need for an occupational information program. It is important to establish a need for the program and thereby gain community support. Good public relations is necessary to the success of any career education program.

Step 2: Selecting a planning team. The second step is to select a planning team composed of school personnel selected by the administration because their teaching assignments place them in an advantageous position for possible implementation of the program. Sometimes teachers exhibit interest in career education concepts and become valuable members of the team because of this. Administrators should select high school students, parents, and other community people as part of a team because these people reflect the needs of students as perceived by the community.

One person is designated as team leader. The team leader may be the career education coordinator or director who is hired to develop curriculum and to organize and implement K-12 career education programs into sequential, viable programs. Whoever is team leader, it is most important that this person be cognizant of possible career education ideas and that she or he believe firmly in the value of the overall concept. Although the team leader is an important part of a team, the success of the program depends largely upon the involvement of teachers, upon the support of the administration, and upon the assistance of parents and other community people. The team members are collectively involved in planning the overall scope and sequence of the program. Teachers are individually responsible for career education planning at their respective grade levels.

Planning time must be allocated by the administration. A K-8 career education program should be included within a school district's goals for curriculum improvement.

Step 3: Planning process. After establishing a need for the program and securing school and community support on a working team, the next step is to develop goals which will serve as curriculum guidelines and emphasize career education. The goals may be achieved through a separate course; they may be integrated into the existing curriculum by enriching the established disciplines; or career education learning may combine both of these approaches. Nevertheless, it is necessary to form goals and objectives that are compatible with the needs, interests, and abilities of the students.

Herr and Cramer (1972) define goals as general objectives. Performance objectives are guideposts that lead both the teacher and the student to the general objective—a learning conclusion.

The four basic elements and criteria of behavioral objectives are: (1) expected student performance; (2) content of the learning to be achieved; (3) evaluative criteria to assess the performance; and (4) the student's opportunity to demonstrate behavior (Campbell, Walz, Miller, and Kriger 1973, p. 174).

The K-8 Occupational Information Program at the Southern Community Unit District #120, Stronghurst, Illinois, can be cited as an illustration of the planning process. The program, now in its fourth year, is increasingly meeting the needs of the students. The planning team, consisting of the principal, coordinator, teachers, and community people, is gaining a wider scope of understanding and an increased appreciation for the program. They realize that the ongoing program requires continuous appraisal and that it grows with the understanding of the people involved. Flexibility in program planning is a key to meeting needs of both students and instructors. In a recent visit, a state evaluation team concluded that: "The K-8 Occupational Information Program is developing very, very well" (Division of Vocational and Technical Education 1974, pp. 344-5). However, as always in education, much more can be done. The planning team realizes that continued or changed planning, modified implementation, and ongoing evaluation is necessary to improve the program and to meet educational needs more adequately.

Levels of Objectives

The planning team at Southern, Stronghurst, used the Illinois Occupational Curriculum Project materials to form the program management objectives. After listing perceived needs, they made a priority rating and agreed upon the program management objective, or the one overall goal for the sequential program. The program management objective should have a target date, an outcome statement, and a criteria statement of proof that the outcome has taken place (Borgen and Davis 1972a, p. 40). An example is: by September 1, 1975, articulate the K-8 career information program with the secondary vocational program by choosing a major emphasis for each grade level based upon developmental needs and by writing student performance objectives for each grade level. Related data will be on file.

Following the identification and selection of the program management objective, the team identified a major emphasis for each grade level:

Kindergarten—self-image
First grade—families
Second grade—needs of people

Third grade—living and working together (interdependency)

Fourth grade—developing positive work attitudes (job image)

Fifth grade—responsibility for self and others

Sixth grade—self-discipline and peer-group alliance

Seventh grade—decision-making, values, goals, and use of individual human resources

Eighth grade—career exploration

Each major emphasis is implemented through the selection of related resource materials and textbooks. Teachers have much flexibility in this selection. Commercial firms produce world-of-work information materials which are adaptable to local programs, and many materials are available from community agencies.

After identifying a major emphasis to meet the needs of the students at each grade level, the planning team listed general objectives under each grade as guidelines to the planning of student performance objectives. General objectives also serve as vehicles for curriculum choice making.

Gysbers suggested that objectives for grade levels may be contained within three broad learning phases. The first learning phase begins at the kindergarten level and continues through grade three, during which time the child may perceive world-of-work related concepts (Gysbers 1969). Examples of such objectives are:

- Children should explore who they are, how they are alike, and how they are different from others.
- Children should find satisfactory places for themselves in school and home so they may be able to relate more effectively to others.
- Children should have a range of experiences concerning the world of work so they will acquire the skills to begin to understand the work world and their place in it.
- Children should explore home, school, and surrounding community to perceive the wide variety and interrelatedness of occupations.

Gysbers indicated that during grades four through six, the students should have opportunities to conceptualize the world of work by utilizing simulation techniques. Some examples are:

- The students should develop a self-concept relating to the world of work by exploring a wide range of occupations.
- Students should explore values of work and reasons why people work.
- Students should acquire basic competencies for the work world through a study of effective time organizational patterns, efficient work habits, cooperation with others, and constructive attitudes toward work.
- The student should develop an understanding of work situations including the behavior of workers through simulated work experiences such as applying for a job, interviewing for a job, and working on a job (ibid.).

In the seventh and eighth grades, Gysbers suggested that the students use their repertoire of career education concepts to begin to generalize about the world of work. Examples are:

- The students should begin to develop a self-concept relating to the world of work by exploring types of educational opportunities which will prepare them for the occupational world.

● Students should view a wide range of occupations, and requirements for entering these occupations, using the job family approach.

● Students should have simulated experiences which promote understanding of the factors that govern success in the world of work.

● The student should use individual resources in decision-making processes, and should practice setting goals relating to values (ibid.).

The general objectives contain world-of-work generalizations and concepts related to the major area of emphasis. Examples are shown for different grade levels:

Kindergarten (Major emphasis—self-image)

Objective: To provide experiences to help children find out who they are, how they are alike, and how they are different from others.

Generalization: People tend to succeed when they have a realistic understanding of their abilities.

Concepts: Everyone is a special person. People are different. I am a special person. I am me.

Seventh Grade (Major emphasis—decision-making, values, goals, and use of individual human resources)

Objective: To involve the student in decision-making experiences relating to values, goals, and use of individual human resources.

Generalization: Attaining goals depends upon the individual's ability to make choices based upon values and upon the individual's ability to manage his or her human resources.

Concepts: Goals are reached through the use of resources. Decision-making is affected by the individual's values. Choices are based upon values (ibid.).

The interrelationship of the major emphases, the general objectives, the generalizations, and concepts assist the team in forming student performance objectives. An outline of general objectives also helps the team members determine whether or not the content of the K-8 program is organized as a coordinated, sequential, spiralized program.

Another way planning-team members may decide what should be included in a sequential program is to ask the question, What promotes success for a worker in the real world of work? To answer this question, the team lists competencies which promote success for the individual on a job, e.g., punctuality, dependability, self-confidence, cooperation, honesty, friendliness, courtesy, initiative, and enthusiasm. Understanding these proficiencies helps children develop related values and attitudes. Answering this question also helps the team identify cognitive, manipulative, and social competencies and to key these to the appropriate grade level. Competencies, which carry over and are reinforced in succeeding grade levels, are the performance abilities of the student. For example, the young person who is socially adept has acquired these skills over a long period of time.

Performance Abilities

Atherton and Mumphrey (1969) indicated that certain personal and social competencies are basic for the individual to acquire before she or he can initially be employed and then can grow and progress as a successful worker. Further, it has been estimated that more workers are fired because of a deficiency of desirable social qualities than for all other reasons combined. The failure to adjust to the job and its surroundings can lead to serious consequences. There are expectations of workers for job performance and for personal conduct.

Cognitive aspects of career occupational information programs can be included in teaching the basic skills of learning to read, compute, write, and communicate successfully. This helps the learner understand the past and present more fully as well as possibilities for the future environment. Atherton and Mumphrey view the intellectual effectiveness of a person as dependent upon several factors, including emotional health, physical well-being, social adjustment, and "the facility to perform as a member in the group processes" (ibid.).

Thus, it follows that those who plan a career education program should have knowledge of the interrelationships of the cognitive and affective domains. Bailey and Stadt (1973) offer assistance in this area for curriculum planners with examples of instructional objectives and behavioral terms for the cognitive and affective domains of the taxonomies. It is important that student performance objectives include values and attitudes as well as the attainment of intellectual knowledge and psychomotor skills.

Writing student performance objectives can be facilitated by the use of a form and guidelines such as the Illinois Occupational Curriculum Project materials. The task, or outcome statement, the conditions statement, and the criteria statement are headings for three columns. The *outcome statement* is appropriate when it specifically states in a short sentence containing an action verb, the activity, skill, ability, or attitude expected of the student. The *condition statement* is appropriate when it indicates (if relevant) time limits, place of performance, the type of materials or equipment the student will use, and any special conditions under which he or she will be working. The *criteria statement* is appropriate when it indicates the quality of the outcome, the quantity that must be achieved for minimum success, and other relevant qualifications, i.e., time allowance, number, proportion, or percentage of attempts and results that are acceptable (Borgen and Davis 1972a p. 58).

Student performance objectives for the first grade, third grade, and sixth grade in the affective domain are shown in Table 6-A. The major emphasis and the teaching concept are included for each objective.

Student performance objectives serve dual purposes. The teacher and the students are guided toward a goal, a task, or outcome. Also, criteria are the preplanned guidelines to measure the outcome and become the basis for evaluation. When the required performance is in the affective domain, it may be necessary to evaluate the student through careful observation.

Evaluation

What should be the guidelines for forming the criteria of an objective? In completing a performance objective which states that the student is courteous to the peer group and to adults, is 100% of the time expecting too much? Can the teacher settle for 90% or 80% of the time and feel that the student has progressed toward a commendable outcome? The child must be treated as an individual. The child who has had experiences with courteous people in his or her home will be nearer the completion of the task than the child who is shouted at or who never hears the words please and thank-you.

Evaluation is determined by the teacher through: (1) an ongoing assessment of the written performance objective as a teaching tool (Does it measure exactly what it proposes to measure? Is the objective appropriate for the grade level? Is it usable? As the objectives are used, make notes in the margins.); (2) an evaluation of the teaching methods used to

TABLE 6-A.
Student Performance Objectives

Major emphasis: Families Concept: Someone has to provide for families.		First grade
Task or outcome	**Conditions**	**Criteria**
The student displays a sense of responsibility toward the care of a family.	In the classroom, caring for a family of hamsters, using certain types of feed and specific measurements.	Show concern for the welfare of the family by regularly feeding and properly caring for the animals 100% of the time.

Major emphasis: Interdependency Concept: People have many friends who help each other in a neighborhood.		Third grade
Task or outcome	**Conditions**	**Criteria**
The student justifies the importance of friends who protect other people.	In the classroom, with paper and pencil and a bulletin board showing a doctor, nurse, policeofficer, safety inspector, lifeguard, and firefighter.	Explain why it is important that people like and appreciate the friends who protect them, as previously taught by the teacher.

Major emphasis: Self-discipline and peer-group alliance Concept: A person must discipline self for appropriate behavior.		Sixth grade
Task or outcome	**Conditions**	**Criteria**
The student displays an understanding of the concept of self-discipline for appropriate behavior patterns.	In the classroom, with checklist type of test and a story illustrating how discipline of self will help a person reach desired goals.	Correct responses to a test which assesses comprehension of concepts of self-discipline as illustrated by a story. Related concepts studied at a prior time form basis for responses.

reach the objective (Are tests written toward the objectives, and are the teaching methods consistent with the required performances?); and (3) an evaluation of student performance, using the stated criteria as a basis for testing.

A wider evaluation of the total K-8 program is necessary. Are students involved in the career education concepts to the extent that they carry ideas home? Are teachers enthusiastic? Do parents exhibit interest? Is the advisory council functioning? Is the planning team involved with continuous activity and communication? Are local newspapers featuring career education articles? Someone has to be interested enough to write the articles. Does education week exhibit career education concepts? Is there a vocational show?

In summary, career education should begin early in the life of the child and continue through the elementary school years so that the child will attain values, attitudes, and skills for occupational preparation. Educators must find ways and means for planning, implementing, and evaluating an occupational information program. Identifying goals and their means of achievement is an essential component of all three facets of program development. Some of these ways have been explored. Many key ideas are involved in developing and achieving instructional goals in a career education program at the elementary level. Educators are challenged to provide career education occupational information programs to meet needs of students at the local level.

EVALUATION OF CAREER EDUCATION: IMPLICATIONS FOR INSTRUCTION AT THE ELEMENTARY SCHOOL LEVEL

Kenneth B. Hoyt

Author of six books and numerous articles on career education, Kenneth B. Hoyt is the most prolific writer in the field. Since 1974 he has served as director of the Office of Career Education, Office of Education, Department of Health, Education, and Welfare. Dr. Hoyt is also professor of counselor education at the University of Maryland. This article was written in 1975.

The birth of a new idea is followed by its expansion into an educational concept. The concept must next be tested for its effectiveness before it is finally implemented in educational practice. The critics of a new idea in education typically use, as one weapon, a call for research results even before the idea has been developed into a tentative concept form. This short set of generalizations could, I believe, be illustrated repeatedly by those who study the history of new ideas in American education. Career education is only the latest example.

Former United States Office of Education (USOE) Commissioner of Education, Dr. Sidney P. Marland, Jr., first introduced the term career education in 1971. It is important to note that Dr. Marland introduced an *idea,* not a *concept.* His idea was that the world of schooling needs to be brought into closer relationship with the world of work. In introducing this idea, Marland called for the definition of career education to be developed in the hard crucible of educational practice. The idea was not new, having been stated as one goal of American education in explicit form by the Morrill Act of 1865. Just prior to Marland's pronouncement, the idea had been well illustrated in books by Venn (1964), by Pucinski (1971), and by Rhodes (1970).

Thus, while the idea was not new, there were two new circumstances surrounding it. The first was the term, career education, which was used to express the idea. The second was that, for the first time, the idea was championed by a USOE commissioner of education and made a top priority of the USOE. Bolstered by these two new aspects, the idea attained quick approval and endorsement throughout the land of educators, parents, students, business people, and the general public. School systems in all parts of the country adopted policy statements supporting career education and initiated efforts to implement such policies. The USOE earmarked several million dollars to demonstrate the concept.

We were caught in a chicken-or-the-egg situation. That is, we were attempting to conceptualize career education by relating education and work. The facts used to promote career education pertained much more to the need to relate education and work than to our demonstrated ability to do so. Given the history of new ideas in American education, this should, it seems, be viewed as neither surprising nor necessarily distressing.

The amount of progress made in the name of career education in the early 1970s was substantial and most encouraging. During this period, the idea of career education was effectively converted into a concept. A multiplicity of methods was devised and field-tested for the implementations of career education. Public enthusiasm for, and acceptance of, career education has continued to grow. More recently we have found ourselves beginning the hard task of evaluating the efficacy of the career education concept. This, of course, is not to say that the task of conceptualizing career education has been completed. Any viable educational concept must be a continually evolving one, and career education must not become an exception. I am only saying that, if one studies the consensus tables that are appended to the current USOE policy paper entitled *An Introduction To Career Education* (USOE 1975), it seems apparent that consensus has been found for a current effort to state the concept of career education.

The purposes of this article are to: (1) provide a short capsule summary of the concept of career education in a form that will hopefully be meaningful to professional persons in elementary education; (2) summarize evaluative criteria now being proposed for career education and identify those that seem most appropriate for use at the elementary school level; (3) illustrate currently available results pertaining to evaluation of career education in elementary schools; and (4) present some brief thoughts regarding our current and future needs for evaluation and research of career education in elementary schools.

The Concept of Career Education

Readers are urged to study carefully the USOE policy paper on career education referred to above. Here, only particular aspects of that paper that pertain specifically to the elementary school will be considered. The following discussion assumes readers to be familiar with the USOE policy paper on career education.

First, it is apparent that career education has been conceptualized around the four letter word work. The word work, moreover, has been defined so as to reflect the need of all human beings to do—to accomplish—to achieve. It is a very humanistic concept indeed. As such, it includes both the world of paid employment and the world of unpaid work, including the work of the volunteer, the full-time homemaker, the pupil, and work in which individuals engage in the productive use of leisure time. It is a concept that obviously applies to all pupils at all levels of education.

Second, with this definition of work, career education is clearly a developmental concept beginning in the preschool years and continuing, for most persons, well into the retirement years. That is why we say kindergarten is very late to begin career education. There is no difficulty justifying a strong conceptual case for career education in the elementary school. As a developmental concept, career education has leaned heavily on the process of career development over the life span, including career awareness, motivation, exploration, decision-making, preparation, entry, progression, maintenance, and decline. The elementary school years have, in this framework, been singled out for particular attention with reference to career awareness and career motivation.

Third, career education has been organized conceptually around the career development process. At the same time, the teaching-learning process has been the prime vehicle utilized for implementing the concept in the elementary school. Here, the rationale has been taken from efforts to reduce worker alienation in business and industrial settings. The classroom is a workplace too. Career education has attempted implementation strategies that it is hoped will reduce worker alienation among both pupils and teachers in the elementary school classrooms. If pupil learning is to improve, pupils who really want to learn must be coupled with teachers who really want to teach.

Fourth, the prime methodology devised for implementing career education has been that of collaborative relationships among the formal educational system, the business-labor-industry-professional-government community, and the home and family structure. By viewing the total community as a learning laboratory and persons from that community as resources for implementing career education in classrooms under teacher direction, the result has been a vast expansion of means, materials, settings, and resources for making learning more appealing and meaningful to pupils and to teachers.

Evaluative Criteria for Career Education in the Elementary School

The USOE policy paper on career education lists nine learner outcomes considered appropriate for use in evaluating career education. Of these, four criteria, while not limited in usefulness to the elementary school, seem particularly appropriate for use at this level (USOE 1975).

The first calls for students to be *competent in the basic academic skills required for adaptability in our rapidly changing society.* At the elementary school level, this can be translated to mean a primary concern for helping pupils learn the basic skills of oral and written communication, of mathematics, and basic science. The importance of this criterion stems from a combination of reasons. One reason is that employers have complained that youthful job applicants coming to them are often deficient in such skills. A second reason is that many persons will change occupations several times during their adult lives and will need these basic skills as a prerequisite for doing so. Many pupils and teachers apparently are not sufficiently motivated to either acquire or impart these essential skills.

The concept of career education calls for two broad approaches to increase pupil achievement in the elementary school. The first is to show pupils how adults need and use skills in the work that they do. The second is to increase the variety of means and settings for use in helping pupils acquire basic academic skills.

The second criterion in the USOE policy paper requests that students be *equipped with good work habits.* The work habits we refer to are those that, over the ages, have been positively related to productivity—to output per person hour. They include such habits as: (1) coming to work (to school) on time; (2) doing one's best; (3) finishing tasks that are begun; and (4) cooperating with one's fellow workers. Again, we find employers asserting that youthful job seekers are coming to them unequipped with such habits. If these habits are to become part of one's life-style as an adult, it would help if they were acquired early in life. The concept of career education calls for elementary school teachers to emphasize consciously the importance of good work habits to their pupils and to provide students with assistance in, and credit for, their acquisition. Hopefully, if this occurs, it, too, will contribute to pupil achievement in the classroom. Additionally, it will serve as a valuable adaptability tool to be used in the adult world of rapidly changing occupations.

The third criterion in the USOE policy paper is the student's *capability of choosing, or having chosen, a personally meaningful set of work values that foster in them a desire to work.* In a generic sense, work values can be thought of as the constellation of reasons individuals give when answering for themselves the questions: Why should I choose to work? What work should I choose to do? We clearly want pupils to work in their roles as students. Thus, in part, our concern is to provide students with multiple reasons why they might choose to master the subject matter we are teaching. Additionally, we seek to help pupils understand the work values of adults now employed in the world of paid employment. That is why, for example, elementary school field trips in career education emphasize work, not occupations—the ways in which workers contribute to society's goals rather than a study of their specific job functions. The worth, value, and dignity of any occupation is brought to that occupation by the human beings doing that work. We seek to help pupils understand the worth of workers—with special emphasis on their parents as workers—through helping them understand the many ways in which each worker contributes to society and so receives personal benefits for herself or himself. It is important for our pupils to want to work.

The fourth criterion considered particularly appropriate at the elementary school level is the students' ability to be *successful in incorporating work values into their total personal value structure in such a way that they are able to choose what, for them, is a desirable life-style.* In applying this criterion to evaluate elementary school career education efforts, we are certainly not thinking of using specific occupational choices as the measuring stick. Rather, we are thinking more of measures that would reduce race and sex stereotyping in prospective occupations. Work values, like other personal values, are highly influenced by early life experiences. Our elementary school textbooks have for years been filled with examples of both race and sex stereotyping when occupations are described. To open up full freedom of choice in later years for both minority persons and for females, these problems must be attacked in the elementary school. Further, the wise use of one's leisure time demands that consideration be given to activities which, because they are productive, result in personal satisfaction and a sense of accomplishment for the individual. This, too, is something career education has said should begin to be communicated to pupils in the early elementary school years. We have reasoned that the best of all possible times to acquaint pupils with the positive connotations of work is when, in their own life-styles, they have difficulty separating it from another four letter word called play.

Examples of Evaluations of Elementary School Career Education Efforts

Of the four criteria discussed above, the first must take priority in our attempts to evaluate the effectiveness of career education efforts at the elementary school level. That is, much as parents favor our efforts to increase student understanding of relationships between education and careers, their basic reasons for sending their children to the elementary school are much more related to education than they are to work. Parents and the general public want elementary school pupils to learn to read, to perform simple arithmetic operations, to acquire the basic skills of oral and written communication, and to acquire a general understanding of, and appreciation for, the world in which we all live. If in the process they learn something about careers, parents will be pleased, but that is not basically why pupils are sent to the elementary school. No new educational idea can succeed if it fails to recognize the importance of this basic educational function. It is the responsibility of any new idea to make some positive contribution toward the general education goal. The old saying that the tail cannot wag the dog is appropriate to remember here. Unless career education can demonstrate that, when applied, pupils in elementary schools increase their levels of academic achievement in the basic skills, it will have trouble justifying itself long enough to be concerned about the remaining criteria.

Thus, it is encouraging to find that, among those few career education programs where conscientious attempts have now been made to engage in some form of "product" evaluation, increases in academic achievement have been observed. It is further encouraging to see that, at least with the few examples now available, the results look more positive than negative.

One example is found in a monograph written by Dr. LaVene Olson (1974) of Marshall University. Using elementary school pupils in Lincoln County, West Virginia, Olson found that when pupils who had been exposed to a career education effort were compared with another group who had not been so exposed, the career education pupils (grades 1–6) scored 11% higher in language achievement and 24.5% higher on mathematical achievement than did the control group.

Similar results were reported in capsule form by Clifford Purcell (1974) of the Santa Barbara, California, career education program. He reported that when the reading ability of second graders from a class emphasizing career education approaches was compared to that of second graders not involved in such an approach, the reading scores on the Cooperative Primary Reading Test were significantly higher in the class using a career education approach.

A letter to me from Dr. E. L. Whigham, superintendent, Dade County Public Schools, Miami, Florida provided data on results obtained from efforts to use a career education approach to teaching mathematics to fourth, fifth, and sixth graders at the Drew Elementary School (Whigham 1974). Comparing gain scores from data collected in 1973 and 1974, he reported mean gains (in the form of grade equivalents) for the fourth graders as 1.96, for fifth graders as 1.52, and for sixth graders at 1.30. The conversations with Dade County career education personnel made these gains seem even more impressive when they related that among inner city elementary schools, such as the Drew Elementary School, the average mean gain in mathematics achievement for the year was less than .50 when expressed in the form of grade equivalents.

A report on evaluation of career education efforts in Prince George's County, Maryland, showed similarly positive results (M. F. Smith 1974). When elementary school pupils who had been exposed to a career education approach were compared with pupils who had not been so exposed, the career education pupils scored significantly higher on both reading and mathematics in grades 3 and 7. In the other elementary schools where comparisons were made (sixth grade), the career education pupils scored significantly higher on math but showed no statistical differences when compared with the control pupils on reading.

One study which has come to my attention failed to show any statistically significant differences between elementary school pupils exposed to a career education approach when contrasted with pupils who were not so exposed. This was reported in a Minnesota study (Brandon Smith 1974). When results from this study were analyzed, it was found that the career education treatment consisted of somewhere between one and two hours per week. This is far from what the concept of career education calls for.

These are all the results, related to the first criterion, that so far have been reported to USOE's Office of Career Education for elementary school pupils. It is, of course, negative and discouraging to see so few results available. On the other hand, it is positive and encouraging to see that at least to date the results do appear to support the rationale utilized in the formulation of the career education concept.

The Future of Evaluation of Career Education in Elementary Schools

On August 21, 1974, President Ford signed into law the Education Amendments of 1974—PL 93-380. Section 406, Title IV, is entitled *Career Education.* The Congress in its wisdom chose to make this first piece of congressional legislation for career education a demonstration act rather than a program implementation act. Thousands of school systems across the land feel that they had already demonstrated the viability and acceptance of career education in their communities. Many seem to feel the Congress erred in not providing the hundreds of millions of dollars required for implementing comprehensive career education programs throughout our nation. Personally, I understand and identify with the desire and commitment expressed by such practitioners. At the same time, when I face the hard question of evaluation, it seems to me that the Congress acted wisely by asking that we demonstrate the effectiveness of career education prior to requesting large sums of money for its programmatic implementation. It should be obvious from what has been said here so far that we have yet to do so on a comprehensive and obviously clear-cut scale.

The truth is, the so-called demonstration projects in career education, funded from 1971 to 1974, were much more demonstrations of the struggle to develop and attain consensus on the career education concept than they were actual demonstrations of the effectiveness of that concept when applied in educational settings. Only now have we reached a point in time when the concept is sufficiently understood and a sufficient degree of consensus has been reached so that we are in a position to test the viability of the concept through evaluation of results of demonstration efforts. In saying this, I have no intention of being either critical or lacking in appreciation of these earlier efforts. On the contrary, it seems to me miraculous that they were able to advance the concept so far in so short a time. They deserve credit from all of us, not criticism from any of us.

Now, however, we must turn our most serious attention to problems involved in demonstrating and evaluating the effectiveness of career education. To do so, it seems to me, our efforts must be directed simultaneously in three basic directions. First, it will be essential that demonstration projects make clear the full career education concept, including its rationale, basic nature, and implementation strategies. We can never really say how good career education is until we are willing and able to define in specific programmatic terms what we mean by exerting a career education effort. We have now reached a point in time when we should be able to do this.

Second, we must devote serious and concentrated attention to the problem of constructing and validating assessment instruments and devices appropriate for use in the evaluation of career education. Much remains to be done before we will be able to say we have adequate devices available for measuring growth in such phases of career development as career awareness, career exploration, career motivation, career decision making, and career maturity. With all of our rhetoric about the nature and importance of work values, we still have far to go before we will be able to say we have reliable and valid instruments available for measuring the existence of such values—or the ways in which they change. Most instruments used to date in evaluation of career development goals were originally intended for other purposes. This is a serious problem.

Third, it seems to me we must all support and encourage efforts of the Education and Work Task Force of the National Institute of Education, as well as efforts of university researchers and those in other parts of society, to hasten the basic research that will be essential to the long run future of career education. I am speaking here about such matters as studying the basic nature of sex stereotyping in occupational decision making, the viability of work experience as a supplement to classroom instruction, the use of performance evaluation, and the approaches used for expanding educational opportunities for all persons. These and many other segments of the career education concept are still based much more on philosophical belief than on hard evidence. One can reach the outer limits of utility for words alone in a very short while.

Concluding Statement

This article has attempted to take a positive, rather than a negative, approach to current problems facing our attempts to evaluate career education at the elementary school level. While I have tried to acknowledge that we still have a very long way to go, I hope I have also communicated my feeling that career education has come a very long way in recent years. We have moved from the idea to the concept stage. We have been able to maintain and expand the enthusiasm and support for career education essential for its continuance. We have attained a degree of consensus among career education leaders that allows us to talk about the topic in definitive terms. We have been able to identify at least some of the criteria appropriate for use in evaluating career education. In the few instances where the basic criterion of career education's effectiveness in increasing pupil achievement has been applied, we have found generally positive results.

At this point in time, I find myself feeling proud of career education's past achievements, more confident than ever of the need for career education, and eager to get on with the task of evaluation.

REFERENCES

Atherton, J. C., and Mumphrey, A. *Essential Aspects of Career Planning and Development.* Danville, Ill.: Interstate, 1969

Bailey, L. J., and Stadt, R. W. Career Education: *New Approaches to Human Development.* Bloomington, Ill.: McKnight, 1973.

Beck, C. *Philosophical Foundations of Guidance.* Englewood Cliffs, N. J.: Prentice-Hall, 1963.

Blocher, D. *Developmental Counseling.* New York: Ronald Press, 1966.

Bonser, Frederic G. and Mossman, Lois C. *Industrial Arts for Elementary Schools.* New York: The Macmillan Company, 1923.

Borgen, J. A., and Davis, D. E. *Illinois Occupational Curriculum Project.* Vol. M. *Management Strategies and Guidelines for Using IOCP Manuals.* Springfield, Ill.: Division of Vocational and Technical Education, 1972a.

Bruner, Jerome. "Continuity of Learning." *Saturday Review of Education.* Vol. 1, February 1973.

Campbell, R. E.; Walz, G. R.; Miller, J. V.; and Kriger, S. F. *Career Guidance: A Handbook of Methods.* Columbus, Ohio: Merrill, 1973.

Combs, A. "An Educational Imperative: The Humane Dimension," pp. 173-188, in *To Nurture Humaneness.* ASCD Yearbook 1970, Washington: Association for Supervision and Curriculum Development, NEA, 1970.

Conant, James. *Slums and Suburbs.* New York: McGraw-Hill, 1961.

Cross, F. R. *Elementary School Career Education: A Humanistic Model.* Columbus, Ohio: Merrill, 1974.

Dewey, John. *School and Society.* Chicago: The University of Chicago Press, 1900.

Division of Vocational and Technical Education. *Evaluation Report of the Occupational Education Program Southern Community Unit District No. 120.* Springfield, Ill.: Division of Vocational and Technical Education, 1974.

Division of Vocational and Technical Education, Special Programs Unit. *Elementary Occupational Information Program Keystone to Career Development.* Bulletin No. 51-374. Springfield, Ill.: Division of Vocational and Technical Education.

Downs, William A. "The Role of Industrial Arts in Career Education at the Elementary School Level." *Some Relationships of Elementary School Industrial Arts to Career Education.* Washington: The American Council for Elementary School Industrial Arts, 1973.

Erikson, Erik. "Identity and the Life Cycle." Psychological Issues Monograph 1. New York: International Universities Press, 1959.

Fulton, B. "Career Development of Children." In *Developing Careers in the Elementary School,* edited by N. Gysbers et al. Columbus, Ohio: Merrill, 1973.

Gysbers, N.C. "Elements of a Model for Promoting Career Development in Elementary and Junior High School." Paper presented at the National Conference on Exemplary Programs and Projects. 1968 Amendments to the Vocational Education Art. Atlanta: March 1969.

Herr, Edwin L., and Cramer, S. H. *Vocational Guidance and Career Development in the Schools: Toward a Systems Approach.* Boston: Houghton-Mifflin, 1972.

Hershenson, D. "Life-style Vocational Development System." *Journal of Counseling Psychology* 15 (1968): 23-30.

Keller, Louise J. "What A College Can Do To Provide Teacher Preparation for Career Education." *Journal of Career Education* 1 (Fall 1974).

Limbacher, W. *Becoming Myself.* (Reference to Teachers' Edition.) Part of the graded series titled *Dimensions of Personality.* Dayton, Ohio: George A. Pflaum, 1970.

National Standard Career Education Model—Kindergarten Through Adult, The. Educational Properties, Inc., P.O. Box DX, Irvine, Calif. 92664, 1972.

Olson, LaVene A. *A Study of Elementary and Secondary Career Education in Lincoln County.* Huntington, West Va.: Marshall University, 1974.

Pucinski, Roman. *The Courage to Change.* Englewood Cliffs, N. J.: Prentice-Hall, 1971.

Purcell, Clifford, ed. *Focus on Career Education.* 5 (1974).

Rhodes, James A. *Vocational Education and Guidance: A System for the Seventies.* Columbus, Ohio: Merrill, 1970.

Roe, A., and Siegelman, M. *The Origin of Interests.* APGA Inquiry Series, no. 1. Washington: American Personnel and Guidance Association, 1964.

Scobey, M., and Graham, G., eds. *To Nurture Humaneness.* ASCD Yearbook. Washington: Association for Supervision and Curriculum Development, NEA, 1970.

Severinson, K. N. *Career Guidance: An Individual Developmental Approach.* Columbus, Ohio: Merrill, 1973.

Smith, Brandon B. *A System for Evaluating Career Education in Minnesota: 1972-73.* Minneapolis: University of Minnesota Research Coordinating Unit for Vocational Education, 1974.

Smith, Midge F. *Interim Study of the Effects of Career Education in the Prince George's County Public School System.* Upper Marlboro, Md.: Prince George's County Public Schools, 1974.

Super, D. "A Theory of Vocational Development." *American Psychologist* 8 (1953): 185-190.

Super, D. E. *The Psychology of Careers.* New York: Harper and Brothers, 1957.

Super, D. et al. *Career Development: Self Concept Theory.* New York: College Entrance Examination Board, 1963.

Sylvester, R., and Matthews, E. "Peacemaker, Plumber, Poet, Drummer?" *The Instructor,* February 1972, pp. 45-56. (Also in *Developing Careers in the Elementary School,* edited by N. Gysbers et al. Columbus, Ohio: Merrill, 1973, pp. 97-110.)

Tiedeman, D., and O'Hara, R. *Career Development: Choice and Adjustment.* New York: College Entrance Examination Board, 1963.

Tyler, L. "Toward A Workable Psychology of Individuality." *American Psychologist,* 14 (1959): 75-81.

United States Office of Education. *An Introduction to Career Education.* A policy paper of the USOE (OE 75-00504). Washington: Department of Health, Education, and Welfare, 1975.

Venn, Grant. *Man, Education, and Work.* Washington: American Council on Education, 1964

Whigham, E. L. Personal letter to Kenneth Hoyt, Officer of Career Education, United States Office of Education, 10 May 1974.

Yearbook of the National Society for the Scientific Study of Education, Part 1. Chicago: University of Chicago Press, 1903.

CHAPTER

7

Career Education in the Junior High School

Unlike career education at the elementary level, which has some limitations in terms of exposing children in actual work situations, junior high school students are and should be exposed to a wide variety of these, not as participants but as observers. This idea is consistent with that of career exploration which is so central to the junior high school experience. In junior high schools the theory of career education is most often put into practice.

This chapter is made up of three articles written in 1974, 1975 and 1977 by one administrator and two practitioners. At that time, the main thrust of career education was implementation. Paul B. Salmon offers straightforward, pragmatic views which, at that time, were representative of many school administrators. Marjorie M. Kaiser presents an interesting account of unintended career education in her English classroom. Her view might have been that of any practicing teacher at the junior high school level, and she offers an approach usable by any English teacher at that level. S. Theodore Woal assesses the information available to junior high school students about the world of work, about occupations, and about the most significant influencers of students in terms of vocational interests. This simple study reveals some interesting results.

IMPLEMENTING CAREER EDUCATION

Paul B. Salmon

Executive director of the American Association of School Administrators, Dr. Salmon has also served as superintendent of schools in California. This article was written in 1975.

Most long time observers of American elementary and secondary education are struck by two things: the many innovations which have been tried over the years and what seems to be an almost constant changing in the focus of the schools. For instance, progressive education moved toward traditionalism, which in turn moved toward open education, which is now returning to more rigidity. The open classroom concept made way for flexible space which too soon gives up its flexibility because of a rigid program or rigid educators. Educational leaders, giant private foundations, and reformers of all sorts seek to institutionalize innovations and procedures which seem to hold promise for better results, but these often return to the traditional modes when the initiator leaves.

Classroom teachers and others responsible for implementation justifiably ask why continuity can't be pursued until proper evaluations are made. Why do we depart from the traditional programs and activities? One suspects that many of the innovations undertaken failed to take root because the supporting constituency was narrow and derived its power from those in high positions. When the leader departs, the program reverts to homeostasis, i.e., traditionalism, to await another reformer.

Most administrators seek continuously to find better programs—programs that will sustain present gains, achieve results in deficient areas, and enlist broad support among students, staff, the public, and governmental agencies. In short, they seek programs which will become institutionalized as a vital part of education.

I believe strongly that career education is a concept which can become such a program. It has an unusual number of dynamic factors which I believe will move it forward more rapidly than many other concepts. Among them are:

● Broad public support for having careers and education joined so that each graduate will have a saleable skill.

● The importance of an individual's job as a determiner of self-respect, social and economic well-being, and political power in American society.

● The common sense decision-making process which career education develops and which life-long learning and anticipated career changes require.

● The relevancy which career education contributes to the rest of the curriculum.

● The scope and sequence of career education which takes it eventually beyond the school's confines into society at large.

● The reasonable ease with which career education should and can be implemented within a school system.

The Broad Public Support of Career Education

Administrators seeking to innovate have frequently had to build the constituency for the idea from themselves outward because the concepts were often complex and the changes brought about were often viewed with suspicion. The business of constituency building is difficult and often impossible. Career education is not that kind of concept. When career education is mentioned, there is often an almost synaptic response by listeners. They know that the students in our schools will have to work in order to sustain themselves and amount to something. They also know that in the past, students have sometimes graduated from our educational institutions without a reasonable idea of what is entailed in holding a job and with few specific skills to offer potential employers. It's true that some will confuse career education with vocational education, but in my judgment that difficulty can be remedied in time.

The United States Office of Education (USOE) began its thrust for the nationwide adoption of career education as a concept undergirding American elementary and secondary education in 1971. This movement continues to be a high priority item for the USOE and the United States Congress. The Chamber of Commerce of the United States, supported by a multitude of other organizations, has enthusiastically embraced the idea of career education and has issued numerous publications supporting the concept. Local chambers of commerce, PTAs, and other organizations have enthusiastically supported career education. The problem of constituency building for this program should not be difficult.

The Importance of an Individual's Job in American Society

Peter Drucker, the industrial philosopher and management consultant, in his book, *The New Society; The Anatomy of the Industrial Order,* emphasizes that in the industrialized world the divorce of the worker from the product and the means of production is essential and absolute. What Drucker observes is that in an industrialized nation with its mass-production processes, most individuals must work as a component in a production unit, access to which must be given by an organization. The work of an individual is most often obscure in the final product. The day of the artisan who took a product from idea to completion has been totally eliminated from most of the work force. Drucker observes that organizations, rather than individuals, produce. Since this is so, then social status, social prestige, and social power cannot attach to the individual's work; they can only attach to the individual's job (Drucker, 1950).

American society has increasingly reflected this condition. Jobs now are much more than economic necessities. They are the source of social status, social power, and self-respect. This explains why unemployment is often a more personal and social tragedy than an economic one. Drucker notes that during the depression of the 1930s we were able to keep a great majority of the chronically unemployed and their families on an economic level well above physical subsistence and probably well above the level all but the very rich lived only a century ago. The depression's major effects were social, psychological, and political.

Jobs are important to us all. Junior high school and middle school students are particularly concerned about their future in the world of work. They recognize keenly the relationship between life-style and income. They are much less aware of work demands on life-style, self-perception, physical and mental stresses, and social status and power. Hoyt and others state that students ask these kinds of questions: What am I like? Why? What can I become? What am I to do to be worthwhile? How do I get there from here? These questions reflect concerns of the students for the careers they will pursue. They are the engines that can make the concept of career education vital to all education. They are incipient questions in the minds of the very young, and they will intensify as the students grow older. They become critical as preparatory career decisions are required. They will even continue through the working years and into retirement. The cry for a relevant education so forcefully brought to the educational decision makers in the late 1960s was born in these questions. Career education is a way of seeking answers to them.

Career education is a concept which must be adopted in integrated fashion throughout the educational programs of the school system. It must extend from bottom to top. The success of each succeeding new task depends on the thoroughness of the foundation building effort which preceded it. It begins with building awareness of the student's self. At the same time the awareness building program must extend to careers and what they require. During the first seven years of school, kindergarten through grade six, awareness building of career/self is a major task of the school. It helps the students to analyze strengths, weaknesses, likes, and aversions. It helps the student relate this information to information gained about careers.

The Common Sense Decision-making Process Which Career Education Requires

In the 19th century it was not uncommon for a person to work a lifetime at one career. Mobility did not really begin until specialization, which came with the industrialization of the western world. Now it is common to hear speakers say that career changes during a person's life will be manifold. They must be expected and planned for. One of the basic elements of career education embraces the idea that a career is not forever and that a job on a career ladder may be highly temporary. In order to accommodate this ever changing environment, it is essential for the person to have a well-developed and carefully designed decision-making procedure for considering career changes. This procedure must include information gathering skills which will provide raw material for self-assessment in terms of interest and capability, as well as other information gathering skills which focus on career options and the demands those options place on an individual.

Carefully developed guidance programs, which are an important component of career education efforts, are some of the most exciting elements to come out of the career education movement. Often these guidance components will include advanced technology. For example, in the Covina Valley, California, Unified School District the guidance program is computer assisted and integrates the educational achievement with career interests. It allows the guidance counselor to manage the guidance program by exception. The computer itself is able to reinforce students who make good decisions. If schools teach pupils how to make career decisions, those skills should be retained and used for the remainder of the individual's life. In later life, when the individual is considering a career change, the decision-making process may be used again and again.

The Relevancy Which Career Education Contributes to the Rest of the Curriculum

In the late 1960s the cry for a more relevant education was heard on virtually all of the campuses of the land. Thousands of pupils were alleging that what they were required to study was irrelevant to their personal, social, cultural, and economic needs. They urged that educational reform be undertaken so that the curriculum would become relevant to their needs. Career education makes a major step in that direction. Beginning in kindergarten and extending upward through the grades, students are led to see that the basic tools of learning, the social and physical sciences, and the arts are all relevant to careers. By examining careers closely in an exploration phase at the middle and junior high school level, students see workers and others using the subjects that they are learning in school as an integral part of their work.

Career Education at the Middle and Junior High School Levels

Building upon the already established base of self-awareness/career-awareness, the major task of career education in the middle and junior high school is exploration—exploration of self as well as exploration of careers. It is here that the student tests perceptions gained in the awareness building program.

Explorations are conducted in several ways. In a well-developed and integrated career education program the instructional materials in all subjects will have a career orientation. Traditional textbooks will be augmented by specifically developed career-oriented supplemental material; consequently, the student at every turn will be confronted with the idea that what the student is studying is relevant to his or her career and will eventually be necessary to success in the chosen career. Special sections of the school resource center will possess printed and media presentations about different careers and the kinds of skills and attitudes required by them. Students have wide latitude to explore careers through this type of experience within the walls of the school. In addition, opportunities will be provided for career representatives to appear before students to discuss their careers and the personal and other attributes which the individual needs to be productive and happy in it. A continual stream of community visitors will be found on the campuses of middle and junior high schools where there are effective career education programs.

In addition to visitors, there will be external visits by the students to job sites where the student will observe and talk with workers. These opportunities will be extensive. Always before the student will be the questions: What am I like? Why? What can I become? What am I to do to be worthwhile? How do I get there from here? Moreover, as the student watches the workers or reads about a career, the next question must be: Is this a possibility for me?

The Implementation of a Career Education Program

Because of the ease of building an external constituency, often the major problem faced by an administrator who wishes to implement a career education program will be with the staff. After all, staff members are the ones who will be involved in the changes. Staff members who do not feel the necessity for the change will resist it.

At this point it is necessary to identify the three elements which must be present if a problem is to be solved by a group. These elements can best be visualized by an equilateral triangle. Each side of the triangle will represent an element. One side is *authority,* another is *program,* and the third is *commitment.* If the career education program is to be implemented successfully, it is essential that somebody be in charge, that there be a well-developed and understood program, and that those involved in implementing it be committed to its success. This is the task which faces the administrator.

To organize the resources necessary to get this job done, I would recommend the establishment of a project team made up of representatives of all the types of employees who will be touched by the program. The team will be a large one because the program will extend from the bottom to the top of the system. The team's first task is to study the feasibility of a career education program for the district. Adequate resources, both human and financial, must be provided for the team. Planning time, too, must be adequate so that the team can determine the feasibility of such a program and make a sound recommendation to the superintendent, to the board of education, to the staffs of the schools, and to the public.

Once feasibility has been established, the team must develop the program. The program must have appropriately defined objectives, adequate budget, appropriate materials, and human resources. It must be explicit as to the duties of all; it must establish the structure in which the implementation will take place. The project team should oversee the implementation of the program and should be available to eliminate the bugs that are sure to appear. Finally, the project team must be an important element in the evaluation of the program. The team must have representation from administrators, parents, students, teachers, and support staff. The time frame for implementation must be established in the feasibility program. Implementers must think in terms of years rather than months to have the entire program flowing smoothly.

I believe career education is here to stay. I think that it will be beneficial to American education generally, for it gives us a focus and has wide appeal. I believe we should get on with the task of implementing it in all school systems of the nation.

UNINTENDED CAREER EDUCATION IN THE ENGLISH CLASSROOM

Marjorie M. Kaiser
Dr. Kaiser is assistant professor of education at the University of Louisville. Her professional emphasis is in English education. This article was written in 1977.

Although the term career education was not really coined until 1970, career education has always permeated the public school curriculum. This permeation has not been visible in the manner of the current organized awareness, exploration, and orientation programs and popular school-wide efforts to infuse academic subject matter with career education concepts and information. It is common knowledge, however, that students in our schools, as in the culture at large, have traditionally been educated toward certain attitudes, predispositions, and stereotyped notions of the world of work and of the possibilities for them in it. The present national emphasis on formalized career education programs (K-12) represents a response to the need not only to provide new information, attitudes, skills, and insights but also to counteract the misleading notions which have prevailed.

In the last five years, various academic areas of the curriculum have been examined to determine how they can aid in the facilitation of career education goals, and, indeed, much has been done to redesign and refocus basic subjects with career education concepts and information in mind. In the English-language arts curriculum, in particular, to which students are subjected during every year of public school, an abundance of material has been created which has the potential of aiding students in making connections between their work with language arts skills and the world of work. Very little, however, has yet been produced by publishers or in-service teachers and other professionals to tap the rich reservoir that is the literature study portion of the English curriculum. Students spend typically over 50% of the time in English classrooms reading, analyzing, discussing, and enjoying literature (Squire and Applebee 1968). With the current refocusing in many public schools on basic language skills, this percentage may be decreasing; nevertheless, it is likely that literature study will always be an important part of any English-language arts curriculum.

Of course, much literature can be read and explored from a career education point of view, and students can be encouraged to consider the importance of work in human lives as it is presented in fiction, poetry, drama, and nonfiction. They can examine varying attitudes toward work and be helped to discover the intricate interaction between human beings and their work—both how human factors affect the quality of the work performed and how the work performed affects these human factors.

But whether students are actively engaged in this kind of exploration of literature or not, they are bound to be affected, in subtle ways perhaps, by what they read and discuss, just as they are by their families' values and attitudes and the mass media surrounding them in their daily lives outside the classroom. Television, films, radio, and periodicals, all enjoyed outside schools, have played their part in building the knowledge and attitudes students develop toward the world of work and toward their place in it. If classroom teachers make no conscious effort toward integrating career education into literature study, it is likely that students will still pick up information, values, and attitudes from what they read.

Eighth Grade Literature Anthologies

What then do the literature books in use in English classrooms contain that may be indirectly educating young people across the country? In an attempt to answer this question, this author analyzed in detail six of the most popular basic eighth grade literature anthologies currently in use in public schools (Kaiser 1976). These six anthologies (Carlsen 1969; Cline 1972; Kitzhaber 1968; Littell 1971; Pooley 1967; Purves 1973) appear on state textbook adoption lists of 23 states. The analysis was limited to the eighth grade level for four important reasons. First, in general, students at this level are at their peak reading interest. From the eighth or ninth grade on, both interest in reading and amount of reading decrease (Carlsen 1967). Secondly, this level is specified in career education programs as part of the exploratory phase, and if classroom teachers chose to make a conscious effort to facilitate career education aims through literature study, this level would seem the most appropriate at which to begin. Third, since the same publishers and series of literature anthologies tend to be adopted by an entire school division, certain generalizations reached about the eighth grade books might likely be true about the seventh and ninth grade anthologies in the series. Finally, the middle or junior high school level may well be a more critical level for students, when their attitudes may still be somewhat malleable. They are apt to be less rigid in their notions about the world of work and about themselves than they are at the senior high school level when in most school divisions they must declare themselves as college bound or vocational.

The importance of these basic literature texts cannot be underestimated. Aside from the fact that supplementary text materials, paperbacks, and hardbounds are used in many school divisions, the basic literature in eighth grade English classes does come from these standard anthologies. In many not so affluent communities, the literature anthology and a grammar-composition handbook comprise the only materials students are issued for their work in English.

Analysis of these six basic literature anthologies revealed a surprising amount of unintended career education. Among the many findings of the analysis, the most important areas include: (1) the number of selections showing work in the anthologies and its importance to theme and characterization; (2) the racial and sexual representations of working characters; (3) the attitudes expressed toward work, the values in work, and the concept of occupational choice or options; and (4) the degree of reinforcement of selected basic career education concepts. These aspects of the anthologies have no doubt played an indirect part in helping to reinforce or negate information, concepts, and attitudes about the world of work that students bring to them.

Selections Treating Work

Because the total number of selections varies from book to book, from 48 to 112, a percentage system was used to present the findings of the analysis. In order for a selection to be considered to show work or present it as significant background, the principal character or narrator had to be actually engaged in his or her work in the selection, or the work of the character had to have background importance to theme or character. In either case, to be fair to the selection as a whole, a teacher could not fail to include some discussion of the work itself and its relation to character or theme, and a student would be apt to see the work as a necessary part of the selection. If work was included incidentally in any selection, as it was in many, the piece was not considered a work selection.

To illustrate this distinction, two selections will serve as examples. In Stephen Crane's short story, "The Bride Comes to Yellow Sky," which appears in two anthologies, Jack Potter's work as a marshal is a major focus in the plot, is important to Jack's character, and has some bearing on themes of the story. On the other hand, in many selections the work of the principal character or narrator is simply mentioned in passing as the character returns home from work to engage in leisure or interacts with other individuals in some way that is unrelated to her or his work. Work is presented in this manner in a selection entitled "Discovery of a Father" from *Memoirs* by Sherwood Anderson. The father's work, running a harness shop, is referred to but is only incidental to his character and is unimportant to the basic subject and theme of the story, a boy's growing appreciation of his father.

In the six anthologies the percentage of selections treating work ranged from 30% to 53%, the mean being 42%. These percentages reveal that a considerable number of the literary selections do involve work to some extent. Literature deals with life, and part of life for nearly all human beings is work. The literature in these anthologies clearly reflects this aspect of life. The work content is clearly there in the anthologies. It is not, however, always critical to the theme or characterization of the selections.

Importance of Work to Theme and Characterization

In judging the importance of work to the theme of a selection, the following rationale was used. If the theme or main point of the selection stated in a sentence centered on work, the work was considered essential. If the statement of theme did not center on the work, per se, it was considered to have only some bearing on theme. For example, "Alone," an autobiographical sketch about Admiral Richard Byrd, solitarily performing his work as a weather scientist in Antarctica, clearly presents a theme that involves the frustrations, dangers, and rewards of this kind of work. The work is essential to the theme. In *The Diary of Anne Frank,* on the other hand, Anne's schoolwork and her writing, while essential to her character, are not the focus of the theme of the play, which speaks rather to the broader themes of the dignity and courage of the human spirit.

In judging the importance of work to the characterization in a selection, a similar kind of reasoning was employed. If the work of a character was central to his or her characterization, then it was considered essential. For example, in Reginald Rose's drama, *Twelve Angry Men,* the work of the principal character, serving as a juror in a murder trial, is intricately connected to the characterization the dramatist creates. His basic character qualities of honesty, justice, and responsibility are illuminated by his contributions as a juror. If the work was important to character but not central to it, then it was considered simply to have some bearing on characterization. For example, in John Clarke's short story, "The Boy Who Painted Christ Black," a young black boy works as a student but takes his leisure activity of painting much more seriously. The desire to create art provides his motivation and expresses his feelings, beliefs, and attitudes much more than his schoolwork does.

In selections in which it was determined that the work presented was essential to theme or characterization, work was shown as very important in life, and it would be difficult for student or teachers to read and discuss them without carrying away a feeling for or a thought about the significance of work to characters or narrators in the various genres of literature. Four of the six anthologies had higher proportions of selections in which work featured prominently in terms of both theme and characterizations (Carlsen 1969; Kitzhaber 1968; Littell 1971; Purves 1973).

Racial Representation of Workers

In the selections treating work, the mean proportion of Caucasian principal characters was 85%. The two anthologies with the highest proportions of non-Caucasian principal working characters (37% and 22%) are texts specifically designed for unmotivated learners and/or students with learning or reading difficulties (Cline 1972; Purves 1973). The one anthology in the group specifically aimed at accelerated or advanced students presents not a single non-Caucasian working principal character (Kitzhaber 1968). Those anthologies in the middle range, designed for students of average and above average ability, present 79%, 92%, 97% Caucasian principal working characters.

These proportions clearly indicate the bias of editors in compiling the anthologies. First of all, the inclusion of selections with non-Caucasian working principal characters in the anthologies designed for unmotivated students and/or students with learning or reading difficulties suggests that many non-Caucasians would be apt to use these anthologies. Conversely, not many non-Caucasians would be apt to use the anthology designed for accelerated students.

The mean representation of Orientals and American Indians, in particular, were both 2%, but four of the six anthologies presented no Oriental and no Indian working characters. This imbalance of the races in several of the anthologies appears even more potentially damaging to student readers when one examines the particular work of the non-Caucasian characters who are included. The non-Caucasian characters or narrators number 20 out of a total of 171 characters considered. The work of these characters is broken down by group in the following way: 15 Negro characters are portrayed as three farmers, three comedians, three domestic workers, three athletes, one carpenter, and two students. Two of the three Negro domestic workers are the only Negro women represented in the anthologies.

Orientals account for three principal characters. These characters are one male student, one female in unclassifiable work, and one male animal keeper. There are two American Indians in all the selections showing work; one is a farmer, while the other is a medicine man.

The anthologies as a whole clearly tend to reinforce traditional and/or stereotyped occupational roles for non-Caucasians, while Caucasians are shown in a wide variety of occupational roles. Such stereotyping in the anthologies distracts greatly from the usability of the books in any career education-literature effort, to say nothing of the subtle and depressing effects it must have on the developing self-concepts of non-Caucasian students and the reinforcing effects on Caucasian prejudice.

Sexual Representation of Workers

Male principal characters dominate the six anthologies, with a mean of 86% male in all selections. Inasmuch as women comprise 51.4% of the population (1970 census), this representation of the real world is a gross distortion. The mean proportion of male characters shown at work in the six anthologies is 89%, while the female representation is 11%. This finding, too, in view of the working world is a serious underrepresentation for women. As of 1974, women between the ages of 16 and 70 made up 39% of the civilian labor force.

Surely, if students consistently read about and identify only with male characters, with a few exceptions, they will carry away the notion that this is the way things are or perhaps even should be. The anthologies in general imply that men are more worth writing about than women, they do more interesting things in life, and that men, rarely women, do the work of the world.

Of the women shown working in the anthologies, 18 in all, their work may be categorized in the following types: 11 workers in the home, one in business, four students, and two in nonclassifiable work. Clearly, this picture of women workers is a stereotyped view. As of 1974, 35% of working women were in clerical positions; 18% were service workers outside the home; 15% were in professional-technical positions; 13% were operatives in factories; 7% were in sales; 5% were in management and administration; 4% were in private household work; and 3% were in other occupations (U.S. Department of Labor 1975).

The obvious stereotyping of occupational roles for women characters again underscores the bias of editors. Literature is available in quantity now that not only shows women in a diversity of occupational roles but also possesses literary merit. With a conscious effort, more selections could be included which would help present a more realistic view of women in the world. Without this inclusion, female students will continue to see a distorted view of themselves in life and a restricted range of occupational opportunities.

Attitudes Toward Work

The bulk of the selections treating work in the anthologies, over two-thirds of them, present characters or narrators who express a mild or strong liking for their work. The character expresses his or her attitude toward work in dialogue, in thoughts, or in behavior. An author may also comment in descriptive or narrative passages in such a way as to reveal an attitude. Examples of strong liking abound. There is Bill Cosby in an autobiographical sketch expressing his joy in being a comedian; there is Charlie Gordon in "Flowers for Algernon" delighting in his janitorial work with his buddies; there is Buddy's distant, aged cousin in Truman Capote's "A Christmas Memory" who takes great pride and pleasure in her domestic work, including the baking of Christmas fruitcakes.

Many characters or narrators express mild liking for their work. Jesse Stuart's young hero works happily enough as a blacksmith to earn money for college in "Winner at the Fair." Somerset Maugham's George Ramsay in "The Ant and the Grasshopper" is a hardworking, decent, respectable fellow who enjoys his work to some degree, looks forward to retirement, and is forced to help support a n'er-do-well brother who despises work. Characters with neutral, accepting attitudes toward work include Steinbeck's cotton pickers in an excerpt from *Grapes of Wrath,* Saroyan's young boy in "The Parsley Garden," who works as a stock boy to pay back a store owner for merchandise he has stolen, and Robert Frost's young farmhand in "Out, Out,—," who in the late afternoon of a long day, lets his mind wander from the sawing of logs only to have the saw cut off his arm.

Practically no characters express mild disliking for work, but there are among the selections several that express strong disliking. These include characters such as Curly Kid in "Why Rustlers Never Win" by Henry Felson. Curly Kid is a young cattle rustler who has such trouble and suffers such pain getting rid of stolen cattle that he comes to hate his work and finally accepts a position as a truant officer. Mr. Hinds, in V. S. Naipaul's "The Raffle," is a primary teacher in Trinidad who hates teaching and his pupils and thus flogs small children at any opportunity.

Building positive attitudes toward work is one of the very important goals of career education programs, and assuming that students can pick up attitudes from what they read, this aspect of unintended career education is a plus factor. By and large, characters like their work, and there is little variation based on race, publication period, or career cluster in which the workers can be classified. There is noticeable variation in attitude toward work according to sex and age group. Out of the total of 18 female working characters, eight of them expressed neutral attitudes (44%), while of the male working characters only 19% were in the neutral category, while 67% fell into the positive categories. This finding, in spite of the small numbers, does suggest less positive attitudes toward work from females than from males. In view of the limited types of work in which women are shown, this finding is not surprising.

Even though the attitudes are predominantly positive, there is also some variation by age group. Age groups used in the analysis were as follows: 6-12, 13-18, 19-35, 36-50, and over 50. The age groups with higher proportions of working characters expressing positive attitudes toward their work are the elementary school age group and the mature adult age group. The largest representation of age groups in the work selections, however, is in the young adult and middle-age groups. Consequently, though the attitudes toward work are most positive in the elementary school and mature adult age groups, there are fewer of those characters in the anthologies. Since students during adolescence tend to identify most readily with students close to them in age or a bit older, this enthusiasm for work on the part of young children and people over 50 years of age may have a negligible effect on eighth grade students. Still, overall the attitudes tend to be in the positive range.

Values in Work

Characters in literature find a variety of values in work just as people in real life do. Many workers find more than one value in their work, but typically one chief value dominates. The chief values or redeeming qualities of work may be classified in the following seven categories: (1) the work environment; (2) supervisors and associates; (3) hours; (4) material gains; (5) pride, prestige, and dignity; (6) solace and therapy; and (7) service and the pursuit of truth.

In all the selections from all anthologies the chief values of work indicated by the working principal characters were, in order of importance: (1) material gains; (2) pride, prestige, and dignity; and (3) service and the pursuit of truth. These three categories account for 80% or more of all the work selections in all the anthologies. In general, the other four categories are not represented sufficiently to be important. Very few characters saw no value whatsoever in work, and few indicated the work environment or supervisors and associates as a chief value. No characters found the chief value of work to lie in working hours or solace or therapy. In only one anthology did material gains not take first place in the ranking of values. Sixty percent of the working characters in this book revealed pride, prestige, and dignity as the chief value of work. This anthology is one of the ones designed for unmotivated students and/or students with learning or reading difficulties, the same anthology with the highest proportion, 37%, of non-Caucasian characters (Cline 1972). While it is doubtful that conscious decisions were made by editors compiling this anthology to present non-Caucasian working characters who see the value of work in the pride, prestige, dignity category, it is certainly a plus feature that this is true. Non-Caucasian students reading the selections would be apt to sense a conviction in the literature that one's work can help enhance one's self-image and image in the family and community.

Occupational Choice

Career education programs emphasize the concept of occupational choice, the belief that "every individual in a culture can find an occupation which is suited to him, which he is suited to, and in which he can achieve satisfaction of his basic needs" (Roe 1956, p. 252). This definition implies a consciousness on the part of the individual, an active planning and decision-making process in regard to her or his work role. Most of the selections in the anthologies (81%) express a negative attitude or no attitude toward occupational choice. The categories used in the analysis were four: (1) affirms the possibility of occupational choice; (2) affirms the possibility but accepts limits; (3) negates the possibility and accepts the inevitable, fate, or destiny; and (4) expresses no attitude toward occupational choice.

The characters who tend to negate the concept accept the work they do in life as something predestined for them by family, by geography, by economic conditions, by history, or by a combination of these forces. In the positive categories, characters express the attitude that they are in control of the kind of work they are engaged in or will be engaged in, perhaps within certain limits. By and large, the anthologies do not support the possibility of occupational choice. Students reading these anthologies would sense a lack of conscious participation on the part of characters in their own careers.

Career Education Concepts

Although there are many concepts which career education experts find basic to the establishment of formal career education programs, the ten concepts selected for use in this analysis were chosen with a specific rationale in mind. The concepts selected were those most often identified with the exploratory phase (middle or junior high school); concepts which applied only to actual work experience and not to what might be communicated through literature were eliminated; likewise, concepts of a strictly

TABLE 7-A.
Reinforcement of Career Education Concepts

Career education concept	Mean proportions		
	upholds	ignores	negates
1. There is dignity in work.	62	23	15
2. Persons need to be recognized as having dignity and worth.	58	39	3
3. Society is dependent upon the work of many people.	42	58	
4. Work means different things to different people.	31	69	
5. An understanding and acceptance of self is important throughout life.	32	68	
6. Individuals differ in their interests, abilities, attitudes, and values.	73	27	
7. Education and work are interrelated.	13	82	5
8. The occupation one chooses affects his/her total life style.	57	43	
9. Satisfying and rewarding work may bring self-fulfillment.	44	56	
10. Such factors as age, sex, race, or religion no longer limit career possibilities.	1	76	23

informational nature having to do with job classifications of one kind or another were eliminated. The final list of ten concepts used are basic ones relating to attitudes toward self, work, the value of work, and occupational choice.

In the analysis a judgment was made about whether each work selection tended to uphold, ignore, or negate each of the ten concepts. Table 7-A will give an impression of the degree to which the anthologies as a group reinforced the concepts.

The concepts ignored by the highest proportion of selections are 4, 5, 7, and 10; the concepts upheld by the largest proportions of selections include concepts 1, 2, 6, and 8. The concepts upheld by the smallest proportions of selections are 10 and 7. While the concepts upheld by high proportions of the selections focusing on work are important concepts, those that are ignored or negated may be more important. Concept 10, a basic principle and belief of those in the field of career education, implies that artificial barriers to career opportunities no longer exist in the world of work. Clearly, the selections analyzed in this study do not uphold this concept. They either ignore it or negate it. Concept 7 is perhaps the single most important concept in terms of what career education attempts to do in relation to the entire school curriculum. *Education and work are interrelated.* This concept was upheld by a small mean proportion of selections; it was ignored by a high mean proportion. These two concepts are conspicuous in their mean proportions.

The impact of these findings lies not so much in the lack of reinforcement of some of the concepts as in the negation and ignoring of some of them. It is likely that student readers, without the benefit of conscious exploration of work in literature and without the guidance of a teacher concerned with promoting the concepts of career education, would leave their literature study with many of the same stereotyped notions about the world of work and the meaning of work that they brought to it. Further, and perhaps more critical to many English teachers, the gap between life in literature and life itself will remain as great as it has always been for many students.

Conclusion

Underlying the reporting of these findings are two important assumptions. First, it is assumed that career education is a respectable and essential means of making academic education meaningful to a great many students. Secondly, the author has worked with the conviction that the aims and principles of career education should be supported by the literature study portion as well as the practical skills portion of an English program. The analysis described here provides career education program leaders as well as classroom English teachers with an indication of what is contained between the covers of the literature books. Whether the literature is consciously used with career education in mind or not, unintended career education is bound to be taking place. Some of this education, as in the case of attitudes toward work, is of a positive nature, while some of it, as with racial and sexual representation and stereotyping, is bound to be damaging.

Although much research has been done with elementary level texts, especially readers, more research to discover work content and attitudes needs to be done with texts in use in all academic areas of all levels. Until such time as those planning and implementing career education programs know precisely what kinds of and how much unintended career education throughout the curriculum students are experiencing, it seems unlikely that formal efforts in positive directions will bring about completely successful outcomes for students.

QUERIES, INFLUENCERS, AND VOCATIONAL INTERESTS OF JUNIOR HIGH SCHOOL STUDENTS

S. Theodore Woal
Dr. Woal is supervisor of school guidance services in Philadelphia and has recently been appointed a member of the State of Pennsylvania's advisory council on career education. This article was written in 1974.

The current thrust in the area of career education suggests that students have many unanswered questions about work. This report presents data on: (1) what information about the world of work ninth grade students have or desire to have in order to make appropriate subject selections to support their tentative job choices; (2) what information about occupations is of major concern to students (whether student inquiries are directed toward data that will assist them in preparing for and entering jobs or about responsibilities, conditions, and other cogent conditions associated with the jobs); and (3) who the most significant influencers of students are.

Research related to various aspects of this study has been conducted in previous years. Ginzberg (1950) discussed some of the problems of vocational choice. Powell and Bloom (1963), working with 900 students in grades 10, 11, and 12, concluded that youth are frustrated in the intelligent selection of vocation due to lack of knowledge of vocational fields and that, in spite of the emphasis on guidance in school, adolescents have little vocational guidance and seldom is it effective.

Doane (1970) investigated the media and procedures in orienting secondary school students to occupations and the opportunities to prepare for them in 27 schools in grades 8 through 12. The Doane study indicated among other findings that 49% of the students stated parents were the most helpful persons in planning with them for their future jobs and occupations; out-of-school people were most helpful, the percentage decreasing from 77% in eighth grade to 61% in twelfth grade; less than one out of ten felt that the counselor was the most helpful person.

The American College Testing Programs (Prediger 1973) conducted a nationwide survey of career development which involved 32,000 students in grades 8, 9, and 11. Again, over one-half of the eleventh grade students (56%) indicated that they received little or no help with career planning via discussions with counselors, and the percentage is substantially higher with eighth graders. Also, their lack of knowledge of the world of work and the career planning process testifies to the need for help.

Purpose of the Study

This study was undertaken with four subject areas in mind: (1) student familiarity with occupations in the world of work; (2) influencers of the tentative choices of occupations; (3) post-high-school plans; and (4) queries and concerns of students pertinent to preparation for entry into a job.

In addition to the above, it was the intention of this investigation to give direction to teachers, counselors, and school administrators in order that guidance programs be more closely related to the needs of the students.

Procedure

To ascertain the vocational interests and the influences that impinge upon and form the tentative vocational choices of junior high school students, a questionnaire constructed by the researcher was administered to 207 ninth grade students whose median I.Q. was 105 (sigma 3.4). Included were 94 boys and 113 girls with a verbal ability and reading comprehension equivalent to ninth grade in a large, urban, integrated school consisting of lower middle-class families. The parents of these students were primarily engaged as skilled or semiskilled workers, and an undetermined number were recipients of welfare supplements.

Findings

Limited knowledge of the world of work. This study utilized the generic names of occupations and professions rather than the categories of the Bureau of Labor Statistics or other agencies. The reason for this was to ascertain the familiarity of the students with specific job nomenclature, since this is their language, and also the vocabulary of influencers, parents, peers, teachers, counselors, and media.

Significantly, an individual boy or girl could not name a total of three jobs that were of interest at the time the questionnaire was administered. Ninety different jobs were named by boys for a total of 265, or 3.0 per boy. The girls named 64 different jobs for a total of 26, or 2.0 each.

The boys reported vocational interests as follows: engineers, 17%; mechanics, 13%; teachers and lawyers, 15%; chemists, 10%; and scientists, 5%. The remaining 40% were distributed among 36 different occupations including artists, computer programmers, draftsmen, police officers, detectives, and plumbers.

The job interests of the girls were as follows: secretaries, 20%; teachers, 15%; beauticians, 12%; stewardesses, 10%; and social workers (including doctors), 3%. The remaining 40% were distributed among 29 different job areas including fashion designer, salesclerk, armed forces, bookkeeper, waitress, and baby-sitter.

It is interesting to note that the Powell and Bloom (1963) study covered offsprings of parents with a higher proportion of college attendance than the general population. Nevertheless, planned levels of occupations in the Powell-Bloom report and this study are compatible. For example in the Powell-Bloom study, 49% of the boys voted for the professions; in this study it was 47%. For the girls the figures are almost identical: office work and teaching accounted for 36.5% in the Powell-Bloom study, while this study found 35%.

Parental influence greatest. Eleven different persons influenced the girls in their job interest. Students reported more than one influencer. The descending order was as follows: parents, 44%; self, 19%; brothers and sisters, 13%; teachers and counselors, 11%; relatives, 8%; and doctors, dentists, books, and television, 5%. Mothers influenced the girls most with 28% as compared to fathers with 16%. Teachers and counselors representing the school ran a low fourth place.

Fourteen different persons influenced the boys in their vocational interest as follows: parents, 40%; self, 15%; brothers and sisters, 13%; teachers and counselors, 11%; relatives, 11%; and books and television, 10%. Boys were influenced mostly by fathers (30%) as compared to mothers (10%), or in the ratio of 3:1. As with the girls, the school was the fourth place influencer.

A comparison of the Doane (1970) study and this investigation reveals very significant facts concerning influencers of vocational choice. For example, in the Doane study students indicated that the most helpful people in planning for future jobs were parents, accounting for 55% of the influencers. In this investigation, parents were the majority influencers of 40% of the boys and 44% of the girls. Sisters and brothers account for 7% in the Doane study and 13% in this investigation; relatives were 5% in Doane's study compared to 11 and 8% for boys and girls in this study. In the A.C.T. study 50-60% (eighth and eleventh graders) indicated that they discussed career plans with parents and relatives several times.

The socio-economic status of the parents of the students in this investigation is in all probability lower than in the Doane studies. Although Doane does not reference his population, it could be assumed that it came from a more favorable socio-economic condition as compared to the lower middle-class situation of the parents in this study. For example, in many of the families in this study, the mother tongue is still used in the home, and many parents and children are encapsulated in the immediate community. This could lend credence to the fact that in this study sisters, brothers, and relatives were a greater influence on the students. These older brothers and sisters have had a wider exposure to the world of work and, thereby, are more familiar with the working world.

The extended family constellation appears to be the greatest influence on the tentative choices of these students. This situation raised several significant questions: Is the family group adequately prepared to offer guidance in this area? Should the school make programs of information available in the area of career development for the family group?

Another salient point can be drawn from the data concerned with influencers of vocational interest. The teachers and counselors representing the schools are a relatively minor influence in career development activity. In both Doane's and the present study, it was found that school counselors and teachers commanded fourth place as influencers of vocational choice. In both studies, only 11% of the students recorded this. This situation is reinforced by the A.C.T. study which indicated that only 9% of the students in eighth grade (up to 20% in eleventh grade) had any sustained contact with teachers and counselors in connection with career interest and jobs.

The inference is that the school experience does not represent a vital force in forming vocational interests. This is probably due to insufficient emphasis on career education in the school curriculum and should give direction to curriculum revision.

Post-high-school plans. When queried as to expectation for completing high school, all the boys and 92% of the girls expressed themselves affirmatively. Eighty percent of the girls and all the boys planned to engage in some form of higher education. However, the matter of financing continued education beyond high school concerned these students. To this question: If there were no problem of money for going to college, would you go? about 92% of the girls and all the boys answered yes. The inference here is strong in the direction of continuing education beyond high school.

The girls indicated that in college they would pursue studies to become: teachers, 36%; nurses, 9%; doctors, 3%; secretaries, 2%; and such other professions as commercial artist, social worker, stewardess, and designer. However, 40% stated they did not now know what area to follow in college. Ninety percent of the boys referred to lawyer, teacher, doctor, engineer, botanist, and business administration; 10% did not know.

These data reveal that: (1) the boys were surer of their vocational aspirations, and (2) in both sexes the emphasis is on the professions.

Once again, these findings corroborate the Powell-Bloom study (1963). Their population included tenth, eleventh, and twelfth grade students and showed 50% of boys and girls planning to enter professional areas.

Queries about preparation and advancement on the job. Several investigators have reported that the information presented in occupational brochures is not oriented to the facts about jobs that enable the students to make intelligent vocational choices (Hoyt et al. 1972).

To ascertain concerns in the area of decision making, this question was asked of each student: "What do you want to know about your future job interest choice?" They replied as follows:

QUESTIONS PERTAINING TO PREPARATION FOR THE JOB

Girls	Boys
What training is required?	What special training is needed?
How long is the training?	What kind of grades are required?
What is the best school to attend?	What courses do I take?
What courses do I take at high school?	What training is needed?
Do I have to go to college?	How long is the training?
How much does it cost to train for the job?	

QUESTIONS ABOUT THE JOB

Girls	Boys
How does it pay?	What are the requirements?
What are the hours of work?	What is the salary?
What are the advancement possibilities?	What special training is required?
What kind of work will I be doing?	What jobs are open in this field?
Does the college get you a job?	Where is the location?
Is it exciting?	Will there be enough jobs open?
	What hours will I work?

The questions of the students were very specific, and the listing is a compendium of all the individual queries. The concerns of the students about preparation for the job and about the job itself do not differ substantially by sex; however, the above summary may well serve as a basis for the development of relevant career information which would be meaningful to students.

Conclusions

This study indicates several significant areas that require the attention of school personnel engaged in guidance activity in the area of vocational information. Primarily five areas are involved: (1) occupational information must be presented to students; data is needed that will answer the basic questions raised by the students; (2) provision must be made in the school curricula for time slots to develop adequately these data by all available and innovative educational devices; (3) school staff, through staff development programs, must become more knowledgeable about industry requirements, emerging job areas, and school preparation required; (4) counseling activities, both individual and group, must be increased to convey to students the relevancy between school and the world of work in very definite terms; this should be specifically related to their occupational needs; and (5) some provision must be made to include parents in the career education process since they are the major influencers of vocational choice at this time.

REFERENCES

Carlsen, Robert G. *Books and the Teen-age Reader.* New York: Bantam Books, 1967.

Carlsen, Robert G. *Perception: Themes in Literature.* New York: McGraw-Hill, 1969.

Cline, Jay, ed. *Voices in Literature, Language and Composition, Book B.* Lexington, Mass.: Ginn and Company, 1972.

Doane, Raymond C. *Project Guidance Practice.* Storrs, Conn.: University of Connecticut, 1970.

Drucker, Peter. *The New Society; The Anatomy of the Industrial Order.* New York: Harper and Row, 1950.

Ginzberg, Eli, et al. "The Problems of Occupational Choice." *Journal of Orthopsychiatry* Vol. 20 (1950): 166-201.

Hoyt, Kenneth B., et al. *Career Education, What It Is and How To Do It.* Salt Lake City: Olympus, 1972.

Kaiser, Marjorie. *Work Content and Attitudes Toward Work in Eighth Grade Literature Anthologies.* Unpublished Ph.D. dissertation, Virginia Polytechnic Institute and State University, 1976.

Kitzhaber, Albert R., ed. *The Oregon Curriculum: Literature II.* New York: Holt, Rinehart and Winston, 1968.

Littell, Joy, ed. *Man in the Fictional Mode, Book 2; Man in the Poetic Mode, Book 2; Man in the Dramatic Mode, Book 2; Man in the Expository Mode, Book 2.* Four vols. considered as one book. Evanston, Ill.: McDougal, Littel and Co., 1971.

Pooley, Robert C., ed. *Counterpoint in Literature.* Glenview, Ill.: Scott Foresman, 1967.

Powell, Marvin, and Bloom, Viola. "Development of and Reasons for Vocational Choices of Adolescents Through the High School Years." *Journal of Educational Research* 50 (1963): 126-33.

Prediger, D. J., et al. *Nationwide Study of Student Career Development, no. 61.* Iowa City: American College Testing Program, Research and Development Division, November 1973.

Purves, Alan C., ed. *Responding: Basic Sequence Two.* Lexington, Mass.: Ginn and Company, 1973.

Roe, Anne. *The Psychology of Occupations.* New York: Wiley, 1956.

Squire, James R., and Applebee, Roger K. *The National Study of High School English Programs: High School Instruction Today.* New York: Appleton-Century Crofts, 1968.

U. S. Department of Labor, Bureau of Labor Statistics, *Handbook of Labor Statistics, Reference Edition.* Washington: 1975.

<table>
<tr>
<td>

CHAPTER

8

</td>
<td>

Career Education in the Secondary School

</td>
</tr>
</table>

The contributions that career education could make at the secondary school level are enormous in terms of career selection and even, to some degree, career preparation. However, to make these contributions possible, the structure of the secondary school curriculum has to be modified. Wise career choices and preparation are essential to all secondary school students, and the modifications must take into account the needs, aspirations, potential, and interests of all students and not only those who will go on to college or enter the world of work.

Chapter 8 consists of three articles written in 1975 when most of the discussions about career education were centered on curriculum reform at the secondary level and attempts were being made to distinguish career education from vocational education. J. Lloyd Trump addresses the total reform needed, including those administrative changes as may be required. He discusses the aspects of reform and provides suggestions for needed key improvements. Howard M. Johnson approaches the same problem but as it applies to school staff development and discusses the employer-based career education model, one of the four models proposed and supported at that time by career education proponents and by the USOE. Curtis R. Finch and N. Alan Sheppard attempt to reduce the confusion between career education and vocational education and draw distinctions between the two. One of the unique features of their article is the inclusion of the variety of definitions of both career education and vocational education as were prevalent at the time the manuscript was prepared.

TOTAL CURRICULUM REFORM AND SOME ADMINISTRATIVE CHANGES THAT CAREER EDUCATION REQUIRES

J. Lloyd Trump

Dr. Trump is associate secretary for research and development, emeritus, for the National Association of Secondary School Principals. He has authored several books on the secondary schools. This article was written in 1975.

The secondary school curriculum in the United States is not much better today than it was three or four decades ago. The system usually requires or specifies half or more of what students take in high school. The required half is typically oriented more in the direction of college and university attendance than toward real life needs. The present situation exists in spite of a variety of efforts at curricular reform running through the decades from the 1930s to the present. Today's innovations of mini-courses and similar changes largely involve the elective areas of curriculum. What is also needed is a fundamental reexamination of the curriculum that the school requires of all students.

The required and elective system, which became a benchmark of secondary education in the United States, was a revolt against the traditional secondary education of European countries that gave students relatively few opportunities to follow their own interests and talents. That latter route was open only to those students who were not in the *gymnasium*, the *lycee*, the grammar schools, or other forms of pre-university programs that provided potential admittance to the better world that university education opened. The flexibility that the required-elective system in the United States provided for all students was envied by many—and condemned by some—in the educational systems in other countries.

The required-elective system here, however, also had serious drawbacks. University preparation still dominated both types of courses. Elective courses were relatively rigid in that much of the content was predetermined by the school system, and almost all of it was organized into either semester or one-year courses with the same credit system as applied to the required courses.

It was no accident that volume I, no. 1, of the *Journal of Career Education* had as its subtitle, "Focus on Vocational Education." Although the issue contained a number of stimulating and provocative articles, career education too often is synonymous with vocational education instead of being a fundamental part of every academic course that the school offers. The use of the term *academic course* in this article simply indicates how strong the mores are.

Aspects of Reform

This writer's hope is that career education will cause the kind of curricular reform that many thoughtful and imaginative persons have recommended for many decades in this country but with relatively small effect on the total curriculum. Every subject and every division of an education program has three general aspects that every student, parent, teacher, and administrator should understand clearly.

First, there are those aspects in the cognitive and skills areas, and to a great degree in the affective domain, that are essential for everyone in this society. Unfortunately the concept of minimum essentials is deplored by many curricular experts. Probably the reason is that they are reluctant to help determine what everyone really needs to know, be able to do, and to have as a part of his or her values, attitudes, and the like. Who is to make the determination of what is essential and how is it to be done? Franklin Bobbitt and his students at the University of Chicago a half century ago answered the question in terms of the mathematics, the science, the literary skills, and so on that everyone needed in order to comprehend the daily newspaper (radio and television did not complicate their lives). In spite of the complexities of modern society, schools still need to make those decisions today. If the decisions are not made, the required curriculum will remain so extensive that students have neither time nor energy to reach the other two aspects of curriculum needs.

The school's responsibility, of course, goes far beyond the requirement of minimum essentials. Secondly, the program needs to help every student discover areas of special interest and competence that might be called hobbies. These outcomes enrich life, add meaning, encourage productivity, and help each individual throughout a lifetime to keep a variety of doors open to careers that at the moment may not be of interest. Moreover, the activities and knowledge in this second area of curriculum are quite necessary for helping individuals to lead a better life outside the hours that they devote to their careers. The process of discovering these interests and talents also gives the individual something to fall back upon when, for one reason or another, career interests change or society forces change.

The third aspect of education is to help each individual identify career interests and to provide preparation for entrance into one or more of these vocations. Every subject in the school is a vocational subject. Every division of every subject has career implications.

The important curriculum task that each secondary school faces is to develop a curriculum organization in all of the basic fields of learning and instruction that clearly indicates to the students and their parents what is essential for everyone of them to know in order to get along at minimal yet adequate levels in our society. At the same time, every subject needs to be taught in a way to provide hobbies and special interests that students may follow currently and know about for possible later use. Moreover, every part of every subject needs to be taught in such a way as to indicate how people who have acquired those subject skills and knowledge have used them in careers.

These three aspects of curriculum may be illustrated simply; however, in the final analysis, the sophisticated development may be quite complex. Why should anyone study poetry? Is there any aspect of poetry that is essential for everyone? The essential reason to know about poetry is that the use of poetry is the only approved method of expressing ideas without punctuation, capitalization, and the other niceties that English teachers insist upon! One would have little respect for English teachers, however, if they did not attempt to arouse the interests of students in writing poetry as a hobby. Certainly at the career level if a person knows enough and has the skills, she or he can make a living at poetry as a poet, critic, or teacher. There is no point either in boring readers or insulting their intelligence by extending the illustration of poetry, as it can be done, to absolutely every other aspect of curriculum in all of the subject fields.

Hope and Pessimism

The point of this article is to express hope that during the last quarter of the twentieth century teachers and administrators of elementary and secondary schools on a broad base will attempt the kinds of curriculum reform that will identify career opportunities and hobbies related to every topic in every subject of the school curriculum. Unfortunately, this kind of curriculum reform may never come from the subject specialists in higher institutions because they show little interest in this kind of change. These persons could be extremely helpful if they would, but little hope is seen in the immediate future in that direction. That pessimistic statement comes from the fact that Bobbitt and many other curriculum reformers attempted to work along those lines in the early decades of this century without much success and with much opposition by the specialists in the subject fields.

The present rebirth of interest in career education might be the stimulus for basic curriculum reforms. Reforms in mathematics, science, and foreign languages, as a part of national defense, however, did not help much; nor did the reform of social studies help in the effort to reduce crime. However, if those subjects and others were taught in a way that would further career education and the development of hobbies, this might produce the dawn of a new day in secondary education. This might involve dramatic reduction of the required course content, but, in the process, schooling might once again become more attractive to the great masses of young people as well as provide better preparation for advanced studies.

The Key to Improvement

The foregoing goals will be achieved only if basic changes occur in how schools are supervised and administered. The school principal and other members of the supervisory-management team are key factors in stimulating and affecting curriculum reform. Change occurs first in local schools rather than in school systems.

The model recommended for the supervisory-management team is described by Trump (1972). Basically the principal and assistant principals, their number determined by the size of the school, need to devote nearly full time to the improvement of instruction. Key persons in the process are carefully selected and prepared department chairmen who work on curriculum development and teaching-learning methods with cooperative supervision by the principal and assistants. Such administrative tasks as involve visitors, public relations, finance and building management contacts with external persons, organizations, programs, student activities, welfare programs, and others are done by persons with special preparation for their assignments, not by persons with the generalized preparations that most principals have.

Since most principals and assistant principals lack adequate preparation for the tasks of instructional leadership, they need on-the-job training. The job is the most appropriate place for training because they may immediately put into practice what they learn. Also they develop readiness for additional preparation. University professors, central office supervisors, and other appropriate persons need to help the supervisory-management team in the process of continuing development. Career education thus has a chance to make the tremendous contribution that its advocates envision.

STAFFING AND TRAINING REQUIREMENTS FOR CAREER EDUCATION

Howard M. Johnson
Dr. Johnson is associate professor of educational administration at the University of Washington and is currently serving on an exchange position as area superintendent for the public schools. Dr. Johnson has served in an advisory capacity for career education. This article was written in 1975.

The expansion of career opportunities in our secondary schools has received substantial support in recent years; it is apparent that career education is an idea whose time has arrived. Numerous community surveys have demonstrated strong community and legislative support for career and vocational programs, and both federal and state monies have been committed to the expansion of career opportunities for our young people. The more practical concerns inherent in career education programs are clearly a hopeful sign for restoring a greater realism to our secondary schools; however, serious attention must be given to critical staffing factors early in the planning phase to prevent enthusiasm for career education from degenerating into disenchantment for both staff members and students. More specifically, unless we view the career education movement, at least on the secondary school level, as a replacement for certain existing educational formats and involving an entirely different staff utilization pattern, we are likely to observe very little expansion or improvement in this important educational endeavor.

Career Education and the Employer-based Format

The establishment of the secondary school as a separate and distinct institution of learning has been hailed as one of society's great achievements, and yet, ironically, it is the very separateness of that institution which has created a considerable frustration to those interested in expanding the career emphasis in the total educational system. This separateness of secondary schools from the general society is a serious obstacle to expanding career education and must be considered as part of the overall planning process. It is this author's opinion that of the four career education models receiving support in recent years from the United States Office of Education (USOE), only those involving an extensive employer-based component will have any real impact in improving career opportunities for our young people.* This position is based upon a number of factors, some relating to the general structure of our economic and educational systems and some relating to the expressed viewpoints of major school client groups. Let us examine several of these important factors.

---

*USOE has suggested that serious attention be given to four specific training models, based respectively in the school, the employing institution, the home, and the residential training center. Pilot studies involving each of the models were supported by USOE during the early '70s.

Shift to a service economy. Perhaps no change in our economic system over the past fifty years has had a more dramatic impact on educational needs as the definite shift to a service-producing economy. For the first time in history, Americans are spending more money on services than on all nondurable goods, such as food, clothing, fuel, beverages, and tobacco products. Soon it can be expected that the consumer outlays for services will exceed the total for all tangible products, including cars and homes. It is estimated that in the 1980's, seven Americans will be working in service jobs for every three involved in producing goods—just the reverse of the situation at the start of this century (*U.S. News and World Report* 1970, p. 34).

From an education standpoint, this move toward a service-producing economy will require that we train increasing numbers of young people for highly skilled jobs in the medical and dental fields, machine repair, and research technology. Conversely, we can also expect an increasing number of workers required in service worker areas that involve a bare minimal skill requirement and include such diverse areas as cooks, waiters and waitresses, hospital attendants, and janitors. Certain of these jobs will require little more than an eighth-grade education, and many of our present and future students may choose to fill these employment categories during the time they are completing requirements for high school and college degrees. Others may choose to leave the formal schooling experience and engage in full-time employment in areas requiring a minimum of special skill development and training. At any rate, it is clear that many of the rapidly growing service employment opportunities involve a rather minimal skill component for entry level jobs, and there is very little point in designing extended school-based programs directed toward these positions.

Cost of equipment. The increasing costs of equipment make school-based programs in some occupational areas prohibitively expensive. Because of the equipment required in such fields as medical research, data processing, and electronics, serious attention will have to be given to moving more and more of the actual training out of the school and into the institutions already utilizing the appropriate equipment. Cooperative vocational programs, particularly in rural areas, have already utilized extensive on-the-job training as a means of reducing overall program cost.

Student concern for a real experience. The claim that school is an unrealistic and irrelevant activity has been made by increasing numbers of students in recent years. Much of this concern about irrelevance stems from the students' view that school tends to be an isolated experience far removed from the realities of life. As Harold Howe, a former U. S. commissioner of education, stated:

> Many of the resources that are potentially most stimulating, both for the general learning of high school students and for their occupational concerns, are just not in the school. To some extent this difficulty can be solved by bringing outside resources into the school, but there are serious practical limitations in this approach, (Howe 1972).

That this separateness of the school environment is perceived by students can hardly be questioned. In a survey in suburban Seattle involving a cross section of secondary students in nine districts, additional on-the-job experience was selected as the most important factor in improving present vocational programs (Northeast Vocational Advisory Council 1971). Only one other factor—the teaching of more job skills—was selected from the list of eleven items by more than 50% of the student respondents.

Employer viewpoints. In addition to the perceptions of students, it is important to look at the expressed views of employers and employees as they examine the merits of extending employer-based educational opportunity. In a statewide survey of employers in Washington State involving a sampling of opinion from central office managers, line supervisors, and nonsupervisory employees, more related on-the-job experience was selected as the single most important factor in improving vocational preparation (Washington State Advisory Council for Vocational Education 1972). The more detailed results of this survey are presented in Table 8-A.

TABLE 8-A.
Greatest Needs in Vocational Preparation*

Areas of need	Percent of respondent group			
	Central management N-63	Line supervisor N-69	Non-supervisory employees N-57	sample Total
Provide more related on-the-job experience	44.4	60.9	63.2	56.0
Teach more personal relations skills	50.8	49.3	49.1	49.7
Teach more job skills	36.5	47.8	31.6	39.2
Emphasize more organizational skills	28.6	39.1	45.6	37.6
Use more resource persons from occupational fields	27.0	20.3	21.1	22.8
Teach more math skills	28.6	18.8	15.8	21.2
Teach more writing skills	25.4	21.7	10.5	19.6
Teach more speaking skills	15.9	15.9	22.8	18.0
Teach more reading skills	25.4	11.6	15.8	17.5
Provide greater variety in program's curriculum	11.1	8.7	14.0	11.1
Other	3.2	2.9	3.5	3.2

* Respondents from 63 major employing agencies in the state of Washington were surveyed. Each was asked to circle the three items considered to result in the greatest improvement in present vocational programs.

TABLE 8-B.
Barriers to Expanding Work Experience*

Barriers as identified by respondents	Percent of respondent group	
	Central office managers and line supervisors N = 132	Nonsupervisory employees N = 57
Inadequate funds	18.9	7.0
Opposition by organized employee group	15.9	3.5
Limited time for supervision	6.8	1.8
No need for trainees	5.3	3.5
Limited facilities	3.8	—
Scheduling problems	2.3	—
Trainees lacking in skills	1.5	1.8
Other	4.5	5.3

* Respondents were asked to list any significant barriers to the expansion of work experience programs. The numbers as presented here represent the percentage of the designated respondent groups choosing a response in each of the barrier categories as listed. Many respondents, particularly in the nonsupervisory category, felt there were no significant barriers or simply chose not to identify any.

Barriers to Extension of Employer-based Learning Formats

Having examined some of the factors supporting the employer-based learning format, one can reasonably ask why schools have not already experienced substantial growth in the number and size of employer-based programs. After all, the economic factors leading toward the service-producing economy and the cooperative and apprentice models for vocational training have been in existence for many years. Information obtained in recent interviews with employer representatives indicates that the prime reasons for only minimal utilization of the employer-based education models are resistance by employee groups (within both industry and the education profession) and an unwillingness by the public to provide needed financial support. No other barrier was mentioned by more than 10% of all respondents. It seems appropriate to examine each of these prime barriers in more detail (Table 8-B).

Funding Problems. Inadequate funding was most often cited as a barrier to expanding work experience programs. While it is certainly true that neither the employing agencies nor the general public has been willing to commit any considerable additional funds to the cause, it is contended that funding for any program viewed as an addition will almost always seem inadequate. It is the very notion that using the employer-based model must be an addition rather than a replacement for our present educational offerings that makes funding the most important barrier to employer-based learning. One need only look at the historical percentage of our gross national product committed to education to know that we are not likely to spend a substantially higher percentage of our economic growth on expanded educational services.

The employer-based training procedure, even on a per day or per hour basis, will be more expensive than the conventional school-based procedure. Since many young people in their high school and college years are still exploring potential career possibilities, extra counseling services will be required for those students needing a change in their work or training station. Others will be faced with employer-employee disagreements which require intervention by a school training supervisor. For these reasons, any plan for the expansion of work experience must be based upon a somewhat higher staff/student ratio than that which exists in the typical school-based program. This differential cost factor, however, can be at least partially offset if we simply replace parts of the present program with employer-based learning situations rather than wait for additional outside funding. This position gained strong support from the National Advisory Council on Vocational Education (1971) when it expressed the concern that far too many local school districts and colleges have viewed federal and state support for vocational education as a ceiling for expenditures rather than as an incentive for development of more diversified and useful programs at the local level.

As a final note on this funding problem, it must be stressed that any move to extend the employer-based model must involve some transfer of monies into the employing institutions themselves. Even an imaginative school-operated social service program of the type proposed recently by David Brison (1972) is likely to involve some transfer of school monies to a variety of public and private agencies. Certain of the new funding sources, as well as these funds redirected from existing school programs, must be used to offset the cost of resource and supervisory persons within the nonschool segment of our economy. Placement of large numbers of students in employing stations (or in exploratory relationships in various occupational areas) will simply not be accomplished without some support to the cooperative employing agencies or firms. A survey of representative employers throughout the state of Washington indicates that their willingness to accept trainees increases rather substantially if outside public support is available to offset additional supervision costs (Northeast Vocational Advisory Council 1971).

Resistance by employee groups. It is entirely understandable that workers would see expansion of employer-based training opportunities as a threat to their employment security. This is particularly true in light of the current high unemployment rates. Tight limitations on the number of job trainees are already part of negotiated agreement in many firms and industries, particularly in manufacturing and construction firms. Any effort to expand training opportunities on an employer-based format must realistically consider the opposition generated by potential loss in job security and will probably have to build in certain controls to satisfy labor unions and other groups representing employee interests.

Another employee interest group threatened by expansion of employer-based instruction is found within the education profession itself. The tradition of having students educated in a separate institution or school and the teaching positions assured by this tradition is perhaps the most significant of all barriers to the expansion of the employer-based training format. History has shown that the industrial revolution (and its removal of the demand for child labor) was more responsible for the rapid growth of both secondary school and college enrollments than any sudden support for education during the early part of this century. This increased enrollment was accompanied by a general expectation that students will be educated almost entirely within the school environment; thus, the schools themselves have grown possessive of their unique and understandably important role in the education process. Given this growth in acceptance of the school-based learning model and the subsequent need to preserve school-based teaching jobs in our society, it is only reasonable that both teachers and administrators will look questionably at any extensive effort to either reduce or alter the role of the secondary school.

Staffing Requirements for an Employer-based Training Format

In a senior high school with a reasonably comprehensive program, we might expect to find approximately 15% of the students enrolled in programs with a high vocational emphasis (Northeast Vocational Advisory Council 1971). Most of these students in vocational programs will be juniors or seniors enrolled in traditional vocational programs like business and office occupations, distributive education, home economics, and auto mechanics. The largest number are likely girls enrolled in either business and office or home economics.

The overall staffing ratio is typically somewhat greater in the vocational areas than in the general school program, and the staff allocation for a 1200-student high school might correspond to the breakdown shown in Table 8-C. In this table, the overall staffing in vocational programs is figured at a 20/1 student to teacher ratio whereas the regular programs are figured at 25/1. This differential is usually made possible through special state and federal funding programs in vocational subjects.

Now, before returning to the basic argument of this paper, namely, that any acceptable extension of career and vocational opportunities will require a change in present staffing patterns, we must first make some assumptions regarding the number of students to be enrolled in vocational and career programs and the percentage of their total programs so committed. It would be wrong to assume that all students should be placed immediately in a specific employer-based training format. This is clearly an age for expanding alternatives and not a time to establish rigid and unified programs for all secondary school students. Logically, while part of the student body would be involved in some kind of employer-based learning program, the majority of those would only be involved for approximately 50% of their time in school, with the remainder of students being in an employer-based learning station. These proportions could be expected to change as shifts occur within the working world itself. At any rate, the assumptions mentioned here might lead to the enrollment pattern (in the sample 1200-student high school) as presented in Table 8-D.

The school-based staff computed in Table 8-D is again figured on a 25/1 ratio of students to teachers. Note that the total school-based staff has dropped from the total of 54 full-time equivalent (FTE) personnel in Table 8-C to only 35.5 in Table 8-D. This loss in school-based staffing is more than compensated for under the model proposed here by the expanded staffing need of the employer-based learning programs. If 550 students of the 1200 are involved in either half-time or full-time employer-based learning experiences and are served by both job coordinator/teachers and employer supervisors, the breakdown might typically approximate the presentation in Table 8-E. The actual allocations are dependent upon the assumed learning model. For purposes of the presentation here, we assume that the vast majority of the 550 students are involved in observation and orientation-type activities, and only a small number are in specific programs designed to give training for

TABLE 8-C.
Typical Staffing Pattern
for 1200-student High School

Student group	Number of students	Staff allocation	
		Teacher	Counselor
Vocational	180	9	1
Regular/academic	1020	41	3
Total	1200	50	4

TABLE 8-D.
Proposed School-based Staffing Pattern
for 1200-student High School

Student group	Number of students enrolled	School-based student full-time equivalents	School-based staff allocation	
			Teacher	Counselor
Employer-based (50%)	300	150	6	1
Employer-based (full time)	250	0	—	.5
Regular/academic	650	650	26	2
Total	1200	800	32	3.5

particular jobs. Note that the employer-based portion of the staffing allocations calls for a total of 22 FTE personnel, with the major part of that allocation going to employer supervision. Adding the 22 FTE staff of Table 8-E to the 35.5 FTE in Table 8-D, we arrive at an overall staffing requirement of 57.5 FTE, which exceeds the current staffing pattern requirement of 54 FTE by 3.5. This addition of 3.5 FTE professional staff will require some additional expenditure for the overall secondary school program, but the major cost of the employer-based learning programs is accommodated through a shift in present funding patterns. In short, what we are calling for is a reduction from the 50 teachers presently employed to a total of 40 teachers (32 FTE assigned to regular programs and 8 FTE working in a new role as job coordinator/teacher).

This 20% reduction in teaching staff is recognized as an important obstacle for implementation of employer-based vocational programs; however, the thrust of this position is that some reduction approximating this figure will be required for reasonable and realistic expansion of the career and vocational opportunities. Some perceptive critics have

TABLE 8-E.
Proposed Employer-based Staffing Patterns
for 1200-student High School

Employer-Based Instructional Format	Full-time equivalent students	Employer-based staff allocation	
		Coordinator/ Teacher*	Employer Supervisor**
Observation/orientation (425) (250 half-time and 175 full-time students)	300	6	12
Work-study (125) (50 half-time and 75 full-time students)	100	2	2
Total FTE (550)	400	8	14

* *It is assumed here that one job coordinator/teacher will be required for each 50 student FTE. It will undoubtedly require more coordinator/teaching time per FTE in working with half-time students, but since each coordinator/teacher will have a reasonable distribution of half- and full-time students, the distribution seems appropriate for this presentation.*

** *It is assumed here that ⅕ of an employer supervisor allocation will be assigned to each 5 student FTE in the observation/orientation format and for each 10 student FTE in the work-study format. While this assignment ratio assumes that supervisors will spend approximately ⅕ of their time in supervision and ⅘ on their regular jobs, these ratios may vary according to the nature of the industry and the needs of students.*

argued that such reductions in teaching staff might occur even without a plan of the type presented here simply because fewer students are likely to bother with a formal schooling experience unless something is done to make it more suitable to their perceived needs. There is already a tendency for increasing numbers to drop out of our schools and colleges, and the public is not likely to maintain the cost of present staffing levels when faced with such declining enrollments.

In actuality the 20% reduction in school-based teaching staff as called for in this model might not be as serious a problem as initially envisioned. For one thing, normal attrition rates will assist in the adjustment. It is also quite probable that the employing businesses and industries will want to hire a certain number of these displaced teachers to serve in employer supervision roles. We can also expect that the school's acceptance of this greater responsibility for career education will lead local communities to commit additional monies for secondary schooling, thereby permitting a somewhat better overall staffing pattern than that described in Table 8-C. Whatever the additional funds, however, it is presumed that some substantial reduction and redistribution in present school-based staffing will be required.

Before proceeding to an examination of the role changes and training requirements associated with the proposed staffing model, it might be well to comment on the suggested need for three components—school-based, observation/orientation, and work-study—as part of the overall school program. The preference for preserving all three components results from the conviction that any group of secondary students will reasonably require a broad spectrum of educational opportunities. While some students desire specific job skills at the high school level, others simply aren't ready to make a serious commitment to learning skills associated with specific jobs or even clusters of jobs. For this latter group, the observation and orientation may be extremely important, but the job commitment expectation so often associated with work-study formats is probably unfounded. In one statewide study of senior high students enrolled in a broad cross section of vocational courses, only 48% indicated that they had made any serious vocational program or job commitment in the area of their study (Washington State Advisory Council on Vocational Education 1975). Certainly, if students in designated vocational classes are still exploring possibilities for careers, we can expect no greater job commitments from students not enrolled in classes designated as vocational. It is important that the school-based, observation/orientation, and work-study options be combined in varying proportions according to the needs of each individual student and not based upon some prior decision to provide a particular ratio of the three components for all students. Imposing any set pattern on all students is likely to be just as unsatisfactory as the system which we are attempting to change.

Role Changes and Training Needs

In the employer-based model (Tables 8-D and 8-E) we observe that only 32 of the 40 teachers will be involved in traditional school-based roles. The remaining eight will be full-time job coordinator/teachers with one such person serving each 50 FTE students. These job coordinator/teachers will be responsible for the placement of students and will work both individually and in groups to meet the students' educational and career needs. In essence, the person filling this role is a counselor and teacher to each of his or her fifty-plus students and will meet with the entire group only on occasion to provide general occupational and career information. This coordinator/teacher works with students in both full-time and part-time job placements but is probably assigned to a limited number of occupational clusters for the major part of the work. Because of the wide variety of job placements involved among the fifty-plus students, the job coordinator/teacher tends to be a generalist and leaves the specialized training needs to the employer supervisors.

The employer supervisor is the real key to success in the proposed staffing model. It is this person who establishes a close identification with each of five to ten workers. Since one-fifth of the employer supervisor's salary (assuming the specific model of Table 8-E) would be paid through public funds for the specific purpose of assisting student learning programs, we can assume that the employer supervisor will commit considerable time to the student's orientation and/or specific training needs. The relative proportion committed to these two functions—orientation and specific job training—will depend upon the nature of the industry and the perceived needs and interests of the student. The student's coordinator/teacher will assist in developing a plan most suitable to the student and will work with the employer supervisor in implementing that plan. The suggestion that employer supervisors spend only 20% of their time in supervision responsibilities and the remainder on their regular jobs is designed to avoid the pitfalls of our traditional separation of work and education and to assure a minimum span of students for each employer supervisor. Using this assignment pattern, the 14 FTE personnel committed to the employer supervision category would actually represent 70 different persons in widely scattered businesses and industries, each committing approximately 20% of his or her working day to supervising five to ten student workers.

The school administrator's role is also changed considerably under this employer-based staffing model. Since approximately one-third (400 of 1200 FTE students) are educated in the employer-based learning programs, it would be advisable to assign a significant portion of administrative time to the program. In most schools of 1200 students, a full-time assistant principal might be assigned to direct the program. Whatever the administrative configuration, it is evident that a much closer liaison between school and community is implied. The identification of student work stations, even with the additional funding, will take considerable time and effort. The business community must be fully oriented to its expanded role in meeting the educational needs of our young people, and the system for transferring public financing into the private sector will no doubt require administrative and legal know-how.

These role changes for both teachers and administrators call for certain new directions in professional training. Not only will professionals in the future have to be much more aware of the working world, but they must also become more adept at working with employers and supervisors in a wide variety of public and private agencies. Perhaps internships in the business world would make good training experiences for job coordinator/teachers and administrators. Persons filling both positions must be prepared to work closely with employers in diagnosing student career needs and in providing appropriate observational and work experiences for students. They must also work at interpreting the employer-based experiences to the school-based staff, thereby assuring articulation between the two programs.

New Financial Base—Prime Benefit

A prime advantage of this proposed staffing plan is the new financial base provided for the employer-based experiences. Under present conditions, and in part due to limited funding, the school administrator and teacher coordinators are required to prevail strictly upon the good will of a few local employers to obtain a limited number of student training stations. Understandably, employers cannot afford under existing conditions to identify very many training stations simply because the rate of return for the supervisory demand is minimal. The staffing pattern proposed here should make this identification of training positions more advantageous to the employer, particularly if some of the rigid minimal wage restrictions can be removed for students whose program emphasizes observation/orientation activities. Admittedly, the financial base represents no panacea for the expansion of work training stations; it does, however, place the public school in a position to pay at least something for a service which the business sector of our economy is uniquely capable of providing.

Before concluding this discussion of a proposal for staff differentiation, it should be stressed that no school has, to this author's knowledge, seriously attempted implementation of this particular plan. The federal government is giving some consideration to providing financial incentives for moving in the direction implied by the model (Report on Education Research 1974), but no real empirical evidence exists concerning the effect it might have on meeting the career education needs for which it is designed. Despite this limitation, it must be stressed that the key concern here is not the implementation of a specific plan but rather a willingness to address priorities seriously in the overall mission of the secondary school. In a sense, we are faced with a choice of continuing to tamper with the mechanics of educational technology (e.g., team teaching, flexible scheduling, and individualized learning packages) or to decide seriously whether the purpose or content of the schooling experience itself should be changed. Meeting the career education needs of our students cannot be accomplished by merely changing the technology of instruction but must involve change in both the location and responsibility for education rather than the implementation of any specific staffing plan which is of prime importance.

Conclusion

The need for expansion of career training in our educational systems is unquestionably great. Both the changing nature of employment opportunities and the perceptions of various school client groups (and particularly those of the students) suggest that increased attention and funding should be directed to this important educational component. Of the secondary school training programs supported by recent federal and state funding programs, the employer-based model seems to hold the greatest potential for meeting the present and future vocational requirements of our society. Anything approaching a full implementation of this employer-based model, however, will require a distinctly different staffing plan and one which transfers present funds and staff allocations into the employing institutions themselves. A realistic and relevant career orientation program is simply not going to take place within the confines of the school building, and due to obvious funding limitations, we cannot expect this career education need to be accomplished as an extension of present services in an already overburdened secondary school program. We must establish priorities for the school program, and if career education is one such priority, monies must be transferred into those elements of the economic system best equipped to provide the educational service. Only by implementing such a transfer of educational resources at the local level can we hope to accomplish the broad goals of career education.

CAREER EDUCATION IS NOT VOCATIONAL EDUCATION

Curtis R. Finch and N. Alan Sheppard

Dr. Finch is professor and chairman of general vocational and technical education at Virginia Polytechnic Institute and State University and has authored numerous publications on vocational education.

Dr. Sheppard is associate professor of education at Virginia Polytechnic Institute and State University, and is currently on educational leave to serve the Department of Education's Federal Council on the Aging. He is founder and past president of the National Association for the Advancement of Black Americans in Vocational Education. This article was written in 1975.

During the early 1970s, as career education began to emerge representing a new and exciting focus for education, many observers became confused by this rather broad, elusive term. Did it represent all of education or merely that portion which has been traditionally identified as vocational education? Persons writing about career education during this formative period certainly did not pour oil on the stormy waters of definition. For example, Loomis (1971) seemed to speak of career education as vocational education with a new wrapper. On the other end of the continuum, Herr (1972) wrote about career education as derived from complex historical and philosophical antecedents. To make matters even more difficult, a key leader and proponent of the career education movement did not offer to identify its specific parameters or relationships with other aspects of education (Marland 1971).

Although these are but a few of the many factors which contributed to a lack of agreement about what constitutes career education, they are perhaps representative of the inputs educators and the lay public have been examining for some time. These inputs raise a key question that must be asked by vocational educators and general educators alike: To what extent does vocational education relate to career education?

Recognizing that it is easy to incorporate one's personal biases into the process of seeking an answer to this important question, the authors felt the need to employ a systematic examination process which would, hopefully, uncover the most meaningful information about these two important areas and their commonalities. The initial portion of this paper examines how career education and vocational education have been defined by different persons, organizations, and agencies. Next, a description is provided of how these important areas interact. Finally, the relationships between career education and vocational education are explicated and their commonalities further explored. It is hoped that in this fashion educators and lay public alike will develop a clearer understanding of career education and recognize its potential as a viable education movement.

Vocational Education: An Historical and Contemporary Perspective

There has been a good deal of debate, misunderstanding, and shifting of ground over the relationship between career education and vocational education.

Vocational education has been defined by people, organizations, agencies, and through legislation as follows:

• That education which is under public supervision or control; that the controlling purpose of such education shall be to fit for useful employment; that such education skill be of less than college grade and that such education be designed to meet the needs of persons over fourteen years of age who have entered or who are preparing to enter work (Smith-Hughes Act 1917).

• A basic obligation of the public school system is the preparation of all young people for effectiveness in the world of work. . . . Modification of many traditional definitions and requirements of vocational education is needed to allow for expansion and variation. . . . Vocational competence involves much more than what is generally called occupational, vocational, or technical education. . . . Too exclusive an emphasis on the building of a specific set of skills must be avoided in vocational education (Draper 1967).

• Education designed to develop skills, abilities, understandings, attitudes, work habits, and appreciations needed by workers to enter and to make progress in employment on a useful and productive basis (American Vocational Association).

• The totality of activities and experiences through which one learns about a primary work role (Hoyt 1974).

Based upon the foregoing, it appears that vocational education includes (at least) the following basic characteristics:

- Education of less than college grade or baccalaureate degree.
- More emphasis on fitting a person for a job and less emphasis on exploring and establishing one's self in a career.
- Preparation for gainful employment.
- Activities and experiences through which one learns about a primary work role.
- Preparation for careers which require less than the baccalaureate degree.
- Emphasis on skill development or specific job preparation.
- Focus of attention is at the upper middle grades, senior high, and two-year college level.
- A physical entity or program rather than an educational philosophy viewed as a vehicle for bringing about major educational reform.

Career Education: Some Definitions

Career education is not a totally new concept. Many of its basic tenets have permeated education for years. What is career education? Obviously, it means different things to different people. It has about as many definitions as there are definers. To illustrate the diversity of current interpretations, selected definitions are provided below:

> Career education is an organized, comprehensive, educational, instructional program designed to facilitate the self and career development of students (State of Georgia).

> Comprehensive career education includes a sequentially developed educational program offering career orientation and awareness, career exploration, and job preparation for all individuals (State of Missouri).

> Career education is a concept (not a program), a comprehensive educational thrust with impact upon instruction at all grade levels and in all subject matter disciplines. The purpose of career education is to provide each student with a coordinated educational experience consisting of career awareness, career exploration, career guidance, and career preparation to the end that all students are prepared for employment immediately upon graduation from high school or to go on to further formal education (State of California).

> Career education is a concept of relevant and accountable education centered on the individual, which provides the opportunities for educational experiences, curriculum, instructions, and counseling leading to preparation for economic independence. The development of this concept is a lifelong process which involves a series of experiences, decisions, and interactions that provide the means through which one's self-understanding can be implemented, both vocationally and avocationally (State of New Hampshire).

> Career education is the term denoting the total effort by educational agencies and communities in presenting organized career-oriented activities and experiences to all persons from nursery school through adulthood and orienting the entire educational plan into one unified, career-based system (State of Illinois).

What the term *career education* means to me is basically a point of view, a concept—a concept that says three things: First, that work-related learning will be part of the curriculum for all students, not just some. Second, that it will continue throughout a youngster's stay in school, from the first grade through senior high and beyond, if he so elects. And third, that every student leaving school will possess the skills necessary to give a start to making a livelihood for himself and his family, even if he leaves before completing high school (Marland 1971).

Career education is an integral dimension of the nursery through adult curriculum which provides for all students a sequential continuum of experiences through which each individual may develop a more realistic perception of his capabilities and prepare him for entry and re-entry into employment and/or continuing education (Doherty 1972).

Career education consists of all those activities and experiences through which one learns about work. As such, it makes no restrictions in meaning whether one speaks about the work of the homemaker, the musician, the lawyer, or the bricklayer. Some work will require advanced college degrees while other work may require no formal schooling of any kind. To the extent that work is judged successful, it does typically—and, in these times, increasingly—require some learned set of vocational skills (Hoyt 1974).

A selection of definitions gleaned from a variety of sources provides other illustrations:

● Career education can be defined as that part of the total school curriculum which provides the student with the knowledge, exploratory experiences, and skills required for successful job entry, job adjustment, and job advancement. It can also be defined as an organized K-12 program to provide every student with an understanding of, and preparation for, the world of work.

● Career education may be defined or described as a comprehensive educational program which gives attention to preparing all people for satisfying and productive work in our society.

● Career education is that part of the total education process which focuses on the successful adaptation of the individual to the world of work.

● Career education is the systematic development of the natural powers of a person over an entire lifetime for his or her life's work. It involves body, mind, and spirit and is commenced in the home where the child's will and intellect are nurtured through love and example by parents and family members.

● Career education encompasses all education in that it is that part of learning experience that assists one to discover, define, and refine talents and use them in pursuit of a career.

● The purpose of career education should be to help people develop human resource competence along with a holistic understanding of the world of work or wage employment system, i.e., the socio-economic institution or working for pay in modern industrial society—to become competent as workers and comprehending as men and women.

Drawing from these definitions, we can see that career education:

● is an educational concept of philosophy rather than a physical entity, program, or department

● begins at grade K and continues through adulthood

● has to do with work but involves more than strict preparation for work

● has strong orientation toward a life ethic and/or work ethic

- encompasses at least a large part of education
- consists of all those activities and experiences through which one learns about work
- provides an awareness, exploration, and preparation function instead of just fitting a person to a specific job
- prepares students for successful and rewarding lives by improving their basis for occupational choice
- is not limited to any particular group or segment of society
- is directed at bringing about educational reform, without adding another discipline, that will bring benefit to the entire population

Career Education and Vocational Education: Points of Clarification

As can be seen, career education has been implicitly defined in many ways. To some, it has been only a new term for vocational education, and to others it has described all of education. For many it has meant a new emphasis on existing programs, while some have seen it as completely new programs or courses to be added on or to replace traditional content. Of course, others view it as synonymous with vocational education; however, this is not the case. Although vocational education is a necessary component of career education, career education is not vocational education. All vocational education is a part of career education; however, career education goes beyond vocational education, since it links learning activities with jobs along the entire range of skills—from the subtechnical to the professional career (requiring a baccalaureate degree). In addition, career education emphasizes self-awareness, career awareness, and decision-making skills to improve individual choices concerning work and education or training.

Career education then is more than vocational education. A key difference is between preparing for a single job or occupation and a concern for how education affects the sum total of one's lifework. The concern of career education is more than that of developing mere economic producers. Rather, its focus is on people who are workers as well as consumers, members of family groups, citizens of the community and the world, and individuals striving to fulfill the best that is in them or becoming all that they are capable of becoming.

Career education, then, is rather inclusive in that it encompasses all of vocational education and much of general education, plus career exploration, career selection, career entry, and career progression. By way of contrast, vocational education has a unique but more limited mission of skill development or specific occupational preparation.

At the same time, career education is not synonymous with all of education. Career education involves that portion of the educational process which relates to the preparation for work and/or that which relates to career development. Education, on the other hand, relates to all of the roles, settings, and events of a person's life. Career education is not seen as synonymous in meaning with education. Education is more concerned with the cultivation of those artistic and moral sensibilities and qualities of intellect that mean success in living in the larger context. This includes transmission of diverse cultural heritages and full participation of individuals in their society as consumers, members of family groups, and citizens of the community and the world.

The Domain of Career Education

Although definitions can provide a useful means of comparing and contrasting career education and vocational education, they are somewhat limiting from a conceptual standpoint. This is especially true when one considers how these two areas relate to general (academic) education, particularly across the K-adult educational continuum.

In a graphic sense, we can perceive career, vocational, and general education more meaningfully contrasted in Fig. 8-1. Even though the domains are represented in a relative manner, one can readily observe how each fits into the total educational scheme. Career education represents the largest domain and extends from K through college to adult education and perhaps beyond. For example, an elderly person might pursue coursework and/or experiences which assist in a smooth transition from work to retirement and prepare him or her for making a continued contribution to society during the later years. This might involve volunteer work with church or civic groups or part-time employment to supplement an otherwise fixed income. Although the career education domain shares much with general and vocational education, it also reflects a certain uniqueness which consists of formal and informal career-related experiences that take place away from traditional educational settings and do not involve educators per se. These might include horseback riding, swimming, scouting, gardening, and other experiences which provide youngsters and adults with serendipitous exposure to many career areas. Although one would not (and probably could not) formally assess the outcomes of these experiences, they are, nonetheless, important contributors to many youngsters' and adults' career repertoires.

The domain of vocational education reflects both shared and unique experiences. The bulk of vocational education can be aligned with career education in terms of career

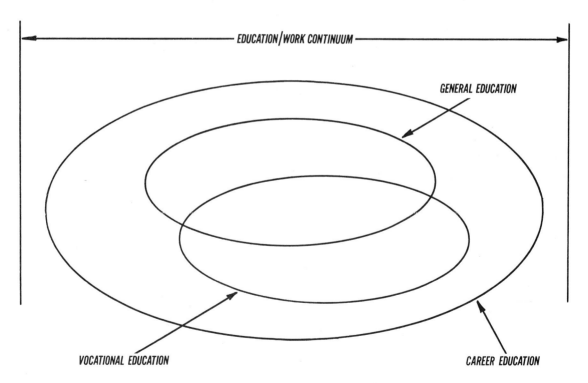

8-1.   *DOMAINS OF CAREER, VOCATIONAL, AND GENERAL EDUCATION*

exploration and career preparation experiences. Most of these shared experiences are associated with career preparation ranging from tenth grade to adult but below baccalaureate level. Unique experiences in the vocational education domain consist of exposure to education which enhances one's employment opportunities and other activities not considered part of a formal education program. For example, a person who has worked in the military as a baker might utilize this experience to excellent advantage upon completion as an associate degree in quantity food preparation. Part-time employment as a service station attendant might well increase a person's options after he or she has completed a high school auto mechanics program. Obviously, employers give at least subjective credit for life experience when adults who have been recently prepared for skilled occupations are considered for certain positions.

General education is very closely aligned with career education in that, conceptually, it serves as a framework for experiences in a variety of career education contexts. Areas most commonly associated with this infusion of domains are explanation, self-awareness, educational awareness, career awareness, economic awareness, and decision making (Center for Vocational and Technical Education 1972). The general education domain, however, contains some unique experiences which do not relate specifically to career education. These experiences are designed to prepare a person for life but would not focus on developing purely survival skills. For example, although one may not necessarily consider selection of leisure reading materials directly related to career education, it is of significant importance from a personal standpoint. This would also apply to other areas, such as entertainment, and other uses of leisure time.

Yes, career education is more than vocational education. It embraces vocational education and general education in a way that has much potential for improving society. Perhaps as educators and concerned citizens recognize the many benefits career education can bring to society, it will gain the momentum needed to accomplish widespread implementation. If career education is to succeed, it is imperative that all persons associated with education understand where career and vocational education align.

REFERENCES

American Vocational Association. *Definitions of Terms in Vocational, Technical, and Practical Arts Education.* Washington: American Vocational Association, n.d.

Brison, David W. "Restructuring the School System." *Interchange* 3 (1972): 63-85.

Center for Vocational and Technical Education. *Developmental Program Goals, Comprehensive Career Education Model.* Columbus, Ohio: Ohio State University, 1972.

Doherty, P. *Answers to Five Basic Questions about Career Education.* Trenton, N.J.: Department of Education, State of New Jersey, April 1972.

Draper, D. *Education for Work—A Report of the Current Scene in Vocational Education.* Washington: The National Committee on Secondary Education, National Association of Secondary School Principals, 1967.

Herr, Edwin. *Review and Synthesis of Foundations for Career Education.* Columbus, Ohio: Center for Vocational and Technical Education, Ohio State University, March 1972.

Howe, H. H., II. "Implications of Career Education." *Proceedings of the Conferences on Career Education.* Educational Testing Service, 1972.

Hoyt, Kenneth B. "An Introduction to Career Education." Draft position paper, Office of Career Education. Washington: USOE, 1974.

Loomis, W. "Career Education." *American Education.* (March 1971): 3-5.

Marland, Sidney P., Jr., "Career Education Now." Paper presented to the National Association of Secondary School Principals, January 1971, in Houston, Texas.

National Advisory Council on Vocational Education. *Fourth Report.* 16 January 1971.

Northeast Vocational Advisory Council. *Phase I Report.* Prepared by the Bureau of School Service and Research, University of Washington, May 1971.

Report on Education Research, 6 (1974): 9-10.

Trump, J. L. "Principal Most Potent Factor in Determining School Excellence." *The Bulletin of the National Association of Secondary School Principals,* 56 (March 1972): 3-9.

U. S. News and World Report. 9 November 1970.

Washington State Advisory Council on Vocational Education. *Report on Senate Concurrent Resolution Number 23.* Submitted to the Washington State Legislature, December 1972.

Washington State Advisory Council on Vocational Education. *Vocational Education Success Measures and Concerns.* January 1975.

Career Education at the College Level

A close examination of what transpired during the first ten years (1970-1980) of career education reveals that most efforts have been directed toward the elementary and secondary school levels and limited attention has been given the college and university level. Some educators claim that for most individuals, if not for all, career decision-making has been completed once they enter college. Furthermore, the careers requiring a college education are well defined and require limited change once you enter. However, such arguments do not entirely justify the resulting neglect.

Chapter 9 consists of four articles written in 1976, '77, and '78 by individuals who were concerned about the implications of career education at the college and university level. Sidney P. Marland, Jr.'s article explicates the relationship of liberal education and work and how they in turn are related to career education at this level. He argues for unity between liberal education and work, with career education serving as the catalyst of that unity. Donald A. Casella and Sandra Samples present an updated analysis of the literature related to career education at the college and university level. C. B. Darrell provides an excellent account of how career educators can be used successfully in college English departments, whereas George E. Leonard and H. Splete present the various aspects of implementing career education within the college or university structure.

THE FRUITION OF CAREER EDUCATION: LIBERAL EDUCATION AND WORK

"... united from the beginning and for all." John Dewey, 1915

Sidney P. Marland, Jr.

Dr. Marland served as United States commissioner of education from 1970 to 1972. During that time he was instrumental in the development and implementation of landmark legislation for career education. From 1972 to 1973 he served as the nation's first statutory assistant secretary of education in the Department of Health, Education, and Welfare, and from 1973 to 1978 was president of the College Entrance Examination Board. This article was written in 1978.

Liberal education in America should not need defenders. Commencing in the upper grades of the schools and continuing through two to four years of higher education, the liberal arts stand as the centerpiece of our educational system. They are the core of learnings on which most other learnings depend, and upon which our society relies for the development of free, informed, and participating citizens whose values derive from cultivated minds and spirits. Yet there seems to be a pervasive anxiety, especially in our colleges, that liberal education is in decline. Some attribute this decline to the public's increased expectations for education that produces occupational outcomes. Since I have been a party to the federal initiative that sought to advance career education, I endeavor in these pages to illuminate John Dewey's quotation. Liberal education and work are inescapably interrelated and interdependent.

To the extent that liberal education is threatened by a preoccupation with vocation on the part of the learner (or indeed on the part of institutional planners and faculty), the issue is real. If the liberal arts are in decline, their place at the center of learning must be restored and safeguarded. If the concept of work has mistakenly been perceived as antithetical to the health of liberal education, the misperception must be righted.

In acknowledging the various forms that liberal education takes from campus to campus and from teacher to teacher, one sees that it does have its roots and its history. We are familiar with the trivium (grammar, logic, and rhetoric) and the quadrivium (arithmetic, geometry, astronomy, and music) of the Middle Ages. The seven branches of learning were the academic equipment and occupational requirement of *freemen.* The work of the clergy, merchants, clerks, physicians, government officials, and cathedral builders resided in the liberating power of learning. While the flexible sweep and scope of the liberal arts today reach beyond the "seven branches" competencies of the ancients, a major purpose remains: that of equipping free men and women with the competencies for contributing to society and to their own fulfillment through work.

New Definitions

There are definitional problems, to be sure. The term "work" needs clarification, as does the phrase "liberal education." Furthermore, the term "career education," not unlike "liberal education," the "humanities," and "general education," means different things to different people. It is quite likely that on any lively college campus one can find as many meanings for liberal education as there are departments. Indeed, it is fair to say that *within* departments scholars will, and with reason, differ in their definitions of the adjectives liberal, humanistic, and general as modifiers of *education.* Yet it is also fair to say, as is the case with career education, that the *concept* of liberal education and the *concept* of work can find a general consensus, allowing for the inevitable small definitional discrepancies.

As with liberal arts, there are many definitions (differing at the margins) for career education. For our purposes, the definition offered by Kenneth B. Hoyt, director, Office of Career Education, United States Office of Education, may be useful: "[Career education is] an effort aimed at refocusing American education and the activities of the broader community in ways that will help individuals acquire and utilize the knowledge, skills, and attitudes necessary for each to make work a meaningful, productive, and satisfying part of his or her way of living."

This takes us back to the perceived antithesis cited above. The word work is too quickly and carelessly equated with occupation or job. Thus the pejorative term "vocationalism" has been raised as the enemy of the liberal arts. Work is much more than job or vocation; and here is the point at issue when we introduce the term career education. A *career,* properly examined, is a lifetime of many parts—*all* of a lifetime. *Work* is a very large, and, under good conditions, a very satisyfing and rewarding *part* of the life or career, and work need not necessarily relate to an occupation or to economic reward. As O'Toole argues, it is faulty to assume that ". . . people work only to make money. . . . No doubt the prime needs of all people are the food, clothing, and shelter that only money can buy. . . . But money is not all that motivates people" (O'Toole 1977, p. 45).

Hoyt (an ardent defender of liberal education) in his illuminating writings on career education adds insight to the meaning of work as an essential outcome of formal education:

> Work is conscious effort . . . aimed at producing benefits for one's self and/or for one's self and society. . . . Since work includes unpaid activities as well as paid employment, it extends to the work of the student as learner, to the growing numbers of volunteer workers in our society, to the work of the full-time homemaker, and to work activities in which one engages as part of leisure and/or recreational time. . . . Career education is the totality of experiences through which one learns about and prepares to engage in work as part of his or her way of living (Hoyt 1975, pp. 3-4).

Returning to O'Toole, he finds corollaries (or perhaps antecedents) with our career education concept in the current thinking of certain of Europe's leading educators:

> The Europeans do not even talk of 'career education;' rather they speak of creating a 'learning society.' To achieve this, they propose the following kinds of goals for education and work:
> - the integration of education, work, and leisure
> - the integration of theory and practice of liberal and technical education
> - the integration of social classes in education and at work
> - an emphasis on continuing education or lifelong learning
> - an emphasis on education for leisure as well as for work
> - preparation of youth for the world of work acquired through actual work experience
> - a deemphasis on educational credentialism
> - a focus on learning and individual growth as the goals of life
> - an emphasis on school as a joyful place where one learns how to learn
> - the integration of age groups (O'Toole, p. 139).

It is noteworthy that all of the perceptions drawn by O'Toole in 1977 from the European models are, in one form or another, cited in my 1974 book on the same subject that deals with American education, *Career Education, A Proposal for Reform.* The spontaneous correspondence of ideas affecting education's evolution between and among countries of Western Europe and the United States is an interesting phenomenon, not limited to career education. That the correspondence is often coincidental and unplanned condemns our mutual isolation and our ethnocentrism. That it occurs suggests a common cultural response to common social needs evolving over time in different countries.

O'Toole observes that "these aims are not yet realized in any country, but in one form or another they seem to run through the writings of educators, futurists, and philosophers in Western Europe. In the United States, however, these goals are less well received. . . . Still, they do appear consistent with an American definition of career education. . . . (ibid.).''

Issues Considered

If work is so much a part of life and career, what, then, troubles us about its relationship with liberal education? The issue is well stated by Walter E. Massey, dean of the college, Brown University:

> At a selective institution such as Brown this questioning of liberal education as a preparation for work is both more and less urgent than at some other institutions . . . there is little doubt that the fear of [underemployment] and the desire for a secure future drives many of our students into a premature professionalism which may be destructive of the goals of a liberal education. Perhaps more significant than either of these problems, however, is the demoralizing effect the negative publicity about liberal education can have on students. . . . (Brown University 1976).

The concerns of Dean Massey were well illuminated by a *New York Times* piece in the spring of 1975 that described the circumstances of recent women graduates of Yale:

> Six years ago Yale University enrolled its first undergraduate women, and the expectations of the 278 who were accepted from a pool of 2,850 applicants were high. . . . Now the women . . . have graduated and entered the working world. . . . Many have found . . . that . . . their education left them unprepared for today's job market. . . . Other women echoed these feelings. . . . Said Linden Havemeyer, a 1974 graduate, "Both men and women feel ill-prepared, and the university is paying more attention to this problem now". . . . "Colleges speak one language and the world speaks another. Students think in terms of a field and their commitment to it. The world outside requires interdisciplinary skills—how to get along with people, how to take responsibility and make decisions."

The issue, oversimplified, resides in differences of perception between faculty and students. The faculty, rightly, holds high the eternal and essential values of the liberal arts as a foundation for the development of civilized men and women. The students (and society, it seems) insist on pragmatic outcomes in occupations, security, and income. The student's disposition is very likely exacerbated by current and continuing unemployment levels and by the steadily rising costs of higher education. These differences of perception need not create a stand-off.

The schools and colleges cannot take on the burden of solving national unemployment problems. They can, however, equip young people to ready themselves for the working world in many ways. This is not to invoke the dread term "vocationalism." Vocation, occupation, and job are terms used in education that have to do with a single, generally narrowly focused task. Education for a vocation is normally aimed at the entry level. The vocation may be that of bricklayer, violinist, college professor, or surgeon. The *readying* for work is an important part of formal education's responsibility—whether in the high school, undergraduate college, or graduate school—quite apart from entry-level competencies. Work is not, and must not be antithetical to the liberal arts. This is where career education—not a program nor a curriculum, but a way of thinking and behaving—finds its application. The concept facilitates the articulation of liberal learning *and* occupation. When the liberal arts and occupational preparation are harmonized, both in the policies of the institution, and in the perceptions of teachers and learners, they comprise the reality of career education. The unity of educational purpose achieved through preparing well-developed and purposive individuals for careers that are built upon liberal learning and occupational fulfillment is the essence of career education.

Institutional Response

But some institutions are responding creatively to the expectations of students and society, and appearing to do so without diminishing their devotion to scholarship in the liberal arts. Glenn S. Dumke, chancellor of the 19 campuses of the California State University and Colleges, declared some years ago: "A baccalaureate degree from our State Universities and Colleges should embrace now, as in the past, a dual approach: a foundation of liberal education, and, based upon that, a specialized program enabling the student to fit himself with the economy or society in a practical way (Dumke 1972)."

The Association of State Colleges and Universities adopted a strong affirmative position on the subject at its annual meeting in November, 1976. The position derived from a Delphic analysis of members' judgments:

> Four-year colleges and universities have an important role in preparing students for careers in the present and projected labor market. Emphasis on career education will grow in our ever-changing technological society. As this occurs postsecondary institutions have a growing responsibility. . . . Educational programs should stress the importance of skills, knowledge and attitude, and the importance of the work ethic and the dignity in all types of work. (American Association of State Colleges and Universities 1977).

Many other illustrations of responsive attention to occupational outcomes in institutional policy can be cited. In the fall of 1977, the National Council of Teachers of Mathematics adopted a detailed resolution that began, "In recognition of the prime importance of work in our society and the role that mathematics plays in the lives of all individuals, the National Council of Teachers of Mathematics supports the position that career education should be a major goal of all who teach and learn mathematics."

The difficulty of achieving balance, however, continues to plague us, as institutions and faculty struggle to elevate academic standards amidst diverse goals. Again, the sustenance of the liberal arts and the need for rigorous institutional policy for their support is argued by Phi Beta Kappa:

> When students are permitted to choose all their courses in areas that interest them and in which they are likely to do well, they obviously will get higher grades. It is clear that more troubling than inflated grades are the implications of this condition for traditional scholarship. Dropping the core of required work in the humanities, the social sciences, and the natural sciences and eliminating foreign language and mathematics requirements threaten the basic definition of liberal learning. (The Key Reporter 1977).

Federal Support

Public policy, including federal law, seems to be facilitating the harmonization of education and work. The passage of the Career Education Incentive Act of 1977, which authorizes $400 million over the next five years, is explicitly directed toward the articulation of academic learning with occupational development at all educational levels. While the Act gives primary attention to the elementary and secondary schools and builds upon the past five years of development and demonstration, it also authorizes $75 million over the next five years for higher education. There is an implicit message in the law that notes the phasing of the concept from the precollege years, where it has had a period of trial with promising results, to the college years, where federal support has been absent. In reporting the bill to the Senate, Senator Hathaway declared:

> The committee views career education at the postsecondary level to be fully as important as at the elementary and secondary levels . . . under the present system, it is clear that many students . . . have no firm idea of their purposes or objectives. The committee . . . realizes that career education concepts must be infused into postsecondary institutions if the overall goals are to be met. (Career Education Incentive Act 1977).

The new law, as it pertains to colleges and universities, provides that interested institutions be invited to seek "demonstration" funds for faculty development, curricular adaptations, increased counseling services, increased placement services, increased articulation between the institution and the business, labor, and industrial communities. This five-year, postsecondary authorization could, as in the case of elementary and secondary education, demonstrate sufficient promise of useful changes and lead to general support of postsecondary programs and services five years hence.

Applying the Concept

I have consciously concerned myself chiefly with the implications of career education as a concept in the higher education setting. I now suggest possible programs, curricular adaptations, and services to be considered beyond the generalizations drawn from the new law. The language of the law is sufficiently flexible to afford institutions of higher education freedom for imaginative responses to the challenge of linking liberal education and work. It should not go unnoticed that the Congressional votes on this policy for educational reform were virtually unanimous in the House and in the Senate. This must tell education planners and faculties something.

The infusion of career education into postsecondary programs would change liberal education administratively and instructionally. Both categories of change are essential. Career education at the college level assumes that higher education aims to afford the learner systematic support in helping him or her decide what to do as a useful citizen after college, and to provide opportunities for readying the learner to do what he or she wants to do. Components of the administrative category are relatively easily identified. They should be disposed generally under the heading of student services and include an enlarged counseling function that includes more systematic arrangements for self-assessment by students, placement services integrated with academic departments, and formal institutional linkages with business, labor, government, the professions, and the community for the identification of internship or other work-site resources for experiential learning. Another important feature of career education in the administrative context is the conscious and deliberate development of institutional policies that would redress occupational stereotyping by sex, race, economic conditions, or handicap in student services and instruction.

Given the institutional commitment to the *administrative* or *student services* aspects of career education, the following types of activities would be established or strengthened and made available systematically to all students:

• Services, including appropriate instruments and counsel to help students understand themselves, appreciate themselves, and comprehend their occupational interests and aptitudes and the related academic corollaries to be fulfilled in preparing for work

• Services that will provide students with a comprehension of the wide array of occupational opportunities, related educational expectations, and a systematic design for taking counsel with practitioners in the fields of interest

• Services that will provide systematic training in decision making, not only for occupational choices, but also for planning one's educational options and personal life as a unit

• Services that will afford students an opportunity to comprehend the meaning of work in our culture, leading to a valuing of work and to the honoring of work well done, no matter its level of craft, service, or profession. The student should learn of the obligations and standards implicit in the behavior of all effective workers, calling for self-discipline, good work habits and attitudes, and relations with others

• Services that will provide planned work experience with or without pay for all students in the fields that seem to interest them, allowing for trial and error, and alternatives

• Services that will afford students the necessary training and counsel for seeking employment, preparing the resume, communicating with potential employers, taking part in the interview, and making the decision

All of these are activities that, in one form or another, are probably present on every campus. However, they are not likely to be systematically arranged in an integrated organizational structure with strong support from institutional policymakers. The items cited above are offered not as a comprehensive listing, but as examples of services that people in college need. They are typical of the changes that would be supported financially by the Career Education Incentive Act of 1977 as demonstration projects. They seem to call for institutional changes, at least in terms of priorities and staffing.

The infusion of career education into instructional programs is not as readily illustrated. Teaching faculty ultimately will determine whether or not the career education concept is to be effectively implemented no matter how ardent the expression of institutional policy. Both by attitude and teaching performance they can either derogate or enhance its administrative effectiveness. They can dismiss the administrative services as irrelevant to their teaching, or they can extend themselves to engage supportively with student services.

Career education *can* enhance the classroom. Given good models of curricular design and teaching strategies and style (also supportable as demonstration projects under the new law), faculty may well choose to adopt the career education concept as a means of improving instruction. This may not be a wholly altruistic choice. If students perceive the liberal arts as extraneous to their own momentary materialistic objectives, it may become clear to teachers that conscious and thoughtful attention to the relationships between education and work can be infused into their subject matter, and that the subject matter is no less worthy or scholarly.

This is not, by any means, to say that all fields of learning and all academic content should be shoehorned into a work-related rationalization. Yet, it is fair to say that creative initiatives by individual professors and departments can and, in many cases, do lead to much clearer work-related connections in the eyes of the learner. Subject areas such as English, the modern foreign languages, mathematics, psychology, economics, history, philosophy, the fine and performing arts, speech, and the natural and social sciences, come quickly to mind as possessing tempting opportunities for thoughtul scholars to turn their talents to the articulation of their fields of learning with appropriate uses beyond the *work* of the professorship and teaching itself. In this way, career education is not added to the curriculum, but rather becomes a way of thinking and behaving about the curriculum.

There are grounds for suggesting that the academic performance of the learner will increase in quality, given the explicit or implicit purposiveness that the teacher can bring to his or her teaching. The motivation of the learner, given the meaningful and useful relationships between the academic content and the individual's life goals, cannot fail to be enhanced. The evidence of this assertion is now being clearly demonstrated in the application of the career education concept to basic instruction in the elementary grades. It is fair to say that the more mature and rational judgments of the better motivated student in college would lead to at least a corresponding increase in teaching effectiveness.

Toward a New Unity

In terms of both administrative services and instructional programs, then, the infusion of career education into an institution's policies, procedures, and curriculum must be justified as a design for improving the quality of education. Better occupational counseling, better decision-making by students, and greater self-awareness and purposiveness on the part of the learner can make the institution a better place. Further, if the faculty accepts the learner's desire to relate learning to lifetime goals and aspirations, better motivation and purposiveness should follow.

If this article has addressed its task effectively, only one simple concept should emerge: liberal education and the development of people for life's work are compatible. Liberal education must be sustained and indeed must be elevated in the arrangement of values we attach to schooling. Thoughtful faculties can elevate the place of the liberal arts by helping the learner to perceive them as essential to the career of a well developed person. Trimming the balance between the pragmatic expectations of the learner and society (including Congress) on one hand and the elevation of the liberal arts disciplines to their deserved level of honor and scholarship on the other can occupy the best of our philosophers and practitioners for years to come. This is not a contest in which one part must lose, and one part must win. It is an elegant marriage, yet to be fulfilled. And, like any good marriage, the whole is greater than the sum of its parts. As Dewey admonished us in 1915: "A democracy which proclaims equality of opportunity as its ideal requires an education in which learning and social application, ideas and practice, work and the recognition of the meaning of what is done, are united from the beginning and for all." (Dewey 1915, p. 316).

The times seem now, threescore years and more since Dewey, to be propitious for creative action. For if we do not act, the transient impulses of the youthful learner, given his or her choice, may indeed lead to the decline and disappearance of what we have known as liberal education. Some institutions, faced with marketplace trade-offs, could trade off their principle capital—the intellectual heritage of a free people—on momentary job-getting accommodation. This would be a national disaster of immeasurable scale; it would mark the beginning of the descent of American education.

CAREER EDUCATION IN UNIVERSITIES

Donald A. Casella and Sandra Samples

Dr. Casella, who is associate director of the Career Planning and Placement Center at San Francisco State University, is active in career education at the college level and has received funding for education work programs. Sandra Samples was a graduate assistant. This article was written in 1976.

Today a college student almost anywhere in the nation might make a request like the one that follows. Wanted: An education that will assist me in learning about myself, my abilities, and my values and interests; that will enable me to acquire the skills to cope with the rapid pace of change in the world; and, most important, that will adequately prepare me for a satisfying and productive career. Would there be many institutions of higher learning that could respond to this request focused on career interests? The answer to this question might well indicate the need for higher education to join elementary and secondary schools in the growing movement to implement career education.

A Richer Concept of Career

There has been a tendency in the past to define the word *career* as simply one's job or occupation. This narrow definition leaves out the further human dimensions which are inevitably linked with a choice of work. *Career* can be expanded to include the life-style, leisure activities, studies, hobbies, community pursuits, and cultural seekings which form a total life pattern. The National Vocational Guidance Association defines career as "a time-extended working out of a purposeful life pattern through work undertaken by an individual" (NVGA-AVA 1973).

Just as career is often defined in a narrow sense, so too is the concept career education frequently limited to that of job training or vocational education. In accordance with the idea of career as previously stated, career education can be considered as "the totality of educational experiences through which the individual becomes knowledgeable about work and is equipped with the skills to be productive" (Hoyt 1975). Marland addressing the 1971 American Vocational Association convention, touched on this point:

> Career education must go beyond occupational needs to what we can think of as survival skills—the interpersonal and organizational understanding without which one simply cannot exist in a modern nation-state, addressing effectively the matter of living itself, touching on all its pragmatic, theoretical, and moral aspects (Marland 1972).

The meanings of career and career education are, therefore, directly dependent upon the meaning of work. We in the United States are experiencing the evolution of a post-industrial understanding of work values. In the process of career development, educational institutions play an important role in value formation and clarification. It is not the purpose of these institutions to impose any particular set of work values, but rather to provide students with the opportunity to develop their own personal work priorities while making career plans and decisions.

Contemporary work values are reflected in the following definition: work is "the conscious effort, other than that involved in activities whose primary purpose is either coping or relaxation, aimed at producing benefits for oneself and/or others" (Hoyt 1975).The values an individual has about work are part of his or her total life-style, and attempting to isolate these work values would be to fragment or divide a personality to the detriment of any growth and learning. It is very possible that in the future the ideal career will be more and more a function of the personal value system of the worker, i.e., one which is of maximum meaningfulness to the person's total life-style.

The process of career development, therefore, is an integral part of human development. Career education, which is intended to facilitate this process, acknowledges the developmental principle and should not end with secondary schools. It is an on-going, comprehensive, integrated, and sequential approach to preparing individuals for life in an ever changing world. This includes higher education.

Mayhew in *Higher Education for Occupations* noted that:

> Educational theorists from Plato to Rousseau to Whitehead to Dewey have posited that learning should be ordered and consistent with the psychological stage of students. While theorists have interpreted the needs of various stages differently, they all suggest that some method of ordering experiences is better than others. Yet when one examines the ordering of courses in baccalaureate programs for vocations and careers, no evidence can be inferred that courses are placed in time to conform to the psychological needs of students (Mayhew 1974).

Universities are long accustomed to providing leadership for elementary and secondary education. In career education, however, the roles are reversed, with universities honestly needing help from their more experienced primary and secondary colleagues! With such cooperation, there are a number of problems in higher education which could be addressed.

Classroom-work Relationship

University students perceive a little relationship between what is taught in the classroom and the workaday world. One of the conferees, Charles Lyons, at a recent Southern Regional Education Board conference on off-campus education stated that classroom theories become meaningful to students "only if they provide a framework through which a person can view, structure, interpret his experiences." In other words, "to understand a theory requires appropriate experience."

> We teach. We try to communicate our own theories and other people's theories. We have students who wait for new schemes, new insight from us. We try. They try . . . . The missing ingredient is experience. Without the meat of experience to interact with and fill out the skeleton of theory, there is no body of understanding.

> Particularly as man's intellect develops and society allows for full-time intellectuals, theories proliferate and become more esoteric. The classroom becomes a place of nonexchange between a professor who may or may not know what he is talking about and a group or students whose inadequate experiential background absolutely precludes a meaningful assimilation of the theories being presented (Cook 1974).

In a report issued by the Southern Regional Education Board conference on off-campus education, the polarization of on-campus and off-campus education was emphatically rejected. It was stated:

> Off-campus and on-campus learning are not dichotomous modes of learning. On the contrary, off-campus learning merges the processes of off-campus student experience with the traditional on-campus classroom processes in a complementary way. The off-campus experience can be viewed as the site of learning, the classroom the place of development and reflection. The classroom can thus serve as either preparation for evaluation of off-campus experiences, just as it has traditionally, if unconsciously, served as preparation for or evaluation of the student's total off-campus life experience. Thus, the off-campus experience is a part of and necessary to the total education process and must be evaluated in that light (ibid.).

In addressing this point, Newman, chairperson of the noted Newman Task Force commissioned by the U. S. Office of Education, asked:

> Why is it that professional training comes only after liberal arts education? For many of these students it might be much more practical to have the entire process reversed, particularly as we begin to make liberal arts education available throughout life. Not only must all of education be restructured but so must the broad range of careers (Newman 1972).

The advantages of a career-dimensioned program of integrated education and work are numerous. For students it can mean a more realistic understanding of an occupation's demands and the opportunity to test and deepen or to revise the career commitment. There is also the opportunity to interact with strong role models and to experience involvement as a catalyst for decision-making and a source of higher motivation. Further, such experiences can function to make job hunting less traumatic because of a more realistic view of what to expect.

> Employers who have learned by sad experience that many young people fresh from college regard their first job as temporary, moreover, are apt to prefer an applicant whose choice is based on experiential knowledge of what the job will be like and a firm sense of commitment and who has had an opportunity to begin developing the necessary skills (Cook 1974).

Related to this point Newman stated that:

> Studies suggest that the men who get to the top in management have developed skills that are simply not taught by formal education. Finding problems and opportunities, initiating action, and following through to attain the desired results requires behavior which is neither measured by examinations nor developed by discussing in the classroom what someone else should do (Newman 1972).

The community at large also benefits from students' work experiences. As Cook stated:

> Apart from these fairly obvious benefits to the students, there are also some readily apparent returns for the large community to be had from college students becoming involved in the world of work. In addition to the fact that these young people have a better chance of identifying their particular gifts and matching them to societal needs, even in the process of learning they often are already contributing fresh perspectives and extra manpower to the community (Cook 1974).

Work Values

A second problem is students' need for more opportunities to form and test their work values. In Yankelovich's study, work did not rank particularly high as an important value in the lives of those college youth surveyed; it fell far below the emphasis placed on love, friendship, education, self-expression, family, and privacy. In 1971 a significant number of students, 61%, felt that hard work does not always reap benefits. A marked change is seen only when this figure is compared to the 31% who felt this way in 1968 (Yankelovich 1972).

It is probable that we are moving toward a future where the idea of a work ethic will be replaced by a pluralistic view of work values, offering a wide variety of ways in which work can become a meaningful and rewarding part of an individual's total life experience (Hoyt 1973). Students need opportunities which will enable them to develop their own attitudes toward the personal, psychological, social, and economic significance of work. By providing these opportunities, career education endeavors to help make work satisfying and meaningful for students. In addition, thinking about work will go a long way toward helping students discover things about themselves. It will help them determine the activities that will bring the greatest meaning to their lives and to find concrete ways to demonstrate their worth through work.

Transferable Academic Skills

A third aspect of the overall problem of student career disorientation is that students need skills which are transferable among career choices. Career choice is a continuous, developmental process, in fact a sequence of choices which forms a career pattern throughout an individual's lifetime. Labor statistics suggest that the average adult male may have eight different occupations in his one career. Students need to be aware that collectively their future working lives will differ radically from past and present patterns; that they will change jobs more often, relocate more often, and change their type of work more often; and that they will require updating at one or more times in their lives to remain employable—all within one career.

Data on college majors supports the fact that vocational interests may change frequently. In a study of the relationships between post-high-school educational programs and occupations, Astin noted that "high proportions of both men and women shift in and out of various occupational groupings during their undergraduate years." A related fact is that:

> Many college graduates who enter the labor force go into occupations that do not require degrees in the particular field in which they receive their bachelor's or master's degrees. Of those men with the baccalaureate degree who were employed full time five years after college graduation, only about three-fourths who were engineering majors reported being employed as engineers; about the same proportion who majored in education reported that they were employed as teachers. Only one-fourth of the natural science majors worked in that field. Slightly over half of the business majors were in business or commerce; and less than five percent of the social science majors had positions as social scientists. Women with the bachelor's degree tend to be even less likely than men to go into the professional field that corresponds to their undergraduate field (Astin et al. 1970).

All of these factors, the changing nature of the work world, the indecisiveness of students in choosing majors, and the frequent choice of jobs which are not related to majors, are significant reasons for students to develop transferable skills. Astin, in fact, stated that one solution to the problem as reported in the University of California study would be to concentrate on development of skills that can be transferred from one field or occupation to another (ibid.). "In essence the courses can be designed to develop competencies in mathematics, languages, and communication, as well as interpersonal skills and skills in systematic inquiry or research." This list of competencies is intended to include those that could be important in performing tasks in many occupations that persons might enter after they complete college (Magarrell 1974b).

Critical Career Skills

A further enumeration of those skills college students need to develop includes: job skills, so that the individual can perform entry level tasks in one or more jobs enabling her or him to grow with the job and to make transfers to other occupational areas in the future; decision-making skills, applicable to many aspects of daily living and working; job-seeking and job-securing skills, sufficient to obtain employment appropriate for the individual's preparation and abilities; industrial discipline, that is, attitudes and habits necessary to maintain and progress in a job; adaptability skills, to pursue learning as a lifelong process and to adjust to changing jobs and job requirements; and interpersonal relationship skills, in order that the individual can function as a follower, co-worker, or leader in work (Bottoms 1973).

Students need opportunities to adapt their skills to changing needs, changing technology, and their own changing interests. These skills would not prematurely force an individual into a specific area of work but would expand his or her ability to choose widely from a broader range of options.

Career Self-concept

At the heart of career development is the individual's self-concept. The essential elements of a fully functioning individual in career development were identified by the Alabama State Department of Education in its position paper on career education:

> It is believed that the key to a full life is to become a self, to learn what you want to be; to believe that you can become what you want to be; to relate your experiences toward the roles that you want to assume; to provide a balance in your living; and to become a fully functional person. We refer to this, becoming a personality, as self-awareness—leading to self-identity (Alabama State Department of Education 1972).

The identification of self cannot be considered apart from the career process. Sadly, the word career is often used synonymously with the words *vocation, job,* or even *work,* and it is not surprising that students often confuse the idea of career with choosing one precise direction in life and having to persist in it regardless of its accord with their true selves. It is important that students not be so bound, but be able to conceive of career as an exciting, dynamic, and continuously developing part of their total being. It is one of the goals of a career education program to encourage and foster this attitude and thinking about career, which places the self at the center of the process.

Accurate Career Information

A sixth aspect of the problem of student career disorientation is that many students lack accurate and current career information. Our nation is a nation of employees. People work for other people in a cycle of production and services that is continuous. It is essential that all individuals understand this system so that they can effectively make decisions about the work they do, where they do it, and for whom. An effective career education program reduces the differences between individual aspirations and the reality of manpower needs. In so doing the individual becomes aware of opportunities for future employment and is more capable of making realistic decisions (Heilman and Goldhammer 1973).

In his commencement address at Ohio State University, President Ford stated:

> Your professors tell you that education unlocks creative genius and imagination and that you must develop your human potential. And students have accepted this. But then Catch 22 enters the picture. You spend four years in school, graduate, go into the job market, and are told the rules have changed. There is no longer a demand for your speciality—another educational discipline is now required. And so one or two more years of study follow, and you return again to the job market. Yet, what you now offer is saleable except that competition is severe. To succeed, you must acquire further credentials. So you go back to the university and ultimately emerge with a master's or even a Ph.D. And you know what happens next? You go out to look for a job—and now they say you're over qualified (Ford 1974b).

The necessity for accurate career information is obvious when considering the technological changes that occur. New jobs are created yearly; old jobs disappear; and others undergo specific modifications. Some have estimated that automation will affect 60,000,000 jobs within the next generation (Shertzer and Stone 1971).

Also, the Bureau of Labor recently estimated that the supply of college graduates may exceed the demand for college-educated workers by 10% between 1980 and 1985 if present patterns of education and work continue without major changes. Putting it another way, American colleges and universities are expected to produce twice as many graduates in the thirteen years following 1972 as they did during the preceding thirteen years, but the number of jobs requiring college degrees is not expected to double (Magarrell 1974a).

Addressing the October, 1974, meeting of the College Entrance Examination Board, Willard Wirtz, president of the National Manpower Institute, pointed out that too many people are training for jobs that do not exist. He urged educators to become more sensitive to the realities of the job market. At the same conference U. S. Commissioner of Education Terrel H. Bell stated that each year students are more undecided about their careers (Bell 1974). "Most young people are not clued in to the available choices and the needs of the future," the commissioner noted.

A Promising Approach and a Worthwhile Investment

Muirhead (1973) has referred to career education as a "promising approach to education" which can serve the needs of a post-industrial society. The career education concept can bring the educational system into a proper balance by affording at least equal importance to the role of work while at the same time emphasizing the importance of a person's being a truly educated citizen who can cope with a rapidly changing world.

During National Career Guidance Week, President Ford stated:

> There is no greater national responsibility than that of helping young Americans find their way to productive and personally rewarding jobs. . . . I urge America's industry, labor, and professional and community leaders to join with high schools and colleges in helping to make students better aware of the many careers that are available.

The opportunities are there. What we need is a systematic way to assist our young people as they decide what to do with their adult lives. . . .

There could not be a more worthwhile investment than this (Ford 1974a).

CAREER EDUCATION AND THE COLLEGE ENGLISH MAJOR

C. B. Darrell

Dr. Darrell is professor of English and director of a developmental education center at Kentucky Wesleyan. He has also served as a consultant in program development. This article was written in 1976.

The Hue and Cry Is On

The hue and cry is on! For more than twenty-five years English departments have serviced the college and university through freshman English courses—presumably designed to assist students in achieving a basic competency in written expression. Needless to say, departments have offered all sorts of courses under the rubric "Freshman English." The course offered most often, however, has focused on developing the habit of good writing (for further discussion, see Wilcox 1973, pp. 62-102). Recent events have indicated that colleges and universities are failing to accomplish this central task. Though many factors enter into the growing crisis about Americans' inability to use the language proficiently, *The Chronicle of Higher Education* recently published an article entitled, "Drop in Aptitude-test Scores Is Largest on Record" (1975). The story indicates that verbal scores fell ten points in just one year (verbal scores dropped from 444 to 434; the math profile dropped eight points, 480 to 472), and that the decline has accelerated steadily since 1963, the all-time peak. According to the same news release, the American College Testing Program (ACT) has encountered a parallel decline in the scores of students it has tested in English. Clearly, since the great majority of students sitting for such examinations are college-bound, colleges and universities face a more difficult task in achieving written proficiency, a goal many authorities believe undergraduate education already has failed in significantly. As we mentioned, the issue has reached crisis proportions. Indeed, *Newsweek* magazine's cover story, "Why Johnny Can't Write," devotes itself to a journalistic analysis (some persons think it an exposé) of the inability of college students and graduates to pass even basic literacy tests. For *Newsweek,* Merrill Sheils begins her article by declaring:

> If your children are attending college, the chances are that when they graduate they will be unable to write ordinary, expository English with any real degree of structure and lucidity. If they are in high school and planning to attend college, the chances are less than even that they will be able to write English at the minimal level when they get there (Sheils 1975).

Other major magazines and newspapers in recent months have limned in the details of the worst crisis in the teaching of English, perhaps, in a half century!

These research studies and the popular outcry about the high school and college graduates' inability to write even minimally effective English does not mean writing the polished English of Bacon, Macaulay, Churchill, Hemingway, or E. B. White; rather, concerned spokespeople refer to the simple need to read a driver's license, an income tax form, or a typical newspaper.

The Traditional English Major

English departments face an equally troubling problem, perhaps one requiring more radical surgery than is needed to improve the teaching and learning of effective writing. That problem is the traditional major or concentration combined with the massive decline in the numbers of undergraduate students electing to concentrate in English. For some time now, undergraduate English faculties and the public school teaching profession have been glutted by qualified candidates seeking jobs with but marginal success. No longer a joke or random truth but painfully true, there are college graduate English majors who drive cabs these days. Trained in traditional departments of English both at undergraduate and graduate levels, college teachers of English have not sympathetically responded to the new students or nontraditional students now appearing on college campuses—those students who have accumulated only average high school records and whose parents most likely did not attend college. That is, English departments have not altered their curricula to accommodate these students, much more vocational, uninclined to traditional liberal arts studies, and practical career-minded. Such students find unattractive the traditional major in English. After all, "English is for those who will teach it."* The work of such persons as Berry and Orange, however, remains a tangential effort at dealing with the chief issue, namely, that college English departments have not faced the issue of career education's place in literature, language, writing, film studies, and whatever else English departments do with and for their students.

Career Education and the Traditional College Disciplines

Career education, a new item on the agenda of traditional college disciplines, is not new to education in America. Former Commissioner of Education Sidney Marland, Jr., lent enormous personal support and won millions of congressional dollars to establish career education in elementary and secondary school curricula across the United States. If I may mix a metaphor, career education is a household word in public school education today, the newest family member of school subjects, and likely to remain around a long while.

Career education means essentially a systematic, pervasive attempt through all educational activities of the public school system to provide a ladder of opportunities for awareness, exploration, preparation, and selection of careers among high school graduates, whether or not they enter college. Increasingly, these ladders of career education include a systematic involvement of fifteen or so occupational clusters delineated by the U. S. Office of Education and adopted by various state education agencies and systems.

Surprisingly, career education has received scant attention from the higher education community, except from an occasional teacher education department—usually at the

---

* Though not at all true—most English concentrators enter business, industry, and the professions other than teaching—this myth manages to survive, indeed prosper. For solid evidence to refute the myth, see Elizabeth Berry's National Council of Teachers of English study, *The Careers of English Majors* (Berry 1966). Linwood Orange's booklet, *English: The Pre-Professional Major,* also tries to sketch the scope of career opportunities available to graduating English majors (Orange 1973).

insistence of the state department of education, requesting that prospective teachers receive some innoculation regarding concepts and practices of career education in that state.

Career education may offer English departments a fresh—pardon the phrase—golden opportunity to attract, once again, significant numbers of majors and to provide for business, industry, and the professions that valuable educational experience unique to persons majoring in English. Furthermore, we can do this without losing that uniqueness in the context of liberal arts education.

College teachers of English need models of career education functional in department offerings, congruent with faculty personnel as far as possible, and clearly able to produce increased numbers of graduates highly and especially attractive to nonteaching career options.

A Proposed Model of Career Education for College English Majors

In that light and in the spirit of experiment, I suggest the following model, not because it represents the best model nor because I have seen it work, but because it constitutes an initial contribution to discussion and creation of models worthy of implementation and evaluation.

The basic ladder model utilized in thousands of public schools constitutes a promising structure on which to develop an English major career education program; I refer, of course, to the awareness, exploration, preparation, and ultimately selection paradigm. Further, this pattern will work smoothly if we can correlate it with particular college years such as freshman, sophomore, and so forth. Finally, we need to insure a mixture of theory and practice, of representativeness and numbers of actual career options available to the English major, and of individual evaluation and institutional review of the program.

Before we turn to the model, three questions deserve our attention because they focus on the issues likely to assure success or failure of the program. First, is the program relevant? Whatever the specific content of a career education program for college English majors, it must reflect institutional goals and mission, involve and appeal to the special yet restricted competencies of the English faculty, attract English major interest, and meet societal career needs. Second, does the program provide for—indeed nourish—flexibility, creativity, and adequacy? The program must be flexible to the institution's students and community. Further, it must encourage and release creativity, and it must be adequate for each student's needs. Third, in retrospect is the experience worthwhile? Evaluation by the business and professional sector, faculty, and students, as well as by those entrusted with responsibility for institutional development and evaluation, remains essential to a successful program.

The curriculum pattern outlined below, designed with the small, as well as the large, department in mind, should allow both to benefit maximally from the resources of both academic and business communities.

Essentially, the program extends four years and implements the awareness-exploration-preparation-selection model. During the freshman year, while the student takes the freshman English course, the staff will invite selected business and professional persons on perhaps a biweekly basis to participate in a news-conference format, during which students ask questions about the visitor's work, particularly as it relates to problems, requirements, and advantages of good writing and speaking. Carefully chosen community representatives can emphasize effectively the significance of writing and can motivate the typical student in ways teachers cannot. This stage constitutes the first rung of the career education ladder—*awareness.*

During the sophomore year, awareness intensifies, and the next rung begins—*exploration.* Probably English majors participate in an in-depth study of career education options as indicated by those participating. In both this course and the next one English majors continue to receive the benefits of presentations of other options offered because of other seminar members. Students research thoroughly the career qualifications, prerequisites, advantages, limitations, life-styles, etc., of career options they find appealing. Each person reports on his or her investigations, and seminar members help weigh and evaluate the discoveries. For each occupation cluster represented by each participant, one representative would visit the seminar for a session to share insights, experiences, forecasts, and recommendations. This step leads to *advanced exploration* and *beginning preparation.*

During one semester of the junior year, the English major participates in a career education experience composed of both additional theory and limited practicum involvement. That is, this level provides consideration of theory related to a series of brief, (mini-practicums) on-site visits to businesses and industries selected by, and of specific interest to, student participants.

The final stage, *selection,* occurring during one semester of the senior year (preferably the first) would find each student participating in an intensive internship of from three to fifteen hours credit (from one course load to a total course load commitment) in the career option selected. Perhaps the company actually employs the student, part-time or full-time, for the internship. Needless to say, internships could, preferably should, I think, work throughout the country, not merely in the immediate vicinity of the college. This kind of off-campus education has been implemented by several institutions, both in this country and in Europe; Peabody College, Drew University, Antioch College, and Stanford University offer off-campus experiences not limited to classroom instruction or narrowly conceived academic experiences.

At any rate, the English faculty, the student, and the intern's host—whether employer or supervisor—have carefully tailored a potentially informative, varied, and challenging series of educational and career activities for the student and have decided on methods and instruments for multiple-party *evaluations.* The final stage of this career education program would, most likely, occur during the final semester of the senior year, when the student devotes one credit hour to discussing with his or her career education advisor the implications of self-evaluation, internship evaluation, and the advisor's reflections of the student's experience, both in internship and in total college experiences.

In diagram, such a sequence of studies for career education for the English major would look like this:

English 1301/CE–1: Freshman English (indicating that one hour of freshman English is career education)

English 2–CE–3: Seminar in Career Awareness and Preparation (indicating three hours credit)

English 3–CE–3: Practicum in Career Preparation (three hours credit)

English 4–CE–3–15:   English Career Education Internship (three to fifteen hours credit)

English 5–CE–1:   Evaluation Tutorial (one hour credit)

As the reader can readily see, such a program requires from eleven to twenty-three hours of the time available to the undergraduate. According to department policy, these hours could substitute for regularly scheduled courses, could supplement them, or do both.

To plan wisely, to obtain maximum cooperation from business, the professions, industry, and labor, each department should establish a liaison committee composed of the institutional development officer, selected faculty, representative community leaders, and students. This committee should represent one of the earliest steps a faculty takes in designing a program similar to the one described above. Too, this committee and the chief academic officer should provide an ongoing evaluation of the program and periodic intensive evaluations to insure maintenance of quality and reduction of weaknesses.

In my judgment, such a program recognizes the legitimate concerns of students about reaching informed career decisions. Moreover, it provides flexibility in that the institution and the community utilize the available resources and talents. The program encourages creativity, individuality, and adequacy in that students help select much of the content of the career education courses; they research careers attractive to them in terms of how their English major will help them. While doing so, they learn what other courses will enrich their career options. During this process, students are constantly relating their English studies to career options. I suspect rather strongly that faculty, too, will begin to design and alter courses so that students sense and respond to the closer tie of English courses with the world of work. I do not mean to suggest, needless to say, that all courses should relate intimately, woodenly, and literally to that world; I do mean to say that more courses could demonstrate the relevance of literature to career, life-styles, etc. Such a program encourages college-level individualized instruction in one of the areas we most need it, I think—career awareness, exploration, preparation, selection, and evaluation.

The two major problems facing English departments today would threaten us less if we could realize the increasing importance of career education and if we could take concrete steps to provide an English language and literature curriculum more responsive to student concern for career guidance and career education.

Summary

During the ten years I have taught college English, I have heard business persons, doctors, attorneys, labor leaders, and government personnel declare again and again that written and spoken English are most essential to obtaining desirable jobs and to advancement. I have heard that so frequently I believe it is true. Our curriculum, however, does not reflect that fact. We continue to offer courses and employ teaching methods as if we were preparing all majors to enter graduate studies in English. It is time we broadened our college English curriculum to invite more students to consider the English major as an undeniably attractively and solid cornerstone for hundreds of successful careers. Lamentably, our professional journals have all but ignored career education and the English concentrator. The Modern Language Association, the National Council of Teachers of English, and the College English Association would assist this country's colleges and universities immeasurably if at least one of them would schedule an annual meeting devoted to the topic discussed in this paper.

CAREER EDUCATION IN COLLEGES OF EDUCATION: A NEGLECTED RESPONSIBILITY

George E. Leonard and Howard H. Splete
Dr. Leonard is professor of educational guidance and counseling at Wayne State University and a consulting psychologist.

At the time this article was written in 1978, Dr. Splete was a professor in the College of Education at Wayne State.

Introduction

In the past, colleges of education have attempted to use their resources to meet the human needs of our society; yet it appears that these colleges have neglected and continue to neglect a crucial concern—that of aiding our population to prepare for and assume desired life-styles.

Career education is an integral part of each individual's career development. Career development is an ongoing process that occurs over the life span and includes home, school, and community experiences related to an individual's self-concept, life-style, and work. Colleges of education must help their graduates respond to the career development needs of those with whom they work. This aid can, and should, be given through the implementation of career education in both pre-service and in-service programs.

A Change in Mission for Colleges of Education

There are several ways in which colleges of education can reorganize their basic functions to serve the needs of career education. This reorganization, in our view, is more than simply preparing certain individuals as career education specialists. We believe that all college of education programs must be affected and involved. Then, and only then, can colleges of education meet current needs.

Pre-service Programs

Preparation of teachers within the career education program should emphasize acquiring knowledge and competence to assist all students, kindergarten through adult, to meet their developmental needs. Teachers involved in career education must be prepared to use knowledge instrumentally to help students achieve their purposes. To accomplish this, the preparatory curriculum for teachers must develop performance skills, not just emphasize academic scholarship.

Secondly, the preparatory curriculum for all teachers should provide background and skill training in helping students acquire those competencies needed to meet their responsibilities at work, at home, and at play. Students will need fulfillment in their life roles. This means that all teachers must know and understand life roles so that they can promote the skills needed for these roles.

Third, within the career education model all teachers, prospective or present, will need to understand the nature of work in contemporary society. Neither Puritanical nor imperialistic attitudes toward work are realistic today. In thinking about work teachers must deal with many philosophical questions if they are to guide children effectively.

Fourth, teachers must have basic knowledge of occupational clusters. They should be familiar with the structure of the occupational world, of employment entry requirements, and especially the style of life associated with occupations.

Fifth, all teachers should learn to coordinate their skills with the skills of other personnel in order to achieve their goals. There should not, and cannot, be a standardized teaching methodology for career education. Individual teachers will be more comfortable and effective in implementing their career education practices in their own individual ways; however, procedures should be closely coordinated by the faculty as a career education team. Teacher specializations should be utilized. Great care must be taken to include and use the expertise of guidance and counseling personnel, as well as other resource specialists available. Through counselor involvement, teachers can become aware of all of the specialized resources available and learn how to use them.

Sixth, vocational education as part of career education plays a new and more important role in the schools. There is a welcome reemphasis on teacher preparation in vocational education areas. These areas include specialized programs to prepare individuals for professional productive and service occupations. This reemphasis on vocational education teacher preparation needs to be examined within the total framework of career education. There is a definite danger in our educational preparation programs of placing undue emphasis strictly on vocational education. We have previously done this with academic education, with the college preparatory programs unduly influencing educational curriculum offerings and programs.

In looking at education as a means of helping people find their chosen places in society, differences between the academic and the vocational must be eliminated, with all subjects related in some fashion to the future career needs of the individual.

Seventh, teachers need to help students explore professional fields and gain the background knowledge and skills they need for entering specific programs. Subject matter must be relevant to the world outside of the classroom. Classes can be taken to community settings where occupational and life roles can be seen and evaluated. Individualized instruction can also be used to allow students to pursue their own individual interests in subject areas and in field investigations.

In-service Programs

It is clearly evident that the in-service needs of current practitioners, who lack the appropriate background and skills in the career education field, are critically important. Colleges of education provide for the in-service needs of the educational professions on more than the peripheral basis which now exists. A number of factors to be considered in college of education in-service programs need to be considered.

Initially, schools of education need to gain the understanding, acceptance, and support of the administration, staff, parents, and community representatives of the area served. Too often, a few individuals from the college and the community make the decision to present an in-service program to a certain population without their understanding and involvement. Programs will, of course, be more successful when key personnel at both institutions are involved from the inception of the program. Both educational institutions need to recognize their involvement as an established and legitimate part of their educational responsibilities.

Second, the needs of the in-service population must be recognized as the starting point for the planning and implementation of the program. Local school districts and communities may have unique needs and perceptions of their participation in career education. Colleges of education must work on a collaborative basis with their in-service constituents throughout the entire in-service process.

Third, all of the pre-service aspects that have been discussed should be reviewed as to their inclusion in an in-service program. We believe that all of them could be included and even expanded upon in an in-service program.

Fourth, there must be even more involvement of parents, students, and business and civic leaders from the community in an in-service program. The role of the home and the community will take on new dimensions in the life and activities of the in-service program and in the school itself. The whole concept of the community school will have to be applied to career education programs, in respect to both the needs of children and to the retraining needs of adults. Teaching staffs and their students will have to be much more involved in activities with persons from the school and the community.

Fifth, this community involvement in a career education in-service program can be especially relevant in providing for needs of culturally diverse and economically disadvantaged children and adults. Special programs for developing appropriate strategies for dealing with the problems of cultural pluralism and disadvantagement should be extended. It appears that many of the educational staffs will need extensive preparation in these areas.

Sixth, this in-service type of program should be viewed as a continuous process by both the community and the school of education. Too often one-shot efforts die aborning because of lack of continuing support and effort.

Seventh, the in-service effort should look closely at coordinating all of the educational programs in the community, from preschool through adult and continuing education. Although adult and continuing education programs may be designed to meet the career needs of individuals who have not been able to achieve their desired ends through normal schooling, they need to be included in the community's appraisal and involvement in a career education in-service program. This is consistent with the career education concept that educators have a responsibility to aid individuals in their career development over the life span.

Continuing Education

The last point regarding educational aid to individuals over the life span needs to be reviewed in the context of college of education services to teachers. Perhaps the distinction between pre-service and in-service programs needs to be eliminated. It is more than likely that what is most needed in preparing teachers for emerging career education programs is a concept of continuous professional education—the never ending process of maintaining currency of knowledge as new knowledge is available and social imperatives shift.

The proprietary professions have been able to take long steps toward a concept of continuous education because the competitive nature of their service requires that practitioners not fall behind. The salaried professions become more protective and seek security measures which shelter practitioners from competition and from the need to remain professionally current. Perhaps the opportunity to develop a meaningful system of professional renewal, such as in the area of career education, constitutes the greatest current challenge to colleges of education.

Field Relationships

There is a distinct need for greater cooperation among schools of education, state boards of education, local school districts, and the community. In order to fulfill the needs of the career education program, teachers need more than theoretical knowledge about teaching, learning, and subject-matter content. In order to deal adequately with individuals, the teacher needs not only knowledge but also the experience and the guidance received from experienced competent teachers. In many ways, little is known concerning the experiences which will result in the superior teacher. We do know that the preparation of the teacher must provide real life experiences over a period of time. We would suggest this cannot be accomplished by traditional practices. The goals of career education can only be achieved with the assistance of schools of education which provide a broader overview of the effective means and processes needed to help students become all they are capable of becoming.

Schools of education have often allowed themselves to become isolated from the community. Also, local school districts have allowed themselves to become isolated. Few school districts in the country have the skills, knowledge, and capabilities to implement a career education program, and only a few schools of education have attempted to perform all of the program functions without the involvement and assistance from agencies external to it. We need to provide practical and real life settings through which the individual matures as a professional teacher. We must also provide opportunities to gain the knowledge and skills needed by a professional person.

Our preparation programs, in order to conform to the real world, should establish ongoing relationships with other agencies which have additional resources that can be used to further the development of teachers. We recognize that, for colleges of education to accomplish their objectives within the career education framework, there will be a great deal of expense involved in terms of needed equipment and facilities.

In the same vein, it should be noted that teachers who can relate to all individuals from childhood to adulthood are needed. As the college of education becomes more involved with diverse populations, it needs to review the attributes and qualifications of its staff in working with these populations. Perhaps colleges of education may in the future employ persons who do not have college degrees yet possess the cultural and vocational backgrounds, experiences, and expertise which can be used effectively in working in the overall career education enterprise.

Research Need

Colleges of education need to examine the effectiveness of their contributions more than ever in this era of accountability and scrutiny by funding agencies. Research provides the schools of education with the means to show something for their efforts.

Career education is geared toward providing teachers with knowledge and skills to aid human function and develop in their life roles; thus, it is important that we research how teachers can be more effective in the teaching process itself and in understanding how humans approach preparation for their occupational goals and life-styles.

Certain priority areas with which schools of education need to be concerned include: greater emphasis on the career development process; the development of programs that effectively deal with our culture; and the educational problems that are connected to the changing nature of our American society.

Teachers need to know much more about the development of personality, how individuals internalize values, how values affect the behavior and career choices of individuals, how individuals achieve a state of self-awareness and self-discipline, and those barriers which prevent individuals from achieving their personal and occupational goals.

Certainly, one of the most serious deficiencies of education is that the processes of teacher education have not been scientifically examined in spite of the fact that teacher education is one of the largest single professional university programs. This must be remedied through researching college involvement and teacher preparation in the field of career education.

Summary

Colleges of education need to be involved in the preparation of teachers for their participation in career education. This responsibility to meet societal needs has been sadly neglected by schools of education. We suggest that colleges of education review their entire teacher preparation programs and revise their training procedures so that their faculty and graduates can work effectively in career education.

It seems extremely important that colleges of education look at their role in career education as it relates to: (1) a continuous educational process through both pre- and in-service teacher training programs; (2) a collaborative relationship with local and state educational agencies and also business and community leaders; and (3) an intensive research effort in the area of teacher training.

It has been said the educational lag in relation to societal needs has been of fifty years duration. Colleges of education need to accept their responsibility to career education now, not in 2020 A.D.

CAREER EDUCATION IN THE COMMUNITY COLLEGE: AN EVOLVING CONCEPT

Kenneth B. Hoyt

Author of six books and numerous articles on career education, Kenneth B. Hoyt is the most prolific writer in the field. Since 1974 he has served as director of the Office of Career Education, Office of Education, Department of Health, Education, and Welfare. Dr. Hoyt is also professor of counselor education at the University of Maryland. This article was written in 1977.

The philosophical foundations of the community college movement and the career education concept have much in common (Hoyt 1973). As a result, it would be difficult to identify any community college where no "bits and pieces" of career education exist. Unfortunately, this leads to a "we're already doing it" kind of reaction when the topic of career education is raised with many community college experts. To offset this, I would like to begin with a bold assertion that, so far as I know, comprehensive, bonafide career education efforts are extremely rare in community college settings today. I hope these remarks will hold greatest meaning for those who disagree violently with that assertion.

It would be both foolish and futile to construct and defend an idealistic model for career education in the community college at the present time. Too many variables including: (a) the great diversity of kinds of students served in one community college as opposed to another; (b) the large number of unknown factors that will determine the future of the community college movement in our nation; and (c) the still evolving nature of the career education concept. On the other hand, to use such variables as an excuse for failing to devote serious thought to the problem is to engage in professionally irresponsible behavior.

Thus, these remarks are aimed at identification of several major problems that appear to be common in most community college settings. For each, I will attempt to outline my own *current* position. My hope is that by doing so, all of us will be better equipped to help each other develop better and more defensible positions. I, for one, readily acknowledge my own personal need for such help.

Many of the thoughts to be expressed here represent things I have learned from participants in two of the Office of Career Education (OCE) "mini-conferences" held during the 1976-77 academic year. One involved 12 community college career education "experts" identified through a nationwide nomination procedure. The second involved four additional community college career education experts identified by The American Association of Community Junior Colleges (AACJC). While the help of these mini-conference participants is gratefully acknowledged, I hasten to add that none should be held accountable for the remarks presented here.

I want to begin with a brief discussion of several variables that combine to prevent us from formulating a single community college career education model at the present time. This will necessarily be accompanied by some predictions regarding the future nature of the community college student body. Following this, I would like to comment briefly on the significance of the word "community" for career education in the community college. Finally, I will offer some thoughts on what I currently regard as basic elements in a comprehensive community college career education effort.

Variables and Predictions

Community colleges, because each aims to serve a different community, are necessarily more distinguished by their diversity than by their similarities. Several of these diversities hold direct implications for those concerned with developing a model for community college career education efforts. The three most significant sources of variation to consider here are: (a) size and geographic location; (b) age levels of students served; and (c) the relative emphasis placed on occupational education as opposed to the liberal arts. To attempt to use a single model for the community college in Hutchinson, Kansas and in Dade County, Florida would be doomed to a failure both because of differences of size and the rural, as opposed to the urban, setting. Even within the large urban setting, it seems fruitless to attempt to impose the same model on LaGuardia Community College in New York City—where 80% of students are recent high school graduates—and Wayne County Community College in Detroit—where only 25% are recent high school graduates. The strong liberal arts emphasis found in the community college in Ocean County, New Jersey, as opposed to the strong occupational education emphasis present in Kirkwood Community College at Cedar Rapids, Iowa pose very different implementation problems.

Of these three variables, the most significant, in terms of implications for career education efforts in community colleges are concerned, is the age distribution of students who choose to enroll. While, of course, numerous exceptions can be found, it seems safe to venture a few generalizations regarding needs of younger students, as opposed to older adults, for career education in the community college.

The young high school graduate seeking admission to the community college is often unsure regarding career goals. At the same time, strong societal pressures are brought to bear urging him/her to make career decisions. Some students succumb by immediately enrolling in a specific occupational education program. Others resist by enrolling in only the liberal arts offerings which, they contend, will be helpful to them no matter what kind of occupation they eventually enter. The need to traverse the "rites of passage" from youth to adulthood lead a great majority of these students to seek college credit for almost any kind of educational experience they undergo at the community college. Increasingly, this is including requests that they receive academic credit for experiences aimed at such goals as career awareness, exploration, planning, and decision-making—including those activities having some work experience component.

The older adult, on the other hand, is very often an individual who enrolls in the community college for purposes of broadening his/her total lifestyle, not for purposes of acquiring entry-level occupational skills. Somehow, it seems to have become respectable to value the broader array of educational goals if one is firmly established in an occupational role. Partly, perhaps, because they *are* adults, older students seem less worried about whether or not a particular learning experience carries academic credit and more worried about whether or not it meets their felt educational needs. I have a distinct feeling that adult students in the community college who enroll for specific purposes of making mid-career occupational changes are in the minority—even among those called "adult students." That is, among the total population of adults who could benefit from community college attendance, I believe the problems of those faced with traumatic decisions regarding mid-career specific occupational change have been overemphasized. Important as these problems and these persons are, they do not seem to me to be either the most important or the most numerous.

As an outsider to the community college movement, I feel free to make some predictions regarding the future nature of community college students without being inhibited by specific knowledge regarding the community college movement. These outsider predictions may find their primary utility in serving as attack points for rebuttals by community college experts. Even that would, it seems to me, be useful.

First, I predict that the average age of community college students will increase substantially in the next ten years. In addition to the usual actuarial reasons for making this prediction, there are two other factors operating. One is the current rapid growth of vocational/technical education institutions which, increasingly, serve both secondary and postsecondary students. I have a feeling that they can be expected to draw significant numbers of both recent high school graduates and adults who seek specific occupational skills required for immediate job entry. The second is what I regard as an inevitable move on the part of our system of state colleges and universities to seek to attract liberal arts students during the freshman and sophomore years. They almost have to move in this direction in terms of their own survival needs. I have a distinct feeling that the current trend toward placing limits on community college enrollments may well be related to this need. Both of these will, it seems to me, tend to cut into what would otherwise be a continuing increase in community college enrollments.

Second, and related to the first, I predict that, increasingly, community colleges will find the career education needs of their older adult students centering around (a) the need for upgrading in occupational skills related to their current occupations, and/or (b) the need to acquire skills and knowledge useful in helping them make more productive use of leisure time—to help them lead fuller, more satisfying lives. To the extent that this prediction is accurate, it may well be that the goal of education as preparation for work will, for many adult students, be translated primarily into terms of unpaid work carried out as productive use of leisure time—not as preparation for the world of paid employment. When applied to the world of paid employment, that goal, it seems to me, will, for increasing numbers of adults, be translated into terms of acquiring skills required for adapting to changes within their chosen occupational fields rather than in seeking a new and completely different set of occupational skills.

To the extent to which either of these two predictions is accurate, career education in the community college will certainly be much different in nature than those efforts now serving as models at the K-12 level.

The "Community" in Community College Career Education Efforts

The concept of collaboration was a key ingredient in career education when the movement was launched in 1971. That concept was picked up by Willard Wirtz and his associates when they produced *The Boundless Resource* several years later. It is currently being further championed through creation of a number of demonstration community education/work councils funded largely with Department of Labor funds. A recent DOL grant to AACJC has resulted in an important effort to demonstrate a leadership role for the community college in the community education/work collaborative effort. Because the total effort is so directly tied into career education, OE's Office of Career Education is investing a substantial amount of funds into the total National Manpower Institute project. Whether or not some of these OCE funds is used in those five communities where community colleges are taking leadership roles has yet to be determined. In any event, there are four aspects of this total concept that deserve discussion here.

First, and most important, I would hope that no community college engages in such a total community effort without starting from an internal frame of reference. The effort cannot hope to succeed unless the need for internal change among community college staff members—and especially among the teaching faculty—is recognized and acted upon. To whatever extent such an effort does not include concentrated attempts to create changes in the attitudes—and thus the actions—of the teaching faculty, it will have missed the basic point of career education as a refocusing of American education. If this happens, the best that can be hoped for will be creation of a series of new specialists, new courses, and new services within the community college—and that is the add-on-approach, not true career education. At worst, unless careful thinking is devoted to the topic, a so-called community education/work council might try to operate as though the community college itself will remain as is—and that would surely be disastrous. I see no good way the full potential of the community college for playing a leadership role in establishing and coordinating the work of a community education/work council can be realized unless and until the community college commits itself to the kinds of internal changes called for by the career education concept.

Second, for community colleges to play a leadership role here, the past and present contributions of the K-12 system of public education must be recognized and used, not ignored nor replaced. Of the approximately 9,300 K-12 public school districts that have, to date, initiated some kind of career education effort, there may be as many as 1,000-2,000 who have already established some kind of community career education action council. Such entities, where they exist, have typically already begun some systematic efforts to identify, catalogue, and utilize resources in the business/labor/industry/professional community for career education. If a community college operates in a community where the K-12 system has initiated this kind of action, it seems to me both appropriate and desirable to try to join forces—not compete with—such an effort. Any community college can make substantial contributions to helping such K-12 school systems improve their initial data bank and operational relationships with the broader community. Whether or not the K-12 school system has initiated such an effort, it seems especially obvious to me that any such efforts on the part of any community college must be planned in ways that include, rather than exclude, the K-12 public school system.

Third, any community college considering an expansion of collaborative relationships with the broader community in the arena of education/work efforts must, it seems to me, recognize the need to include the many important community segments who, for years, have wrestled with these problems on their own. I am referring here to such efforts as those of local service clubs (Rotary, Kiwanis, etc.), local chapters of Scouting USA, Girl Scouts of the USA, Junior Achievement, Chamber of Commerce, The National Alliance of Businessmen, Business and Professional Womens' Clubs, Women's American ORT, local Council of Churches, local AFL/CIO affiliates, local NOW chapters, the American Legion and Legion Auxiliary. Most of these efforts have concentrated on younger students and have not considered devoting similar amounts of energy to the community college setting. For some, it would be admittedly inappropriate to do so. That is not the point. Rather, the point is that each represents an existing community resource both interested in and holding high potential for making positive contributions to the total career education effort. Many of their efforts could be, and should be, put in a career development perspective that recognizes the need for extending services and concerns to at least the younger students in the community college. It is a set of resources that should be fully utilized.

Finally, any such effort must recognize the broader community as a learning laboratory for community college students—just as the community college has viewed itself as a learning opportunity for all segments of the community. The "information rich/experience poor" charges that have been leveled against American education are not entirely without validity. The concept of experiential learning has yet to be converted from a series of course opportunities for a minority of students to an educational methodology available to all. The hard questions of who will determine, supervise, grade, and credit experiential learning in the broader community are ones that will, I hope, be answered with the help of community education/work councils. The necessity for recognizing this as a major direction for change cannot be ignored in any such effort.

Basic Elements of Career Education in Community College Settings

For all of the reasons discussed earlier—plus more—it seems likely to me that career education efforts in community colleges may well vary considerably from those at the K-12 levels. The earlier K-12 experience, on the other hand, can and should be utilized in thinking about dangers to be avoided in initiating career education in community colleges. As a final part of this presentation, then, I would like to outline what, at this point in time, I consider to be basic elements of career education in a community college setting. I do so with the obvious note of caution that these elements will have to be applied in different fashions—depending on the characteristics of the community college, its students, and the community in which it operates.

First, and most important, a community college career education effort must, it seems to me, start with a full and careful consideration of community college educational goals. The goal of education as preparation for work must be considered as one among several basic goals of the community college. It should not be allowed to take precedence over other basic goals. Rather, it should be recognized as one among several to which the community college is committed.

Second, with respect to the goal of education as preparation for work, career education asks for an expansion in meaning of that goal beyond the conventional interpretation as specific vocational skill training required for entry into the occupational society. In addition to this interpretation, this goal must take on two other important meanings. One concerns itself with helping students acquire adaptability skills (including work habits, work values, decision-making skills, etc.) required for changing with change in the occupational society. The second concerns itself with expanding the meaning of this goal so as to include unpaid work as well as paid employment—including both productive use of leisure time and the changing meaning of work in today's home/family structure. The community college engaged in true career education will accept and find ways of implementing this expanded meaning of the goal of education as preparation for work.

Third, the community college's career education efforts will expand greatly the means utilized for helping students in the career awareness, exploration, planning, and decision-making process. In too many community colleges, these functions are today seen as the prime responsibility of student personnel workers. This, I feel, must change in several ways. One way can easily be seen if we consider current priorities for use of occupational education facilities. Too often, these are reserved—either by law, policy, custom, or tradition—primarily for use by those preparing for specific job entry in a particular area of occupational education. Career education calls for such facilities to be made equally available to the liberal arts student who wants to acquire only enough skill in a particular area so that skill can be used in productive use of leisure time. They should also be made available to the occupationally undecided student who wants some "hands on" exposure to several areas of occupational education before making firm career decisions. In my ideal career education program, students will receive academic credit for such experiences.

A second expansion will be seen in greatly increased faculty participation in the career guidance process. I see no way of fully implementing career education unless the teaching faculty are regarded as key participants. Each can and should know the career implications of his/her speciality—in terms of both paid and unpaid work—and be prepared to discuss them with students. Obviously, this will require both (a) in-service staff development for the teaching faculty and (b) specific assigned time for faculty members to participate in these kinds of interactions with students.

A third area of expansion in this area will be involvement of persons from the business/labor/industry/professional community in the career guidance process. Whether involved in small group seminars, as resource persons in classrooms, or as members of a counseling team in the student personnel offices, such persons can and should be utilized in the career guidance process.

Fourth, a community college career education effort should, it seems to me, involve some form of work experience opportunity for all students. I am, of course, here thinking primarily about the younger students who come to the community college directly from high school. Those enrolled in such liberal arts programs as pre-law, pre-medicine, pre-engineering, etc. are as deserving of work experience opportunities as are those enrolled in pure occupational education programs. Whether that work experience is paid or unpaid will depend on the total set of reasons why it is undertaken—i.e., to the extent productivity for an employer is involved, then pay should also be involved but, to the extent the primary goal is career exploration, unpaid work experience may be justified. This is a good example of an area where implementation should be done only with the full participation of organized labor in basic policy determinations.

Fifth, a community college career education effort should, it seems to me, be built and operated within the framework of career development as a lifelong process. If this is done, then that effort will surely be intimately tied to career education efforts at the K-12 level. It will also be tied to adult/recurrent/continuing education efforts and with career education efforts at the four-year college/university level. A community college that has not considered and established such linkages cannot, in my opinion, be considered to be operating a comprehensive career education effort.

As part of this linkage effort with other segments of education, it seems particularly crucial that the generic problem of stereotyping, as a deterrent to full freedom of occupational choice, be considered and acted upon. This includes problems of race and sex stereotyping as well as stereotyping with respect to handicapped persons and to older Americans. For example, it is difficult to believe that a Title IX Coordinator in a community college would have no interest or involvement in efforts of local elementary schools to reduce sex stereotyping in textbooks and in classroom practices—for it is at these early ages where neglect is most damaging and help is most rewarding.

Finally, it seems to me that, if a community college is engaged in a comprehensive career education effort, the liberal arts faculty will be deeply involved in providing students with knowledge and experience required for actions the student will take to humanize his/her total lifestyle. There is much talk today about dehumanizing conditions in the world of paid employment—and, to be sure, such conditions do exist. At the same time, the individual does have some control over the extent to which such conditions will be personally dehumanizing. If the liberal arts are the "liberating" arts, then they should make a conscious attempt to help individuals find a personal meaning and meaningfulness in life that will allow them to cope successfully with many of the dehumanizing conditions they are likely to find in the world of paid employment. I would consider such attempts an integral part of the total career education effort.

Concluding Remarks

In my opinion, career education is much needed on the campus of every community college. Perhaps you can see, from these remarks, why I feel there is still much to be done before this becomes a reality. I very much hope that some will be inclined to devote their energies into making career education—comprehensive career education—a reality on the community college campus.

REFERENCES

Alabama State Department of Education. *Career Education in Alabama.* Alabama Appalachian Career Education Project. Division of Vocational Education and Community Colleges. Montgomery, Ala.: Alabama State Department of Education, 1972.

American Association of State Colleges and Universities. *Career Education at the Four-year College and University Level.* Washington: American Association of State Colleges and Universities, 1977.

Astin, H. S.; Folger, J. K.; Bayer, A. E. *Human Resources and Higher Education.* New York: Russell Sage Foundation, 1970.

Bell, T. H. *APGA Guidepost.* November 1974.

Berry, Elizabeth. *The Careers of English Majors.* Champaign, Ill.: National Council of Teachers of English, 1966.

Bottoms, J. E. "Employability and Work Adjustment Skills." *Career Guidance.* Eds. Norman C. Gysbers; Harry N. Drier, Jr.; Earl J. Moore. Worthington, Ohio: Charles A. Jones, 1973.

Brown University. *Report on the Liberal Education and the World of Work Conference.* November 19-20, 1976.

Career Education Incentive Act, Committee Report, to Accompany S. 1328, October 17, 1977. Washington: United States Senate, 1977.

Cook, M. A., SND. *The New Vocationalism: Challenge to Liberal Learning.* Submitted to the American Council on Education, 1974.

Dewey, John. *Democracy and Education.* New York: E. P. Dutton, 1915.

"Drop in Aptitude-test Scores Is Largest on Record." *The Chronicle of Higher Education.* (15 September 1975).

Dumke, Glenn S. "The Future of General Education in the California State University and Colleges," April 1972.

Ford, President Gerald. *APGA Guidepost.* November 1974a.

Ford, President Gerald. Commencement Address to Ohio State University. 29 August 1974b.

Heilman, C., and Goldhammer, K. "Career Education's Psycho-social Foundations." *NASSP Bulletin,* March 1973.

Hoyt, Kenneth B. "An Introduction to Career Education." A Policy Paper of the Office of Education, U. S. Department of Health, Education, and Welfare, November 1975.

Hoyt, Kenneth B. "What the Future Holds for the Meaning of Work." *American Vocational Journal,* January 1973.

Key Reporter, The. 43, Autumn 1977.

Magarrell, J. "College Graduates Seen Exceeding Demand by 10 Percent Between 1980 and 1985." *The Chronicle of Higher Education,* 24 June 1974a.

Magarrell, J. "Students Shift Job Goals and Demands on Curricula." *The Chronicle of Higher Education,* 10 June 1974b.

Marland, S. P., Jr. "Career Education: Every Student Headed for a Goal," *American Vocational Journal,* March 1972.

Mayhew, L. B. *Higher Education for Occupations.* Atlanta: Southern Regional Education Board, 1974.

Muirhead, D. P. "The First Steps Show Promise." *Phi Delta Kappan,* February 1973.

Newman, F. "A Preview of the Second Newman Report." *Change,* May 1972.

NVGA-AVA Commission on Career Guidance and Vocational Education. *Position Paper of Career Development.* Washington: National Vocational Guidance Association, 1973.

Orange, Linwood. *English: The Pre-professional Major.* New York: Modern Language Association of America, 1973.

O'Toole, James. *Working, Learning, and the American Future.* San Francisco: Jossey-Bass, Inc., 1977, p. 45.

Sheils, Merrill. "Why Johnny Can't Write." *Newsweek,* 8 December 1975.

Shertzer, B., and Stone, S. C. *Fundamentals of Guidance.* Boston: Houghton-Mifflin, 1971.

Wilcox, Thomas. *The Anatomy of College English.* San Francisco: Jossey-Bass, Inc., 1973.

Yankelovich, D. *The Changing Values on Campus.* Boston: Washington Square Press, 1972.

CHAPTER 10

Career Education for Individuals with Special Needs

With the passage of Public Law 94-142, career education for individuals with special needs, especially the handicapped, took on new significance. This area of education has been emphasized at all levels of formal schooling, and it is consistent with our society's concern with providing for the handicapped and disadvantaged. In the last few years career education has played an important role in assisting the handicapped with career exploration and preparation and will continue to do so.

This chapter contains two articles written in 1977 during the debate over education for individuals with special needs. Charles Kokaska and Oliver P. Kolstoe present the role of special education in career education, including how career education may contribute to the handicapped and how special educators may implement it in existing programs. Gary D. Meers and Charlotte Conaway delineate the vocational educator's role in career education for the handicapped. Their article clearly distinguishes between career education and vocational education as they involve handicapped learners and provides useful suggestions for implementing both in programs for the handicapped.

Special Education's Role in Career Education

Charles Kokaska and Oliver Paul Kolstoe
Author of many publications on special education, Dr. Kokaska is professor of special education at California State University.

Dr. Kolstoe is professor of special education at the University of Northern Colorado. He is nationally recognized for his many contributions to special education and teacher education and for his publications in the field of special education. This article was written in 1977.

Psychologist Hermann Ebbinghaus once remarked that psychology had a long past but only a short history. One can also state that exceptional individuals (including handicapped and gifted) have existed since the first humans, but the special education which enables them to manifest their potential is a recent development.

Special education's infancy can be traced to the works of Jean Marc Itard and his student Edouard Sequin in the 1800s. The toddler years began with the first public school special classes established in such cities as Chicago, New York, and Worcester, Massachusetts, in the early 1900s. Special education developed slowly through the ensuing decades only to be ushered into the adolescent years with a surge of activity and federal funding during the administrations of Presidents John F. Kennedy and Lyndon B. Johnson. The vigor of those years was reflected in the rapid expansion of training programs, research centers, parent organizations, publications, and services to the handicapped, and the activity has not subsided. Every one or two years one witnesses a growth spurt occurring in another program dimension—early childhood, normalization, mainstreaming, and advocacy, to name a few. The latest development, Public Law 94-142, the Education for All Handicapped Children Act, may be an indication that special education is approaching a stage of maturity at which professionals, parents, and consumers will use every resource necessary to obtain a continuum of appropriate services for the handicapped.

Career education does not seem to be new for special educators, as there has always been a concern for the success of the adult handicapped individual as an employee and consumer. Indeed, there have been many secondary programs for the handicapped that were established because the schools were not doing much to prepare the handicapped for successful adult roles.

Although the vocational aspect of career education has often been emphasized, career education has assisted special educators by including concepts about the totality of life within the curriculum. Since the handicapped often need longer periods of intensive teaching, career concepts can be used to lend continuity to a curriculum that extends from early childhood through the adult years.

Finally, while preparing for work and holding a job have been of interest to a great many people, the total field of special education has been lacking in its efforts to provide handicapped students with coordinated programs which prepare them for competition in the labor market. Career education, therefore, has provided a boost to those special educators who have long promoted the development of a continuum of experiences leading to successful employment.

The Education for All Handicapped Children Act

There is no need to discuss the law in its entirety, but it is a logical beginning, as a great deal of time and effort is used to develop regulations and state and local school district plans to meet the legal provisions. Hopefully, this is one of the best opportunities for the infusion of career education concepts into the plans which will provide the structure for the education and training of the handicapped.

One of the main concepts which has emerged in the field of special education is the application of the *least restrictive alternative.* The concept can be traced to the legal case of Brown vs. Board of Education (1954). Reynolds (1962) and Deno (1970) basically advocate that handicapped individuals should be in that educational environment which provides the least deviation from the regular classroom but still meets their needs. Deno identified a continuum of settings ranging from the most restrictive, such as hospitals and treatment centers, through special classes and resource rooms, to total integration in regular education. It is this latter alternative that gave rise to the term *mainstreaming* for special class students.

Public Law 94-142 specifically requires the local education agency (LEA) to establish or revise individualized programs at the beginning of each school year and to review educational provisions periodically but not less than annually. Such programs are to include a written statement of the:

- Present levels of education performance.
- Short-term instructional objectives and annual goals.
- Specific-term instructional objectives and annual goals.
- Projected date for initiation and anticipated duration of services.
- Appropriate objective criteria, evaluation procedures, and evaluation schedule.

It is in the drafting of the individual education program that the team of professionals with the consent of the parents will determine the best educational setting. The law not only requires the individual program but also provides some financial resources so that education agencies can support several alternative environments in which the student will be able to pursue the instructional objectives. The individualized program and the services which will facilitate its achievement are the very heart of the legislation.

One implication of the law is that career education can receive increased attention in the assessment, program planning, instruction, and evaluation sequence. This emphasis will be evident at the elementary and secondary levels.

It is one thing, however, to say that career education can receive increased emphasis and quite another to implement that intent. One problem centers around the skills of the instructors. For example, it is possible that the special child or adolescent will receive instruction from several teachers in a school day. This is usual for the average student in the high school setting, but it is confounding for certain children if they move between instructors. It has been in an effort to minimize this problem that the previous history of special education has been characterized by the self-contained classroom in which one teacher (and an aide if funds are available) was responsible for the bulk of the curriculum. It is this kind of all or none situation, i.e., the child either fails in the regular class or is maintained in the segregated setting, that has led to the inflexible programs which have met with disfavor among educators and parents. A second problem is that the segregated classroom requires low teacher-pupil ratios. College/university training programs could not

2

produce enough teachers to meet the needs of the identified handicapped students based on those ratios even if the school districts were able to finance the classes, which is an additional problem.

By introducing the individualized program, it is expected that these problems will be eliminated. It is obvious that the skills of a variety of professionals can be utilized to their maximum, but it is not obvious which professionals will be most skilled in providing career development for the handicapped. We know that many special educators are deficient in including career education materials and lessons in the curriculum, but we have also encountered situations in which regular classroom teachers, although knowledgeable with career education, hesitate in their efforts with the handicapped students because of their inexperience with these students. Nevertheless, individualized programming is a promising start.

A second development is that the law requires each state department of education to develop a plan with descriptions of programs and procedures for the comprehensive training of personnel. The plan must include provisions for in-service training of general and special educators as well as support personnel. This training will, in all likelihood, concentrate on the assessment, program planning, instruction, and evaluation components. Career education, as an integral part of the above components, would then become a specific area of attention in the in-service training.

Through these in-service training plans, we expect to witness improvement by regular and special educators in integrating career education objectives into the individual programs. The training packages should also include the roles and services provided by counselors, teacher aides, and other faculty and support personnel.

There is no one professional who can be designated as the person responsible for the career development of the handicapped, given the multitude of possibilities, including the child's development level, the educational setting, and the skills of the professionals. In some instances, the special class teacher must assume that responsibility; in others it may be the regular classroom teacher or counselor. Regardless of who accepts the responsibility for the instructional phase, the individual education program manager must be sure that this element, career education, receives continuous attention.

Exemplary Programs

Several publications have identified career and vocational programs for the handicapped (Bureau of Education for the Handicapped 1973; Lake 1974). Most are established at the secondary level and often emphasize certain disabilities. Overall, there are not as many programs as we would like to see which include all areas of exceptionality and extend from the elementary years to adulthood. It is a tall order and indicates some of the future needs in this area of special education. The following examples have not appeared in previous collections and illustrate attempts to cover a wider range of ages and disabilities.

A Teacher's Handbook on Career Development for Children with Special Needs: Grades K–6

At this writing the *Handbook* has been field tested at two career education model demonstration sites in Arlington Heights and Tamms, Illinois (Illinois Office of Education 1976). The field tests are a result of three years of planning and development initiated by the Illinois Office of Education. Over the years several pioneering efforts in work experience, curriculum development, and training of personnel have emerged from the state of Illinois and this publication is in that tradition.

It is directed at identifying practical and effective means for meeting the career awareness and development needs of three groups of handicapped: hearing impaired, physically impaired, and visually impaired.

The *Handbook* includes chapters on career education activities for the above children, resources, curriculum planning, and parent activities, as well as sample lesson plans developed by teachers in association with the demonstration centers. This represents one of the few efforts to design career awareness activities for these three types of disability and will most likely set the pace for other state departments of education.

A Career Training Center

The Kern High School District, Bakersfield, California, covers a geographic area of nearly five thousand square miles and includes a cross section of secondary school situations which range from an urban population to rural farm and mountain communities. The district established a career training center to provide prevocational preparation in ten job clusters and eventual integration of the students into work stations in the community (Kern High School District 1976). The center operates its own transportation system in order to relay a wide range of handicapped students from their regular high schools to the center.

The students are involved in a program of concentrated instruction in specific work skills on job stations that replicate sites in the community. Upon completing instruction, the center staff places students in some of the three hundred plus work stations that have been developed with community employers.

Of special note is that the center staff consists of a core of faculty, while other members from the several high schools accompany their students during the training period. These faculty members observe and instruct their own students during the vocational training sequence and are able to relate the center experiences to the classroom instruction at the regular high schools; therefore, a measure of continuity is maintained for the student while an element of in-service training exists for the high school instructors.

Career Education Through Multi-experience Centers

The Quincy, Illinois, public schools under Title III of the Elementary and Secondary Education Act (ESEA) reorganized their educational offering beginning in 1970. Called *Education by Choice*, the plan now offers seven alternative education programs ranging from a very traditional program which stresses the three Rs to a fine arts school. Included is the career education program which uses multi-experience centers. Located in various schools in the community, each center focuses on a set of experiences which are different from but complementary to all the other centers. They are: (1) upholstery shop; (2) food services; (3) production; (4) health careers; (5) laundry; (6) construction; (7) grooming; (8) maintenance and repair; (9) horticulture; and (10) career city (Career Education Through Multi-experience Centers 1975).

Weld County Board of Cooperative Education Services (BOCES)

In Weld County, Colorado, the BOCES developed a career education for the mentally retarded program in 1974 with funds from Title III of ESEA (*Career Education for the*

Mentally Retarded 1975). The materials are for the primary, intermediate, and junior and senior high levels. At the primary level the materials are puzzles, posters, puppets, and costumes for career role playing skits. The most unique aspect of the program consists of booklets and stories designed to foster self-understanding. The major vehicle is a booklet called *All About Me.* It is marked "Private," "Personal," and "Not To Be Read by Anyone Else Without the Express Permission of _____." It is clearly explained to the child that it is his or her property alone because it will be all about the child.

The booklet is in question or short-answer form with space underneath each statement for an adequate response. It starts with a personal statement, "My Name is _____," which establishes ownership, but immediately gets into the personally revealing information like who the child is named for; if the child likes his or her name; if the child is proud of the name or would rather have a different name; and in each case, why? Next the booklet turns to role playing but with a twist. It asks the child what he or she would like to be if the child were a sound, a book, a color, a movie, a hero, a month, a week, a day, a flower, a food, or a television show. Somewhat later in the booklet they are asked to tell what has made them feel best, worst, shy, mad, sad, nervous, worried, and happy.

A series of stories relating to self-understanding have been developed to illustrate behaviors. Mad Mabel, Greasy Gretchen, Walked-on-Wanda, Scared Scott, Sad Sam, Nervous Nellie, and B. O. Barney allow the youngsters to relate to being mad, sad, or having a noticeable body odor. Other stories teach decision-making by presenting alternatives and then using discussion groups to examine the pros and cons of each alternative.

Problems of driver education and group living are also present in story-discussion form along with job application and job requirements. With all the materials, the unique feature is the interactive story-discussion format which forces the youngers to become personally involved during the lessons.

Future Developments

There is little doubt that the handicapped will receive increased support in the broad area of career education. This support will be fostered by the activities of some of the following groups.

The President's Committee on Employment of the Handicapped. The committee has been expanding its efforts to facilitate the interchange of ideas among the many professionals involved in obtaining successful employment of the handicapped. This includes representatives from vocational rehabilitation, veterans administration, employment services, vocational education, sheltered workshops, and special education. One example of this interaction was the National Forum on Pathways to Employment held in November, 1976, at which professionals, parents, and consumers identified barriers to employment and recommended actions by which various agents who provide services to the handicapped could counteract the obstacles. The projected publication of the document produced by the several committees within the forum will assist school and agency personnel, employers, and members of the governors' committees on employment of the handicapped in their efforts to improve programs and tactics.

Parent Organizations. These organizations are devoting more attention to the vocational futures of the handicapped. Their efforts have a direct influence upon schools and government agencies through cooperative agreements that are established to facilitate training and placement of the students. For example, since 1966 the National Association of Retarded Citizens (NARC) and the Department of Labor have been involved in a series of contracts which are designed to encourage industry to employ the retarded. The on-the-job training project has been one of the most successful endeavors by the NARC, with over ten thousand persons hired since its inception (NARC 1975).

Because of the success of the NARC efforts, the Department of Labor awarded a somewhat similar contract to the Epilepsy Foundation of America (EFA). The contract provides assistance in employment preparation and placement for six hundred youth in cooperation with the school districts of Cleveland, San Antonio, Portland (Oregon), Atlanta, and Minneapolis/St. Paul. One could expect that these kinds of contracts will be expanded to other organizations like the NARC and EFA.

Professional Organizations. The organization which speaks for all areas of the handicapped and gifted, the Council for Exceptional Children (CEC), has established a Division of Career Development (DCD), as it recognizes that this need exists across all exceptionalities. Most of the remaining eleven divisions in the CEC are founded according to areas of exceptionality, i.e., gifted, mental retardation, etc. The organization of the new division is closely followed by the funding of the Vocational Education Policy Project, which has as its goal the development, assessment, and dissemination of a locally focused administrative policy manual. This manual will provide guidelines for appropriate vocational education to all handicapped students.

Paralleling the DCD is the establishment of the National Association of Vocational Education Special Needs Personnel (NAVESNP) which is affiliated with the American Vocational Association. Some of its initial goals are to identify methods and procedures for improving and expanding the delivery of services to the handicapped through coordinating and consolidating resources of related agencies and groups. It is very likely that these two organizations (DCD and NAVESNP) will attempt to maintain a close relationship to one another as they serve the same population of consumers and strive for similar goals.

VOCATIONAL EDUCATION'S ROLE IN CAREER EDUCATION FOR HANDICAPPED STUDENTS

Gary D. Meers and Charlotte Conaway
Currently secretary of the Division of Career Development within the Council of Exceptional Children, Dr. Meers is also associate professor of special vocational needs at the University of Nebraska.

Charlotte Conaway is program specialist for Vocational Education for the Handicapped, U.S. Department of Education and acts as a regional consultant. This article was written in 1977.

Vocational education's role in career education for the handicapped, stated in its simplest form, is to provide experiences whereby the handicapped students are trained for gainful employment. This simple statement has many far-ranging ramifications that must be explored before the reality of this statement can be fully achieved.

Terms Defined

Career and vocational education have been defined and delineated by a number of authors including Hoyt, Finch, and Sheppard. The purpose of these efforts has been to illustrate clearly that the terms career education and vocational education are not synonymous but are complementary and compatible.

Career education, as defined by Hoyt . . .

> includes all those activities and experiences through which one learns about work. As such, it makes no restrictions in meaning whether one speaks about the work of the homemaker, the musician, the lawyer, or the bricklayer. Some work will require advanced college degrees while other work may require no formal schooling of any kind. To the extent that work is judged successful, it does typically—and, in these terms, increasingly—require some learned set of vocational skills (Hoyt 1974).

With this definition as a basis, the following are components of the universal concept of career education (Finch and Sheppard 1975). Career education:

- Is an educational philosophy rather than a physical entity or single program.
- Begins at grade K and continues through adulthood.
- Is concerned with learning about work and involves more than preparation for work.
- Provides an orientation toward a work ethic.
- Is encompassed in the totality of education.
- Consists of all those activities and experiences through which one learns about work.
- Provides an awareness, exploration, and preparation function instead of just equipping a person for a specific job.
- Seeks to prepare all students for successful and rewarding lives by improving their basis for occupational choice.
- Is for all students.
- Benefits the entire population.

Vocational education has been defined by the American Vocational Association (1971) as "education designed to develop skills, abilities, understandings, attitudes, work habits, and appreciations needed by workers to enter and make progress in employment on a useful and productive basis." With this definition as a framework, vocational education includes the following basic characteristics:

- Preparation for jobs requiring less than a baccalaureate degree.
- Activities and experiences through which one learns to assume a primary work role.
- An emphasis on skill development or specific job preparation.
- A focus of attention at the upper-middle grades, senior high, and two-year college level.
- A physical entity or program, rather than an educational philosophy, with the major goal of gainful employment (Finch and Sheppard 1975).

It is obvious from the definitions and characteristics that career education and vocational education are not synonymous, but vocational education can be regarded as a specific, special component of career education. In order to provide comprehensive program offerings to all students, however, vocational education is integrated within career education.

In order to understand some of the problems facing vocational education's role in career education of the handicapped, it is important to consider its history.

In the past, many parents have held a negative image of vocational education because they wanted something that was supposedly better for their son or daughter than they had during their education and work years. This something better was associated with a college education. Administrators often viewed vocational education as a dumping ground for students judged to lack ability in academic education. By placing these students in a vocational education program, they were out of the mainstream of the academic program for three-hour blocks of time, with little if any thought given to their vocational aspirations or aptitudes.

By providing longitudinal experiences for both students and parents, the career education movement has done much to eliminate this negative image. In addition, career education has provided a basis for more realistic career decisions and increased acceptance of vocational programs. This is not to say that the negative image problem has been totally eliminated, but the problem has been minimized. With increased visibility and acceptance for vocational education and more informed career decisions, greater emphasis must be placed on programming for total student involvement.

Students' Rights Movement

A parallel movement encompassing the educational rights of the handicapped has also influenced the expansion of vocational education's role. Public concern grew to the point that federal legislation, entitled the Equal Rights to Education for All Handicapped Children Act (P.L. 94-142), was passed in November, 1975. This legislation specifically outlines the rights of the handicapped to quality academic and vocational education; thus, vocational education has a new role in the process of educating handicapped persons. In addition, vocational legislation in the form of the 1976 amendments to the Vocational Education Act of 1963 set aside specific dollars for vocational programs for the handicapped; thus, through legislation vocational education now has a mandated role in the career development process of handicapped persons.

Establishment of Vocational Education's Role in Career Education for the Handicapped

Specific components of vocational education affecting its role in the career education process of the handicapped must be delineated. These components include:

- Vocational teacher preparation
- Educational planning team
- Coordination of services
- Physical modifications
- Architectural barriers
- Educational programming

Vocational Teacher Preparation. Vocational teachers have had a commitment to provide educational experiences to all students. Many times in the process of program placement, scheduling, and other teaching duties, this commitment has slipped down the priority list to the point where handicapped students have been omitted from programs, or if admitted, isolated within the classroom. The need to prepare vocational teachers to teach the handicapped effectively has led to their inclusion in vocational education programs.

With the enactment of the Equal Rights to Education for All Handicapped Children Act, and the amendments of 1976, as well as the increased public advocacy for the rights of handicapped persons, neglect will no longer be tolerated. Vocational teachers must renew their commitment to total student programming. With this renewed commitment come some teacher preparation issues that must be dealt with in order that vocational education teachers have the skills and strategies necessary to work with handicapped youth. These issues include:

1. *Vocational teacher attitudes toward handicapped learners.* Many teachers, including vocational teachers, have preconceived ideas about the handicapped. These ideas may be based on previous experiences, or a lack of them, with the handicapped. Teachers' experiences may have been limited to meeting an orthopedically handicapped person on the street, a mentally retarded person at a public gathering, or a casual observance of a special education class in their school. Many vocational education teachers have not been provided the opportunity to gain personal experience in teaching and working with handicapped persons.

Vocational teachers must have experiences that will lead to positive classroom or laboratory programming for handicapped students and bring about eventual attitudinal changes.

Positive learning experiences can be provided in a variety of ways. First, through in-service educational activities, vocational teachers can be oriented to the needs, interests, and abilities of handicapped students. These in-service sessions must concentrate on the development of strategies needed for work with the handicapped. When vocational teachers understand their role and feel competent to assume that role, programmatic changes will be forthcoming in the best interest of the handicapped students (Meers 1976).

Administrative support is an important factor relating to teacher attitudes. If support for serving the handicapped student in vocational education is not present throughout the administrative hierarchy, the vocational teacher will quickly become discouraged and attitudes will revert under this kind of stress. Fiscal support for equipment, supplies, personnel, and services is also important.

Since the basic premise of programming for the handicapped learner is to meet individual needs, a concentrated effort must be made to apply this premise to the teacher as well. The teacher needs to be shown how teaching can and does help the handicapped student and how the program or course offering fits into the future aspirations and successes of the handicapped based upon other school offerings. Each teacher needs to understand the contributions he or she can make to the handicapped students' education and be provided opportunities to develop his or her unique capabilities.

2. *Vocational educators from industry with minimal teacher preparatory training.* The vocational teachers who come from industry or the trades learn strategies used in regular instructional programs. The specific programming skills needed to work with handicapped students must also be included in the basic teacher education program required for certification. To meet certification requirements in most states, vocational teachers from a trade area are required to take between 9 and 20 semester hours of course work. Teacher education institutions must see that during part of this teacher education course work, teachers become familiar with the needs, interests, and abilities of the handicapped as related to vocational programming. In addition, in-service workshops can help vocational teachers develop the ability and confidence to teach handicapped persons.

3. *Degreed vocational educators received their training before the emphasis was placed on special needs learners.* In-service workshops are needed to provide updated information to those teachers who completed their education prior to the present emphasis

on teaching the handicapped learner. Efforts must be made to provide these workshops for vocational teachers in every district in every state. The workshops should include attitudes, program development, curriculum modification, and work role identification as they apply to preparing the handicapped for gainful employment. Course work should also be provided on teacher education campuses for those teachers returning to update their transcripts for certification requirements.

Educational Planning Team. As vocational education teachers assume their role in career education of the handicapped, they must become part of a comprehensive educational planning team. The educational planning team should consist of teachers, administrators, counselors, psychologists, social workers, rehabilitation counselors, and other appropriate specialists. This team will assist in the development of the student's educational plan and coordinate the educational experiences of the handicapped students.

Since career awareness and career exploration experiences are prerequisites to the student entering a vocational program, the vocational teacher needs to be an informed participant in planning and conducting these experiences. The vocational teacher can build on the student's previous experiences. The result will be a much smoother transition into the skill development courses.

Vocational teachers do not have, nor should they be expected to have, all the skills and expertise necessary to work with all handicapping conditions. What they do need to know is where and how resources can be secured to assist them. The educational planning team can assist in this effort. Vocational teachers will become aware of the resources available from the special education teacher, resource teacher, speech therapist, counselor, and other team members. If the required assistance is not available within the team, the knowledge base of the total team can serve to locate the needed resources. Many teachers will need to overcome the feeling that to seek assistance is an indication of incompetence or inability to do the job.

The end results of this total team planning process will be more accurate placement of handicapped students in vocational programs plus a feeling of more personal involvement by the vocational teacher. Vocational teachers will see themselves and vocational education as essential ingredients in career education programming for handicapped persons.

Coordination of Services. An important component that will affect vocational education's role in career education for the handicapped is the coordination of services for students. The average handicapped student is the recipient of services from four agencies. Vocational teachers and administrators need to be aware of the services provided, who is providing them, and how these services relate to those provided by the vocational program. The vocational teacher should promote interagency cooperation. These efforts will reduce the incidence of multiple placement, duplicate services, and client/student confusion. This is an example that can be used to plead the case for the establishment of educational planning teams.

Physical Modification. The excessive cost of making modifications to laboratory equipment is an argument often used to exclude handicapped students from vocational classes. Vocational teachers and administrators will find that in most cases the only modifications necessary are raising desks by placing blocks under the legs, lowering workbenches, or arranging tools in a specific and set pattern for easy identification. Consultation with state and national agencies, such as the President's Committee on

Employment of the Handicapped; Mainstream, Inc.; or the local vocational rehabilitation office, will provide the vocational teacher or administrator with the information to make the necessary physical modifications within the vocational setting.

Architectural Barriers. The removal of architectural barriers has been mandated by law, so this obstacle to handicapped student involvement in vocational programs is fast being overcome. Vocational education, in its concern about cost of these modifications, can look to industry for some reassurance about the expenditures.

Kaiser Aluminum and Chemical Corporation, for example, decided to revamp its twenty-seven-story headquarters in Oakland, California, to help handicapped workers gain easy access. There was concern that the costs would run into the hundreds of thousands of dollars, but after consulting with Mainstream, Inc., a nonprofit organization dedicated to getting handicapped persons into jobs, it was found the work could be done for less than $8,000. As an example, Braille numbers can be placed on every selection button in an average elevator for approximately $3. There are many examples on how architectural barriers can be overcome.

Educational Programming. Careful and concise educational programming is needed. As mentioned before, everyone must work together toward the goal of acquiring a saleable vocational skill for each student. In many cases, the nonvocational teacher involved in programs for the handicapped may not be familiar with teaching methods to accomplish this goal; therefore, a process must be undertaken that will enable all teachers to contribute their special skills toward helping handicapped students acquire saleable skills.

Upon acquiring a saleable skill, the handicapped student should be placed on a work site that is compatible with his or her vocational expertise. This requires that the vocational coordinator, in conference with the educational planning team, make a careful match between student and job. This will include a balancing of many important factors, such as transportation, work location, safety hazards, and job skills to the point that the student will be able to perform satisfactorily on the job. Since gainful employment is the expected end result of vocational training, the analysis of job sites, student placement, and employer satisfaction must not be perceived as an add-on role but as one crucial to total program success.

Personal Characteristics of Handicapped Students

Personal characteristics of students are an important but often neglected consideration in vocational preparation. Vocational educators must include in their teaching/learning sequences opportunities and experiences that will allow students to strengthen those characteristics that are complementary to the job, to minimize those characteristics that are not, and to develop, if possible, those needed.

The vocational teacher, in an effort to provide all the necessary skill development experiences, may overlook the important part personal characteristics play in the employment success of an individual. Human attributes such as self-expression, sociability, work independence, appearance, and cooperation can be demonstrated, practiced, and utilized by students throughout the training program, as demonstrated in a program at the Eaton Rapids (Michigan) High School. The students in this unique program have organized and are operating an ice cream parlor within the school. The Cold-Tongue Ice Cream Parlor sells ice cream products to fellow students, teachers, and visitors during lunch hours and for an hour after school each day. The students involved in this operation are acquiring and utilizing those personal characteristics that will allow them to progress toward their end goal of gainful employment (Reed 1976).

Conclusion

Career and vocational education have been defined in light of their respective contributions to the educational process. With the expansion of career education to include the handicapped, the role of vocational education is expanding.

Career education is for every student. Vocational education is for every student desiring to learn a saleable skill requiring less than a college degree and who can profit from vocational education if provided the opportunity. The vocational teacher's role is to provide the learning experiences so that self-direction and job fulfillment through gainful employment are within the grasp of this challenging, unique, and worthwhile population.

REFERENCES

American Vocational Association. *Definitions of Terms in Vocational, Technical, and Practical Arts Education.* Washington: American Vocational Association, 1971.

Brown vs. Board of Education, 347 U.S. 483 (1954).

Bureau of Education for the Handicapped. *Selected Career Education Programs for the Handicapped.* Washington: Government Printing Office, 1973.

Career Education for the Mentally Retarded. Brochure of the Weld County Colorado BOCES, 1975.

Career Education Through Multi-experience Centers. Application for continuation grant. Submitted by Quincy, Illinois, Public Schools, 29 May 1975.

Deno, E. "Special Education as Developmental Capital." *Exceptional Children* 37 (1970): 229-237.

Finch, Curtis R., and Sheppard, N. Alan. "Career Education Is Not Vocational Education." *Journal of Career Education* 2 (Summer 1975).

Hoyt, Kenneth B. "An Introduction to Career Education." Draft position paper, Office of Career Education. Washington: USOE, 1974.

Illinois Office of Education. *A Teacher's Handbook on Career Development for Children with Special Needs: Grades K-6.* Springfield, Ill.: Superintendent of Education, 1976.

Kern High School District. *Vocational Guide for the Handicapped.* Bakersfield, Calif.: Kern High School District, 1976.

Lake, T., ed. *Career Education: Exemplary Programs for the Handicapped.* Reston, Va.: The Council for Exceptional Children, 1974.

Meers, Gary D. *Vocational Teacher Attitudes Toward Special Needs Youth.* Unpublished research project. Lincoln, Nebr.: University of Nebraska, 1976.

National Association for Retarded Citizens (NARC). *Mental Retardation News* 24 (January 1975): 1.

Reed, George R. "Sundae School for Special Education Kids." *Phi Delta Kappan.* 58 (October 1976).

Reynolds, M. "A Framework for Considering Some Issues in Special Education." *Exceptional Children* 28 (1962): 367-370.

CHAPTER 1

Evaluation of Career Education

A persistent argument from the critics of career education has been that there is not enough empirical evidence to support the emphasis on it, and, therefore, we may be investing our resources in something that is not as effective as we think. This argument and the need for more reliable data makes evaluation a key issue. For career education to develop conceptually and programmatically, we must evaluate its strengths and weaknesses, thus making more reliable decisions about it. Evaluation, however, is not easy. Our skills and knowledge, even though they are growing daily, are not adequate, and more emphasis needs to be placed on initiating new programs or managing existing programs.

This chapter is made up of four articles written in 1976 when our knowledge of the processes of evaluation was relatively limited. Reginald Corder and Gail Hare provide an excellent account of evaluation through ethnography. Bill and Carolyn Raymond provide an excellent approach for evaluating career education at the local level, which is where it should be evaluated. However, the reader should refer to Chapters 2, 4, and 10 for more comprehensive definition of career education. Robert J. Rossi and Donald H. McLaughlin offer a detailed account of evaluating career education through longitudinal studies, a method which ultimately will determine whether career education makes a difference. Terry Newell's article provides a long-range evaluation plan which could have excellent results.

SPECIFYING AND STUDYING THE CAREER EDUCATION TREATMENT

Reginald Corder and Gail Hare

At the time this article was written in 1976, Reginald Corder and Gail Hare were professional associate and administrative assistant, respectively, for the Educational Testing Service in Berkeley, California. This article was written in 1976.

In this article we report on our experience in using three different approaches to the study and documentation of processes used in an experimental career education treatment. The three approaches are: ethnography; systematic observation of student behavior in natural settings (i.e., those settings which are a part of the student's planned career education program); and in-depth interviews with students.

The treatment under investigation was a career education model (experience-based career education) developed over a three-year period by four different agencies in four widely separated geographic locations. Development activities of these agencies were funded by the National Institute of Education. The institute also funded our role as external evaluators during the third developmental year.

We hope to provide interested readers with a straightforward but relatively modest account of the contributions of ethnography, systematic observation, and in-depth interviews to our understanding of the processes that were actually used and valued in the treatment model. We will not present the argumentation for including an adequate description of the treatment under investigation as a part of evaluation reports.

We would like to suggest that certain frequently made assumptions about what constitutes an adequate description of treatment are not warranted. Among these assumptions are that: (1) treatments may be adequately described by merely providing a label for the treatment with no other detail (e.g., the inquiry process was used); (2) teacher reports about the extent to which they have followed a desired treatment can be accepted at face value (Medley and Mitzel 1963, pp. 249-250); and (3) when teachers are given specially prepared, experimental materials and instruction about how to use them, they will use the materials in the prescribed fashion. We believe that the failure of much educational research to present consistent cumulative findings is due, in part, to the failure to document the nature of the treatments under study (Corder 1971). In response to the need for adequate description of treatment, educational researchers have begun to give increased attention to process documentation and evaluation. Those methods usually employed in this increased effort include classroom observation by nonparticipant observers and/or videotaping the educational processes under study.

In any attempt to document the nature of the treatment provided, the question will arise as to how much detail or specificity is required. It is probably impossible and even undesirable to document what occurred to the extent that exact duplication could be achieved in a replication site. Education cannot be prescribed like the instructions in an automotive repair manual; it is necessarily a human endeavor. In fact, the experience of the authors is that teachers will tend to resist instructional procedures which they feel overprogram them; therefore, treatment to be used in a classroomlike environment cannot be specified to the extent necessary for experiments in a chemical laboratory or conditioning experiments in a psychological laboratory. For any understanding of a treatment and for any study of the relationship between processes and outcomes, however, it is necessary to provide more detail than that given in a research report by one of the agencies that is developing the treatment. A report by one of the agencies involved with the treatment that we studied said simply that the treatment evaluated was the career education program developed by the agency. This we regard as simply an exaggerated example of labeling, where no useful information is provided.

This introduces one of the problems posed to us as external evaluators: to conduct a study which would provide programmatically useful information on the relationships between student performance and the kinds of experiences that students received in the career education program to be evaluated. In order to fulfill this purpose, we had to have considerable information about what was actually occurring at the four treatment sites.

Some of this needed information was given to us at the outset. For example, all pupils were of high school age and were self-nominated for the program. The programs were conducted as alternatives to the regular high school programs available to these pupils. The programs were individualized, i.e., constructed around pupils' individual needs and interests, although some similar requirements were made of all pupils. At least some of the learning experiences for all pupils were conducted in employer and community settings outside the school. Whether these characteristics were integral to the treatment under investigation was unknown at the beginning. The original request for evaluation required an assessment of the differential effectiveness of the treatment across treatment sites. This requirement was later removed from the contract, but had it remained, it would have been necessary to determine whether the characteristics of the model indicated above constituted anything more than surface similarities.

In short, since the requirements for external evaluation, as amended, included a determination of effective processes used at the individual sites, it was necessary for the evaluator to know what was going on at each site in order to be able to integrate process and outcome data.

The three approaches we used are not new but have been used in other research and evaluative investigations. Our approaches did contain some unique features, however, and it is in the description of these unique features that we hope to make our contribution to the reader.

The Ethnographic Approach

The term *ethnography* lies within the discipline of anthropology. Both its meaning and the research approach associated with the term are likely to be much less familiar to educators than are systematic observation or in-depth interviewing (Wolcott 1974). In recent years, however, interest has developed in ethnographic research in schools to the extent that ethnography is included in a number of both large and small investigations.

An ethnography is an anthropologist's descriptive account of the way of life exhibited by a group of individuals. Ethnographers are concerned with culture and the social environment which surrounds and influences its members. Schools, like any structured institution, are social environments. An anthropologist conducting ethnographic field work in a school setting is thus concerned with observing, recording, and analyzing the behaviors of those individuals (students, staff, and others) connected with the school. People, their environments, and their interactions and adaptations are the foci of the ethnographic investigation.

Ethnographic research demands a degree of personal and contextual involvement uncharacteristic of other fields of social science. In contrast to educational psychologists and others who speak of *data gathering* in their approach to research, the anthropologist conducting ethnographic research refers to his or her activities as taking field notes. The ethnographic researcher attempts to immerse herself or himself in the lives of those under study. This we find to be an additional contrast to some educational researchers who might never see the individuals whom they are studying. Instead of relying on a number of research assistants, the anthropologist generally assumes responsibility for both the recording and analyzing of data related to the particular study; thus, the ethnographer himself or herself is the primary instrument for the research.

The anthropologist lives in at a site for a considerable period of time. Through the process of participant observation (i.e., by entering as fully as possible into the everyday activities of those under study), he or she establishes rapport with the informants (i.e., the principal persons providing information). While in the role of participant-observer, the anthropologist is continually observing, asking questions, and using other field work methods in an attempt to understand and describe the setting adequately.

The product of ethnographic research is a report called an ethnography. This report tells how and where those studied spend their time. (In the language of ethnography this is time-space mapping.) The structure of the culture is also described in these reports. We observed that anthropologists think in terms of two kinds of structure: an *overt structure* (the formal pattern and mode of operation) and a *covert structure* (an informal set of rules concerning interpersonal behavior which conditions interaction). By request we asked the ethnographers to observe discrepancies between the actual (overt) structure of the treatment and the theoretical or stated treatment and, if possible, to indicate reasons for these discrepancies. As we understood ethnography, this was an extension of the usual role of an ethnographer. We also asked the ethnographers to report on the programs particularly from the students' point of view. In so doing, the ethnographers were able to determine what the students felt was important about the program. This provided a detailed description of the treatment as it was actually applied. In addition to material presented throughout the reports, case studies on selected students were completed by the ethnographers. These case studies are unlike the case studies of many psychologists. The case studies completed for these reports are concerned with student perceptions of their experiences in the program, reasons for entering the program, and achievement made as a consequence of their participation.

Readers will recognize from our description that the work of an ethnographer is highly subjective. Everything is translated through the eyes of the ethnographer; therefore, it was a concern of ours and others that their reports might be biased. The ethnographers themselves protect against bias by utilizing a number of informants, selecting them to give varying points of view, and checking information and sources of information against each other. For example, the case-study students reviewed and approved the case studies about themselves before the ethnographies were released.

We have attempted to determine the validity of the reports by submitting drafts of the reports to the developing agencies. It is interesting to note that the critiques of the ethnographies by persons in these agencies point to very few factual inaccuracies in the reports. Most of their comments were directed to alternate interpretations of some of the conclusions. One of the advantages of an ethnography, however, is that a great deal of information is presented without interpretation, thereby giving readers a chance to draw their own conclusions which they can check against those of the ethnographers.

In addition to submitting the drafts to the developing agencies, we also submitted them to a panel of distinguished educational anthropologists. This panel, while offering some criticisms about the organization of the reports, in general felt that by anthropological standards all judgments rendered in the reports were supported by sufficient documentation.

Is there one way to do an ethnography? We feel the answer to this question must be no. Several factors prompt this answer. Three teams of ethnographers were hired to conduct the ethnographic research at the four sites. We observed that each team took a somewhat different approach to the investigation, and there are differences in the reports each produced. We also observed that the members of our distinguished review panel criticized different elements of the reports. This suggests to us that there is not one way to do an ethnography, and yet ethnographers do have their discipline. This leads us to a second question: can anyone be an ethnographer? We, at least, would not want to make such an attempt, yet anthropologist Wolcott (1974) indicates that some educational scholars have made contributions to the descriptive literature without having satisfied all the usual criteria of ethnography. We think the point is that the discipline of anthropology teaches what to look for in analyzing a culture. Educators, for example, do not have this background. The other important consideration is a question of domain, or turf. An educator in a school is in her or his own terrain and thus probably takes most of what goes on for granted. Ethnographers, on the other hand, especially ones with cross-cultural field experience, are trained in different ways of perceiving culture. And since ethnographers have not been trained as educators, they are able to take note of the "culture-shock" phenomenon in their work.

While the ethnographic reports are not discussions of the achievements of the programs, they provide three basic kinds of information: (1) descriptive information on processes; (2) a discrepancy analysis of the treatment in terms of actual versus theoretical models (as noted above, this was provided on specific request); and (3) some estimates of the most valuable components of the programs as perceived by the students.

Systematic Observation

In contrast with the ethnographies, which provided a holistic description of the entire program structure and treatment, we used systematic observation to provide highly detailed description of selected elements of the treatment. Specifically, the behavioral observations were used to obtain detailed information about pupil activity both at the school settings and at the employer/community resource settings—the two principal settings in which the planned treatment and learning were to occur. Also in contrast to ethnographic methods, observers were nonparticipants in the activities observed and attempted not to interact with the students or others.

Systematic observation generally means observation in which the anticipated behaviors are carefully defined and the observed behaviors then coded into the set of categories based on these definitions. Systematic observation, as usually done by live observers, requires the observer to make instant judgments about the behavior he or she is witnessing and to record these judgments concurrently on some instrument. The recording is often done by checking the cells of a matrix.

Our approach to recording behavior was, however, different. The observers wrote a running commentary about what they observed as it happened. The emphasis was on description rather than judgment. The completeness of their written description was limited only by their ability to observe in detail and write rapidly. An observation was the written description of one student's activities and interaction with others. In the process of watching the student, the observer separated the description into events. An event was considered to end (and the next to begin) whenever a student's activity changed or the persons interacting with the student changed. The time at which each event began was recorded so that event durations could be calculated.

When an observation was completed, it was transmitted to a coder, whose first task was to study the event structure of the observation. Coders were instructed to separate an observer-defined event into two or more events whenever it was apparent that the student's activities had changed within the observer-defined event or whenever an event seemed to be of undue length. Having resolved any such problems which might have existed within the event structure of the observation, the coder next encoded the nature of each event. To do so, the coder relied upon a collection of descriptive code words—the lexicon.

The lexicon consisted of four types of words, each category descriptive of a different aspect of an event. The four types of descriptors were: (1) context, which relates to the input and output of work and information during an event; (2) person, which is descriptive of the people with whom the student is engaged during the event; (3) materials, which describe tools, books, or equipment used by the student during the event; and (4) activities, which are descriptive of the student's behavior during the event.

The category scheme and the lexicon were developed and the descriptors which formed the lexicon were based on actual occurrence in the observations, but they were related to the pupil outcome goals of the projects for the purpose of analysis. The authors worked in cooperation with persons from the developed agency to establish the appropriateness of the language of the lexicon.

The lexicon is an open rather than a closed system for classifying observable behavior. The lexicon can be augmented by the addition of new entries within a category or with new categories at any time that an observable set of behaviors with similar characteristics cannot be adequately assigned an existing lexicon term or where new categories of observable behavior are required.

The analysis of the coded observations was done using a system called *APPLE*. The acronym APPLE decodes as Anecdotal Processing to Promote the Learning Experience. The software for the system was developed by F. L. Converse and E. K. Converse, School of Education, University of California, Berkeley. Written in COBOL programming language, the APPLE system is readily transported to a number of computers of different model and manufacture.

The product of the analysis was a computer record showing, for each student and for all students, the number and duration of events related to the stated instructional goals of the treatment. This summary related student activities to the desired outcomes, offering a way to compare the two. If, for example, no activity was ever observed on obtaining skills in career decision making, how could students be expected to learn anything in this area?

Systematic observation and the flexible APPLE system were ideally suited to evaluating these career education projects. Rather than testing a relatively small number of predetermined observational categories as defined in most category systems, all of the observable student events recorded could be examined for their relationship to the goals of the treatment. A maximum amount of information was recorded, each item of which was available for analysis.

In-depth Interviews with Students

The interview obtained information about the students, the program goals, and the most helpful school procedures. The student in-depth interview occurred as a one-time, end-of-year event.

Since the external evaluation project was to provide information on the achievement of at least some of the treatment goals, it was necessary to have some kind of a career decision-making model from which the interview questions could be derived. The model would be useful in producing questions about the goals and the particular approach to career education under study. An idealized model of career decision making was developed as a part of the external evaluation effort. This model identified seven major stages, the first five of which might be reached by students in grades 9-12. The model was used in defining the general structure of the interview.

Two kinds of questions were included in the interview. Five questions sought information about student progress in each stage of the career decision model. The other seven questions covered those procedures (school and nonschool) which were most helpful in making this progress. The interview, therefore, was another attempt to integrate process and outcome information.

Since the interview was to be about career decision making, it seemed important to let each student choose the career topics to be discussed. This individualized approach to the interview would make group analysis of the resulting data difficult to complete. Nevertheless, it seemed the only approach that would be consistent with the individualized nature of the treatment under study.

All the hazards of self-reported information are present in this type of data gathering. Appropriate statistical approaches were used for the determination of the reliability of the interview data. Estimated reliabilities varied on selected aspects of the interview. The general finding is that nearly all scales had adequate reliability for group analysis.

Conclusions

This article represents our experience in studying the treatment developed at four career education sites. While the treatment came from one particular concept of career education, there was some question about the similarities at each of the four sites.

The three approaches we used have provided significant information. Much of the information in any one approach is complementary to information provided by the other approaches. Our reports provide to potential adopters of this career education model valuable information concerning not only the effective and ineffective processes but also the limitations in developing and carrying out such treatments.

By combining information from the ethnographies, the systematic observations, and the student in-depth interviews, a relatively integrated description of the processes used and valued in this treatment is obtained. At the present time we make this integration by logical rather than statistical inference.

As in most investigations of this kind, hindsight shows that some things could have been done in a slightly different way. We wished, for example, that we had provided for a better statistical integration of the information gained from the various sources.

While we were involved in the study of this career education treatment at the summative evaluation stage, we would like to point out that any of these approaches to describing and determining the effectiveness of processes could be well utilized by developers of career education programs in the formative stage; however, we caution that these approaches are expensive. All involve the time of professional staff. The question is: how good (complete, valid, and reliable) do you want your information to be? Cheap alternatives to the approaches described here are not readily available.

A series of reports which provide the detail for this summary have been furnished to the National Institute of Education. These volumes are recommended to interested readers who seek further information on these approaches.

EVALUATION CONCERNS FROM THE LOCAL PRACTITIONER'S POINT OF VIEW

Bill Raymond and Carolyn Raymond

At the time this article was written in 1976, Drs. Bill and Carolyn Raymond were director of planning and evaluation and director for the center for career development, respectively, for the Mesa, Arizona public school system.

It is the intent of this article to present the more common obstacles encountered in the evaluation of career education programs, as seen from the viewpoint of a local practitioner. Although the emphasis here is on the negative, we feel that much evidence exists regarding the progress being made in the career education field with respect to evaluation. It is hoped the reader will keep this in mind as the various concerns are presented.

As we began to write this article, it became immediately apparent that no particular logical sequence of presenting the problems seemed to exist. Moreover, what we really were creating was a series of concerns, many of which seemed no more important than another or necessarily related to one or the other. As a result, what will be presented is a potpourri of problems which all career education practitioners must face as they become more deeply involved in the evaluation of their programs. Also, at the end of most major concerns, we have prepared a recommended *do* list for the practitioner.

Concern One: Bits and Pieces versus the Whole Pie

One of the major evaluation problems facing the career education practitioner as he or she attempts to determine program effectiveness is, in many cases, the lack of program definition. Since its early beginning, the career education movement has been plagued by a lack of definition. *Ed. note:* This lack of definition was intended by the originators. See Herr, p. 55; Hoyt, p. 176; Meers and Conaway, p. 264; and Rossi, p. 290, for definitions and goals. The early conceptualizers provided the canvas and the first few brush strokes, but the picture's final composition was intentionally left to others. The first project funded by the U.S. Office of Education (USOE) had a golden opportunity to help supply the needed composition, but through a series of events (some mistakes and some intentional) combined with a sudden shift of responsibility to the National Institute of Educators (NIE) and a reduction in program emphasis, this much needed composition failed to mature.

One inherent danger in this situation is that the local practitioner, in an attempt to provide the funding source or administration with a project evaluation, tends to confuse project evaluation with program evaluation. It is one thing to be able to evaluate effectively an instructional or field trip activity, or even a combination of activities comprising what might be called a career education project, but this should not be confused with the ability to provide an evaluation of a comprehensive career education program. The evaluation of a career program must lie in its total impact upon students as demonstrated in their accomplishment of identified behaviors and attitudes, none of which would be dependent upon the successful completion of a single unit or activity of the program, but would represent the successful attainment of an entire curriculum. Many projects have opted for proving their worth in evaluating the bits and pieces, i.e., units of instruction, training activities, usage of resources, etc. These are important aspects of formative evaluation endeavors and play a vital role in developing more effective delivery systems and/or longitudinal evaluation.

In an informal survey we conducted, we found very few projects which defined their program by using a set of identified, measurable, student objectives for all grade levels. Furthermore, those programs which had started to develop and/or adopt a series of student objectives to represent their basic program rarely included objectives from all of the dimensions normally associated with career education. We have also been working recently with a few of the newly funded (OE—$10 million) career education projects to assist them in this endeavor.

One of the problems in obtaining what we are calling program evaluation, rather than the bits and pieces, is that funding agencies often will not provide resources for its development. In Mesa we have on two occasions submitted to one of our funding agencies a request which, if approved, would have permitted us to spend time preparing a set of minimal student objectives with appropriate assessment tools for each grade level. In both instances, our request was rejected. As a result, we have had to work on this endeavor on a catch-as-catch-can basis.

This situation is most unfortunate, because new programs with different competing emphasis may soon absorb many of the dollars currently allocated to career education. No doubt many of the people who help establish educational priorities feel they have given us enough money and time to prove ourselves. The most important thing we can bring to a school system, therefore, is an accountable comprehensive career education program with objectives, test items, and monitoring systems for each grade level. This is one way for us to move career education from a project status to a permanent district/college status.

Note the emphasis we have placed on each grade level rather than two (i.e., sixth and ninth) or four grade levels (i.e., third, sixth, ninth, and twelfth). We believe that if one waits to measure student attainment in the third grade, no one really accepts responsibility for these student outcomes. A workable accountability program will have each teacher responsible for a certain amount of student growth. In addition, allowance for individual student ability and achievement and a set of minimal objectives for all grade levels, with measurement tools at appropriate reading comprehension levels, are needed. Students can be diagnosed at the beginning of each year and the teacher given a profile of his or her students. This focuses the responsibility on the teacher for helping each student achieve the next set of objectives.

Also, note the use of the word minimal. Many projects, in trying to define career education, have developed reams of objectives covering the waterfront. We know of several projects that have listed over a thousand objectives. This approach might demonstrate the comprehensiveness of career education, but in our opinion, will fail to give focus and direction to teachers' activities regarding overall program accountability. We feel that anywhere from ten to thirty terminal objectives for each grade level is sufficient.

Suggested Do's for Concern One

● Measure bits and pieces of your program during formative evaluation stages, but begin developing those objectives and measuring tools at the beginning to allow for program evaluation at each grade level.

● Develop your program evaluation around measurable student outcomes which will focus on each teacher's responsibility for delivery of a certain number of the objectives and also allow for individual student growth.

● Refrain from developing a large number of objectives. Provide a small number of terminal student objectives with accompanying testing tools.

● Continue to press funding agencies for time and financial resources to be spent on this endeavor.

● Don't be fooled by your own reporting of evaluation of the bits and pieces as being adequate. If you do, we predict that limited program outcomes will be left in your system when the funding period is over.

Concern Two: Ignoring the Nonsignificant Differences (NSD)

Picture the unfortunate practitioner who has labored for months only to come face-to-face with the fact that few differences exist between programs. It is interesting to watch a normally objective professional under stress, who rationalizes rather than investigates why significant differences were not obtained.

We've all heard snap pronouncements like these: "The instruments weren't sensitive enough to pick up the true differences that must exist," "The teachers were lackadaisical about administering the instruments," "The observers didn't take their job seriously," "The evaluation design was so complex with so many variables that the data was highly subject to contamination."

A few of the more sophisticated practitioners might reason that the treatment (program activities) was not well enough defined or controlled to expect to measure significant differences. Some might even determine that their instruments were measuring the correct program outcomes, but the treatment was not delivering the outcomes. Others might find that the treatment was not delivered (actual transactions differed from intended transactions).

In today's tight money market for educational programs, the practitioner responsible for an innovative program is ultimately brought to the court of justification to account for funds. At this point he or she confronts other innovations which compete for the classroom teachers' time or available funds. Critics who feel that the taxpayers ought to be getting a fair shake for their dollar may also be encountered. When this occurs, evaluation can be the practitioner's best friend, or it can be the straw that breaks the camel's back.

The educational practitioner should be his or her own severest critic. In the final analysis, all the rationalization in the world will not continually be able to prop up a bad program or one that needs major surgery. Even a seven percent gain in student growth, which is considered to be significant by many, may not be justified if the dollars needed to obtain that gain are excessive.

Suggested Do's for Concern Two

- Recognize that NSD's are your concern and not to be rationalized away.
- Refine and revise measurement tools and/or program activities (treatment) until you can prove without any doubt the effectiveness of your program.

Concern Three: More of the Same or They Get It Anyway

Quite interestingly, whether many practitioners want to admit it or not, a goodly portion of the objectives that many programs include would be achieved by the students whether or not they were active participants in a career education program. This is evidenced by one statewide evaluation effort with which we are acquainted. Although there were significant differences between the control and treatment groups, the control group still scored very high (in the seventieth percentile) on the knowledge and attitudes evaluated. This problem is not peculiar to career education. A few students enter the first grade knowing how to read, and some can print their own names; however, after years of much educational chest beating regarding the development of educational programs tailored to fit individual educational needs, very few school districts have devised programs to fit the needs of those students who can read prior to their entry into school. So it is with career education. Many students come from environments in which they already have learned many of the concepts presented in some career education projects. In like fashion, if students stay in that environment, they may grow in their understanding of career-related information and attitudes regardless of the institutional program offered.

Moreover, much of what practitioners are calling career education already exists in the schools. For example, consider the following objective commonly used at the second or third grade:

> Given several workers in the community with whom the student is familiar, the student will describe how he or she benefits from their work.

When one examines the test item used to measure this objective, one usually finds the commonly known ten to fourteen service workers, such as policeman, nurse, lawyer, etc. This objective, upon examination, has been taught in the schools for years at these grade levels. Consequently, it is no wonder there are no differences between treatment and nontreatment of participants. Most students score correctly on the test item.

Evaluational efforts must help the practitioner identify entry level skills and attitudes as well as determine focus areas so that energy and resources are spent to the best advantage.

Evaluation then must assume the major responsibility for assisting practitioners in the identification of appropriate program objectives as well as their attainment.

Suggested Do's for Concern Three

- Focus your program objectives on those learnings which are of high value but which are not already part of an existing program and, therefore, apt to be taught without your program emphasis.
- Use evaluational efforts to identify entry level skills and attitudes and areas which produce significant growth so that your energy and resources are well spent.

Concern Four: The Test Buying/Developing Dilemma

Although many tests are commercially available, a critical examination of the items reveals that many target on superficial behaviors rather than significant outcomes. Some test items have been constructed at such a low level of sophistication that the more knowledgeable student with the thoughtful answer may actually respond incorrectly if, in fact, the identified correct answer is the one requiring less sophisticated knowledge. For example:

Which of the following occupations would be chosen by someone who likes to use his or her hands?

_____ Nurse   _____ Typist   _____ Teacher   _____ Forester

Tied closely to the above concern is that many of the commercial materials we have examined tend to focus on one or two of the broad dimensions of career education. Several programs we have been associated with identified at least ten career education dimensions. Quite possibly all of these dimensions should be an integral part of any comprehensive program. Most commercial tests explore student knowledge of specific occupational information and more often than not ignore or just give tokenism to such dimensions as worker adjustment, psychology of work, social contribution, planning, school work relationship, organizational structure, economic trends, etc.

Often a commercial test may be incongruent with the stated philosophical underpinnings of a career education project. For example, while most commercial test producers give lip service to the concept of the dignity and worth of all workers, when it comes down to the preparation of specific test items, many of them invariably focus on the professional or highly technical occupations. One must ask if this is indirectly teaching that other workers are not as important and, therefore, have less dignity.

As much as producers wish their material to be free of bias, the bias of their test writers is slipping through. Biases concerning the middle-class socio-economic status, sex occupation stereotypes, educational level of workers, and, unfortunately, though on an infrequent basis, ethnic bias can all be found.

Bias is also related to changing society structures. For example, attitudes about the family may reveal the stereotyped bias of the writer. If a test item asks for the occupation of the child's father, it ignores the fact that some children do not even know who their fathers are. A more realistic test item might ask the student to name occupations of three adults he or she knows.

Seldom is it possible to find a test item dealing with high level cognitive behaviors; yet these are the behaviors practitioners are attempting to develop and measure. This is especially frustrating since the cognitive area is infinitely easier to measure than the affective domain. If commercial test producers are obviously fumbling in this area, how can they possibly hope to address the affective concerns adequately?

Affective items are few and far between in the tests we have examined. In fact, many of the items which are labeled as affective are really cognitive measures in the self-awareness dimension. We need these cognitive items in this dimension, but we also need affective measures which cover the entire gamut of a student's career development.

Local practitioners need to examine all test items carefully to insure that they are not controversial in the eyes of the community which they serve. Apparently commercial test item writers have not sufficiently field-tested their material in order to red flag those items which might create potential problems for practitioners in conservative communities. We know of one project director who set his project back in time, and personally was in trouble, because he administered a test with such items as:

- Is your father satisfied with his job?
- Do you have any friends?
- Do you get along with your parents?
- How often do you attend church?
- Would your parents get upset if you didn't go to college?

Not only did this create a stir in his general geographic area, but it had statewide ramifications due to the fact that a member of the state legislature interjected himself into the fray with vigor.

Unfortunately, there are few commercially prepared tests that are appropriate at all grade levels. This means that these materials must be adapted in order to test reliably at all instructional levels.

Of all the commercial tests brought to our attention, most are of the paper and pencil variety. Also, the apparent reading level is aimed at the average or above average reader; therefore, it is logical to assume that probably a third or more of the students tested are going to experience such difficulty with the reading content that little, if any, information regarding their career development will be gleaned.

Some companies in areas other than career education produce testing devices which allow selection from a pool of items, thus increasing the congruency between the evaluation device and program efforts. This practice needs to be refined and encouraged in the career education area.

Based on these concerns and others, the practitioner may use a criteria checklist to examine all tests closely. The practitioner, however, may decide that none of the commercial tests suit his or her needs and decide to produce tests in order to measure desired student outcomes. This approach has its problems too. The most immediate problem is often the lack of trained personnel to accomplish the task. Normally, training of this type is not required for most of the practitioners unless they have been preparing for a specialized field. Also, acquisition of the necessary skills requires far more than just reading a few basic documents. It is not a simple task to develop valid, reliable, discriminatory, administrable test items. The evaluation test item writer needs a reservoir of experiences upon which to draw in preparing the product. The same concerns listed earlier about commercial tests should also be considered when developing one's own tests.

Another concern with the do-it-yourself approach is that few funding agencies or school districts are willing to allocate the resources needed to develop well-written items correlated to desired student outcomes. In most situations, test development is an expensive process. This is a fact that has apparently escaped the attention of most administrators charged with the responsibility of allocation of funds.

Another obstacle is time. Most projects operate with certain time reporting requirements. Carrying out a program and involving the students are time consuming. Since funding agencies seem to place a higher priority on these than on effective evaluation, the latter may not receive enough attention. Often the result is that practitioners turn to inferior testing products and are rarely held accountable for the outcome.

We have had direct experience with one rather large project which determined that, in order to solve this problem, they would approach a large testing service and have them prepare test items to measure predetermined student outcomes. Even though a sizable contract was signed, which should have guaranteed a quality product, the results were disappointing. In fact, 80% of the items were never used. The project director has stated that they have rewritten, tried out, and revised so long that, in essence, there are few original items left which are of any value. Most of the current items were written by his staff.

We are concerned at this time about giving the wrong impression. Commercial tests can be a reasonable option. Undoubtedly, under the right circumstances with the right people involved, this approach may be highly successful; however, the three different projects we were involved with were not able to resolve their student outcome evaluation problems in this manner. On the other hand, we have seen this successfully handled with another consulting firm. We guess it is a matter of knowing with whom you are dealing. We have often found that bigness and known names in the field are not necessarily important criteria in selecting a firm.

We would like to mention one final concern. Our involvement with one statewide project shows that the early development of an inadequate instrument, whether commercially or locally produced, can have long-lasting, serious consequences. The project we have in mind spent a substantial amount to develop a series of test items that we would judge to be seriously deficient. This test has most of the characteristics mentioned as concerns under the commercial testing section. Its initial limited introduction into the state program was through an inexperienced local practitioner who sent glowing reports of its virtues back to the state department. Moreover, the final report, capitalizing on the utilization of this poor instrument, was so beautiful and graphically illustrated that it found immediate acceptance at the state level. The state administrators, in their desire to obtain statewide baseline data for a longitudinal study, hastily agreed to push for statewide evaluation using the instrument. We can only guess that they never really examined the content of the instrument but accepted it on the basis of an artist's ability to display the data.

Suggested Do's for Concern Four

- Develop a criteria checklist of important concerns regarding testing products, and examine both commercial or locally produced products to determine the best to use.
- Include in the checklist criteria on such areas as depth of content; comprehensiveness of career development concepts and careers covered; congruency with project philosophy; bias such as socio-economic, sex occupation stereotypes, educational levels of workers, ethnic, and changing social structure; level of cognitive domain; controversial items with respect to community political base; reading level; diagnostic and summative

purposes; pool of items for self-selection; and, finally, and perhaps most importantly, compatibility with desired student outcomes.

- If the choice is to contract out test development, examine carefully the qualifications of the individuals who will actually be preparing the test items—not the salespeople.

Concern Five: The Affective Cop-out

Another concern which involves measurement of student outcomes is what we call the *affective cop-out.* Some practitioners, inexperienced in evalution and threatened by its effective application, feel that much of what they want a student to acquire is not observable and, therefore, not measurable. For several years, those practitioners with a limited understanding of what evaluation is all about have divided the whole problem into two camps. They view evaluation as the measurement of student outcomes against specific measurable objectives, while, on the other hand, they recognize the problems inherent in the measurement of attitudes. Then, in the final analysis, they identify their career education program as one concerned primarily with self-awareness and attitudinal factors and, therefore, reject many of the proven techniques that evaluation has to offer. Somehow many practitioners do not seem to be able to accept what evaluation can do for them in proven areas, while at the same time pioneer those areas where techniques might still be considered to be primitive. Evaluation is not an either-or situation. It is a quest for the selection and application of the best as we know it to exist.

Suggested Do's for Concern Five

- Continually search for ways to measure those changes which one intuitively thinks are taking place.
- Be innovative. Some of the best evaluation ideas originate in the most unlikely places. Sometimes *knowing* that something won't work places such constraints on the thinking process that nothing happens; while the uninitiated, not hampered by such knowledge, experiments and develops something useful.

Concern Six: All Things to All People, or a Man for All Seasons

Local practitioners should not attempt to promise results or take credit for student gains in subject areas for which they do not have direct program input or have the primary responsibility for evaluation. For example, while the assumption may be valid that if you make reading more relevant to the student, his or her potential for increased reading achievement is significantly improved, it may not be valid that the changes in reading are a function of a career education activity. Since a host of other activities not directly related to career education are also affecting the students' motivation and achievement in the basic skill areas, the career education practitioner should be extremely cautious in taking credit for student growth in these areas.

Suggested Do's for Concern Six

- Be cautious in using increasing student basic skill knowledge as a program outcome unless you are directly attempting this through specific program activities. Be cognizant of other district curriculum efforts in this same area, and be sure, if you make positive statements, that your activities are the ones bringing about the results.

Concern Seven: The Instrumentation Saturation Enigma

In the past few years, there has been a noticeable amount of resistance from classroom teachers regarding the use of evaluation devices. This resistance has also been reflected by administrators, both at the local as well as the district level. Many reasons can be advanced for this reluctance. When the federal government started, around 1965, providing more funds for specific programs, almost invariably an evaluation of some sort was required. Many districts and states have also initiated new and broader evaluations of their own programs and staff. In many states, citizens have clamored for a higher degree of accountability, and these demands have proliferated into a wide variety of accountability laws throughout the nation.

The end result of all this activity is that a significantly higher percentage of time is now required for the administration and tabulation of evaluation data. Quite understandably, these activities have been accompanied by a certain amount of resistance. It would appear that this resistance is gaining momentum and has found support from some professional organizations.

Unfortunately, as a direct result of many poor evaluative efforts in the past, much of this resistance may be justifiable. As in most instances when an injustice has been created, however, an overcorrection of greater magnitude often occurs. Consequently, many well-planned and potentially useful evaluations are condemned along with their ineffective brothers. Guilt by association is not an infrequent happening in America, and the same may be true for the evaluation of career education efforts. Practitioners in this area are definitely suffering from the poor efforts of early projects, not only in career education but also in other areas.

Practitioners have the professional and moral responsibility to curb this situation. It is imperative that an evaluation plan be examined to insure that only data which is meaningful and can provoke significant program changes be sought. Enough attitudinal questionnaires may have been administered over the years in career education for us to know that effects can be obtained without a certain program and that program efforts should not be undertaken.

In fact, we have seldom seen data from questionnaires serve much value to decision makers.

Part of the disillusionment of evaluation stems directly from the fact that much of the data which is collected is never reported in a meaningful manner to the classroom teacher or unit administrator. With this situation in mind, it is certainly not difficult to understand why classroom teachers grow weary of participating in data collection efforts, for seldom are they provided with any feedback or, if it does come, it is too late.

The same problem exists for district level administrators as they attempt to cooperate with state and federal data gathering efforts. In our own district, an agreement was made to cooperate with a large, well-respected consulting firm that had a federal contract to gather data from sites that had been early participants in the career education movement. The district, in an attempt to reduce duplication of efforts in its own data collection, decided to use part of the data to be collected by the outside agency, since it would be virtually the same as what we had intended to collect. We had planned to use our data as part of a quasi-experimental study of various promotional effects on career education usage. The outside agency verbally guaranteed a fast turn around time if we would only cooperate with their effort. The results of the study were to help make significant program changes on a definite schedule. Unfortunately, the data was not delivered on time, and most of our efforts in trying to control the study were for naught. Once again, intuition was used to make a program decision.

We would suggest that an evaluation of evaluations is in order. Included in this evaluation should be the nonrecipients of data from which the original data were generated. We need a continual examination of how project directors and contracting agencies use or don't use previous results. We earnestly feel that if we can start demonstrating that data collection efforts do result in program improvement, that most of the resistance to the administration or completion of evaluation tools will melt like a block of ice on a hot August afternoon.

Suggested Do's for Concern Seven

● Check existing data you could have access to which may relate to program outcomes.
● Check the data collection plan and instruments to be utilized to insure there is no redundancy within them.
● Look with a critical eye toward each source and type of data to determine whether it is truly needed for improving the program or proving program effectiveness.
● Use unobtrusive measures whenever possible.
● Utilize population sampling techniques, as well as matrix sampling techniques, so that all participants need not respond and those responding need only respond to a few evaluational segments.
● Collect, whenever possible, classroom data which can have direct application as a diagnostic tool for teachers and insure quick turn around time.

Concern Eight: The Transaction Travesty

One of the paramount problems facing a local practitioner as she or he prepares to evaluate a program is that many programs have activities so loosely defined that one cannot establish which program activities or combination of activities are leading to the achievement of the objectives. Even in some programs where well-defined student outcomes exist, it has been our experience that all too often the same scrutinizing attention has not been paid to the development of well-defined program activities. In fact, there is often little evidence that any of the outcomes were indeed a function of program activities but may well have been a function of other intervening variables.

Very rarely is any attempt made to record deviations individual teachers make as they substitute their own activities for those suggested instructional activities in the program. This, by no means, implies that the substituted activities are inferior to the originals, but if there is no record kept, then it is impossible to identify which activities are actually accomplishing the outcomes. It is important, therefore, to devise some system of monitoring actual classroom activities so the program director can identify the most effective transactions and be sure the intended transactions are taking place.

A similar problem exists in trying to assess the effectiveness of the promotional efforts of staff on the implementation of a program on a districtwide basis. Quite frequently, little attention is paid toward the accurate documenting of the strategies used in promoting teacher utilization of resources (brochures, training, demonstration of resources, model teaching, etc.) and in having the program accepted by classroom level educators.

A still larger problem is not recording those activities accomplished by a program director in attempts to promote a program on a districtwide basis. Since promotional strategies at this level are neither well defined nor an accurate accounting of them made, it is virtually impossible for the program director to identify later which were the most effective in getting the largest number of classroom level practitioners to participate in the program with enthusiasm. For instance, how does the project director know whether the district-sponsored career days or the two-day career orientation teacher seminar was the most effective in bringing about teacher involvement in the program?

Suggested Do's for Concern Eight

- Define all program activities in detail, insuring that each individual implementing these activities is aware of the intended transactions to take place.
- Monitor program activities to be sure that the intended transactions do indeed take place.
- Design evaluation plans in order to be able to determine which program activities are bringing about the desired outcomes.

Concern Nine: The Old Correlation versus Causation Catastrophy

After years of screaming by college professors and highly trained practitioners at the local level that correlation does not prove causation, we still find a significant number of practitioners who have fallen into this trap. It's understandable how this happens. Good evaluation studies, which identify those causal factors to which significant student growth can be attributed, are difficult to design and accomplish. Even when a project initiates evaluation utilizing experimental or quasi-experimental designs, including repeated measures in time series designs, often the logistical problems of data collection, or keeping the treatments free from contamination, are so complex that it's impossible to sort out what treatment caused which outcomes. Often, after much energy is expended and when all the data is finalized, one becomes so exasperated that correlation data analysis is undertaken. Then, when one resorts to correlation data, one still cannot infer much, and decision making continues to be done by the seat-of-the-pants approach. Unquestionably, correlational data can identify program areas in which program decisions need to be made; however, it's certainly not the best decision-making mode on which a practitioner should rely.

In a recent meeting, we heard one project director indicate that his evaluation determined that field trips were ineffective at a given grade level in bringing about desired student knowledge, and, therefore, no longer would he support field trips as an effective instructional activity for students at this grade level. This was quite a revelation, and, if true, would have great impact on all of our projects; so we decided to examine carefully how this statement was derived. We found that the evaluator had correlated questions on type of instructional experiences students had been involved in with some cognitive test items of knowledge regarding the world of work. What had actually happened was that all of the students, whether they scored well on the knowledge items or not, had taken few field trips; therefore, it wasn't that field trips were ineffective in bringing about the desired student learnings but rather that they had not taken place. We know of two practitioners who left that meeting and used the information, which was stated in a causative fashion, to make a decision to cease the support of field trips for that grade level. What lasting effect this may have, we may never know.

We, as practitioners, are so eager to get information to help us make program decisions that we often will give credence to data from other programs without thoroughly examining the data.

Suggested Do's for Concern Nine

● Carefully examine all evaluational efforts to determine whether it is correlational or causational data.

● Refrain from making causative statements about the data when it obviously is not.

● Work hard to collect causational data whenever possible. Do not be satisfied with correlational data even though it may have to be used initially.

● Carefully examine statements made by other practitioners or evaluators regarding their data. Accept it only after proof. Do not accept it on faith.

Concern Ten: The Bebop Syndrome

The career education practitioner, like any other practitioner charged with the responsibility of proving the worth of a new program, soon finds that the political ramifications of his or her evaluations are such that if there is a wish to survive, he or she had better accentuate the positive and eliminate or hide any negative evaluation data that might prove embarrassing.

The impetus for sweeping the dirt under the carpet is usually indirect and inferred rather than directly ordered; however, on two occasions we have been personally requested not to discuss the facts, as legislatures may be listening. The local practitioner is deluged with reminders from many funding offices that state or federal legislatures are observing with great interest the birth and development of career education. Occasionally, remarks are heard that the economy is bad and that the dollars for education are limited; therefore, only those programs which are able to prove their significant worth to the educational growth of students have any chance of surviving. It doesn't take long for an educational practitioner with much political savy to comprehend that the economic future is intimately related to program results, and if the practitioner and career education itself are to remain, then evaluation data had better be well accentuated on the positive side and virtually eliminated on the negative.

Even without formally communicating this message to anyone, it is amazing how everyone involved in the process seems to understand clearly the importance of accentuating the positive. This system inherently defeats the objective collection of data which would ultimately improve a program. This situation causes one to speculate about whether or not education is prone to a never ending parade of fads. Is it that everyone is so busy pretending that there are no clouds in the sky that no one gathers the formative evaluation data required for significant program revision and improvement? The consequences is that in a few months, after everyone is tired of the new fad, it is relatively easy to displace, because new practitioners, wishing to implement another new program, begin to ask some rather embarrassing questions about the current fad and a new cycle begins.

One must not judge too harshly the creator, the promoter, even the practitioner who falls into this syndrome. To make the program go, he or she must devote much positive energy to the positive vibrations. Somehow she or he must be reinforced to look inwardly for change and growth. Those of us who are devoted to making career education a long lasting concept in the curriculum rather than a fad must insist that we be objective in all we do and report all the facts.

Suggested Do's for Concern Ten

● Identify not only successes but failures, and examine carefully these failures (temporary setbacks) in order to refine your program.

● Report all findings and concern yourself with several hypotheses as to the results, but refrain from rationalizing away the findings which were those you hoped to find.

● Remember that your credibility in the long run is much more important than political ploy.

● Be realistic about what you can accomplish—do not over-promise.

● Encourage funding agencies to be credible also to those they serve.

● Lastly, be your own harshest critic.

LONGITUDINAL EVALUATION IN CAREER EDUCATION

Robert J. Rossi and Donald H. McLaughlin

Dr. Rossi is research scientist and director of the Social Indicators Research Program at the American Institutes for Research in the Behavioral Sciences. He is author of numerous articles and books on social indicators.

Donald H. McLaughlin is senior research scientist and director of the Statistical Analysis Group in Education at the American Institutes for Research in the Behavioral Sciences. Dr. McLaughlin directed the 1975 nationwide survey of career education and has played a major role in the 1979-80 evaluation of the effects of the Career Education Incentive Act. This article was written in 1976.

In this paper we wish to distinguish between short-term and long-term evaluation designs. We will discuss the usefulness of long-term designs in assessing the effects of career education programs and in validating short-term designs. By *short-term evaluations* we mean those which involve minimal delay between program participation and evaluation data collection and which measure predicted performance. *Long-term longitudinal evaluations*, on the other hand, refer here to studies which involve the direct relating of program participation to ultimate criteria by using a design, such as a panel design, which allows for the same individuals to be followed up for a period of years. Since the use of one or the other of these evaluation procedures depends both on the practical and on conceptual considerations, we begin by weighing the practical advantages and disadvantages of using each type of evaluation design and by examining some recently stated career education goals. What emerges from this examination is evidence that a longitudinal evaluation of career education can benefit both practitioners and theoreticians if it is undertaken on a nationwide scale and if results are used to assist in the development and validation of short-term evaluation procedures for assessing the progress toward long-range career education goals. We then describe in general how such a longitudinal evaluation of career education can be carried out and what roles career education participants at all levels will have to play to make possible its success.

Short-term vs. Long-term Evaluations in Career Education

The type of evaluation procedure employed depends in most cases on the scope of the program objectives and on a consideration of the costs involved. Where budgets, personnel, or time constraints will not allow for either short-term or long-term formal evaluations to be undertaken, then informal or more subjective ones will have to do. Likewise, where there is not a clearly defined or agreed upon set of program objectives, any evaluation, formal or informal, will be difficult to perform. At present and for the near future it is doubtful that local education agencies (LEAs) can bear the costs of carrying out longitudinal evaluation of career education formally. This kind of evaluation is perhaps the most expensive and requires a level of commitment and constant support beyond the capabilities of most schools. For example, early results from the nationwide survey and assessment of career education supported by the U.S. Office of Education show clearly that the number of districts in the nation having carried out formal evaluations is not large and, of those having performed such evaluations, the majority employ short-term procedures only; thus, while informal follow-ups may be made of alumni, perhaps at class reunions, it is more reasonable to expect LEAs to rely on short-term designs when they do carry out formal program evaluations.

Problems arise, however, when LEAs must evaluate the effectiveness of long-range goals they may establish for students in career education. Evidence that such long-range goals for career education are strongly supported by education personnel at various levels throughout the country is presented in the appendix to the 1975 U.S. Office of Education policy paper entitled "An Introduction to Career Education." In the appendix to that paper, evidence was reported of the overwhelming agreement of local and state career education practitioners across the country on the *nine learner outcomes and societal and individualistic objectives for career education* listed below. Students should be:

- competent in the basic academic skills required for adaptability in our rapidly changing society
- equipped with good work habits
- capable of choosing and who have chosen a personally meaningful set of work values that foster in them a desire to work
- equipped with career decision-making skills, job-hunting skills, and job-getting skills
- equipped with personal vocational skills at a level that will allow them to gain entry into and attain a degree of success in the occupational society
- equipped with career decisions based on the widest possible set of data concerning themselves and their educational-vocational opportunities
- aware of means available to them for continuing and recurrent education once they have left the formal system of schooling
- successful in being placed in a paid occupation, in further education, or in a vocation consistent with their current career education

● successful in incorporating work values into their total personal value structure in such a way that they are able to choose what, for them, is a desirable life-style (Hoyt 1975)

The societal objectives of career education are to help all individuals: (1) want to work; (2) acquire the skills necessary for work in these times; and (3) engage in work that is satisfying to the individual and beneficial to society.

The individualistic goals of career education are to make work: (1) possible; (2) meaningful; and (3) satisfying for each individual throughout his or her life (ibid.).

Such phrases as capable of choosing, that will allow them to gain entry into and attain a degree of success in the occupational society, successful in being placed in a paid occupation, able to choose . . . a desirable life-style, engage in work that is satisfying and beneficial, and to make work (1) possible; (2) meaningful; and (3) satisfying for each individual throughout his or her life are indicative of the long-range goals of career education and clearly imply that post-school or work-world experiences are involved. If LEAs are to do more than pay lip service to these goals, they must design and implement career education programs which will have long-term effects on their students' lives. This cannot be done unless the post-school or work-world effects of these programs are understood—that is, unless a longitudinal study of program effects is undertaken. Faced with this compelling list of career education goals on the one hand and the reality of limited resources on the other, LEAs have three possible courses of action open to them.

● They may choose to redefine their career education program objectives to include only goals that can be measured using short-term evaluation designs such as end-of-course tests.

● They may choose to seek out state-level or federal support to follow up their students systematically over the long term to determine whether their career education programs have prepared students to establish productive and rewarding careers successfully.

● They may choose, if there were a short-term measurement design which was validated as predictive of long-term career development effects, to use that validated short-term design to evaluate their career education programs.

The first alternative seems to us to be without real merit since it is just these long-range goals that make career education a positive force for bringing education and work together. Saying this, however, a cautionary note must be interjected. We do not wish to give the impression that there are no important short-range career education goals. Competency in basic skill areas and possession of good work habits, for example, are necessary for students' eventual success and satisfaction in their work-world roles. The issue is, thus, not that schools must choose either one or the other type of career education goal or that they must choose some of each of these types. Rather it is, first, that school personnel must define clearly what their career education program objectives are and obtain agreement on these goals within their communities and, second, that they must realize that long-range goals cannot be assessed as easily at the present time as can short-term goals. What is important is that if long-range goals are defined and agreed upon for a career education program, they should not be ignored due to expected problems in assessment.

As to the second alternative, there is nothing new in LEAs obtaining government support to improve their educational programs, but consider for a moment the difference between requesting funds for building or conducting staff development activities and requesting money to perform a longitudinal study of alumni. Project TALENT, a nationwide longitudinal study of over 400,000 high school students in the 1960s, has required thousands of hours of staff time and the constant support and attention of the federal government over a sixteen-year period. While we would expect the number of students to be smaller in individual districts' evaluations, consider if every LEA decided to perform this sort of formal longitudinal study of its graduates! The costs would be staggering and not, it seems, wholly justifiable. How much coordination between LEAs would be needed to insure communication, that is to insure that methods and findings could be shared? How much of the information collected would be so different in one LEA than in another to warrant each LEA undertaking such a venture? Finally, how many school districts could count on the consistent and continuing federal or state, community, and staff support for a period of from five to ten years? It seems, then, that state or federal support of LEAs for their individual performance of longitudinal career education evaluations is an infeasible approach.

A related matter may be raised here concerning the feasibility of individual state education agencies (SEAs) carrying out longitudinal evaluations of a sample of ongoing career education programs in their states. Questions of cost and redundancy must also be raised here, however, and in addition there are problems regarding graduates who move to different states to work and live—should they be followed up? Also, how useful can such longitudinal data on students from one state be to other SEAs who cannot afford their own evaluations—that is, how generalizable will the results be? It would appear, as before, that the expected costs outweigh the potential gains.

There is, however, the third alternative described above to consider. This approach we take to be the most promising one for career education practitioners and theoreticians interested in the evalution of long-range goals, provided that there are validated predictors of long-range career education goals available; however, there are none available, and to obtain them it is necessary to collect long-term data on the careers of individuals who have taken batteries of tests likely to include a set of valid predictors. Consequently, a single longitudinal evaluation of career education is necessary in order to provide the necessary validation of instruments that can be used in short-term evaluation designs. In this way the replication or duplication of long-term studies by either LEAs or SEAs could be avoided without these agencies losing the ability to assess long-range career education goals. If the one longitudinal evaluation that is conducted is sufficiently comprehensive (as it must be), a wealth of information about how career education experiences can affect career development could be acquired.

The major factors to be considered in determining the scope of such a longitudinal study are what career education practitioners on the one hand and theoreticians on the other want in terms of information and instrument development. Given that the validation of short-term predictors of long-term career education goals for use in LEAs nationwide is a primary concern of such a study, the sample population on which the validation study will be based must be representative of school-age persons in the different geographic regions of the United States. The sample, therefore, will have to be drawn from the population of all persons in the nation, and the scope of the study will, by necessity, be nationwide rather than district or statewide. For theoreticians, whose primary concern is for understanding what the construct, career education, involves, the in-depth examination of the continuing effects of various career education experiences provided by a longitudinal study of nationwide scope should be immensely valuable and more useful than any empirical results so far available. Consequently, a single nationwide longitudinal evaluation of career education programs and their effects on individuals' development can provide tools for use by LEAs in their own evaluations of the long-range career education goals they may have adopted and make the seemingly infeasible proliferation of longitudinal studies at either the LEA or the SEA levels unnecessary. In addition, a single study of this scope, conducted formally and with the cooperation of career education practitioners and theoreticians across the country, would be likely to provide much more adequate and accurate data about the effects of career education on individuals, schools, and the work world than would be possible by any other, more limited means.

It should come as no surprise, then, that it is our feeling that career education participants at all levels should take responsible roles in performing this evaluation. Since these roles are described in greater detail in the next section, along with a plan for conducting such a longitudinal evaluation of career education, it seems appropriate to conclude this first section with a review of the possible gains these participants may expect from performance of a longitudinal evaluation of career education.

Students who are involved in a longitudinal study of career education can gain some perspective of how education and work are, or can be, related for them as they respond to follow-up questionnaires. Participation in such a study can also give them an opportunity to have a positive influence both on the educational system and on the educational and work experiences of future generations.

LEA personnel involved in such a long-term study can gain important feedback on the effectiveness of their school programs. This information should not only be helpful for program design but should provide these agencies the opportunity to make inputs into both local and national education and work policies. An important aspect of LEA participation—one not often mentioned explicitly—is that aiding in the location and follow-up of alumni can help schools maintain a link with their graduates in a way that both enhances the school program and helps in the maintenance and strengthening of support for local education efforts within communities. Of course, as has already been noted, a major result of this kind of study would be to provide all LEAs, participants as well as others, with the means to evaluate the long-range effects of their career education programs while students are either in school or at the point of graduating.

Researchers in university and institutional settings stand to gain opportunities for very useful, exciting, and continuing research into relationships between education and work if a *career education data bank* is established on the basis of longitudinal study. The availability of such a career education data bank would also provide colleges and universities with information on which to validate the effectiveness of their pre-service and in-service programs designed to prepare teachers for employing career concepts, methods, and materials in their classrooms. Moreover, the same benefits projected above for LEAs in terms of ties with alumni, increased community support, and availability of valid short-term indicators of long-range effects can be expected by colleges and universities as active participants in a longitudinal follow-up study of their alumni.

SEA personnel, in addition to gains similar to those noted for LEA personnel, can gain a perspective on what is needed in career education in their state, the effectiveness of state career education efforts, and how the relationship between education and work in their state is affecting other aspects of state government (e.g., labor policies, programs aimed at human resources development, etc.).

Business/labor/industry/professional representatives stand to gain knowledge about the effectiveness of career education for enhancing worker satisfaction and about the relationship of career education experiences to such things as turnover rate, community relations, and community development. These representatives also would gain a sense of direct contribution to the improvement of education and work linkages, especially to the extent that the evaluation design included a detailed assessment of business/labor/industry/professional efforts in the areas of school and community relations and worker development.

Federal government representatives may stand to realize the most significant gain of all, namely the strengthened and coordinated cooperation and communication between career education participants at many different levels. Additionally, these representatives can expect to learn about the relative effectiveness of federal policies and programs pertaining to education and work and about the effectiveness of career education in terms of the problem areas for which it is proposed as an instrument of reform.

Implementing a Longitudinal Evaluation of Career Education

Two fundamental issues must be dealt with in the design of a longitudinal study of career education: (1) the need for conceptual clarity in defining what is to be evaluated and (2) the need for a methodological approach capable of reducing the time needed to gather information which can be useful for refining career education practices. If these issues are carefully considered and resolved adequately, it is then possible to focus more specifically on the principal aims of the study:

● to provide validation for short-term measures predictive of long-range career education goals (e.g., career success and satisfaction)

● to provide comprehensive and particular data on the effects of career education on individual development

● to provide a *control group* against which individuals participating in career education programs can be compared

The first and third aims can be accomplished if methodological issues are effectively handled. The second aim requires conceptual clarity about what career education means in the language and, thus, what career education practices can be reasonably expected to accomplish.

Consider first the need for conceptual clarity in order to understand the effects of career education on individual development. This need follows directly from the theoretician's concern for what career education is all about and from the practitioner's immediate concern for what can be done to reform certain conditions existing within the educational/social environment. Conceptual clarity is not just a matter of resolving different individuals' interpretations, although this can be a starting point. Looking to the language itself—that is, to how the term, career education, is used or can be used in everyday discourse—it is possible to see four kinds of activities which can occur at various points in an individual's development. Career education can refer to:

● education about careers or work

● education that is facilitated or made possible by the use of career/work concepts, methods, and materials

● education that occurs when one is in a career or doing a particular kind of work

● education that results from one's career or work

Statements about what is expected from career education activities must be carefully constructed and concise. For example, to say that career education will reduce worker alienation requires, minimally, that the steps to be taken toward this aim be spelled out clearly. It is also necessary, it seems, that *reduce* be defined carefully. Will alienation be removed completely? Will more than half the workers in all kinds of jobs find they are no longer disassociated from themselves in their jobs? Is disassociation from oneself in work synonymous with alienation? These and many more questions must be considered and answered clearly in order to (1) know what aspects of career education should have what kinds of effects and (2) refine career eduction programs as the results of a nationwide longitudinal study become available. Clarity of terminology, of career education goals, and of program expectations is a basic requirement if long-term evaluation of career education programs is to be helpful to decision-makers at all levels. Conceptual clarity is necessary for the selection of adequate tests and for the design of meaningful follow-up questionnaires and interview schedules.

Consider next the aims of this nationwide study (stated above) and how they relate to methodological issues. The first aim follows from (1) a recognition of the need for criterion-referenced measures of career education program effectiveness; (2) a recognition that the appropriate criteria cannot feasibly be measured by local school districts; and (3) a belief that the gap can be bridged by the execution of a sufficiently comprehensive longitudinal evaluation study to find relations between the appropriate criteria and measurements which local districts can perform.

In order to carry out a comprehensive long-term study without taking fifty years (the interval between school and retirement over which careers develop), a simultaneous multiple-cohort design can be used. Such a design is illustrated by the problem of determining what factors at age 20 are predictive of success at age 40. One can accomplish this approximately by gathering initial data on two cohorts, 20-year-olds and 30-year-olds, and following each group up in ten years. Statistically, one finds the best set of variables among the data initially gathered on the 30-year-olds for predicting career success and satisfaction at 40; then these variables are correlated with the data initially gathered on the 20-year-olds. This principle can be used to shorten the time interval of the project further; for example, to find the predictors at age 15 of career success through age 63, one could follow up each of twelve groups of individuals over a period of five years, the ages of the groups initially being 15, 19, 23, . . . 55, and 59.

The problem with this extreme is the loss of predictability due to error variance among the initial groups. We would expect the predictable variance to be decreased with successive steps in the prediction chain:

$$R^2 (20 \rightarrow 30 \rightarrow 40) = R^2 (20 \rightarrow 30) \, X R^2 (30 \rightarrow 40)$$

Furthermore, there may be trends in the environment which tend to invalidate the approximation: for example, in following up two groups, twenty- and thirty-year-olds for ten years, one is assuming that the younger group will follow the same pattern of career attainment over the subsequent ten years that their older counterparts did. This assumption can be relaxed greatly by adding a measure of overlap of age ranges to the project as portrayed in Table 11-A. In this design, age ranges are not confounded with the trends over time. The assumption underlying this model is that either there are no trends over time or any trends can be extrapolated from comparison of relationships between the two successive five-year periods.

In order for this procedure to be valid, great care must be taken in sampling and in follow-up data collection. To return to the relatively simple two-cohort example, the sample

TABLE 11-A.
A Hypothetical Design To Obtain 20-Year Longitudinal Validations in 11 Years: Ages at Data Collection

Group	Year one	Year six	Year eleven
A	Age = 20	Age = 25	Age = 30
B	Age = 25	Age = 30	Age = 35
C	Age = 30	Age = 35	Age = 40
D	Age = 35	Age = 40	
E		Age = 20	Age = 25

of thirty-year-olds must be drawn to match the sample of twenty-year-olds as it is predicted to be ten years later, or at least to contain a subset that will match the younger sample. For example, it would not suffice to choose the older sample from a single community or small set of communities, even if the younger sample would have become geographically dispersed, probably resulting in different predictive relationships. Choosing both samples from within a single country, such as the United States, would be a reasonable procedure insofar as one is willing to ignore emigrants in the evaluation of a career education program. Not only geographic dispersion but also dispersion on socio-economic status; on marital, military, and educational experiences; and on other dimensions must be anticipated so that the older sample must be more exhaustive in its representativeness than the younger sample.

What can be done if the younger sample, when it reaches the age at which the older sample was initially observed, is quite different? If an overlapping design is employed, it is possible to estimate the regularity, or predictability, of that difference; however, if the change is so drastic as to produce little overlap on some important variable, there is a gamble in extrapolating relations observed on part of a dimension to another part of that dimension. For example, suppose the older sample had amounts of education ranging from 8 to 16 years, and the younger sample's amount of education at the same age ranged from 14 to 20 years. We might find that the amount of education is quite predictive of earnings for the older sample, but we would not necessarily expect the same relation for the younger sample. Such differences are, in fact, quite damaging to the design. To avoid them, it is imperative to include extremes on all major dimensions in the older sample(s).

Another constraint on the sample is that it represents as great a variation on (potential) career success for each cohort as one can obtain without knowing exactly what that dimension of variation is. That constraint is necessary to assure that the study will be sensitive to possible sources of predictability of career success and satisfaction; thus, each cohort-sample should be drawn from the (potentially) unemployed and the affluently employed, from the professions and the general labor force, and from different sexes, races, and ethnic groups. Previous information, such as Project TALENT's experience and Parnes' National Longitudinal Surveys, should be used to the fullest to aid in this aspect of the design.

Once we decide upon an ideal design, the data must still be collected. The problem of sample attrition—inability to recontact and gain participation of each subject at the time of a follow-up, say, ten years later—is so difficult that it has discouraged many from the use of longitudinal designs; however, in Project TALENT the research staff members have developed methods for dealing with that attrition, both data collection methods (Carrel, Potts, and Campbell 1975) and statistical methods for correcting the bias created by sample attrition (McLaughlin, Fulscher, and Yen 1974). Methods are now being developed and evaluated for maximizing survey response rates, and special, expensive procedures can be used to locate a small subsample of the nonrespondents to correct for nonresponse bias. To the extent that the overlapping panel design limits the maximum time interval for each individual's follow-up, the attrition problem can be alleviated. For example, in Project TALENT the percentage of regular respondents has decreased as a function of the number of intervening years, as shown in Table 11-B. This decrease, to a great extent, resulted from the loss of forwarding addresses and the increasing desire to avoid possible federal "spying" on private lives.

The third aim of this evaluation study is to provide a comparison group against which local school districts can evaluate the effectiveness of their career education programs. The fundamental problem is that the experimental and comparison groups are not chosen

TABLE 11-B.
Decrease in Response Percentages to Project Talent Follow-up Surveys Over Time

Years Intervening Between Testing and Follow-up	Percentage Responding without Special Follow-up Search
1	61.1%
2	43.6%
3	42.8%
4	40.0%
5	39.0%
6	35.1%
7	32.0%
8	26.6%
*	*
*	*
11	28.8%
12	24.9%
13	22.2%
14	19.6%

randomly from the same population. The question is certain to arise in any local evaluation based on comparison with a nationwide sample of whether the students in the particular local program are comparable to the national average. A large step toward solving this problem is to include in the data set for each individual in the experimental and comparison groups a set of background or input factors (such as socio-economic status) and to match experimental and comparison groups on these factors by some method such as analysis of covariance. In the last decade the use of such matching methods has drawn sharp, and deserved, criticism. The root of the criticism is the use of such matching methods to compare samples drawn from what are actually quite different populations; they lose potency when the experimental and comparison groups can be shown to have similar distributions on the background, input factors. In order to avoid this criticism, another constraint is therefore placed on the sampling for this long-term validation study. The younger cohorts must include adequate numbers in all strata of the various background factors. With that constraint, the problems of matching a particular local school district's experimental group with an adjusted national average comparison group can be solved.

One factor which cannot be as easily matched as others is the temporal context of the groups. An experimental group (the participants in an LEA's career education program) tested in 1980 should be evaluated relative to a comparison group of the same age in 1980. The implication of this constraint is that new younger cohorts must be added to the study every few years. To the extent that the assumption that changes over time do not have large high-order interactions with background variables is valid, these later cohort samples need not be as large as the initial cohort samples. In present-day America, however, changes in potential for career fulfillment are occurring at different rates and directions for different population segments. The design of such later cohort samples should, then, take into account the dynamics of society at the time of the data collection.

The various constraints on the evaluation design together imply that the project would be quite extensive—possibly more extensive than any empirical research study yet undertaken in the area of education. Table 11-C shows estimates of the necessary sample sizes for such a study, to be undertaken over a ten-year period. The study must clearly be undertaken on a national level rather than within the several states, although these states may well have quite different policies for implementing career education.

It must be undertaken with the understanding of its importance not only to a reform movement in education but also to the overall career fulfillment and quality of life of society's participants. The purposes of this project would be to provide the bases for the performance of easy, but valid, evaluations of particular career education programs at the local or state level and to develop and refine the construct, career education. Because the responsibility for its success must lie with career education participants at all levels throughout the country, it is important that some attention be paid to what these responsibilities may involve. Their brief description will tell us where we must start to plan for a nationwide longitudinal evaluation of career education.

LEA personnel must take primary responsibility for administering the tests or test batteries that are to be validated. Depending on the age level of the youngest cohort in the study, the role of these personnel may also include responsibilities for recording carefully the interaction of students with in-school, out-of-school, paid, and unpaid work experiences and the administration of formal follow-up questionnaires to students or scheduling interviews with students. It is possible that LEAs may be needed to assist in both the locating and contacting of students for a period after their graduation from the district.

TABLE 11-C.

Ages of Samples in Proposed Design for a Nationwide Validation Project To Help the Evaluation of Career Education

Sample	Sample size	Age at year 1	Age at year 3	Age at year 5	Age at year 7	Age at year 9
1	5000	15	17	19	21	23
2	2500	19	21	23	25	27
3	7500	23	25	27	29	31
4	4000	27	29	31	33	35
5	10000	31	33	35	37	39
6	5000	35	37	39	41	43
7	15000	39	41	43	45	47
8	7500	43	45	47	49	51
9	15000	47	49	51	53	55
10	5000	51	53	55	57	59
11	10000	55	57	59	61	63
12	5000	59	61	63	65	67

NOTE: *The samples should all be stratified on sex (2), race (4), geographic region (4), socio-economic status (3), and type of career (50), yielding a total of some 5000 strata.*

Personnel in the district should also be able to describe carefully what school-centered efforts are being made in the area of career education; what are the aims of these efforts; and which students participate.

University or college personnel must take primary responsibility for assisting and/or possibly conducting follow-up activities of LEA-originating students as well as for administering tests or test batteries for use with college-level students that are to be validated. They can expect to help with the locating and contacting of students and must also be able to describe carefully all aspects of their efforts in the area of career education. Researchers at universities, colleges, and institutions must be relied on to provide technical and theoretical expertise.

SEA personnel must take primary responsibility for coordinating data collection and career education program development activities ongoing in their states. As regional coordinators, they must be able to participate in evaluation design meetings and be able to make on-site visits to LEAs when they are asked to do so.

Business/labor/industry/professional representatives take primary responsibility for describing in detail the kinds of career education efforts made by their companies and firms. These representatives should expect to be involved in helping with follow-up activities and, in some cases, will be involved in the actual administration of tests or batteries of tests for use with mid-career persons.

Federal government representatives must take the primary responsibility for managing all phases of the study and coordinating the efforts of all participants. These representatives must also take the lead in insuring that there will be the consistency and constancy of support for the study necessary for its success.

EVALUATING CAREER EDUCATION: A PLAN FOR POSSIBLE RESULTS

Terry Newell

Dr. Newell is currently chief of the Executive Development Branch of the Horace Mann Learning Center of the U.S. Office of Education. This article was written in 1976.

By almost any measure, the growth of career education since its inception in 1971 has been remarkable. Career education programs have been initiated in hundreds of local school systems. Over forty states have designated career education coordinators and over fifty percent of the states have position statements, state plans, or budgets for implementing career education. Federal legislation has been enacted in support of career education, and a growing number of business, labor, industry, professional, government, and educational groups have come out in support of the career education concept. It is fair to say, however, that career education has, to date, been accepted more on faith than on the basis of demonstrated achievement.

This relatively uncritical acceptance of career education is testimony to the attractiveness of the concept and the creative programs developed by practitioners at all levels. In the long run, however, the growth of career education will depend on evidence of its effectiveness. Both critics and advocates agree that this should be so. The worth of the investment in career education must be proved, and the programmatic development of career education must be based on a firm knowledge base of what works, when, how, and for whom. It is time to devote increasing attention to the evaluation of career education. It is time to turn the creativity of practitioners and researchers loose on the problems of evaluation, much as they were turned loose on the problem of conceptual development a few years ago.

Given this need, the purposes of this article are to: (1) suggest some components of a long-range plan for the improvement of evaluation in career education; (2) outline parameters that might guide a long-range evaluation plan; and (3) highlight some critical problems that will confront any attempt to implement such a plan. As implied by these purposes, improvement of evaluation in career education will take time. It is thus all the more important that we begin now.

Some Action Steps of a Long-range Evaluation Plan

While there is no consensus on the steps that must be taken to improve career education evaluation, much of the current dialogue seems to center on a few major areas. What follows is a suggested set of action steps. These steps may be out of order. Some key steps may be missing. No pretense is made that what follows is a comprehensive approach or the best approach that might be taken. It is an attempt to stimulate constructive dialogue.

Determine important questions. Practitioners, researchers, and policymakers at all levels (and often within the same level of education or government) have varied expectations for career education. Little progress can be made until these groups engage in a joint dialogue to determine the most important questions they want career education evaluation to answer. Once these questions have been explicitly stated and agreed to by all parties, a comprehensive, cooperative evaluation plan will be possible. A consensus on needs is a precondition to a combining of resources. The dialogue must address three major problems. First, how can the large number of questions of interest to different groups at different levels be trimmed to a size that promises to respond to everyone's needs with available resources? We cannot possibly hope to address all of the important questions in a short time. We can hope to address most of the really critical questions. This will mean a conscious decision to leave some questions unaddressed so as to concentrate resources on a smaller number. Second, which questions are capable of being answered with existing technology? The techniques to answer some questions may simply not be available in the forseeable future, however important the questions may be. We must be willing to acknowledge this. Third, what do the questions really mean? We must increase the clarity and precision of our definitions of critical variables. What do we mean by *career decision-making, career exploration,* and other terms? Until we can answer these questions, we cannot build appropriate instruments or research designs.

Develop needed instruments. One area on which almost all practitioners agree is the need for new instruments for use in career education evaluation. While some instruments developed for other purposes are usable in part, there are very few instruments carefully developed based on career education objectives. The new instruments must be based on a sound conceptual base, and they must be technically sensitive to local program effects. Development of such instruments will take time, perhaps three to four years. While the Office of Education and the National Institute of Education have begun cooperative efforts in this area, their resources will need to be augmented by much greater state and local efforts. Some very helpful state efforts are already underway in this area.

Develop new methods. New measurement instruments are necessary but not sufficient for improving evaluation in career education. Effort must also be devoted to the development of more effective research designs and more sensitive research techniques than those traditionally used in educational evaluation. In addition to the standard method of paper and pencil testing, evaluators of career education will increasingly have to rely on such strategies as the use of behavioral indices of change, including unobtrusive measures and sophisticated design and analysis procedures if conclusive evidence about career education's effectiveness is to be obtained under the very unexperimental environment of everyday learning.

Improve the evaluation skills of career education. There is a need for in-service training in evaluation in general and career education evaluation in particular among career education practitioners at all levels. Where practitioners are conducting their own evaluations, they need detailed training in evaluation design and procedures, with a particular focus on career education. Where practitioners contract out their evaluations, they need to know enough to specify the tasks and obtain the high quality services they need. A little consumer education in evaluation could do much to improve the quality of purchased evaluation services.

Develop technical assistance and dissemination. To keep research and practice closely tied and to gather and spread the best of what is available in the way of instruments, designs, techniques, and results, some mechanism is needed to provide action assistance to practitioners. Local practitioners must be given the expertise they need when and where they need it if we expect them to improve their evaluation efforts. This dissemination and assistance function is often overlooked and badly needed.

Synthesize existing evidence. There are some useful data on the effectiveness of career education already available. While these data are not numerous, they do exist in widely scattered places. Other data of lesser quality also contain some potentially useful information on the effectiveness of career education. We must collect and synthesize the best of what information we have to learn what it can tell us. A large number of technically weak evaluations using varied methods which all reach the same conclusions do tell us a little as they corroborate each other. As the quality and quantity of the results improve, the data bank must be continually updated and made more useful.

Initiate longitudinal research. Many of the really important and measurable outcomes of career education can only be realized as students progress in the world of work beyond school. The effectiveness of career education practices can therefore only be determined by relating them to the work experiences of graduates. This requires longitudinal research. An adequate evaluation of career eduation should really begin when a child enters school and can only logically end after that child has spent a number of years in out-of-school work. Such longitudinal evaluation studies should be initiated as soon as possible and must be continued for a number of years. One option would be to build on existing longitudinal studies (e.g., the National Assessment of Educational Progress, the National Longitudinal Study of the High School Class of 1972, etc.); but this could only respond to a small part of the real need.

Parameters of a Long-range Evaluation Plan

The action steps described above are possibilities. An effective long-range plan for the evaluation of career education must come out of a process which draws on the experience and innovativeness of practitioners within and outside of education. Whatever the final plan, however, some parameters seem called for to help guide the dialogue and to assure that the plan responds to common and generally accepted needs in evaluation. What follows is a list of some of these parameters. No inference should be made that this list is agreed on by all those interested in career education evaluation. As with the list of action steps, this list is offered to stimulate dialogue, not to make a pretense of consensus.

● The plan should present a year-by-year proposal for what is to be accomplished and what can therefore be expected. Broad claims for large and positive results in a short time must be avoided. Educators have too often promised more than could be delivered. A plan for possible results is what is needed. It should be cautious, capable of being attained by the dates specified, and progressive (i.e., lead to more and better evidence as time goes by).

● The plan should be communicated in clear terms to all important constituencies, especially decision makers who can affect budgets and legislative commitments to career education. Products resulting from the plan must also be communicated to all interested groups. Feedback on the plan and its results must be actively encouraged. Only with such continuous and open communication can the plan continually evolve, and only with such communication can we restore the credibility for educational claims that is now so frequently lacking.

• The plan must be based on a sensible funding schedule. Asking for too much too soon is neither realistic, necessary, nor wise; yet it must be made clear that this plan for possible results will not be cheap. Funding beyond that presently available for career education evaluation will be necessary for a period of probably ten to fifteen years.

• The plan must yield data useful at all levels of education and government. Local evaluations which look at unique variables of little utility beyond the local level will not meet the broader policy needs of state and federal decision makers. By the same token, national evaluations with data of little interest to local practitioners breed local resistance and seem only to occupy space on the shelf. Local cooperation can only be expected if there is feedback of locally useful data. Similarly, federal and state assistance to local programs can only be expected if variables beyond purely local interest are made part of the evaluation. Cooperative and nonthreatening evaluation must be an underlying principle of whatever plan is finally developed for career education evaluation.

• The plan must provide for different levels of evidence of effectiveness of career education. While educationally and statistically significant results in student performance may be the ultimate criterion (for short-range studies), we must develop a hierarchy of evidence leading to this. This hierarchy might include: (1) testimonial evidence of program success given by parents, teachers, students, and others; (2) changes in performance detected by low-cost, statistically suspect methods and/or instruments; (3) statistically significant changes in performance shown by high-quality, valid, and reliable instruments and techniques; and (4) changes in performance, shown by valid and reliable instruments and techniques, which are educationally as well as statistically significant. Such a hierarchy would have at least two major benefits. First, it would allow us to make more useful judgments about the extent of what we know. Arguments about the value of evaluation results now center on whether the data are *hard* or *soft*. This dichotomy ignores the fact that evaluation data can still be useful even if not rigorously obtained. The dichotomy perpetuates the belief that if the data are not hard, then we know nothing. Second, a hierarchy of levels of evidence would allow decision makers to opt for, pay for, and accept various degrees of rigor in evaluation.

• The plan must also provide for different categories of evidence along an inputs-process-product continuum. Too few evaluations concentrate on all of these variables at the same time. As Charters (1973) has indicated, student learning is the last step in a series of actions and is dependent on them. Such actions include policy statements, structural and program changes, in-service training, changes in staff behavior, changes in student learning activities, and ultimately, changes in student behavior. Evaluation must look at all of these steps and at the linkages between them if cause and effect questions are ever to be answered. As Charters so clearly stated, the conclusion that an educational effort doesn't work cannot be fairly drawn until we have proven that it has actually been tried. Evaluation which focuses only on outcomes begs the question of whether anything different was done which could be expected to lead to the desired outcomes. As in the case of levels of evidence, an evaluation plan which provides for the collection of evidence along an inputs-process-product continuum would clarify, for decision makers, what they can expect at different points in a program's development for different degrees of investment.

Critical Problems Facing Career Education Evaluation

Whatever the shape and content of a long-range evaluation plan for career education, certain critical problems will have to be confronted. Most of these problems have persistently plagued efforts to improve the measurement of the effectiveness of their educational innovations. Some of these problems can be addressed by improving the state of the art of evaluation. Others can be at least partly resolved by changes based on existing knowledge. All of them must be overcome before any plan for possible results in career education can fulfill its promise.

• Traditional evaluation designs, techniques, and instruments do not appear to be sufficiently sensitive to be useful in most natural settings and to detect changes in important career education variables. As a result, common evaluation approaches have often not resulted in the production of positive, convincing evidence about the effectiveness of career education (or other educational programs). Some insist that this lack of evidence proves the bankruptcy of educational innovations. It may well be, however, that the fault lies in the state of the art of evaluation and not in the educational programs. More effective designs, new techniques, and more carefully developed evaluation instruments will be increasingly needed if we hope to show positive results.

• Too few evaluations of educational programs address organizational variables as determinants of change. It is not sufficient to look only at program resources, treatments, and outcomes if we want to understand when and how career education works. We must also analyze the various change strategies used, the organizational climate in which change is attempted, and the interactions between the subsystems of the institution(s) attempting to implement career education. Whether a project uses outside consultants or internal change agents, is characterized by strong staff commitment and good communication or a lack of commitment and distrust, and how internal political factors are influencing the project are just a few of the organizational variables that must be studied in career education evaluation. They seldom are.

• The public, in general, including legislators and top bureaucratic policymakers, does not understand the complexities involved in evaluation. We have simply not communicated that it is a difficult venture that will take a long time, considerable funding, and many mistakes before techniques are perfected and conclusive results can be shown. The public may be unwilling to wait for results because we have never impressed upon them that they will have to wait. Cures for disease do not come overnight. Neither do educational results. The analogy is in some respects unfair, but the basic similarities of time and complexity are real.

• Despite the importance with which they view educational programs, policymakers devote relatively little attention to educational evaluation. Most of the attention that does come is centered around the time at which funding decisions are made. This results in a low priority for evaluation and low funding levels for evaluation research and practice. It also results in viewing evaluation as something to be initiated as a program nears its end rather than before its beginning. Until we can impress upon people at all levels of education and policymaking that evaluation is a management tool for improving programs as well as a consideration in funding decisions and that it must receive adequate time and funding to be done well, we are bound to continue to be asked to deliver too much too fast too late. There are some hopeful signs in this area. The new federal legislation for career education recognizes the importance of keeping a continuous pulse on career education, and local practitioners are devoting more attention to evaluation, but much more needs to be done.

● Perhaps the most difficult problem for career education evaluation lies in the fact that it has been described to many people as a way of improving basic skills. However logical this rationale for career education may be, it will be difficult to support in the short run. Career education is only one of many variables affecting academic achievement. Until we have a better understanding of how to implement career education to maximize its effects on basic skills attainment and until we know how it interacts with other critical variables, it may be necessary to tone down the immediacy of our promises. This presents a very troubling dilemma. On the one hand, we could ask support for career education on the basis that it will lead to positive gains in such areas as career awareness, career decision-making skills, attitudes toward learning, and self-awareness—all without any net loss to traditional academic achievement. On the other hand, it may well be that the public is not content with such gains and will not support career education unless basic skill gains can be shown. It may be the *Catch 22* of career education that we are forced to promise what we know we cannot yet demonstrate. One possible approach to avoid this dilemma may lie in the notion of *functional competency.* This notion would define some career education objectives in terms of real-life skills needed to succeed in the world of work (e.g., ability to fill out job applications; understanding one's rights and benefits in the work place; knowing how to locate work possibilities; etc.). While these functional skills in no way define the totality of career education objectives, they seem to have the advantages of being: (1) important outcomes to the general public; (2) fairly easy to measure; and (3) possible to accomplish in large measure through career education intervention. Such functional competency approaches as used in the Adult Performance Level Study at the University of Texas should be looked at more closely in this light.

Conclusions

Despite problems, the outlook for career education evaluation is hopeful. Some results that point to the effectiveness of career education are available. Consciousness of the need to improve evaluation in career education is growing at federal, state, and local levels. If we address the topic of career education evaluation carefully, with increased resources and with ingenuity, we can develop and deliver a plan for possible results. What we must not do is mistakenly present popularity of the career education concept for long-term support for its development. Only positive results will generate that support. Only action will generate results.

REFERENCES

Carrel, K. S.; Potts, C. A.; and Campbell, E. A. *Project TALENT'S Nonrespondent Follow-up Survey: The 10th Grade Special Sample.* Palo Alto, Calif.: American Institutes for Research, 1975.

Charters, W. W., Jr., and Jones, John E. "On the Risk of Appraising Non-events in Program Evaluation." *Educational Researcher,* November 1973.

Corder, Reginald. *The Information Base for Reading.* Final report. Project No. 0-9031. Grant No. OEC-0-70-4792 (508). United States Office of Education, National Center for Educational Research and Development, 1971.

Hoyt, Kenneth B. "An Introduction to Career Education." A policy paper of the U.S. Office of Education. U.S. Department of Health, Education and Welfare, Publication No. (OE) 75-00504, 1975.

McLaughlin, D. H.; Fulscher, G. V.; and Yen, W. M. *Project TALENT'S Special Sample: Is It Necessary?* Palo Alto, Calif.: American Institutes for Research, 1974.

McLaughlin, D. H., and Tiedeman, D. V. "Eleven-year Career Stability and Change as Reflected in Project TALENT Data Through the Flanagan, Holland, and Roe Occupational Classification Systems." *Journal of Vocational Behavior* 5 (1974): 177-196.

Medley, D. M., and Mitzel, H. E. "Measuring Classroom Behavior by Systematic Observation." In *Handbook of Research on Teaching.* N. L. Gage, ed. Chicago: Rand McNally, 1963.

Wolcott, H. F. *Criteria for an Ethnographic Approach to Research in Schools.* Eugene, Ore.: Center for Educational Policy and Management, 1974. Mimeographed.

CHAPTER 12

Teacher Preparation for Career Education

If career education is to take hold and provide curriculum changes and reforms, teachers and administrators must be prepared to function effectively under the new system. The problems of teacher preparation persist today and undoubtedly will persist in the future simply because institutions responsible for the preparation of teachers are the last to respond to change, if they respond at all. In the mid-1970s, there was movement by many colleges of education to restructure their traditional programs to respond to the trend toward career education. That momentum, however, seems to have slowed, and there is a fear that career education, in spite of the federal and state initiatives, may be in serious trouble because of the limited attention given to the preparation of teachers.

In this chapter, consisting of four articles written in 1974 and 1976, Rupert N. Evans and Wayne N. Lockwood, Jr., provide insightful views on the problems associated with teacher preparation which were as critical then as they are today. Norman Gysbers, Carol Magnuson, and Earl J. Moore offer a conceptual model for pre- and in-service education of teachers. Louise J. Keller presents one of the strongest arguments for what colleges of education can do. Her article has theoretical as well as practical value. John R. Cochran and David M. Weiss present an excellent design for in-service teacher preparation.

TEACHER EDUCATION FOR CAREER EDUCATION: ISSUES IN NEED OF SOLUTIONS

Rupert N. Evans and Wayne N. Lockwood, Jr.

Dr. Evans is professor of vocational education at the University of Illinois at Urbana-Champaign, where he has also served as dean of the College of Education.

Dr. Lockwood is currently associate professor of industrial technology at Illinois State University. This article was written in 1974.

Who Will Assume Responsibility for Teacher Education in Career Education?

The key question in teacher education for career education is who will ultimately assume responsibility for it? To date almost all of this responsibility has been assumed by university departments of vocational education or industrial arts.

In one sense, this has been healthy, since it has broadened the interests and contacts of these departments, but in the long run this is not a satisfactory solution if career education is to permeate the entire school system. Representation from each of the major levels of education and from each of the major subject areas is necesary both for development of satisfactory content and for the acceptance of that content. Maryland, for example, found that industrial arts and home economics teachers plus guidance counselors were not a group with a broad enough base to convince junior high school staffs to install career education.

Early USOE funding of career education with vocational education dollars led to the view that career education is synonymous with vocational education and is controlled by vocational educators. This view remains widespread. The best way to combat this misunderstanding would seem to be to involve other pertinent groups in teacher education for career education.

Awareness, Exploration, Preparation, and Implementation

The five components of career education are classroom instruction, vocational education, career development, interaction with business and industry, and the home and family (Hoyt et al. 1974, p. 14). These components are a part of teaching and learning at every level from early childhood through adult education.

Many of the state guides for career education specify that awareness of the world of work will be taught in the elementary school; exploration in the junior high school; and preparation in the high school. These levels of education may be defensible as places to begin teaching for awareness, exploration, and preparation, but the development of awareness goes on throughout life, and so does exploration and preparation. Vocational teacher education programs should show teachers how to develop awareness and how to encourage exploration, as well as how to prepare students for work.

Career implementation tends to begin in earnest when the student leaves the school setting to enter the world of work. The high rate of unemployment of students suggests that many would like to begin implementation earlier. Adequate career preparation must be made available to all students prior to career implementation. Currently, most career preparation in the form of vocational education is concentrated in the last two years of high school and is unavailable to students who elect to enter the world of work at an earlier point in their life. Moreover, there are too few opportunities for moving gradually and in planned fashion from preparation to implementation.

Teaching Values in Career Education

The teaching of values in any field is a subject for controversy. What values should be taught and how should they be taught are lively questions in career education. Some proponents seem to advocate inculcation of the values implicit in the protestant work ethic. Some skeptics point out the possibility that career education could be used to brainwash youth to accept the values held by employers.

The typical teacher education program teaches very little about values or how to teach them, but since work values are implicit in career education, teacher education programs for career education cannot avoid this subject. Very little has been written about how to teach work values, but an excellent literature has developed on what work is and how people value it.

Departments of Career Education

Because no one is going to have the skills and knowledge to teach teachers about all of career education, most classes and texts in this field should be the product of a team effort. Assembling a team has many good by-products, not the least of which is that the professor of elementary education (or the professor of any other field) whom you ask for assistance will learn more about career education and about you.

The preceding suggests that an ideal teacher education department of career education should include representation from at least the following fields: elementary school education, one of the secondary school academic subjects, vocational education, guidance and counseling, industrial sociology, and home economics. Representation from a number of other specialties would be desirable, with post-secondary and adult education heading the list.

A department of this size presupposes a substantial instructional load. In these times of financial stringency in higher education, it is to be expected that few institutions could move quickly toward establishing a full-fledged department. Nevertheless, this is what seems to be needed, at least on a part-time basis, to do the job. If courses and enrollments in career education continue to grow, it seems reasonable to expect that departments of this size and scope will become common.

The Content of Teacher Education for Career Education

It is widely recognized that a certain amount of general and professional preparation is desirable for all teachers. Beyond that point, teacher education requirements should be determined by the instructional responsibilities to be assumed by each individual.

It is generally accepted among vocational educators that one can no more teach that which he does not know than he can return from a country where he has never been. This led to the employment of specialist vocational teachers. No one would expect the teacher of shorthand to be able to teach welding or anatomy.

Career education requires the support of a great many education specialists, all of whom need some amount of teacher education. Pre-service teacher education programs eventually will provide a major portion of the preparation for some of these individuals, but for the next few years, the pre-service preparation of many of these individuals will be in large measure a local responsibility, most often delegated to the career education teacher who must assume the role of team leader. Instructional leadership must therefore be included in pre-service and in-service programs designed to prepare career educators. For example, the use of community resources is strongly advocated in career education. One way this is accomplished is through the use of resource persons in the classroom. Such individuals need to be prepared if they are to be an effective part of the career education teaching team. Additionally, career educators must be prepared not only to lead the team but to coach its members. If ever there was an opportunity to make effective use of master teachers and differentiated instruction, it lies in the opportunity presented by career education.

In teacher education, however, the need for a team approach has not been recognized or at least has not been put into practice. Too frequently we see departments of vocational teacher education made up of two or three persons who purport to teach teachers for all kinds and levels of vocational education.

Teacher education for career education is even worse in this regard. It is common for a university to assign one or two persons to be responsible for teaching all levels and kinds of career education teachers. Career education begins in early childhood and extends to senility. It demands a knowledge of human development which is greater in range than that required by any other school curriculum. Moreover, consider the five components of career education (classroom instruction, vocational education, career development, business and industrial interaction, and home and family). Each one of these components can serve as a focus of professional study for a lifetime.

Off-campus Teacher Education Programs

An immediate concern regarding the implementation of career education is the in-service education of practicing professionals. For many years it has been a standard practice for universities to teach the same material in off-campus classes that they use in on-campus classes. This was justified as a means of maintaining quality standards. A consequence of this system was to design the setting so that teachers from several schools would attend the same off-campus class; thus, there was no incentive to adapt the course to the needs of a single school system.

Contrariwise, the desire of a superintendent of schools or other persons responsible for in-service education in a school district often is for a course to be developed which would enroll only teachers from that district, all of whom would study material designed to meet their particular needs. Most universities, if they are willing at all to adapt their instruction to one district's needs, were willing to do this only on a noncredit basis.

When it is described in these terms, it is difficult to see why the university view was influential for so long. Nevertheless, it did prevail (except in large cities which had their own teachers colleges) until the 1960s. The circumstance which began to break the back of university opposition to credit courses designed to meet local school district needs was the involvement of arts and sciences (instead of college of education) staff in implementing new curricula in mathematics, biological sciences, chemistry, and physics. Those higher prestige professors were able to develop credit courses off campus to aid a school district to install their particular brand of new mathematics or science.

By the time career education began to require locally designed in-service courses in the 1970s, an additional factor had become important: on-campus enrollments in universities had decreased and they saw a need for additional off-campus instruction to bolster sagging staff/credit ratios.

The limiting factor now in in-service programs for career education is a shortage of university personnel who are qualified to offer such instruction in career education, not the university's unwillingness to offer such programs.

This shortage, plus a general desire for grass roots in-service education is leading to increased amounts of graduate level instruction conducted by local school personnel who are designated as adjunct professors (or some similar title) by the universities. The content is determined locally and local instructors are used, with the university accepting a credit-issuing and quality control monitoring function.

In some places this movement has gone so far that the need for the university as a part of the in-service education delivery system has virtually disappeared. In more desirable situations, local school personnel are working together with university instructors to the long-term advantage of both. The principal advantage to university teacher education personnel is an opportunity to learn more about career education so that this can be passed on to pre-service instructors and to in-service personnel from school districts which are too small to conduct full-fledged in-service programs of their own. The principal advantage to public school personnel is a less frequent rediscovery of the wheel because the peripatetic university professor brings with him word of the trials, successes, and failures of other career education programs encountered in his or her experiences with those programs.

Correspondence Instruction in Career Education

Whenever the exigencies of time or the availability of instruction make teacher education classes difficult to assemble, individualized instruction through correspondence becomes an alternative worthy of study. In recent years, the availability of computer-assisted instruction and instruction via television has added a new dimension to the traditional program of study by mail.

In the 1920s, a combination of vocational instructors who needed courses for certification and an inadequate number of vocational teacher trainers led to the creation of a number of correspondence courses. The Pennsylvania State University was a leader in this movement, and it still has three correspondence courses which are useful to vocational teachers throughout the country.

A principal obstacle to such instruction has been the use of state lines as an arbitrary boundary for teacher training purposes. Too often, a course which is offered in another state is not accepted for certification purposes even if its content is identical to that of a course offered within the state. Since correspondence courses serve widely scattered needs, the limitations of state boundaries are particularly damaging to them.

During 1973-74 the University of Illinois developed three correspondence courses, two for vocational teachers and one for elementary school teachers of career education. All three are usable on the traditional individual basis but are even more effective when several teachers in a school district enroll simultaneously and meet together once a week to discuss the materials. Development of additional such courses has been jeopardized by the dispersal of Education Professions Development Act (EPDA) funds to states and regions which see little reason to use *their* funds for development of courses which may have utility beyond the state or region.

Similar difficulties may cloud the future of the innovative teacher education program sponsored by the Appalachian Regional Commission. This program, conducted by the University of Kentucky, is using a NASA satellite to beam televised courses to teachers in 13 states and to allow these to communicate with teacher educators in Lexington. One course for teachers of reading and three courses in career education (for elementary, junior high, and high school teachers) were conducted during 1974-75.

What Kinds of Associations Will Promote Professional Development in Career Education?

The American Vocational Association and the American Industrial Arts Association undoubtedly have devoted more effort to the promotion of career education than have all other professional associations in education taken together. A few other groups, such as the prestigious Modern Language Association, the National Association of Secondary School Principals, and the American Personnel and Guidance Association, have seen career education as a movement worth encouraging, but most professional groups have acted as if it were a passing fancy, worthy of little or no notice.

One reason for the lack of interest from most organizations in education may be the peripheral interest in career education as compared with the goals for which their organizations were established. The solution may be to establish a national career education association which can interact with other education associations on an equal basis.

In contrast, a number of business and industrial groups, such as the National Chambers of Commerce, the Associated General Contractors, and the National Manufacturers Association, have expressed continuing interest. It may be expected that as the changing birthrate begins to affect the number of entrants to the labor market, they will express even more interest.

Issues in Need of Solutions

The purpose of this article has been to raise some of the important issues that must be resolved if effective teacher education programs for career educators are to be developed. Promising strategies for coming to grips with some of the issues have been suggested, but with no guarantee that the issues will be resolved. Basically, we don't know how to resolve them; however, we in the profession must continue to identify, raise, and attempt to develop solutions for issues involving career education and encourage professionals outside career education as well as nonprofessionals to do the same. It is imperative to the long-term success of career education that solutions be developed.

312

CAREER EDUCATION CONCEPTS, METHODS AND PROCESSES FOR PRE- AND IN-SERVICE EDUCATION

Norman C. Gysbers, Carolyn Magnuson, and Earl J. Moore

Dr. Gysbers is an international consultant in career education and is currently a professor of counseling and personnel services at the University of Missouri at Columbia.

Dr. Magnuson is an educational consultant and a member of the Missouri career education council.

Involved with many federal and state career education projects, Dr. Moore is also associate professor in the Department of Counseling and Personnel Services at the University of Missouri, Columbia. This article was written in 1974.

Career education is a new and emerging thrust in education today. Goldhammer underlined this point well when he suggested that career education has the potential of restoring relevance to the educational process.

> . . . career education constitutes a new, vitalizing thrust in education. There are, of course, those who will say that it is just another passing fancy and if we don't pay much attention to it, it will go away and leave us undisturbed. The evidence mounts daily that this is not the general reaction. The increasing public and legislative reaction to career education is one of hope that a new paradigm for educational operations has finally been found which will not only provide a basic social return consistent with the anticipated human and financial inputs, but a relevance for youth which will help them find their social identification and secure a sense of mission and destiny as participating members of society . . . (Goldhammer 1972).

If we accept Goldhammer's thesis, then the task is one of defining career education and developing appropriate models and resources to implement it fully in the schools. At the present time substantial efforts are directed toward assisting local school districts to develop comprehensive career education programs. Most states as well as the federal government are providing some financial support, materials, and technical assistance to school personnel to reach this goal.

Due to the increasing emphasis given to career education by federal, state, and local agencies, it is clear that teacher, counselor, and administrator education programs also must incorporate career education concepts into their pre-service education curricula as well as initiate vigorous in-service programs to improve and extend the career education competencies of practicing counselors, teachers, and administrators. At the present time, however, most teacher, counselor, and administrator preparation programs are not yet providing sufficient educational experiences designed to prepare these people to develop comprehensive career education programs. Neither are these preparation programs providing the levels of assistance needed to improve and extend the career education competencies of existing school personnel. While many educators recognize this situation and are making substantial strides to overcome it, they are hampered by the lack of well-established career education theory, methods, and resources.

As a partial response to this situation, personnel in the College of Education, University of Missouri-Columbia, under sponsorship of the Research Coordinating Unit of the State Department of Education, carried out a project to develop career education materials for K-6 for use in the pre- and in-service education of teachers, counselors, and administrators. The goal of the project was to develop career education materials for instruction, guidance, and administration to be used in grades K-6.

Career Conscious Individual Model

Because there are many ways of conceptualizing career education, the first step in the development of the materials was to formulate a theoretical conceptualization of career education. After much reading, thinking, and discussion, the word *career* was conceptualized as an integration of all dimensions of a person's life. Looking at the total individual and his or her total development necessitated the adoption of a model to provide a framework around which to organize material ideas and concepts. The model selected was that developed by the Career Guidance, Counseling, and Placement Project at the University of Missouri-Columbia. This model provided four basic domains for organizing the skills, knowledge, and attitudes individuals need to facilitate their total development. The ultimate outcome, career consciousness, focuses on enabling individuals to acquire life career competencies, attitudes, and values; to anticipate possible life career roles, settings, and events; and to relate them to their present situations.

The career conscious individual model is based upon life career development concepts and principals. The word life indicates that the focus is on total persons, on all aspects of their growth and development over the life span. The word career identifies and relates the many settings in which people find themselves—home, school, occupation, community; the roles which they play—student, worker, consumer, citizen, parent; and the events which may occur in their lifetimes—entry job, marriage, retirement. The word development is used to indicate that people are continually changing over their lifetimes. When used in sequence, the words *life career development* bring these separate meanings together, but at the same time they mean more than these words put together in sequence. They describe whole persons—unique persons with their own life-styles. Life career development is defined as self-development over the life span through the integration of the roles, settings, and events of a person's total life.

The four basic domains of the career conscious individual model are: (1) self-knowledge and interpersonal skills; (2) life roles, settings, and events; (3) life career planning knowledge and skills; and (4) basic studies and occupational preparation.

Self-knowledge and interpersonal skills. In this domain individuals learn about themselves, about others, and about interactions between self and others. Concepts in this domain emphasize becoming aware and accepting of self and others and the development of interpersonal skills. Self-appraisal and skills for self-improvement also are introduced. Through an awareness of personal characteristics—aptitudes, interests, goals, abilities, values, and physical traits—growth is begun toward understanding their influence on the person each individual is and can become. Through learnings in this domain, individuals become aware of the ways they interact with their environment, thus leading to the development of a personal identity. A person who utilizes self-knowledge in life career planning and interpersonal relationships and who assumes responsibility for his or her own behavior reflects desired outcomes in this domain.

Knowledge and understanding of life roles, settings, and events. Throughout each individual's lifetime she or he will be assuming a number of roles, functioning in a variety of settings, and experiencing a myriad of events. Learning within this domain focuses on acquiring an awareness of the roles, settings, and events which interrelate to form one's life career. The roles of family member, citizen, worker, and leisure participant; settings such as home, school, community, and work; and events such as birthdays, educational milestones, job entry, and job change are identified and examined in terms of their influence on each person's total life-style. Learning in this domain includes developing a knowledge and understanding of the structure of the education, work, and leisure worlds. The interdependency of workers both on and off the job is considered. The individual learns to relate his or her unique personal characteristics and aspirations to specific occupational requirements and characteristics. The effect of change—natural as well as unexpected, social as well as technological, in self as well as in others—is a major learning. As a result of learnings in this domain, individuals begin to answer the question, "Who am I?" through a developing awareness and exploration of the interrelatedness of roles, settings, and events.

Life career planning, knowledge, and skills. Planning for and making decisions are vital tasks in an individual's life. Every day decisions are made which influence one's life career. Mastery of the decision-making skills and the application of these skills to life career planning are central learnings within this domain. A preliminary task to effective decision-making is the clarification of personal values. The degree of congruence between what one values and the outcome of decisions one makes contributes to personal satisfaction. Individuals learn within this domain to identify the steps necessary in making decisions. Included are the skills for gathering and utilizing relevant information. Understanding the influence of planning on one's future and the responsibility one must take for planning are components of the life career planning process. Life career planning is ongoing. Change and time affect one's planning and decisions. A decision outcome that is satisfactory and appropriate for the present may, with time or change, become unsatisfactory or inappropriate; thus, the ability to evaluate decisions in view of new information or circumstances is vital. Individuals who are able to clarify personal values, identify steps needed to make personal decisions, gather relevant information, and apply decision-making skills to their life career plans reflect desirable outcomes in this domain.

Basic studies and occupational preparation. The learnings in this domain encompass the traditional subject matter areas found in most school programs and represent the largest component of the career conscious individual model in terms of amount of content. Basic to an individual's development is the acquisition of knowledge, skill, and understandings in areas such as language arts, mathematics, social studies, industrial arts, fine arts, vocational-technical education, home economics, and health and physical education. The needs of students have changed, presenting a new challenge to educators and education. It is imperative to look at traditional disciplines in terms of relevancy for pupils and the world in which they live and will live. Basic studies must continue to be an important part of the school program and will take on even greater meaning when related to the roles, settings, and events of a person's present and future life. In a similar manner, occupational preparation must become a significant part of the educational program of every pupil. Based on learnings in this domain, the individual will acquire the basic study and occupational preparation, skill, and knowledge competencies necessary to function in the life-style he or she may choose. In addition, they will be able to incorporate a variety of learning opportunities into their daily living and will continuously be able to acquire and refine basic and occupational skills and knowledge throughout their lives.

Career Education Module Development

Once a career education model was selected, it was then necessary to identify concepts to be expanded into modules of learning activities. When selecting the ideas to be developed, two populations or groups had to be considered—the pupils for whom the activities were to be written and the pre-service teachers, counselors, and administrators who would be implementing these concepts. This presented a dilemma. There was, on the one hand, the desire to formulate a growth-producing developmental continuum of activities for pupils, and on the other hand, the need to provide prospective teachers, counselors, and administrators with an overview of career education which would enable them to develop their own ideas as well as to implement the project's materials. Since the purpose of the project was to provide pre-service teachers, counselors, and administrators with materials which facilitate the development of career education, it was decided to place top priority on developing materials to give these individuals starting points for implementing career education concepts.

With this in mind, it was decided that, as a beginning, concepts would be selected from the career conscious individual model domains of self-knowledge and interpersonal skills, life career planning knowledge and skills, and life roles, settings, and events. Because the intent was for the modules to be starting points, each one was written to encompass a broad developmental level rather than specific grade levels. Modules were developed for the K-3 and the 4-6 developmental levels. Within each module, adaptations for older and younger pupils were provided.

An example of one of the modules which has been developed is titled *Roles, Settings, and Events: An Overview* (developmental level K-3). It was developed for the purpose of providing teachers, counselors, administrators, and the pupils with whom they work an overview of the roles, settings, and events of a person's life.

The first step was to formulate module goals and objectives. This question stimulated goal and objective formulation: "As a result of learnings in this module, what behaviors or concepts will the pupil possess?" For this module the following goal and objectives were formulated:

Module Goal: For the learner to define the meaning of roles, settings, and events.
Objectives: The learner will:
        • identify a variety of roles
        • describe the interrelatedness of roles
        • identify a variety of settings
        • describe the interrelatedness of settings
        • identify a variety of events
        • describe the effect of different kinds of events

The module is divided into three learning sequences with one sequence focusing on the concept of roles, the second on the concept of settings, and the third on the concept of events. Activities within these sequences are constructed to reach the objectives. Each of the modules developed followed the same general framework—the formulation of goals and objectives and the subsequent development of activities designed to provide pupils with the learnings necessary to meet the objectives.

A Perspectives, Methods, and Processes Guide

A vital part of the project's products is the guide for educators to methods and processes of career education. The modules, through the activities contained in them, provide suggested content for career education, while the guide provides detailed discussion of the processes or methods to facilitate the implementation of the module activities. Successful implementation of career education requires a certain amount of risk on the part of teachers, counselors, and administrators. Attempting small group discussions for the first time in a first grade class can be a trying experience, even for the most experienced educator. The guide is meant to give teachers, counselors, and administrators techniques to support their efforts in trying new ideas. Examples of two of the processes discussed in the guide are provided in the following description of one of the most important career education processes—the *exploration of the world of work.*

This process requires that teachers be able to teach the skills of interviewing, to facilitate the planning and the taking of field trips, and to teach the skills of pupil-planned and presented class presentations. Through the guide, educators will be able to attain the competencies neccessary for teaching these skills to their pupils.

Interviewing is the first process skill to be learned and taught. Through interviewing, pupils are able to acquire information from the world about them. They will utilize the skill of interviewing formally and informally throughout their lives. The ability to ask questions of others will facilitate their interpersonal relationships as well as enable them to learn more from and about their environment.

There are several components involved in conducting an interview. Pupils must first have an understanding of the overall purpose of interviewing. This includes knowing the who, what, where, when, why, and how of interviewing. They must know that there are two main types of interviews—group and individual. Group interviews occur when there is more than one interviewer, while individual interviews are one-to-one situations where the total responsibility of the interview rests with one person.

A second important component of interviewing is the ability to record information received during an interview. Developing ability in note taking and the use of video or audio tape recorders and/or photography is essential to the total interviewing process. The information recorded must be accurate; thus, interviewers must be at ease with at least one of the recording methods.

Interviewing is more complex than it first appears. It is possible to provide each child with a printed list of questions to ask in an interview; however, if pupils are to become independent interviewers, they must possess the ability to generate questions and responses spontaneously as the interview is conducted. Interviewing requires the mastery of four subskills—asking, receiving, reviewing, and responding. Once a question has been asked, the interviewer must receive a response—he or she must hear and understand what has been said. The receiving of information is followed by reviewing the information received in order that the inteviewer respond appropriately. Though these may seem like segmented and sequential subskills, all four skills will be in process and interacting at the same time during the course of an interview.

Field trips and classroom visits by resource persons promote use of interviewing and recording skills. Both field trips and classroom visits require skilled teachers and counselors. They must be adept at allowing pupils to help plan even though they provide structure for the learning experience.

Advance preparation for field trips or classroom visits by resource persons requires that all those involved understand their specific roles. Teachers, counselors, and administrators serve as facilitators and organizers. Outside resource persons must be contacted to arrange time and place of visit. If it's a work-site visit, school personnel must plan for appropriate transportation. The pupils have the responsibility of planning and gathering equipment which will be necessary for the visit. If a resource person is making a visit, chair arrangement and where the resource person will sit or stand must be considered. If a work-site visit is to be made, pupils must plan what equipment will be needed and who will be responsible for it.

Students, teachers, and counselors are mutually responsible for talking together about individual and group expectations for visits, for generating possible questions, and for deciding on appropriate behavior.

Teachers and counselors are urged to plan ways that individual interests are met through field trips. If school policy permits, a parent or other adult might take a small group of students on a field trip to a location which a large group couldn't visit. If company policy permits, when visiting a large work site where more than two or three jobs are performed, the large group might be divided into several small groups, each group exploring a different aspect of the work site.

The classroom visit or field trip completed, the pupils must then plan ways of sharing the information they gained with each other. It is important for teachers and counselors to accept the fact that not all class members will be interested in or need the information which every other class member acquired. Pupils should be responsible for planning presentations. Teachers or counselors are responsible for planning ways that pupils may attain the skills necessary to plan and present exciting and interesting classroom presentations. The *Methods and Processes Guide* provides teachers and counselors with suggestions for ways of teaching these skills to pupils. Some of the ways considered are slide presentations, audio or videotaped experiences, display of illustrations, or simulations and experiences.

The process of exploration of the world of work is but one process included in the guide. Methods and techniques for conducting small group discussions, for utilizing puppetry, for role playing, and for creating a positive classroom climate also are included. Through the use of the guide and the modules, educators will be able to begin the development and implementation of a career education program.

A Final Note

Teacher, counselor, and administrator preparation programs must integrate career education concepts and methods into their respective pre- and in-service curricula to support and reinforce the substantial progress that has taken place at state and local levels. Although training programs will repond to this need differently, there are some basic components which form the basis for pre- and in-service curriculum integration and therefore must receive attention if teacher education institutions are to exercise a leadership role. These components are:

● A conceptual model that encompasses the goals of career education in a comprehensive yet easily understood framework. Such a model should represent agreed upon needs and values so that it can be used to guide and structure program development.

• Exemplary packaging of career education content (modules) that can be used to deliver career education objectives. These modules can provide a basis for organizing learning experiences, resource development, and evaluation planning.

• A methods and process guide that describes new approaches to traditional teaching and counseling methods and techniques to facilitate career education content delivery.

The integration of career education content and methods into pre- and in-service preparation programs must be specific and practical but at the same time be open-ended and adaptable to accommodate special program needs and to stimulate individual innovation.

WHAT A COLLEGE CAN DO TO PROVIDE TEACHER PREPARATION FOR CAREER EDUCATION

Louise J. Keller

An early proponent of career development eduction, Dr. Keller has published other writings in the field. Currently she is coordinator of graduate vocational teacher education at the University of Northern Colorado. This article was written in 1974.

A number of meaningful implications can be construed from the literature on what a college can do to provide teacher preparation for career education. This paper addresses two of these implications:

• College faculty will need in-service education if changes are expected in faculty attitudes, programs, and operations.

• There are a number of specific commitments that a college/university should consider if it is to prepare career education personnel.

These two implications provide the bases for some generalization (as well as some specific recommendations) regarding the preparation of teachers for career education.

In-service Education for the College Faculty

Experience with exemplary projects has demonstrated the need for in-service education of all personnel. There are few guidelines available for in-service education at the collegiate level. Much has been written, however, on the topic of in-service education for career education at the elementary and secondary levels. The writings concerning career education for the collegiate level are limited primarily to conference papers and speeches. Hansen (1973) noted in an ERIC Information Series that eight universities had instituted some curricular changes or activities to accommodate the preparation of teachers for new roles and new relationships in career education. It is ironic that many of the spokesmen for career education are from colleges and universities. This is not difficult to understand by those who are associated with higher education. It is easier to conceptualize career education than to implement the concepts of career education. When one considers the very manner by which curiculum is introduced and/or changed within the university, one begins to understand the hurdles career education will have at this level of schooling. Curriculum changes are introduced after a consensus for changes is secured from various committees. Individuals serving on key committees within the university structure are prone to protect their own independent disciplines, especially those with declining enrollments. Survival within the university often depends on the "ownership" of degree programs which stipulate numerous required courses to assure generation of the FTE (full-time teaching equivalent), or bluntly stated, to assure the continual employability of professors. The introduction of new content and processes which may affect programs is often viewed with distrust and suspicion.

Teacher preparation institutions will have to deal with their personnel where they are within the institutional structure. Those who wish to impact change within the system, according to George N. Smith, Suprintendent of Schools, Mesa, Arizona, will need to be concerned with two categories of change: (1) effective or human change (the growth and development of the faculty) and (2) program or procedural change (including organizational direction and programs) (Smith 1973). These changes cannot be accomplished without a comprehensive and coordinated in-service training program.

The following suggestions have been tried with reasonable success as part of an internal service education program for college of education faculty. These suggestions are listed and described briefly.

Organize a task force committee for career education which is representative of all areas/departments/disciplines which prepare teachers, counselors, and administrators. This task force is charged to accomplish a variety of tasks. Task examples are stated below.

● Analyze both the present status and future aspirations of teacher preparation programs on campus.

● Review career education literature, research, models, state exemplary projects, and share findings with members of the committee.

● Visit and assess local educational agencies' needs and concerns regarding career education.

● Communicate with state educational agencies and review the state plan for career education.

● Clarify the role of the college/university in career education.

● Define for the committee such terms as: work, career development, career education, vocational education, and community-based system of education.

● Organize an advisory committee to be composed of elementary, secondary, post-secondary educators, and community lay people to: (1) aid in interpreting implications of career education for the college/university teacher preparation programs and (2) assist with in-service education of the college faculty.

● Establish in-service education priorities.

● Consider in-service education strategies. (Two interesting strategies colleges have considered are: (1) designing career education projects within the college's laboratory school as a means of providing impact on both students and faculty and (2) organizing and training interdisciplinary cadres of college teachers to instruct others on campus and to work with local educational agencies in the state.)

● Organize and coordinate in-service education groups.

● Secure funds to support in-service education and provide released time for key faculty members.

● Cooperate with in-service education groups on campus in the establishment of short- and long-range plans for reforming teacher education to be more sensitive to the career development needs of all students as well as to preparing needed educational personnel for career education.

Establish and evaluate an in-service education program for faculty which will include such topics and activities as:

- A review of the conditions which call for education reform at all levels of schooling.
- The rationale for career education.
- The basic concept assumptions of career education.
- The programmatic assumptions of career education at all levels of schooling.
- The findings and definition of terms adopted by the Task Force Committee for Career Education.
- The competencies needed by personnel for various roles, functions, and levels of schooling.
- The implications these competencies have on existing programs in teacher education.
- The needed commitments to design, implement, maintain, extend, and evaluate a personnel development program for career education.
- A visit with career education personnel from state exemplary projects.
- A review of conceptual frameworks or models for the collegiate level which are concerned with programs for preparing personnel for career education as well as exemplifying or demonstrating a career development process for all its students.
- Endorsement by the in-service groups of basic concepts and the formation of tentative plans for implementing a plan of action for preparing personnel for career education through: (1) pre-service education; (2) graduate education; (3) in-service education; and (4) on-campus and field services.

The above suggestions represent several of the basic steps or procedures for developing and implementing a program of career education at the collegiate level. The first step to be taken should be the establishment of a planning and coordinating task force committee for career education. An early task would be to analyze both the present status and future aspirations of the teacher preparation programs. Looking at where one is in the light of where one would like to be, and vice versa, are mutually helpful ways to analyze problems. Analyzing the facts about where one is can bring to light previously undiscovered student needs, which may necessitate a change in goals and objectives. Analyzing concerns about where one wants to be can make apparent the necessity for collecting facts about the present which were not previously considered important. Planning for career education, therefore, involves needs assessment—the asking of fundamental questions such as: Where are we? Where do we want to go? How do we get there?

It took us fifty years to accept the concepts of the kindergarten, and it probably will take as many years to understand and accept the concepts of career education. Those who perceive career education as a vehicle for educational reform will have to be committed to short-term successes and failures and long-range planning.

Some Specific Commitments for Colleges/Universities Preparing Personnel for Career Education

There are some specific commitments that a college/university should make if it is to prepare career education personnel. These are categorized as: (1) a commitment to a career development process for all students; (2) a commitment to changes in the pre-service teacher education program; and (3) a commitment to supportive services needed to facilitate career development education on campus and in the field.

A commitment to a career development process. Any program in an institution of higher education has the following programmatic responsibilities: (1) facilitate the development of individuals for their career/life roles; (2) provide relevant programs based upon manpower and human needs; and (3) provide adequate counseling and teaching interventions that facilitate and enhance individual career development.

Career education can be examined for its content and process objectives. The process is often referred to in the literature as career development. Theories of career development which have emerged over the past several decades have affected significantly the conceptualization of career education. In an attempt to operationalize the process of career development within the context of an education environment, Keller identified six career development stages which were perceived to be transitional and often cyclic for many individuals:

- Awareness (of self and career/life roles).
- Explorations (to discover self in relationship to careers).
- Identification (with career clustering systems for occupational, home, avocational/leisure, and citizenship development).
- Preparation (for entry into career role[s]).
- Entrance into a new role.
- Assessment of role and possible education recycling (Keller 1972).

Many of the career education models that have been conceptualized show the *awareness* stage to be a primary concern for the elementary school and the *explorations* stage to be the primary concern of the junior high school. Students entering the university who have not been exposed to career education experiences will need to become *aware* of career opportunities in general as well as roles/functions/levels in education. Students will need an opportunity to *explore* these roles as well as *prepare* for specific competency levels and be assisted by the university with job placement and continual professional development through new outreach in-service education programs aimed at all graduates employed in educational institutions within a state.

Four-year teacher preparation institutions need to recognize that their students also need exposure to career clusters, exposure to career models, and utilization of career models on advisement teams to aid career decision making. The process advocating career development at the elementary and secondary levels of education must be exemplified in higher education. The difference is in the level of sophistication and rate of transition. The difference is not in the basic process.

Colleges and universities that are interested in preparing personnel for career education can begin by demonstrating their concern for the career development needs of students. It may be through career development practices that colleges can convey what is meant by career education. Institutions that allow for career options, alternative preparation modes, and provide career guidance services to aid students through the transitional stages are indeed involved in career education.

A commitment to personnel development for differentiated roles. Institutions that intend to prepare personnel for career education face the task of properly perceiving future education roles. The wide range of personnel needs—professional and paraprofessional, in-school and non-school personnel—represents an interesting challenge to colleges/universities that prepare personnel for local educational agencies.

Preparation of individuals for differentiated roles, functions, and levels promulgates: (1) a performance-based curricula; (2) the establishment of a career lattice for education which recognizes those roles which may not need a baccalaureate degree; (3) student selection criteria for specific career programs in education; (4) consortium or partnership arrangements with other institutions for the preparation of personnel for career education; (5) a more interdisciplinary approach to professional teacher education; and (6) the recognition that personnel development is continuous and that perhaps we should perceive pre-service and in-service education as a continuum rather than two separate and unrelated functions.

Colleges and universities have an opportunity to prepare not only professional teachers for career education but also those who will serve in new supportive or ancillary roles as well as adjunct personnel who can bridge the schools with homes, industries, businesses, organized labor, and governmental agencies. Colleges and universities should also give attention to the preparation of volunteers for career education. This is a service that can be provided to a local community through its public school system. The improving of communications between and among community representatives, local school personnel, and college/university personnel holds great promise for moving from a school-based toward a community-based system of education.

The declining enrollments in many institutions of higher education may provide colleges/universities the most advantageous and exclusive opportunity to give serious attention to the dynamics of recruitment and selection of personnel for new career roles.

A commitment to changes in the pre-service professional teacher education programs. Those who have been involved in career education at the local level have learned that there are some special skills needed by all educators to accommodate career education. These skills need to be considered when designing preparation programs for career education. Some of these skills are the ability to:

- Assess the needs of learners, educational personnel, and the needs of the community
- Formulate objectives for career education
- Structure curriculum and instruction around four career cluster systems (home, avocational/leisure, citizenship, and occupational)
- Secure and utilize community resources
- Analyze clusters to determine learning modules/elements for individualizing instruction
- Integrate and correlate subject matter
- Design pupil personnel services
- Evaluate and measure achievement.
- Select, collect, and disseminate career education materials and media
- Articulate curriculum and instruction vertically and horizontally
- Counsel for career preparation
- Manage situations, data, and ideas
- Place students once competency levels have been reached
- Involve volunteer helpers in the educational process
- Work effectively in teams and differentiated staffing patterns

This short article does not permit a comprehensive analysis of needs and the elucidation of prescriptive measures. The following modules or courses are suggested for all education majors and partially answer the question, "What can colleges do to prepare personnel for career education?" These modules relate specifically to career education, K-12/14. It is important to understand that preparation for career education is more than the following modules/courses. In fact, preparation for career education is not a program, but it is a mix of existing and new curricular offerings as well as a mix of existing and new instructional and guidance services and learning activities. It is a professional development system. In brief, the system is composed of learning, guidance, supportive services, and management components. The following modules/courses represent a small part of the learning component directed at preparing all teachers for career education.

Modules for Career Education Teacher Preparation*

Careers in Education. Individuals interested in roles, responsibilities, and relationships in education are encouraged to participate in this awareness and exploration module. Students will have an opportunity to observe all levels of education and areas of specialization and relate these experiences to their own career plans.

Society and Work. This module is concerned with basic knowledge about the institutions and dynamics of our society which generate, define, and lend meaning to occupations. The module provides examples of how such content can be interfaced with subject matter throughout a school system. The module is divided into four units: (1) components of a working society; (2) the economics of work; (3) how work roles and values are defined; and (4) changes in the working world. (Additional information for this module and those titled *Occupational Information and Basic Technology* can be found in a study by Altman 1966.)

Guidance and Counseling for Career Planning. This module is concerned with the role of all teachers in guidance and counseling. Participants are introduced to counseling techniques, the use of information about the world of work, and self-knowledge for making effective career choices and educational/training plans. The idea behind this module is that if students can learn to be good teachers at the undergraduate level, they can also learn to be good counselors. The teacher's role in guidance and counseling must be strengthened for career education.

Basic Technology. This module involves students from all areas of specialization. The module units draw heavily upon findings in the fine arts, engineering, sciences, and humanities for content. Participants have an opportunity to examine and develop for themselves those basic technologies needed by all members of society. These are the informal applications of learning to survive in a modern society and may be grouped as to: (1) general work habits; (2) machines and mechanical principles; (3) electrical principles; (4) structures; (5) chemical and biological principles; (6) numerical operations; (7) verbal communications; and (8) human relations. This module provides students with an opportunity to analyze and synthesize their general education and education specialization and to relate these knowledges and experiences to the educational needs of people in both rural and urban environments for career/life roles.

---

*Editor's Note: Teacher education modules for career education are available at the University of Missouri-Columbia.

Career Education Concepts. The historical antecedents of career education are discussed and related to six cyclic stages for career development: (1) awareness of careers and self; (2) role explorations; (3) cluster identification and orientation; (4) preparation for employability; (5) job entrance and development; and (6) career assessment and recycling. These six stages are associated with the mission and goals of education at various levels—early childhood through adult education. Students visit schools and investigate how these schools have implemented specific career education goals and objectives.

Clustering Techniques for Career Education. Clustering systems are examined for content, learning experiences, and role relationships. Implications for different grade levels are explored (for example: integrated and correlated subject matter, work simulated laboratories, work sampling in the community, utilization of volunteer helpers from the community, and placement of world-of-work bound students). (The U.S. Office of Education has predicted that some eight million teachers will need to be involved in cluster curriculums.)

Occupational Education. The preparation phase of career development is examined in more depth. The units are: (1) basic principles of occupational education; (2) determination of various educational disciplines' roles in occupational preparation programs; (3) manpower needs and predictions; (4) occupational preparation methods; (5) legislation mandates; and (6) purpose and goals of vocational education.

Subject-matter Application. *(This is required of all majors in a college of education.)* This module is concerned with helping the future or present teacher relate subject matter of his or her specific discipline to the career/life realities of people in order to make education relevant, understandable, and even more palatable for some youngsters. Within the context of the subject-matter application module, groups of education students discover underlying themes in the community which could be utilized as a field source for firsthand experience for them and as the most likely means by which their future students might explore the diversity that is in the universe of work.

We are asking teachers in the field today to restructure or adapt their curriculum and instruction around a new theme called career education. If we expect this creativity to take place in the future, there needs to be some preliminary pre-service experiences. Within the subject-matter application module there is an opportunity to bring together learners from many disciplines. We already know from our experience in career education, K-12, that graduates coming from teacher preparation institutions are required to integrate, correlate, and differentiate their subject matter. Academic and general education teachers often find it difficult to relate content and process to occupational environments. On the other hand, vocational teachers find it equally difficult to blend their activities with basic education components. Within the subject-matter application module, strategies for exploring and involving students with other subject areas, thereby blending educational experiences, should be high on the priority list for pre-service education. This kind of interdisciplinary involvement is also important because future teachers will need to be prepared for new coordinating roles and role relationships. Teachers employed today must be trained to plan and work in teams and differentiated staffing patterns. The environment in which they are prepared should contribute to these new working relationships.

The pre-service experience should expose future teachers to instruction in group dynamics, involvement in ethnic groups, planning strategies, and human relations. Students will need experiences as education team leaders, team members, individual unit instructors, social leaders, group counselors, individual counselors, progress evaluators, and school-community coordinators. Future teachers will need an understanding of the total educational spectrum and should be able to relate their specialization to occupational environments. Perhaps one way to bring about change of attitudes on campus is to involve professors from different disciplines in this module.

These eight modules should provide many involvement experiences. Not all undergraduate students will be able to take all the learning and experiencing modules offered by a college; however, these can become a part of the pre-service/in-service education continuum for career education.

A Commitment to Supportive Services

A commitment to career education is an institution's recognition that the professional development of teachers is a continuous process which must be sustained by human development and resource services. Some of these services are briefly described below.

Career Guidance and Counseling Services. A college of education should provide its own career guidance and counseling services. Four goals for this service are suggested: (1) to establish a team advisement system which replaces the present major advisor system: The advisement team would help individuals plan an academic and occupational experience program; the team would be composed of (a) major advisor, (b) field service coordinator for the college of education or department, (c) on-campus member-at-large (could be a nonprofessional staff representative), and (d) world-of-work adviser; hopefully each individual graduating from the college of education would be prepared for multiple career options upon graduation—a position within education as well as for jobs outside the field of education; (2) to provide prospective teachers opportunities to identify with recognized career educators and to discuss personnel development concerns; (3) to measure, review, record, and plan prescribed and discretionary learning experiences to reach specific career objectives; and (4) to serve as a referral agent for students with special needs.

Educational Field Services. Some of the unique services of this component are: (1) job development and placement services; (2) directed occupational experience supervision and coordination; (3) educational internship experiences through centers for teacher education or with LEAs; and (4) student teaching (planning and supervision).

Career Education Resource Center. A resource center will locate, evaluate, select, collect, and disseminate K-12/14 career education curriculum and instruction materials, media, and information. The center would also publish guides and handbooks and possibly a statewide newsletter for communicating and sharing career development activities. The center's foci also would include research activities and services for evaluation, curriculum and instruction development, and to support the in-service education program.

In-service Education. In-service education is provided through career education cadres composed of interdisciplinary teams from the college/university and assigned to communities to assist with local planning and implementation of career education.

Your Challenge

What can colleges/universities do to prepare teachers for career education? You can exhibit a capacity and willingness to:

● become aware of and sensitive to the actual needs and concerns of local communities involved in career education, and restructure to some degree your curriculum

- develop a conceptual framework and organizational strategies for implementing the concepts of career education through program content, learning experiences, and career development services
- develop new communication and partnership systems which will help initiate as well as sustain the career education thrust

The development and installation of a system whose focus is on reforming teacher preparation programs for career education will necessitate major restructuring, value orientation changes, a major realignment of goals, and an internal adaptation to a significantly different set of commitments. Such a massive change is too much to expect over the next few years. Perhaps your challenge is to take the first step by organizing a task force committee and implementing where possible some of the ideas suggested. The colleges and universities that prepare personnel for educational positions should be the leaders in career education. The challenge is yours!

IN-SERVICE PROGRAMS FOR CAREER EDUCATION TEACHERS

John R. Cochran and David M. Weis
Drs. Cochran and Weis are associate professor and professor of education, respectively, at the University of Akron and are involved with in-service education of career education teachers and evaluation of career education programs. This article was written in 1976.

As career education has been introduced into Ohio schools, large numbers of teachers have been called upon to present traditional courses in new ways and to incorporate concepts into their subjects and grade levels which were not previously emphasized. The training of experienced teachers to utilize career education concepts presents many unique challenges. Teacher motivation, time, acceptance, and confidence are a few of the more serious ones. The purpose of this article is to present a description of some of the teacher needs related to teaching career education that have been identified, four types of in-service programs designed to meet these needs, some considerations in planning career education in-service programs, and a model describing the proposed content of a career education in-service program.

Teacher Needs

Three basic needs of experienced teachers new to career education are: (1) an understanding of the basic concept of career education; (2) an increased knowledge of educational and vocational opportunities and entry requirements; and (3) assistance in developing specific classroom application of points 1 and 2.

That teachers need an understanding of the concept of career education may seem rather obvious. There are, however, several inherent problems in accomplishing this teacher understanding. The first is that the concept of career education is often vague and reminds one of the ink blot test in which each person ascribes his or her own meaning. Sometimes career education is thought to be simple preparation for work, educational relevance, or even the same as vocational education. In Ohio career education is more than any one of these. Career education, as presented in our in-service programs, is defined as providing students with the opportunity to cope effectively with an increasingly complex society by helping them acquire knowledge, attitudes, and skills related to the developmental areas of *individual and environment, world of work, self, decision-making, employability and work adjustment, education and training* and *economics.* As teachers learn to apply relevant concepts from the above developmental areas to their own growth, they begin to recognize the need to incorporate these concepts in their teaching. When career education is presented in this way, one finds that many teachers are already doing things in the classroom which could be considered career education and that teachers then have less difficulty understanding the need for their involvement and the ways in which they may become involved in the program.

The second need, an increased knowledge of educational and vocational opportunities and the requirements for entering into them, has not previously been required of most teachers. At the secondary school level especially, teachers have had to know their subject area but have not necessarily been required to consider what careers might be related to the subject, how the subject taught relates to many careers, how the concepts taught relate to everyday living, and what a student needs to do to pursue a career related to that subject. Teachers need a much broader knowledge of the implications of the subject matter they are teaching and must be able to convey this knowledge to students.

The third need, that of assistance in incorporating career education into the classroom, is very important. Teachers are most turned on by how-to-do-it activities. They want to know how to incorporate career education into the classroom by planning activities and identifying resources to help them successfully attain the objectives they have stated. A better understanding of the process of career development is an essential element of this implementation.

Four Types of In-service Programs

Four types of in-service programs have been identified by the authors for the purpose of providing in-service preparation for career education teachers.

The first, and usually most informal in-service program, has been labeled the *career education in-service session.* The in-service session is usually an after-school meeting which lasts for one or two hours. It is usually planned and conducted by the local school personnel for faculty members from one building. The purpose of the in-service session is to introduce teachers to career education materials or to present concepts designed to meet the wants of the teachers in that particular building. The advantage of this type of in-service program is that it provides local coordinators the opportunity to work directly with smaller groups of teachers. It also provides the teachers the chance to share and coordinate career education activities in their building. Finally, it motivates teachers to become more involved in the career education efforts in their classrooms.

The second type of in-service program is the *career education conference.* The conference, which is designed to last one or more days, is often planned by local program personnel to serve fifty to one hundred participants. The purpose is to provide teachers, counselors, and administrators with a basic knowledge in one or two areas of career education. A conference may also be planned around a given theme that assumes that the participants have an understanding of basic concepts of career education. The advantage of the career education conference is that it provides a setting to introduce personnel from several buildings to the concepts of career education. It also provides the participants with the opportunity to share their ideas with teachers from different grade levels, subject areas, and buildings.

A third type of in-service program is the *career education workshop.* This approach differs from a conference in that it offers the participants college or university credit and lasts for longer than one or two days. The purpose of the workshop is determined by the personnel from the schools and the college or university faculty member. Workshops, by design, offer a great deal of flexibility in meeting the needs of the participants. They may provide an overview of career education, or they may focus on an in-depth study of a selected area, with the development of curriculum as an end result. An advantage of the career education workshop is that it may be scheduled for consecutive days or over a period of weeks or months. College credit often acts as a motivator to get the teachers to participate in the workshop. The length of the workshop usually provides the teachers sufficient time to establish an adequate knowledge for them to feel comfortable in implementing career education into their classrooms.

The fourth type of in-service program identified by the authors is the college or university *career education course.* The course is offered on campus and adheres to the regular academic calendar. It is usually planned by the faculty member to meet specific objectives. In other words, the course may be designed to focus on a general knowledge or the development of specific skills. An advantage of the course concept is that it is attended by personnel from a number of different school systems. This provides for a sharing of ideas and a broadening of participants' awareness beyond the confines of their own schools. Another advantage of the course concept for in-service programs is that it lends itself to more structure and allows for more attention to the scope and sequence of following courses.

Considerations in Planning In-service Programs

A number of factors must be considered before selecting the type of in-service program that best meets the needs of the population served. The following list, although by no means all-inclusive, presents some factors for consideration:

Participants
Administrators
Counselors
Teachers
Teacher aides
Others

Participant needs
Basic knowledge
Advanced knowledge
Concepts
Application
Experience
Material by grade level
Material by subject area

Time available
Before or after school
Evening
In-service days
Saturdays
Weekends
Summer
Regular school days

Sites for program
College or university campus
Schools
Resorts, motels, etc.

Motivation to attend
Interest
Stipend
College or university credit

Combinations of the above factors make one of the four types of in-service programs more appropriate than the others. For example an in-service session may be the most appropriate to present general career education concepts to administrators available for only a few hours after school. If, on the other hand, one wanted to train a core of teachers to be leaders in career education curriculum development and instruction, a sequence of career education courses might be more appropriate.

To date, the following activities have been considered most useful by participants in the author's in-service activities: (1) observations and hands-on experiences in business, industry, and vocational laboratories; (2) considering their own career development related to such topics as future shock, life planning, and values; (3) micro-teaching, i.e., present a mini-lesson, having it videotaped, and critiquing it with other teachers; and (4) good lectures, providing plenty of group interaction and relating directly to instruction.

A Model for an In-service Program

The following nine-phase model is designed to provide participants with an appreciation and understanding of career education through developing an awareness of their own career development, gaining knowledge of career education concepts and how they relate to subject matter, and finally, becoming more aware of community resources which may be utilized in providing career education experiences for students. The model is not intended to be presented in any one of the four types of in-service programs. Rather, it is intended to be a source of ideas to help structure in-service programs that meet the needs of the participants:

1. Introduction
   The introductory phase of career education in-service must be dedicated to developing an understanding of the need for career education and commitment to it, an understanding of the concept of career education, and an understanding of local career education programs. At this point, no attempt is made to spell out teaching techniques and specific, detailed methods of introducing career education into the classroom.

2. Career Development
   In this phase participants are introduced to the concept of career development. In addition, they are made aware of essential learning for effective career development. Finally, they are shown how many of these concepts can be incorporated into their classes, in what Ohio labels developmental areas of self, individual and his environment, world of work, decision-making, employability and work adjustment skills, education and training, and economics.

3. Career Education in Specific Subject Areas
   Specific, in-depth training for teachers, showing them how career education concepts can and should be incorporated into specific grade levels and/or subjects, should come next. Teachers need to know relevant teaching principles, techniques, and resources and should have practice implementing them.

4. Guidance
   Teachers, counselors, and administrators need to learn how the counselor can be involved in career education both by working directly with students and by acting as a consultant to teachers. Individual and group counseling, test interpretation, and assistance with career information and decision making are some of the areas which need to be explained.

5. Community Resources

   All members of the career education team need to be aware of resources available in the community, such as industry, service, business, social, and religious organizations. Whenever possible, participants should study these resources by visiting them and, when appropriate, getting hands-on experience.

6. Program Administrators

   Program administrators need additional training in such areas as: how to implement change; local resources; and principles of career program administration, group dynamics, vocational testing, curriculum development, making community contacts, and program evaluation.

7. The Community

   It is essential that community leaders be introduced to the program. Their assistance and cooperation are essential if the program is to be successful.

8. Parents

   Parents usually have great influence upon the career development of their children. They must be involved by learning about the program, understanding the problems and opportunities faced by youth in making career decisions, and assisting in the conduct of the career education program.

9. Program Improvement

   No program can remain static. It is important to enlist administration, counselors, teachers, parents, and community leaders in assessing the program, identifying areas of needed change, and suggesting ways for that change to be accomplished.

REFERENCES

Altman, James W. *Research on General Vocational Capabilities (Skills and Knowledges).* Pittsburgh: Institute for Performance Technology, American Institutes for Research, 1966.

Goldhammer, K. *The Roles of Schools and Colleges of Education in Career Education.* Final Report of the National Conferences on Career Education. Columbus, Ohio: Center for Vocational and Technical Education, September 1972.

Hansen, L. Sunny. *Career Education: Teachers' Responsibilities.* Information Series, No. 93 (VT 020 381) Document, ERIC Clearinghouse on Vocational and Technical Education. Columbus, Ohio: The Center for Vocational and Technical Education, Ohio State University, 1973.

Hoyt, Kenneth B.; Evans, Rupert N.; Mackin, Edward; and Mangum, Garth. *Career Education: What It Is and How To Do It.* Salt Lake City: Olympus, 1974.

Keller, Louise J. "Pre-service Preparation of Teachers for Career Education." Paper prepared for the Sixth Annual National Vocational and Technical Teacher Education Seminar, October 23-26, 1972. Columbus, Ohio: The Center for Vocational and Technical Education.

Smith, George N. *Career Education: Local Administration of Programs.* Information Series, No. 94(VT 020 382) Document, ERIC Clearinghouse on Vocational and Technical Education. Columbus, Ohio: The Center for Vocational and Technical Education, Ohio State University, 1973.